The Interdisciplinary Science of Consumption

The Interdisciplinary Science of Consumption

Stephanie D. Preston, Morten L. Kringelbach, and Brian Knutson, editors

The MIT Press
Cambridge, Massachusetts
London, England

MIT Press books may be purchased at special quantity discounts for business or sales promotional use. For information, email special_sales@mitpress.mit.

Set in ITC Stone Serif Std 9/14 by Toppan Best-set Premedia Limited. Printed and bound in the United States of America.

Library of Congress Cataloging-in-Publication Data

The interdisciplinary science of consumption / edited by Stephanie D. Preston, Morten L. Kringelbach, and Brian Knutson.
pages cm
Includes bibliographical references and index.
ISBN 978-0-262-02767-0 (hardcover : alk. paper)
1. Consumer behavior. 2. Consumption (Economics)—Psychological aspects. 3. Consumers—Psychology. 4. Neuropsychology. 5. Evolutionary psychology. I. Preston, Stephanie D. (Stephanie Delphine) II. Kringelbach, Morten L. III. Knutson, Brian.
HF5415.32.I575 2014
339.4′7—dc23
2013050848

10 9 8 7 6 5 4 3 2 1

Contents

Foreword

Peter C. Whybrow

Reason is, and ought only to be the slave of the passions, and can never pretend to any other office than to serve and obey them.
David Hume, *A Treatise on Human Nature* (1739)

Consumption is the sole end and purpose for all production; and the welfare of the producer ought to be attended to only so far as it may be necessary for promoting that of the consumer.
Adam Smith, *The Wealth of Nations* (1776)

In biological terms it's simple enough: we consume to live. Without sustenance all creatures wither and die. Thus, at the core of consumptive desire is the need for nourishment. Because humans evolved under conditions of privation and danger, the drive to satisfy hunger is a primary passion, a force comparable to seeking sex and security and one powerfully rewarded.

Millennia ago, when finding a fruit tree was a rare delight and dinner had a habit of running away, such brain systems of immediate reward were a survival adaptation, strengthening resolve and enhancing success in the hunt. But now that we live in relative abundance, the whole world is a shopping mall, and our appetites are no longer constrained by limited resources, our craving for rewards—the fat and sugar of fast food, money, the novel gadgetry of modern technology—has become a boundless hunger. In an affluent society, those consuming passions that served so well in earlier times are now suddenly maladaptive. (See the chapter by Knutson and Karmarkar, the chapter by Kringelbach, the chapter by Preston and Vickers, and the chapter by Lea.)

This mismatch is particularly evident in the United States, the paradigmatic consumer culture. The astonishing appetite of the American consumer now determines about 70 percent of all economic activity. And yet in this land of opportunity and material comfort—where we enjoy the 12-inch dinner plate, the 32-ounce soda, and the 64-inch TV screen—more and more citizens are burdened by debt while feeling time starved and overworked. Epidemic rates of obesity, anxiety, and depression are increasingly accepted as normal.

Why should this be? First, living in a culture of material abundance has revealed an uncomfortable behavioral truth. It turns out that, despite our technological achievements and our capacity for reason, the human animal remains an easily seduced, curiosity-driven pleasure seeker with an appetite for excess. This comes as no surprise to the behavioral neuroscientist, for it is clearly established that "overloading" the brain's ancient reward circuits—addictive drugs being the classical example—will trigger craving and insatiable desire. (See the chapter by Robinson, Robinson, and Berridge.) But the broader truth for those confronting the enticements of America's consumer society is that nature provides little in the way of a built-in braking system when it comes to temptation. When presented with the opportunity for personal reward, we routinely discount the future for the present. (See the chapter by Rick, the chapter by Lea, and the chapter by Preston and Vickers.)

The second important element in our search for understanding is one of paradox: the consumer society is constructed upon the same human appetites and penchant for greed that now give us concern. The Enlightenment philosophers whose writings helped to frame today's concept of the free market—John Locke, Bernard de Mandeville, and David Hume among them—had no illusions about the human propensity for excess. They correctly identified individual greed as the engine of wealth creation, but believed that through social constraint and the give and take of the market it could be held in check to serve the greater good. Adam Smith, the patron saint of capitalism, called this drive for personal betterment "self-love." In the parlance of the day, it was "God's incomprehensible remedy"—an acquisitive propensity that, together with curiosity and social ambition, "keeps in motion the industry of mankind." (See the chapter by Preston and Vickers and the chapter by Frank.) Through individual initiative, "universal opulence" would be achieved. Today we call it "human progress."

In the beginning, of course, the paradox was of little consequence. At the start of the Industrial Revolution, few individuals had many possessions, or the resources to buy them had they been available. And in the construction of a social democracy the theory made sense. Consumerism enables us to be different, to distinguish ourselves from others by what we buy and what we choose to display. We call this "self-expression," and it has become the cornerstone of the modern free-market society, embracing widespread competition as a positive force and promoting differentiation through choice rather than through rigid hierarchy. (See the chapter by Frank, the chapter by Saad, and the chapter by Mittal, Griskevicius, and Ellis.)

But during the nineteenth century, with the advent of mechanization and the harnessing of fossil fuels, which offered freedom from the constraints of the planet's solar-driven energy cycle, the production of material goods was transformed. And with that transformation came the progressive growth of everyday consumption. Work, rather than being at the center of a local agrarian economy and of family life, became something apart. It became a means to an end: the purchase of goods. A century later, as mass production hit its stride and human effort was organized to satisfy desires and to generate new ones, it was just a matter of time before consumers' appetites became the primary driver of economic growth. Need fostered desire, and desire begat craving.

Remarkable material progress has followed. Perhaps no nation on Earth has embraced the vision of a technology-driven material future more warmly than the United States, and the twentieth century has rightfully been described as the American Century. But in maximizing material choice America has built a market culture that not only reinforces consumer behavior but also is dependent upon it to function economically. Thus, increasingly, commercial success is measured not by the quality but by the quantity of product sold—by the merchant's ability to maximize profit through increased consumption. The globalized rich world has followed America's lead: economic vitality is now dependent upon inducing and sustaining addictive-like consumer behaviors, and the *amount* we consume has become a standard measure of economic vitality. (See the chapter by Frank.)

The addictive pursuit of economic maximization is compounded by the falling away of many of the physical factors that once bridled human behavior. With the convenience of the World Wide Web, instantaneous electronic communication, and a revolution in transportation, time and distance are no longer barriers to globalized commercial growth. In this competitive "Fast New World" we have become tethered to the workplace around the clock, and time has become the limiting factor in securing financial and social success. In our restless search for more time, more goods, and more money, we forgo exercise, rob ourselves of restorative sleep, and grab food on the go. The media portray this as a world of choice, excitement, energy, and self-actualization, but from the perspective of personal health it is also a world of stress, mismatch, and unintended consequences.

The increasing prevalence of obesity in the United States serves as a disturbing example of how—inadvertently, through the enticements we have conjured—we have become victims of our own consuming passions. (See the chapter by Todd and Minard.) Maximizing profits in the marketplace necessitates creating desire in the mind of the consumer. Fortunately for merchants, this has not been difficult when it comes to foodstuffs. Our primitive affinity for fat, sugar, and salt—all of which were scarce in the ancestral environment—has made it easy for the food industry to stir our ancient cravings. In consequence, in addition to leading the world in material wealth, living standards, freedom of choice, and technological development, Americans now also have the dubious distinction of being among the fattest people on Earth, with millions of citizens predisposed to type II diabetes and to cardiovascular disease.

Comparable examples can be found in the field of economics. The dot-com bubble, the subprime mortgage crisis, the financial meltdown—each of these reflects a similar stirring of our ancient appetites. We have learned from this roller-coaster ride that the market-driven consumer society, in its search for continuous growth, can offer opportunities for great personal benefit. But we have also learned that the same social system, with its capacity to transform need into desire, has the potential to induce insatiable craving in the consuming passions, creating a slippery slope to excess and environmental degradation.

Markets, like living organisms, are dynamical systems that seek spontaneous order. But although a market is a result of self-interested human action, its self-correction does not result from human intention. Rather, in the ideal, through the actions of millions of individuals who have the freedom to choose (equivalent, let's say, to the individual neurons of the brain), a spontaneous order emerges that has a well-structured, dynamic, self-correcting social pattern. This was essentially the thesis that Adam Smith set forth in describing his vision of a self-regulating market society. Although most of us no longer live in a village, we still cling to Smith's ideas as basic to economic life.

But there is a snag. The fundamental and common principle of dynamical systems, biological and social, is that they are regulated at all levels of their organization by mechanisms that provide continuous homeostatic correction. Unfortunately, in our dogged pursuit of material perfection we are perturbing many of those homeostatic mechanisms. Perfection does not exist in nature, or in markets. Rather, such systems are all about balance and dynamic fit, a balance that we now find ourselves losing. And time is growing short. We can no longer afford, to paraphrase Hume, to let reason be the slave of the passions. If we are to change the status quo, we must seek our own counsel: we must stand back and objectively bring together what we know about the science of consumption, at all levels of conceptual organization. In the best Enlightenment tradition, that is what this book is about: seeking new directions through reason and objective inquiry.

Introduction: Toward an Interdisciplinary Science of Consumption

Stephanie D. Preston, Morten L. Kringelbach, and Brian Knutson

In a single news program, one may see segments about the rising rates of obesity, the devastating failure of our financial markets, tips on how to save money and lose weight, and slice-of-life stories about people who compulsively hoard goods in their home. This volume examines whether these stories share a common thread, and explores these commonalities from an interdisciplinary scientific perspective. At some level, all of these behaviors represent *undesirable* resource-allocation decisions. Though these decisions may emanate from fundamental neural and psychological processes that have evolved over hundreds of millions of years to adaptively guide mammals toward resources that are needed for survival, in an industrialized society they may also have unintended consequences.

Evolved and Conserved Mechanisms for Consumption

Shared mesolimbocortical mechanisms

Food, drink, and shelter are necessary for human survival. Money can be used to obtain them. Because of the ancestral necessity of sustenance and of mates, the human nervous system probably evolved highly efficient, conserved, and largely automatic mechanisms that ensure that individuals are attracted toward these critical stimuli. Humans probably share these adaptations with other mammals. From the standpoint of the underlying mechanism, animal research and now human research suggest that the same neural circuits in the mesolimbocortical system—which includes the nucleus accumbens, medial and ventromedial prefrontal cortex, the amygdala, the hippocampus, and the insula—motivate the consumption of diverse rewards across a broad range of species. For instance, evidence for the role of the mesolimbocortical system can be variously observed during single-cell firing studies in rats and monkeys to food rewards (Schultz 2002), lesion studies of animal food hoarding (Whishaw 1993; Whishaw and Kornelsen 1993), the compulsive hoarding of material goods in patients with frontal lobe lesions (Anderson, Damasio, and Damasio 2005), the functional neuroimaging of healthy people while gambling or shopping (Hsu et al. 2005; Knutson, Rick, Wimmer, Prelec, and Loewenstein 2007), as well as during the functional neuroimaging of compulsive hoarders (Saxena et al. 2004). Multiple chapters in this volume (including the one by Kringelbach, the one by Knutson and Karmarkar, the one by Plassmann and Wager, the one by Preston and Vickers, and the one by Robinson, Robinson, and Berridge) discuss the role of these conserved systems in decision processes in many mammalian species to choose, approach, obtain, and consume rewards.

Shared affect-based decisions to share and consume

Humans may also share evolved and simple or "fast and frugal" ways of deciding what to consume. In their chapter, Todd and Minard describe how people and rats use simple heuristics for deciding what to eat, such as eating previously enjoyed foods, familiar foods, or even foods that they have observed others eating. Even in the presence of extensive information, complex decisions about consumption can be made on the basis of much simpler and largely automatic processes that require little explicit comparison or analysis.

These simple decision rules may also extend into the social realm. For instance, even more complex social or "moral" choices related to the distribution of resources may translate across species, at least among primates. As the chapter by Brosnan, de Waal, and Proctor attests, nonhuman apes and monkeys seem to draw upon a sense of fairness and reciprocity when they consider distributing food, which may presage similar moral values in humans. Apes and sometimes monkeys share food with individuals who have shared with them in the past, who have groomed them, or with whom they share a positive social bond.

Together these findings imply that humans and even some nonhumans reciprocate favors through proximate mechanisms related to the giver's affective associations with potential recipients and gifts. Other research suggests that affective states can also guide decisions to consume or to share by indicating current and anticipated problems, as well as by indicating the relative bounty or scarcity of environmental resources. Thus, as outlined by Knutson and Karmarkar, emotional feeling states associated with the items to be consumed and their prices are integrated to predict choice. Moreover, Rick describes how individual differences in the anticipated "pain of paying" can drive individual differences in financial choices of "tightwads" versus "spendthrifts." Preston and Vickers further demonstrate that incidental emotions not related to the decision at hand can bias choice in ways that mimic the influence of those emotions when they are intrinsic to the choice. Moreover, as Plassmann and Wager argue, people can form or be given expectations about choice outcomes that not only shape choices but also shape the experience of consumption—for example, making wine associated with an attractive label and a high price actually taste better than the same liquid poured into a less auspicious carafe.

Shared resource-saving behaviors

As Sherry describes in his chapter, neural overlap between humans and other species extends from affect to memory, since the same neural circuit that humans use to remember where they left their car keys or how to get to work—the hippocampus—is also used by food-storing animals (e.g., Clark's nutcrackers and squirrels) to store and retrieve cached food in order to survive long, resource-scarce winters. The relevance of animals' food storing to human consumption is not always emphasized, yet it provides evidence for the capacity of evolved neural systems (even in birds with brains that are very small compared to the brains of mammals) to optimize decisions about resource allocation. Lea presents a similar view of how optimal decision processes shared between humans and pigeons or rats can bias choice in similar ways and may (or may not) motivate choice over a much longer time period than that of the typical laboratory experiment. Moreover, the ways humans store resources to satisfy perceived future needs—including food pantries, emergency rations, bank accounts, financial investments, and perhaps even social partners, memories, and ideas—are in some ways analogous to the food storage performed by birds, chipmunks, and squirrels. These fundamental resource-allocation decisions appear to be compromised in compulsive hoarders, who acquire and fail to discard excessive numbers of items to the point of distress, impaired daily living, and compromised safety, as described by Preston and Vickers. As basic instincts collide with modernity, an improved scientific understanding of these processes may reduce such pathological negative consequences and—better yet—optimize the use of time and space to promote better resource storage for everyone. As Peter Whybrow so clearly emphasizes in his preface, the mismatch of consumption instincts to modern environments must be recognized before the negative consequences for individuals, society, and the environment can be addressed.

Insatiable Appetite as a Hazard of an Evolved Mechanism to Consume

Although animals possess a basic neural predisposition to seek and enjoy sweet or caloric foods, or to attract and enjoy pleasing social partners and mates, they are not necessarily well equipped to deal with conditions that deviate from ancient resource environments. As Robinson, Robinson, and Berridge explain, modern purified drugs of abuse may exploit these systems, transforming initial enjoyment into need and craving, often to the detriment of the addict's health and quality of life. Todd and Minard similarly describe potential negative consequences of "fast and frugal" food-consumption decisions, including increasing rates of obesity and related morbidities, as well as extensive waste resulting from the acquisition of food that is thrown away.

The exploitation of endowed reward systems can also occur for "supernormal" goods, such as flashy, expensive automobiles and eye-catching women with disproportionately endowed bodies. Kringelbach extends the neural-reward framework of Robinson, Robinson, and Berridge to humans, emphasizing the role of internal pleasurable states that are associated with the activity of the "default" neural network and drive people toward desired products. Kringelbach also points out that these supernormal goods may especially suffer from a failure to adapt insofar as many are never directly or literally consumed, thus bypassing the feedback mechanisms that normally inform people that they have had enough.

Significant evidence presented in this volume by Knutson and Karmarkar, by Lea, and by Webley suggests that money, although an artificial human construct, has obtained a special status as a learned yet direct reward that people may seek for its own sake. Lea and Webley (2006) have previously written about how people are motivated to obtain money as both a tool and a drug, again asserting a cross-domain mechanism for natural and artificial or symbolic rewards. Presumably, combining the serial appetitive-to-consumptive framework of Craig (1918) described by Knutson and Karmarkar with Kringelbach's argument that material goods lack a satiety feedback mechanism implies that financial rewards may be sought and accumulated long after they have ceased to be useful. Indeed, Rick's description of tightwads may bring to mind familiar "Scrooge-like" characters who appear to save for the sake of saving, at the expense of healthy social relationships and a reasonable quality of life. Moreover, the presence of money and the goal of obtaining it may directly inhibit people's prosocial drive (Vohs, Mead, and Goode 2006), and so, by extension, selfishness may increase with financial resources (though philanthropic exceptions may resist this pull). Thus, although people may eat fruit or grains only until they feel full, or drink water only until they are no longer thirsty, people may be less able to moderate their consumption of sugary sodas, cookies, potato chips, electronic media, fast cash, or large homes. However, Webster and colleagues raise some hope for resolving this dilemma in their chapter on patterns of consumption across the life span. They report that older adults consume less in the categories typically seen as most self-gratifying, including goods, vacation, travel, food, and transportation. Of course, some of these changes are attributable to logistical changes associated with aging; however, older adults increased their expenditures on gifts and donations, which opens the possibility that, in general, they become more sensible and/or more compassionate consumers with age. The life-history approach advocated by Mittal and colleagues may predict such changes, insofar as older adults are no longer investing in their own mating and reproduction but can still contribute to the success of their relatives through interpersonal investments.

Consumption Problems Arising from Discounting the Future

A preference for immediate rewards lies at the heart of many of the problems of individuals and of society, and has been labeled temporal, delay, or hyperbolic discounting. When rewards are immediate and obvious, people find them difficult to resist, even in the face of significant long-term costs. For example, Todd and Minard suggest that this pervasive bias in favor of the present causes people to take three times more than they can eat from an appealing buffet, and seduces people into routinely eating enjoyable but unhealthy junk food. Webley further explains that although even young children (e.g., age 6) can understand the concept of saving money and its relationship to patience, control, and the virtuous delay of gratification, they nonetheless detest saving and instead often creatively manipulate parents and grandparents to satisfy their immediate desires—much like the addicts who creatively manipulate friends and family to obtain drug money. Stephen Lea adds that discounting lies at the heart of peoples' inability to save for retirement and can lead to extensive debt. However, Lea also expresses skepticism about whether neural discounting mechanisms, which have been largely studied in brief experimental tasks with rats and pigeons, can extend to major financial decisions (such as planning for a vacation or for retirement, or paying off a credit card debt over months or years). Instead, Lea argues for a need to augment models of human saving to incorporate the unique human ability for "mental time travel," which allows recall of past events and planning for future events. Although mental time travel has the potential to mitigate present focus, it is still imprecise and vulnerable to biases (e.g., optimism and availability). Overall, delay discounting and related biases may encourage people to finish off a can of Pringles today while planning to go on a diet tomorrow, to buy a large-screen television on credit with the plan to pay it off in six months, to drive to work rather than walk, and to take exciting or calming drugs or even part-time lovers at the expense of long-term happiness. In abundant environments, humans still struggle to maintain a balance. The unfortunate mismatch between our neuropsychological endowment and modern environments, eloquently described by Peter Whybrow in the preface above, is relevant to most of the chapters that follow.

The problematic legacy of present bias may worsen before it improves. First, appeals to immediate gratification have grown increasingly sophisticated, and rewarding consumable products are readily available—offering quick and convenient fixes to common problems (as in the case of "no money down" programs with exorbitant interest rates for furniture and televisions). Second, the consequences of consumption are often temporally and even physically distant (Loewenstein 1996), taking place in an uncertain future or in faraway places (for example, in unregulated factories that maintain poor working conditions for laborers and despoil local natural resources). The Nobel Prize awarded to the Intergovernmental Panel on

Climate Change and Al Gore and the recent financial crisis have brought the issue of excessive consumption to the forefront of national politics, but even though some changes have occurred, much remains the same.

Overconsumption Motivated by Social Signaling

Excessive consumption may also serve as a form of social display. Just as male bowerbirds decorate their nests with feathers and shards of glass to attract mates, people appear to acquire objects that maximally project their wealth and their character to others. Some individuals even explicitly report "status" as a reason for possessing a prized object (Richins 1994b). Similarly, people feel most attached to possessions that remind them of their past, of a former self, or of a social relationship (Belk 1988; Richins 1994a). However, this particularly existential role that consumption plays in human life has yet to be empirically studied in economics or in neuroscience and is only beginning to be discussed in relation to consumption in marketing, psychology, and clinical science. Most of the work in this area has been done by contributors to this volume. For example, multiple chapters describe the potential for consumable goods to establish a person's social identity or status. The chapter by Griskevicius, Redden, and Ackerman and the chapter by Saad address human males' use of conspicuous signals of consumption to attract mates. These social signals are apprehended and appreciated by females, who, in turn, are more likely to display their prosocial nature to others. Moreover, Mittal, Griskevicius, and Ellis argue that people adopt life-history strategies that seek faster and riskier approaches to mating when exposed to early environmental stress or deprivation, suggesting a malleable developmental "set point" for consumption. Social influences on personal consumption choices are also discussed by Todd and Minard, who recount how simple evolved heuristics to eat what others are eating might affect what and how much people subsequently decide to eat.

According to Frank, modern consumption operates like a social comparison "ratchet" that increases exponentially over time. In this system, people are less concerned about their absolute level of wealth and about material excesses than with looking better than their immediate neighbors and peers. Thus, newer, larger, and more luxurious homes set new precedents to be reached and exceeded by competing peers, who must subsequently purchase even bigger homes, establishing a new precedent for the scale of luxury, and so on to infinity. Recent economic practices, such as giving people loans that they cannot afford to repay or mortgages that require no down payment, escalate this progression by introducing new standards of living that individuals fight to attain even though they lack the means or the financial security to afford them. Aside from personal and social unsustainability, excessive conspicuous consumption cannot be sustained by the earth, which has limited resources that are being increasingly exploited. Frank recommends an approach that exempts savings from individual taxation, but taxes luxury purchases at a progressive rate. Perhaps because of the compelling drive to acquire more than one's neighbor, though, convincing people to vote for such a measure has proven difficult, even if it would benefit everyone in the long run. The impulse to do better than one's peers, again, hearkens back to the short time horizons that plague many poor decisions.

The Need for an Interdisciplinary Science of Consumption

There is a need for scientists to rise to the occasion and confront these issues by constructing coherent models that can directly address the multiple negative consequences of overconsumption. One way to do this is to develop models that can directly inform novel and efficacious solutions. Careful comparison of the mechanisms underlying seemingly disparate processes may lead to a unified model of resource allocation that can benefit science and society. For example, by understanding the evolution of animal food hoarding, clinicians and marketers may identify environmental triggers for human acquisition, which can in turn be used to develop strategies for reducing consumption that take prepotent and prepared tendencies into account. Further, bringing neuroscientists together with researchers who study shopping and compulsive hoarding may help individuals to better predict their own behavior and to understand the neurobiology of relevant disorders. New neuroscientific knowledge may improve the sophistication of theories of choice, as well as inform marketing, business, and finance applications.

Many fields are already playing with pieces of this puzzle, but typically without connecting them. For example, marketing researchers study behavioral and neural mechanisms of choice using experimental designs almost identical to those used by researchers of pathological human compulsive hoarding. Economists have long studied resource-allocation decisions such as tradeoffs between short-term and long-term gains (delay discounting), giving to one's self versus giving to another (trust games), or allocating one's resources to the community (the commons dilemma). They have also directly studied the influence of possession on people's choices (the endowment effect). Although these topics are highly relevant to daily human consumption, most of them are not typically studied in the context of relevant applied resource-allocation contexts such as animal hoarding, human compulsive hoarding, or public policy scenarios involving consumption and the environment.

As evidence for a lack of interdisciplinary exchange about consumption, consider that no term in psychology refers to decisions about resources, and that almost no psychological or neuroscientific research addresses decisions to acquire or discard material goods, other than the research conducted in behavioral economics and marketing. Psychologists use the term *acquisitiveness*, but a search for this term in the PsychInfo database revealed only 71 articles since 1887, only 13 of which are particularly germane to the topic and most of which were written in the early 1900s (e.g., Cameron 1923). The term *hoarding* is used by animal and human researchers, but with very different connotations. "Resource-allocation decision," a phrase used by economists, is usually reserved for specific scenarios in which people choose whether to keep money or give it to a stranger. A field called "Material Culture" (or "Material Goods") exists, but articles on this topic are mainly restricted to anthropological and sociological treatments. (In June of 2011, a search for the term *psychology* in the *Journal of Material Culture* yielded forty articles published since the journal's inception in 1996.) Together, these disjunctions between fields suggest gaps in communication about topics of common interest.

Final Remarks

To begin to bridge these communication gaps in the academic literature, the authors represented in this volume have created interdisciplinary forums for researchers across domains to interact and discuss commonalities and differences in their fields. So far, these meetings have included two conference sessions (one at a 2009 conference of the Society for Personality and Social Psychology and one at a 2011 Cognitive Neurosciences conference) and two Interdisciplinary Science of Consumption conferences at the University of Michigan (in 2010, 2012, and 2014). Many of the contributors to this volume spoke at these meetings, which focused on mechanisms underlying decisions to acquire or discard valued resources (e.g., money, food, material goods), with the specific goal of examining deep commonalities that cross species, domains, and fields of inquiry.

The overarching idea explored in this volume is that common biological and psychological mechanisms support different domains of consumption. Because these mechanisms have provided adaptive solutions to critical problems in our ancient past (e.g., securing food and mates), they are highly conserved through evolution and difficult to override. However, such powerful mechanisms can generate maladaptive decisions in environments in which rewards are superabundant, emotions are incidental to decisions, and unchecked social competition and display motives inflate expectations for consumption over time. The chapters provide an overview of current research in the various contributors' laboratories and fields, and explain how the work is related to the overarching theme of consumption. The volume concludes with a discussion of broad policy implications of consumption science.

Excessive consumption poses a potential threat not only to individuals but also to humanity by producing environmental waste, encouraging unfair labor practices, and reducing financial and physical well-being. Local and federal policy makers often struggle to encourage financial saving, reduce waste, increase recycling, and promote physical and mental health. Through careful comparison of the mechanisms underlying seemingly disparate outcomes, a unified understanding of consumption might emerge that benefits both science and society.

References

Anderson, S. W., Damasio, H., and Damasio, A. R. 2005. A neural basis for collecting behaviour in humans. *Brain* 128 (1): 201–212.

Belk, R. W. 1988. Possessions and the extended self. *Journal of Consumer Research* 15 (2): 139.

Cameron, E. H. 1923. The psychology of saving. *Annals of the American Academy of Political and Social Science* 110: 156–164.

Craig, W. 1918. Appetites and aversions as constituents of instincts. *Biological Bulletin* 34 (2): 91–107.

Hsu, M., Bhatt, M., Adolphs, R., Tranel, D., and Camerer, C. F. 2005. Neural systems responding to degrees of uncertainty in human decision-making. *Science* 310 (5754): 1680–1683.

Knutson, B., Rick, S., Wimmer, G. E., Prelec, D., and Loewenstein, G. 2007. Neural predictors of purchases. *Neuron* 53 (1): 147–156.

Lea, S. E. G., and Webley, P. 2006. Money as tool, money as drug: The biological psychology of a strong incentive. *Behavioral and Brain Sciences* 29 (2): 161–209.

Loewenstein, G. 1996. Out of control: Visceral influences on behavior. *Organizational Behavior and Human Decision Processes* 65 (3): 272–292.

Richins, M. L. 1994a. Special possessions and the expression of material values. *Journal of Consumer Research* 21 (3): 522.

Richins, M. L. 1994b. Valuing things: The public and private meanings of possessions. *Journal of Consumer Research* 21 (3): 504–521.

Saxena, S., Brody, A. L., Maidment, K. M., Smith, E. C., Zohrabi, N., Katz, E., et al. 2004. Cerebral glucose metabolism in obsessive-compulsive hoarding. *American Journal of Psychiatry* 161 (6): 1038–1048.

Schultz, W. 2002. Getting formal with dopamine and reward. *Neuron* 36 (2): 241–263.

Vohs, K. D., Mead, N. L., and Goode, M. R. 2006. The psychological consequences of money. *Science* 314 (5802): 1154–1156.

Whishaw, I. Q. 1993. Activation, travel distance, and environmental change influence food carrying in rats with hippocampal, medial thalamic and septal lesions: Implications for studies on hoarding and theories of hippocampal function. *Hippocampus* 3 (3): 373–385.

Whishaw, I. Q., and Kornelsen, R. A. 1993. Two types of motivation revealed by ibotenic acid nucleus accumbens lesions: Dissociation of food carrying and hoarding and the role of primary and incentive motivation. *Behavioural Brain Research* 55 (2): 283–295.

Evolutionary Perspectives

1 Reciprocity in Primates

Sarah F. Brosnan, Frans B. M. de Waal, and Darby Proctor

Acquiring food and acquiring mates are probably the two most critical decisions that any animal ever has to make. Without the former, survival is not possible; without the latter, one's genes are not passed on, and thus survival isn't relevant. Why, then, if food is so critical, do individuals of many species share it? In some cases, the answer is quite simple. For instance, in any species with maternal care, mothers share food of some form with their offspring so that they will survive and flourish. This is particularly the case in mammals. Mammalian mothers obligately lactate, providing food for their offspring for days or years (depending on the species). But what about situations in which individuals share food with individuals not related to them? From an evolutionary perspective, food sharing among non-kin should emerge if the benefits offset the costs. In 1971 Robert Trivers proposed the principle of reciprocal altruism, according to which individuals exchange favors in such a way that the short-term cost of individual A's helping individual B now is offset by the long-term benefit of A's receiving help from B in the future.

However, this evolutionary explanation raises the question of mechanism: How do individuals avoid being taken advantage of? Reciprocal altruism works only if favors are returned; otherwise the sharer pays a cost now but receives no benefit in the future. Although one could keep track of favors given and received, this requires significant cognitive abilities (Stevens and Hauser 2004) and is thus unlikely to be a solution in most situations and in most species, possibly including humans. Another possibility is that individuals' decisions are guided by their affect. That is, decisions to share food with another individual are probably based on affective signals related to liking the other, having a bonded relationship with the other, having received from the other previously, and/or using fairness principles that are driven by affect. If this is the case, then reciprocity and food sharing are forms of affect-driven resource-allocation decision making, and clearly share part of the mechanism described in the introduction to this volume, in the chapter by Preston and Vickers, in the chapter by Knutson and Karmarkar, and in the chapter by Kringelbach. That is, individuals may use affect as a guide when deciding how to allocate food to themselves and others—for example, directing resources to valued partners or to those who shared with them previously.

In this chapter, we outline what is known to date about reciprocity and food sharing in nonhuman primates. In short, we argue that the vast majority of reciprocity and food sharing is driven by affect and is based either on the symmetry inherent in a close, bonded relationship or on a mirroring of attitudes. We discuss primarily nonhuman primates, as this is our area of expertise, but we believe that this is likely to be the case across the animal kingdom, as well as in many human decisions to allocate resources to others. We first discuss observational data on reciprocity. We then discuss studies of capuchin monkeys, a species for which there is much experimental evidence. We end by reconsidering how these data provide evidence that using emotions as guides for decisions to allocate food and other resources to others is a shared mechanism across the primates, and probably beyond.

Reciprocity in Chimpanzees

Reciprocal coalitions and revenge

De Waal and Luttrell (1988) applied a matrix permutation technique to correlations between given and received agonistic support in more than 2,000 observations over five years in the Arnhem Zoo chimpanzee colony and in a large sample of interventions in mixed-sex groups of rhesus (*Macaca mulatta*) and stumptail macaques (*Macaca arctoides*) at the Wisconsin Primate Center. In all three studies, agonistic intervention was defined as a third individual responding with an aggressive act against one, and only one, of two participants in a dyadic confrontation. Interventions were recorded as triplets: individual A helps B against C. Reciprocity could occur in the domains of both *pro* interventions (A helps B against C) and *contra* interventions (A supports C against B), and hence may reflect two kinds of *quid pro quo,* as in "one good turn deserves another" and "an eye for an eye." The latter kind of punitive reciprocity has received far less theoretical attention than the first (but see Clutton-Brock and Parker 1995).

However, before one concludes from a positive correlation that giving depends on receiving, the most obvious variable to control for is time spent in association: if members of a species preferentially direct favors to close associates, the distribution of favors will automatically be reciprocal, owing to the symmetrical nature of association. Symmetrical relationship characteristics are (or ought to be) considered in every correlational approach to given and received acts of assistance across dyadic relationships, such as social grooming, food sharing, and agonistic support (Seyfarth 1980; de Waal and Luttrell 1988; de Waal 1989), as well as any kinship, age similarity, or gender similarity. This mechanism for cooperation, dubbed *symmetry-based reciprocity*, must be distinguished from *calculated reciprocity*, which is based on mental score keeping of favors given and favors received (de Waal and Luttrell 1988).

Table 1.1 presents Pearson correlations and partial correlations after statistical removal of the effects of symmetrical relationship characteristics. The analysis controlled for symmetrical characteristics such as time spent in proximity, matrilineal kinship, and whether the individuals were of the same sex. The partial correlations resulted after correcting for all these characteristics at once. These data confirm a significant level of reciprocity

Table 1.1

Pearson reciprocity correlations (*r*) between given and received agonistic interventions for three primate species. The *pro* rate concerns beneficial interventions; the *contra* rate concerns harmful interventions. Partial correlation coefficients (*pr*) have been adjusted for the effects of multiple symmetrical relationships characteristics. Probability levels (*P*) evaluate the partial correlations based on a permutation technique. From de Waal and Luttrell 1988.

Measure	Correlation	Rhesus	Stumptail	Chimpanzee
Pro rate	*r*	0.36	0.35	0.61
	pr	0.28	0.18	0.55
	P	0.005	0.025	0.005
Contra rate	*r*	–0.17	–0.23	0.33
	pr	–0.19	–0.29	0.32
	P	0.005	0.005	0.025

in *pro* interventions among adults of all three species, even after statistical adjustment for symmetrical relationships. The chimpanzees showed considerably higher reciprocity correlations than the macaques, however. An even more significant difference emerged with regard to harmful *contra* interventions. These interventions were significantly reciprocal in chimpanzees but significantly anti-reciprocal in macaques—that is, if macaque A often intervenes against B, macaque B will rarely intervene against macaque A, but if chimpanzee A often intervenes against chimpanzee B, chimpanzee B will do the same to chimpanzee A.

De Waal and Luttrell (1988) explain the absence of reciprocal *contra* interventions in macaques by their stricter hierarchy, which prevents subordinates from intervening against dominants. Most data in their study came from females, however. A similar analysis restricted to male bonnet monkeys (*Macaca radiata*) did yield evidence for reciprocal *contra* interventions, perhaps reflecting a looser dominance structure among male than female macaques (Silk 1992). There is also evidence for indirect retaliation among macaques: defeated subordinates redirect aggression against their opponent's relatives (Aureli et al. 1992). The squaring of accounts in the negative domain, dubbed a *revenge system* by de Waal and Luttrell (1988), may represent a precursor to human justice (de Waal 1996). Justice can be viewed as a transformation of the urge for revenge—euphemized as retribution—in order to control and regulate behavior (Jacoby 1983).

In most species in which reciprocal altruism has been observed—e.g., blood sharing in vampire bats, *Desmodus rotundus* (Wilkinson 1984), and allogrooming in impala, *Aepyceros melampus* (Hart and Hart 1992)—symmetry-based reciprocity has not been excluded and hence remains the most likely mechanism. This is not to say that uncorrected positive correlations are meaningless: obviously, symmetries are part of evolved social life. If they assist reciprocal relations that confer benefits, this is all that matters from an evolutionary perspective. If evidence is limited to positive correlations, however, one should not jump to conclusions about contingencies between giving and receiving. Although we know from experiments (see below) that monkeys are *capable* of contingent exchange, and although analyses that have gone beyond dyadic relationships—for example, in biological markets (Noë and Hammerstein 1994)—show behavioral distributions that seem too finely tuned to the supply and demand of partners and benefits to be accounted for by symmetry-based reciprocity, we would still argue that correlations cannot reveal underlying processes, and that thus it is best to adhere to conservative interpretations.

In view of these problems, observational studies should add sequential analyses, which look at the unfolding of behavior over time. Does a beneficial act by individual A toward B increase the probability of a subsequent beneficial act by B toward A? These analyses get around the problem posed by symmetries. Preliminary sequential evidence for an exchange between affiliative behavior and agonistic support, and vice versa, exists for cercopithecine monkeys. De Waal and Yoshihara (1983) found increased post-conflict attraction and grooming between previous alliance partners in rhesus monkeys. Seyfarth and Cheney (1984) played back calls that vervet monkeys (*Cercopithecus aethiops*) use to both threaten an aggressor and solicit support to gauge the reaction of individuals that had recently been groomed by the caller. They reported increased attention to previous grooming partners. Hemelrijk (1994) examined agonistic support after experimentally manipulating grooming among long-tailed macaques (*Macaca fascicularis*) and found indications that individuals supported those who had groomed them—that is, individual A supported individual B more if B had groomed A, but not if A had groomed B.

Hemelrijk's study comes closest to demonstrating a temporal relation between two services, but what is still missing is evidence of partner specificity—that is, evidence that the return service specifically targets the individual who offered the original service. The alternative is generalized reciprocity, or the "good mood" hypothesis (see below), according to which the receipt of services leads to an indiscriminate increase in beneficial behavior. Our research on food sharing in chimpanzees attempted to address this important distinction.

Food for grooming in chimpanzees

Although food sharing outside the mother-offspring dyad or the immediate kin group is rare among primates (Feistner and McGrew 1989), it is common in both capuchin monkeys and chimpanzees. Food sharing lends itself uniquely to experimental research, because in captive conditions the quantity and type of food available, the initial possessor, and even the amount of food shared can be manipulated by the experimenter. Furthermore, food sharing provides a quantifiable currency. An observer can see exactly how many times the non-possessor obtains food and can estimate the quantity shared. Finally, the observer can tell whether the sharing was active or passive.

Active food sharing, a rare behavior, consists of one individual handing or giving food to another individual. Passive food sharing—by far the more common type—consists of one individual obtaining food from another without the possessor's active help (figure 1.1; see also Jaeggi and van Schaik 2011). Passive sharing is selective, however, in that possessors are not equally tolerant of all individuals; only approximately half of the interactions between a possessor and an interested nonpossessor resulted in an actual transfer of food.

There are three hypotheses that are commonly used to explain food sharing in primates: the sharing-under-pressure hypothesis, the sharing-to-enhance-status hypothesis, and the reciprocity hypothesis (reviewed in de

Figure 1.1
A cluster of food-sharing chimpanzees at the Yerkes Field Station. The female in the top right corner is the possessor. The female in the bottom left corner is tentatively reaching out for the first time, and whether she feeds will depend on the possessor's reaction. Photograph by Frans de Waal.

Waal 1989 and de Waal 1996). The sharing under pressure hypothesis, similar to the tolerated theft hypothesis of Blurton-Jones (1987), predicts that individuals will share in order to be left alone by potentially aggressive conspecifics (Wrangham 1975; Stevens 2004). This hypothesis is contradicted by the fact that the most generously sharing individuals are often fully dominant and have little to fear from anybody around them and by the fact that most aggression in feeding clusters is not directed by non-possessors against possessors but vice versa (de Waal 1989). This confirms the remarkable "respect of possession" (cf. Kummer 1991) already noted by Goodall (1971) in her first accounts of meat sharing among wild chimpanzees. The sharing under pressure hypothesis also fails to explain food transfers in experimental protocols where the negative consequences of non-sharing are eliminated by physical separation (see below).

The hypotheses that remain, then, are the sharing to enhance status hypothesis and the reciprocity hypothesis. The sharing to enhance status hypothesis predicts that generosity increases the altruist's standing in the community (Hawkes 1990), but there is as yet no evidence for this effect in nonhuman animals. The reciprocity hypothesis predicts that food is one component of a service economy, and hence that it is exchanged reciprocally for other favors. These two hypotheses are, of course, not mutually exclusive.

We initially explored food sharing using matrix correlations (de Waal 1989). This matrix approach yielded significant results in the predicted direction. However, food sharing among chimpanzees correlates positively with proximity and grooming, and hence with the amount of time individuals spend together in non-food situations. As was explained above, the effects of association must be removed before any explanation other than symmetry-based reciprocity may be invoked. When the matrix analysis was recalculated to statistically control for the effects of association, the correlation continued to be significant.

However, a more recent study in chimpanzees that also controlled for effects of association (Jaeggi et al. 2013) failed to find evidence of short-term reciprocity of food for grooming in chimpanzees. An important difference between the studies was in the way they measured food sharing. De Waal (1989) included both active sharing (the rarer form) and passive sharing (which is more common in chimpanzees), whereas Jaeggi et al. (2013) measured only active sharing. Nonetheless, bonobos (*Pan paniscus*) did show short-term reciprocity, even when the effects of association were controlled for. Jaeggi et al. posit that this species difference is due to the higher rate of grooming in the presence of large food patches in bonobos than in chimpanzees, which increases short-term reciprocity. Thus in at least some contexts, both chimpanzees and bonobos apparently show short-term reciprocity apart from typical association patterns.

Statistical elimination of a variable is not as powerful as experimentally controlling for it, however. A new experiment was designed to measure temporal patterning within each dyad, thereby holding the effect of association constant. Partner specificity was addressed, i.e., whether a beneficial act by individual A toward B specifically affected B's behavior toward A (de Waal 1997a). The difficulty in measuring food sharing across time is that after a group-wide food-sharing session, as used in these experiments, the motivation to share is changed (the animals are more sated). Hence, food sharing cannot be the only variable measured. A second service that is not affected by food consumption must be included. For this, grooming between individuals before food sharing was used. The frequency and the duration of hundreds of spontaneous grooming bouts among the chimpanzees were measured during a period of 90 minutes. Within 30 minutes after the end of these observations, the apes were given two tightly bound bundles of leaves and branches. Nearly 7,000 interactions over food were carefully recorded by observers and entered into a computer according to strict empirical definitions described by de Waal (1989). The resulting database on spontaneous services exceeds that for any other nonhuman primate.

De Waal (1997a) found that adults were more likely to share food with individuals who had groomed them earlier in the day. In other words, if A groomed B in the morning, B was more likely than usual to share food with A later in the same day (figure 1.2). This result, however, could be explained in two ways. According to the "good mood" hypothesis, individuals who have received grooming are in a benevolent mood leading to generalized reciprocity—i.e., increased sharing with all members of their group. According to the exchange hypothesis, the individual who has been groomed responds by sharing food only with the groomer. The data indicated that the sharing was specific to the previous groomer. In other words, each chimpanzee remembered who had just performed a service (i.e., grooming) and responded by sharing more with that particular individual.

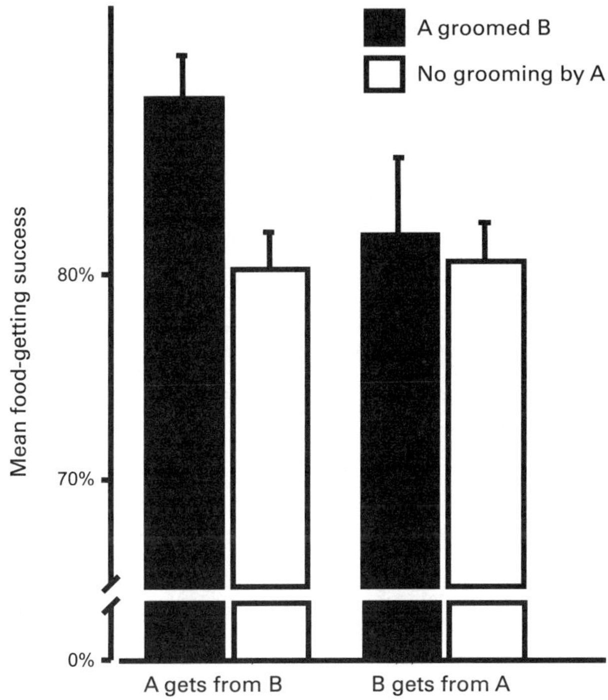

Figure 1.2
Mean (+SEM) food-getting success per dyadic direction between adult chimpanzees during food trials. Two conditions are distinguished: either individual A had groomed B in the hours preceding the food trial or there had been no grooming from A to B. The left graph shows the success of A in obtaining food from B; the right graph shows the success of B in obtaining food from A. Success is defined as the percentage of approaches to a food possessor resulting in a transfer of food (regardless of whether the transfer is active or passive) from possessor to non-possessor. It was found that A's success in obtaining food from B increased significantly after A had groomed B, whereas B's success in obtaining food from A was not affected by A's previous grooming. From de Waal 1997a.

Also, aggressive protests by food possessors to approaching individuals were aimed more at those who had not groomed them than at previous groomers. All this is compelling evidence for the exchange hypothesis.

Further, de Waal found that grooming between individuals who rarely groomed each other had a greater effect on subsequent food sharing than grooming between partners who commonly groomed each other. Among partners in which little grooming was usually exchanged, there was a more pronounced effect of grooming on sharing. There are several ways to interpret this. It could be that grooming from a partner who rarely groomed the subject was more noticeable, leading to increased sharing by the food possessor. Chimpanzees may recognize unusual effort and reward accordingly. Alternatively, individuals who groom frequently tend to be close associates, and favors may be less carefully tracked in these relationships. Close friendships may be characterized by symmetry-based reciprocity, which does not have the high degree of conditionality found in more distant relationships. These explanations are not mutually exclusive: both will lead to less conditionality when exchanges are more common in a relationship.

Of all existing examples of reciprocal altruism in nonhuman animals, the exchange of food for grooming in chimpanzees comes closest to fulfilling the requirements of calculated reciprocity. This study strongly suggests memory-based, partner-specific exchange in chimpanzees. There was a significant delay between favors given and favors received (from half an hour to two hours), and hence the favor was acted upon well after the previous positive interaction. Apart from memory of past events, for this to work we have to postulate that the memory of a received service, such as grooming, induces a positive attitude toward the same individual, a psychological mechanism described as "gratitude" by Trivers (1971) and further explored by Bonnie and de Waal (2004).

One difficulty, however, has been the challenge in demonstrating reciprocity in more carefully controlled experimental studies. Although observational studies in chimpanzees, both those described herein and those conducted in the field (e.g., Gomes et al. 2009; Gomes and Boesch 2009; Watts 2002; Mitani 2005), strongly indicate reciprocal behavior, we can never be fully certain that this patterned behavior is truly reciprocal until studies designed to rule out potentially confounding variables and demonstrate causation have been conducted. Two carefully controlled recent chimpanzee studies have found little or no evidence of reciprocity (Brosnan et al. 2009; Melis et al. 2008), though it is possible that the results were influenced by a short time frame, a lack of partner choice, or other aspects of the more artificial experimental designs.

Sensitivity to partner choice in chimpanzees

If chimpanzees are cooperative and reciprocal, they may be sensitive to how their reward outcomes compare to those of others. Such sensitivity probably would have been essential to the evolution of cooperation and reciprocity, insofar as such information helps individuals recognize when they should seek out new partnerships that might provide more benefit (Fehr and Schmidt 1999; Brosnan 2011). Although evidence for demonstrating sensitivity to others' outcomes has been mixed (e.g., Bräuer, Call, and Tomasello 2006, 2009; Brosnan 2009; Silk et al. 2005; Jensen et al. 2006; Jensen et al. 2007), several recent studies have demonstrated that chimpanzees are sensitive to others' outcomes under certain conditions (Brosnan et al. 2005, 2010; Horner et al. 2011; Proctor et al. 2013). The majority of these studies explore how chimpanzees respond to different rewards, but one recent study added the ability for the partner to alter outcomes after the subject had made a choice. This allowed for an exploration of whether chimpanzees are sensitive to possible recourse by another chimpanzee. Proctor et al. (2013) tested chimpanzees in an ultimatum game and in a preference test similar to the dictator game to test how the possibility of intervention by a social partner in a task altered subjects' behavior. The ultimatum game is a common two-player human economics task used to test for fairness in reward distributions. The first player (the proposer) is given some amount of money and told that he or she may split it with a partner in any way he or she chooses. If the partner accepts the offer, both get the proposed split of money. However, if the partner rejects the offer, both go home with nothing. The dictator game is played in the same way, except that the partner may not reject offers.

In the chimpanzee version of the dictator game, the proposer selected one of two tokens, one representing an equitable split of the rewards and one an unequal split favoring the proposer. When the chimpanzees were paired with passive partners who had no role in the task, they overwhelmingly chose the selfish option, which rewarded them the most. However, when the partners were active in the game and had to accept the proposers' offers in order for either chimpanzee to get anything, the chimpanzees were significantly more equitable. Critically, the subjects changed their behavior without the partner ever refusing, which would have blocked both chimpanzees from receiving any rewards. That is, the subject seemed to recognize the partner's role without overt action (partners did behaviorally indicate frustration with lower offers) and so changed their choices accordingly. Thus, chimpanzees are clearly sensitive to the outcomes of others, as well as to their potential to alter their own outcomes. Such behavior is probably critical for the emergence of reciprocity. Moreover, chimpanzees are not alone in this; capuchin monkeys, too, show abundant experimental evidence of reciprocity.

Studies of capuchin monkeys

Even though laboratory work on primate cooperation goes back to the late 1930s (see Crawford 1937), few experimental studies have been conducted since. Especially lacking is experimental manipulation of "economic" variables, such as the relationship between effort, reward allocation, and reciprocity. Recently, this situation has changed thanks to experiments on brown, or tufted, capuchin monkeys.

The genus *Cebus* seems particularly suited for cooperation research (Brosnan 2010). These monkeys show high levels of social tolerance around food and other attractive items, sharing them with a wide range of group members both in captivity and in the field (Izawa 1980; Janson 1988; Thierry et al. 1989; de Waal et al. 1993; Fragaszy et al. 1997; de Waal 1997b). This level of tolerance is unusual in nonhuman primates, and its evolution may well relate to cooperative hunting. Perry and Rose (1994) confirmed reports by Newcomer and de Farcy (1985) and Fedigan (1990) that wild *Cebus capucinus* capture coati (*Nasua narica*) pups and share the meat. Since coati mothers defend their offspring, it is conceivable that coordination among nest raiders could increase capture success. This has also been suggested for capuchins' hunting of giant squirrels (*Sciurus variegatoides*) (Rose 1997). Rose proposed convergent evolution of food sharing in capuchins and chimpanzees based on group hunting. The precise level of cooperation among individuals engaged in the hunt is not relevant for such evolution to occur; all that matters is that hunting success increases with the number of hunters. In such circumstances, every hunter has an interest in the participation of others, something promoted by subsequent sharing.

Reciprocal food sharing

In the delayed exchange test (DET), two monkeys are placed in a test chamber, separated from each other by a mesh partition that allows for food sharing. Monkey A is given a bowl of cucumber pieces, placed well out of reach of monkey B. After 20 minutes, the cucumber is removed, and a bowl of apples is given to monkey B (second test phase). The same pair is given another DET later, on a different day, with the order reversed between the monkeys (figure 1.3).

In years of testing with this paradigm, our capuchins displayed an astonishing amount of social tolerance, sharing food on a reciprocal basis. Males tended to share more than females regardless of the sex of the partner. A matrix analysis found that, for the 14 female-female dyads in which the possessor was dominant, more sharing occurred between partners who in their group life had fewer agonistic interactions, shorter rank distances (i.e., were close in the dominance hierarchy), and higher levels of proximity and grooming. Furthermore, the number of tolerant food transfers in the first test phase was significantly correlated with the number of tolerant food transfers in the second phase (de Waal 1997b). The most parsimonious explanation of this result is symmetry-based reciprocity, that is, reciprocity

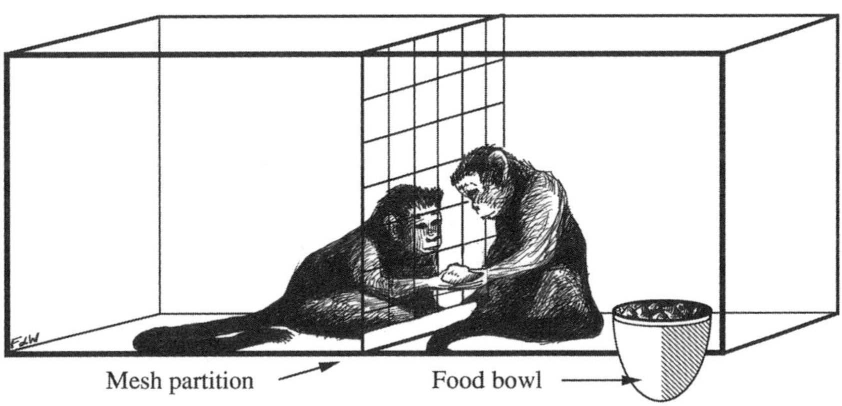

Figure 1.3
A sketch (made from a video still) showing active food sharing by a pair of capuchin monkeys. The monkeys are separated by a mesh partition, and the monkey on the right has access to a bowl containing apples. Active food sharing is rare, but facilitated taking, in which the food possessor drops pieces by the mesh and allows the other monkey to take them, is common. Drawing by Frans de Waal, from de Waal 1997b.

based on the symmetrical nature of relationships. The capuchins were already familiar with each other (pair members lived in the same group), and food sharing may have resulted from a combination of affiliation and tolerance toward conspecifics.

Our next concern was whether or not reciprocity could be attributed to anything besides the symmetry inherent in the relationship. For this, changes within each relationship over time were examined. The test was similar to the previous one, but incorporated six DETs on each pair. For each DET, individual A was given apple pieces for 20 minutes, then these were removed and individual B was given carrot pieces for 20 minutes. The roles between individuals remained the same over the six tests. The results were compared across tests to see how sharing in the second test phase was affected by sharing in the first phase between the same two individuals. This approach allowed us to correlate events over time, rather than across relationships, tightening a possible argument for causality between the behavior in both dyadic directions. Sharing rates were found to covary significantly over time within each pair of individuals, indicating something more than symmetry-based reciprocity (de Waal 2000).

Calculated reciprocity, or mental score keeping, however, may still be too complex a mechanism. To explain these results, de Waal (2000) proposed attitudinal reciprocity—that is, each individual's behavior mirrors the partner's attitude in close temporal succession. Instead of the monkeys keeping careful track of how much they gave and received, they may merely have responded positively (i.e., with proximity and tolerance) to a positive attitude in their partner. To confirm this, Suchak and de Waal (2012) paired capuchin monkeys with either a member of their social group, with whom they had long-term social relationships, or an out-group member, with whom they had no established relationship. One monkey, the chooser for the test session, was presented with a choice of two tokens, one of which rewarded both individuals (a prosocial token) and one of which rewarded only the chooser (a selfish token). The monkeys made the prosocial choice regardless of whether the partner was a familiar group mate or a member of another social group.

We do note, however, that sensitivity to the identity of one's partners probably varies by subjects' age and sex. In a previous study, capuchins showed differences in the frequency of prosocial behavior between in-group and out-group capuchin monkeys (de Waal, Leimgruber, and Greenberg 2008), behaving significantly less prosocially toward out-group monkeys. However, the two studies tested different groups of monkeys. Whereas in the earlier study only adult females were tested, Suchak and de Waal (2012) tested primarily adolescent males, who were nearing the age at which they would emigrate in the wild and who thus may have been inclined to show more positive behavior toward other adolescent males. Thus, the differences in the two studies probably were due to the fact that out-group adolescent males were more affiliative with each other than were the adult females.

After the basic prosocial task, Suchak and de Waal (2012) repeated the task, but let the monkeys take turns making the choice. Monkeys were significantly more prosocial in this reciprocal procedure. Importantly, the monkeys were prosocial to all individuals, regardless of their earlier relationship, which suggests that their prosocial behavior was driven by subjects' behavior rather than by the existing symmetry in their relationships. The increase in prosociality when the monkeys alternated choices further supports the idea of attitudinal reciprocity. When their partner was more prosocial, they too were more prosocial. Such mirroring of social predispositions might explain the reciprocal distribution of food sharing without the requirement of score keeping.

Cooperation

Despite indications of cooperation among wild capuchins, early tests of their cooperative abilities in the laboratory failed. The early tests used electronically mediated or other complex devices that were beyond the monkeys' comprehension (Chalmeau et al. 1997; Visalberghi et al. 2000; Brosnan and de Waal 2002). Adoption of the paradigm pioneered by Crawford (1937), on the other hand, quickly led to success. That paradigm, in which two individuals pull food toward themselves, is entirely mechanical. As such, it is intuitive: the monkeys can see how their pulling causes the food to move toward themselves; they also immediately feel the effect of their partner's pulling.

In our test, two capuchin monkeys had to work together to pull in a counterweighted tray, at which point one or both of them would be rewarded (figure 1.4). Monkeys were situated in the test chamber separated from each other by a mesh partition, so that they had the option to

Figure 1.4
The test chamber used for the cooperative pulling task in capuchin monkeys, inspired by Crawford's (1937) classical study. Two capuchin monkeys are situated in adjacent sections of the chamber, separated by a mesh partition. There is a counterweighted tray with two pull-bars, and each monkey has access to one bar. The bars can be removed. In the solo effort test, two monkeys were in the test chamber, but only one monkey had a pull-bar and only that individual's food cup was baited. In the mutualism test, both monkeys were required to pull their respective pull-bars, and both food cups were baited. In the cooperation test (depicted here), both monkeys were required to pull, but only one individual's food cup was baited. Drawing by Sarah Brosnan.

share food. Each monkey had its own bar to pull in the tray, although these bars could be removed for control tests. Food was placed in transparent bowls so that each monkey could see which one was about to receive the food.

Initially, monkeys were taught to pull in the tray individually, which they learned quickly. At this point (and throughout the experimental period, which lasted three years) each monkey was given regular strength tests to determine how much weight he or she could pull in individually. For trials in which only one monkey pulled, the tray was weighted just under what this individual could pull. For trials in which both monkeys pulled, the tray was weighted more heavily than the strongest individual could pull alone, but somewhat lighter than their combined strengths. Each test consisted of four ten-minute trials conducted on seven same-sex pairs of adult capuchins. The five test conditions were as follows:

Solo effort test (SOL) Only one monkey had a pull-bar, and only that monkey received food, although both monkeys were present in the test chamber. This required no cooperation.

Mutualism, or double test (DBL) Both monkeys were required to pull together, and both cups were baited.

Cooperation test (COP) Both monkeys were required to pull together, but only one food cup was baited. This represented altruism on the part of the helper.

Obstructed view test (OBS) This was the same as the COP test except that the mesh partition was replaced by an opaque one. This eliminated visual communication between the monkeys, but both monkeys still could see both cups on the tray, and that only one cup was baited.

Unrestricted cooperation test (UCP) This was the same as the COP test, except that the partner was free to move in and out of the test chamber, which had an open connection to part of the group cage. This meant that the helper—needed for successful pulls—was not always at hand.

As expected, the success rate of cooperative trials was significantly lower than that of mutualism tests or solo efforts. In the unrestricted cooperation tests, bar-pulling attempts by the food possessor decreased significantly when the partner left the test chamber, which indicated that the monkeys had learned to associate their partners' presence with successful pulling. They may even have made the more complex association that they could succeed only with their partner's help (Mendres and de Waal 2000).

Bar-pulling success also decreased significantly in the obstructed view tests relative to the cooperation tests. In the obstructed view test, vocal communication was still possible and the monkeys continued to make pulling efforts at the same rate they did in the cooperation tests. Since both monkeys could see the food cups, their success rates should not have decreased if the impetus to pull simply stemmed from seeing food. What changed was their ability to see each other's behavior, which suggests that success was at least partially dependent on visual coordination with the partner. The failure to succeed when visual access was cut off indicates that the monkeys were paying attention to each other's actions and coordinating their efforts. This result countered the claim of Chalmeau et al. (1997) that capuchins don't understand the need for a partner in cooperative tasks (Mendres and de Waal 2000).

Sharing after cooperation

The central question underlying this project was whether food sharing would increase in the context of a cooperative enterprise. In a service economy, food can be exchanged for assistance in cooperation, or the converse. Our analyses of the amount of food sharing indicated that capuchins shared significantly more in successful cooperative trials than in solo effort trials in which the partner was present but did not, and in fact could not, assist (de Waal and Berger 2000).

Furthermore, the partner pulled more frequently after successful trials. Since 90 percent of successful trials included transfers of food to the helper, capuchins were assisting more frequently after having received food in a previous trial. The simplest interpretation of this result is that motivational persistence results in continued pulling after successful trials. But a causal connection is also possible—that is, pulling after successful trials may have been a response to the obtained reward and the expectation of more.

The most cognitively demanding interpretation of these results is that the food possessor understands that the partner has helped and that the partner must be rewarded if cooperation is to continue. This would represent calculated reciprocity, in which a one-on-one exchange of favors drives reciprocal altruism. Each individual understands the other's costs (assistance in pulling or loss of food) and, out of gratitude, returns the favor.

However, a simpler explanation of the cooperation and food sharing in these trials is a variation on attitudinal reciprocity (cf. de Waal 2000), in which the possessor and the partner feel closer after a coordinated effort. The attention and coordination that cooperation entails may induce a positive attitude in the partner, which is expressed in social tolerance and mutual attraction, which translate into food sharing. After a food-sharing episode, similar mechanisms lead to increased pulling by the partner and hence to further cooperation.

The conclusion we draw from these experiments is that capuchins are quite good at performing, and probably also at understanding, cooperative tasks. The mechanism most likely to underlie cooperation and sharing in these monkeys is attitudinal reciprocity, in which cooperation partners mirror the attitude shown by their partner toward them. This is different from symmetry-based reciprocity in that reciprocation is not induced by symmetrical relationship characteristics but by attitudes that vary over time. This rather conservative explanation does not preclude the possibility of more complex processes, which may be uncovered in future research.

Expectations about reward division

During the evolution of cooperation, it may have become useful for actors to compare their own efforts and payoffs with those of others. Negative reactions may ensue in case of violated expectations. A recent theory proposes that aversion to inequity can explain human cooperation within the bounds of the rational-choice model (Fehr and Schmidt 1999). Similarly, cooperative nonhuman species seem to be guided by a set of expectations about the outcome of cooperation and about access to resources (Brosnan 2006, 2011). De Waal (1996) proposed a sense of social regularity, defined as follows: "A set of expectations about the way in which oneself (or others) should be treated and how resources should be divided. Whenever reality deviates from these expectations to one's (or the other's) disadvantage, a negative reaction ensues, most commonly protest by subordinate individuals and punishment by dominant individuals."

The sense of how others should or should not behave is essentially egocentric, although the interests of individuals close to the actor, especially kin, may be taken into account (hence the parenthetical inclusion of others). Note that the expectations have not been specified: they are species typical (de Waal 1996). One previous experiment on clumped rewards versus dispersed rewards (de Waal and Davis 2003) supports the role of expected returns in that it shows that cooperation disappears when subordinates anticipate a disadvantageous outcome. To further explore expectations held by capuchin monkeys, we made use of their ability to judge and respond to value. The ability to notice and respond when either reward value or efforts vary promotes cooperation by allowing individuals to recognize beneficial interactions. We knew from previous studies that capuchins easily learn to assign value to tokens, both through direct interaction with the items and through social learning (Brosnan and de Waal 2004b,c). Furthermore they can use these assigned values to complete a simple barter (Brosnan and de Waal 2004c). This made it possible to test whether they also responded negatively to inequity by measuring the reactions of subjects to a partner receiving a superior reward for exchanging the same tokens.

We paired each monkey with a group mate and watched their reactions when their partners got a better reward for doing the same bartering task. This consisted of an exchange in which the experimenter gave the subject a token that could immediately be returned for a reward. Each session consisted of 25 exchanges by each individual, and the subject always saw the partner's exchange immediately before his or her own. Food rewards varied from lower-value rewards (i.e., a piece of cucumber), which they are usually happy to work for, to higher-value rewards (i.e., a grape), which were preferred by all individuals tested. All subjects received four conditions, including the following:

an Equity Test, in which the subject and the partner did the same work for the same lower-value food

an Inequity Test, in which the partner received a superior reward (a grape) for the same amount of effort

an Effort Control Test, designed to elucidate the role of effort, in which the partner received the grape without having performed any task

a Food Control Test, designed to elucidate the effect of the presence of the reward on subject behavior, in which grapes were visible to a single monkey, but were not given to that monkey (or to any other monkey, since they were alone).

Individuals who received lower-value rewards showed both passive negative reactions (e.g., refusing to exchange the token, ignoring the reward) and active negative reactions (e.g., throwing out the token or the reward). Relative to tests in which both received identical rewards, the capuchins were far less willing to complete the exchange or accept the reward if their partner received a better deal (Brosnan and de Waal 2003). Capuchins refused to participate even more frequently if their partner did not have to work (exchange) to get the better reward, but was handed it for "free." Of course, there is always the possibility that subjects were just reacting to the presence of the higher value food, and that what the partner received (free or not) did not affect their reaction. However, in the Food Control Test, in which the higher value reward was visible, but not given to another capuchin, the reaction to the presence of this high-value food decreased significantly over the course of testing, which is the opposite change from that seen when the high-value reward went to an actual partner. In the latter case, the frequency of refusals to participate rose over the course of testing

(Brosnan and de Waal 2003). Moreover, a subsequent study utilized a different Food Control condition, in which rewards were visible but neither member of the pair received them. In this case, subjects' responses to the lower value cucumber were indistinguishable from their reaction to the cucumber in the Equity condition, and were far lower than their responses to the cucumber when their partner got a grape (inequity condition; van Wolkenten, Brosnan, and de Waal 2007). Thus, it is likely that the elevated response seen in the first Food Control condition was an artifact of being tested individually.

Although the capuchins' reactions to this situation do not necessarily indicate a full-blown sense of fairness, as is seen in humans (Brosnan 2012; Brosnan and de Waal 2012), this response fits in well with the proposed evolutionary trajectory of inequity aversion (Brosnan 2006). Like humans, capuchin monkeys seem to measure reward in relative terms, comparing their own rewards with those available and comparing their own efforts with those of others. Moreover, other species that are highly cooperative, including chimpanzees and dogs, respond similarly to this inequity, whereas species that do not cooperate extensively with non-kin tolerate inequity (Brosnan 2011; Price and Brosnan 2012). Although our data cannot elucidate the precise motivations underlying these responses, one possibility is that monkeys, like humans, are guided by social emotions. These emotions, which economists call "passions," guide humans' reactions to the efforts, gains, losses, and attitudes of others (Hirschleifer 1987; Frank 1988; Sanfey et al. 2003). In contrast with primates marked by despotic hierarchies, tolerant species with well-developed food sharing and cooperation, such as capuchins, may hold emotionally charged expectations about reward distribution and social exchange that lead them to dislike inequity.

Summary and Conclusions

Although theories about the evolution of reciprocal altruism are well established, proximate mechanisms have not been studied extensively. There probably are several levels of reciprocity, ranging from the more complex end of the spectrum—such as the kind originally proposed by Trivers (1971), which involves obligations and punishment of cheaters—to reciprocity based on simple social symmetries. The evolutionary perspective postulates that the cost of help given be offset by the benefits of help received, which can be achieved in multiple ways, all of which fall under the general rubric of reciprocal altruism. Two decades' worth of research on coalitions, grooming, and food sharing in macaques, chimpanzees, and capuchin monkeys has allowed us to gauge the cognitive level of cooperation. We have discussed three potential mechanisms, although we cannot exclude the possibility of more—see Brosnan and de Waal 2002 and de Waal and Brosnan 2006.

The least cognitively demanding explanation of reciprocal altruism is that individuals interact on the basis of symmetrical features of dyadic relationships, which cause both parties to behave similarly toward each other (de Waal and Luttrell 1988; de Waal 1992). This mechanism requires no score keeping, as reciprocation is based on pre-existing features of the relationship, such as kinship, mutual association, and similarity in age or gender. It produces reciprocity without a strong contingency between given behavior and received behavior. A certain mutuality in the exchange of benefits is probably required for the stability of any social relationships, but this can be achieved without careful record keeping. All that is required is an aversion to large, lasting imbalances in incoming and outgoing benefits. We believe that moderately conditional mutual aid is common in primates, including humans, not only among kin but also among close friends and associates. The prediction, then, is that the contingency between given benefits and received benefits decreases with closeness of the relationship (cf. Clark and Grote 2003). Conversely, the effect of a single act on future exchanges will be greatest in the more distant relationships, as de Waal (1997a) confirmed for chimpanzees.

The second proposed mechanism is attitudinal reciprocity, in which an individual's willingness to cooperate co-fluctuates with the attitude the partner shows or has recently shown (de Waal 2000). This "If you're nice, I'll be nice" principle divorces cooperative interactions from the symmetrical state of the relationship, making them contingent upon the partner's immediately preceding behavior. The principle appears to approximate mutualism, but with the difference that the two parties do not benefit at the same time. The involvement of memory and score keeping seems rather minimal, as the critical variable is general social disposition rather than the specific costs and benefits of exchanged behavior.

The third and final mechanism is calculated reciprocity, in which individuals reciprocate in a behavioral one-on-one fashion across a significant time interval. This requires memory of previous events, some degree of score keeping, partner-specific contingency between given and received favors, and perhaps punishment of cheaters. The best evidence for this "What have you done for me lately?" principle of reciprocity in nonhuman animals concerns, perhaps not coincidentally, our closest relative, the chimpanzee (de Waal 1997a). Whereas active punishment was not observed in chimpanzees, we did observe aggressive protest against partners trying to obtain services without previous payment. In addition, the demonstrated principle of exchange entails passive punishment in that it predicts the forfeiting of services by those who fail to provide services.

It is logical to expect that calculated reciprocity, with its higher cognitive requirements, will be found only in a few species, whereas cognitively less demanding affect-based forms will be more widespread. For any species in which reciprocal exchange is reported, we suggest that the default mechanism is symmetry-based. The burden of proof rests on those who assume more complex mechanisms. It could be argued that we know enough, from studies such as those reported here, to consider complex exchange to be within the capacity of primates. This sounds reasonable, but it should not be taken to mean that these animals necessarily rely upon these capacities all the time. To reduce memory overload, nonhuman primates, and probably humans, too, can usually be expected to follow processes simpler than calculated reciprocity. We therefore recommend that correlational studies on primate behavior always be complemented by sequential studies in which behavior is tracked over time. Such studies allow a more careful monitoring of exchange, including the establishment of contingency between given and received behavior. Such monitoring is necessary insofar as seemingly complex levels of reciprocity can easily be explained by a combination of symmetry-based and attitudinal reciprocity.

We find, then, that in many, if not most, cases reciprocity is driven by some form of affect, be it the symmetry inherent in bonded relationships or the positive feeling toward another that may spark a return benefit. Thus, food sharing and reciprocity appear to be forms of affect-driven resource allocation in nonhuman primates as well as in humans, indicating that this mechanism is widespread. (See also the chapter by Preston and Vickers.) In fact, this may even be the primary mechanism through which most food sharing and reciprocity occurs, while the more cognitively complex mechanisms (such as calculated reciprocity) are restricted to humans and a few other species. Thus, the study of other species may enrich our view, broadening our perspective on species that share similar mechanisms and our perspective on how such mechanisms may manifest in humans and in other species.

Acknowledgments

We are grateful for constructive comments from Stephanie Preston. We thank the technicians, animal care staff, and undergraduate students who helped during these projects. The capuchin work was supported by the National Science Foundation under a grant to Frans de Waal (IBN-0077706) and by a grant from the National Institutes of Health to the Yerkes Regional Primate Research Center (RR-00165). The Yerkes Regional Primate Research Center is fully accredited by the American Association for Accreditation of Laboratory Animal Care.

References

Aureli, F., Cozzolino, R., Cordischi, C., and Scucchi, S. 1992. Kin-oriented redirection among Japanese macaques: An expression of a revenge system? *Animal Behaviour* 44: 283–291.

Blurton-Jones, N. G. 1987. Tolerated theft, suggestions about the ecology and evolution of sharing, hoarding, and scrounging. *Social Science Information* 26: 31–54.

Bonnie, K. E., and de Waal, F. B. M. 2004. Primate social reciprocity and the origin of gratitude. In *The Psychology of Gratitude*, ed. R. Emmons and M. McCullough. Oxford University Press.

Bräuer, J., Call, J., and Tomasello, M. 2006. Are apes really inequity averse? *Proceedings of the Royal Society B* 273 (1605): 3123–3128.

Bräuer, J., Call, J., and Tomasello, M. 2009. Are apes inequity averse? New data on the token-exchange paradigm. *American Journal of Primatology* 71 (2): 175–181.

Brosnan, S. F. 2006. Nonhuman species' reactions to inequity and their implications for fairness. *Social Justice Research* 19: 153–185.

Brosnan, S. F. 2009. Responses to inequity in nonhuman primates. In *Neuroeconomics: Decision Making and the Brain*, ed. P. Glimcher, C. Camerer, E. Fehr, and R. Poldrack. Elsevier.

Brosnan, S. F. 2010. What do capuchin monkeys tell us about cooperation? In *For the Greater Good of All*, ed. D. Forsyth and C. Hoyt. Palgrave Macmillan.

Brosnan, S. F. 2011. A hypothesis of the co-evolution of inequity and cooperation. *Frontiers in Decision Neuroscience* 5.

Brosnan, S. F. 2012. Introduction to "justice in animals." *Social Justice Research* 25 (2): 109–121.

Brosnan, S. F., and de Waal, F. B. M. 2002. A proximate perspective on reciprocal altruism. *Human Nature* 13: 129–152.

Brosnan, S. F., and de Waal, F. B. M. 2003. Monkeys reject unequal pay. *Nature* 425: 297–299.

Brosnan, S. F., and de Waal, F. B. M. 2004a. Reply to Henrich and Wynne. *Nature* 428: 140.

Brosnan, S. F., and de Waal, F. B. M. 2004b. Socially learned preferences for differentially rewarded tokens in the brown capuchin monkey, *Cebus apella. Journal of Comparative Psychology* 118 (2): 133–139.

Brosnan, S. F., and de Waal, F. B. M. 2004c. A concept of value during experimental exchange in brown capuchin monkeys. *Folia Primatologica* 75: 317–330.

Brosnan, S. F., and de Waal, F. B. M. 2012. Fairness in animals: Where to from here? *Social Justice Research* 25 (3): 336–351.

Brosnan, S. F., Henrich, J., Mareno, M. C., Lambeth, S., Schapiro, S., and Silk, J. B. 2009. Chimpanzees (*Pan troglodytes*) do not develop contingent reciprocity in an experimental task. *Animal Cognition* 12 (4): 587–597.

Brosnan, S. F., Schiff, H. C., and de Waal, F. B. M. 2005. Tolerance for inequity may increase with social closeness in chimpanzees. *Proceedings of the Royal Society B* 1560: 253–258.

Brosnan, S. F., Talbot, C., Ahlgren, M., Lambeth, S. P., and Schapiro, S. J. 2010. Mechanisms underlying the response to inequity in chimpanzees, *Pan troglodytes. Animal Behaviour* 79: 1229–1237.

Chalmeau, R., Visalberghi, E., and Gallo, A. 1997. Capuchin monkeys (*Cebus apella*) fail to understand a cooperative task. *Animal Behaviour* 54: 1215–1225.

Clark, M. S., and Grote, N. K. 2003. Close relationships. In *Handbook of Psychology: Personality and Social Psychology*, ed. T. Millon and M. Lerner. Wiley.

Clutton-Brock, T. H., and Parker, G. A. 1995. Punishment in animal societies. *Nature* 373: 209–216.

Crawford, M. 1937. The cooperative solving of problems by young chimpanzees. *Comparative Psychology Monographs* 14 (2): 1–88.

de Waal, F. B. M. 1989. Food sharing and reciprocal obligations among chimpanzees. *Journal of Human Evolution* 18: 433–459.

de Waal, F. B. M. 1992. Coalitions as part of reciprocal relations in the Arnhem chimpanzee colony. In *Coalitions and Alliances in Humans and Other Animals*, ed. A. Harcourt and F. de Waal. Oxford University Press.

de Waal, F. B. M. 1996. *Good Natured: The Origins of Right and Wrong in Humans and Other Animals*. Harvard University Press.

de Waal, F. B. M. 1997a. The chimpanzee's service economy: Food for grooming. *Evolution and Human Behavior* 18: 375–386.

de Waal, F. B. M. 1997b. Food transfers through mesh in brown capuchins. *Journal of Comparative Psychology* 111: 370–378.

de Waal, F. B. M. 2000. Attitudinal reciprocity in food sharing among brown capuchin monkeys. *Animal Behaviour* 60: 253–261.

de Waal, F. B. M., and Berger, M. L. 2000. Payment for labour in monkeys. *Nature* 404: 563.

de Waal, F. B., and Brosnan, S. F. 2006. Simple and complex reciprocity in primates. In *Cooperation in Primates and Humans*, ed. P. Kappeler and C. van Schaik. Springer.

de Waal, F. B. M., and Davis, J. M. 2003. Capuchin cognitive ecology: Cooperation based on projected returns. *Neuropsychologia* 41: 221–228.

de Waal, F. B. M., and Luttrell, L. M. 1988. Mechanisms of social reciprocity in three primate species: Symmetrical relationship characteristics or cognition? *Ethology and Sociobiology* 9: 101–118.

de Waal, F. B. M., and Yoshihara, D. 1983. Reconciliation and redirected affection in rhesus monkeys. *Behaviour* 85: 224–241.

de Waal, F. B. M., Leimgruber, K., and Greenberg, A. R. 2008. Giving is self-rewarding for monkeys. *Proceedings of the National Academy of Sciences* 105 (36): 13685–13689.

de Waal, F. B. M., Luttrell, L. M., and Canfield, M. E. 1993. Preliminary data on voluntary food sharing in brown capuchin monkeys. *American Journal of Primatology* 29: 73–78.

Fedigan, L. M. 1990. Vertebrate predation in *Cebus capucinus*: Meat eating in a neotropical monkey. *Folia Primatologica* 54 (3–4): 196–205.

Fehr, E., and Schmidt, K. M. 1999. A theory of fairness, competition, and cooperation. *Quarterly Journal of Economics* 114: 817–868.

Feistner, A. T. C., and McGrew, W. C. 1989. Food-sharing in primates: A critical review. In *Perspectives in Primate Biology*, ed. P. Seth and S. Seth. Today and Tomorrow's Printers and Publishers.

Fragaszy, D. M., Feuerstein, J. M., and Mitra, D. 1997. Transfers of food from adults to infants in tufted capuchins (*Cebus apella*). *Journal of Comparative Psychology* 111: 194–200.

Frank, R. H. 1988. *Passions Within Reason: The Strategic Role of the Emotions*. Norton.

Gomes, C. M., and Boesch, C. 2009. Wild chimpanzees exchange meat for sex on a long-term basis. *PLOS ONE* 4 (4): e5116.

Gomes, C. M., Mundry, R., and Boesch, C. 2009. Long-term reciprocation of grooming in wild West African chimpanzees. *Proceedings of the Royal Society B* 276: 699–706.

Goodall, J. 1971. *In the Shadow of Man*. Houghton Mifflin.

Hart, B. L., and Hart, L. A. 1992. Reciprocal allogrooming in impala, *Aepyceros melampus*. *Animal Behaviour* 44: 1073–1083.

Hawkes, K. 1990. Showing off: Tests of an hypothesis about men's foraging goals. *Ethology and Sociobiology* 12: 29–54.

Hemelrijk, C. K. 1994. Support for being groomed in long-tailed macaques, *Macaca fascicularis*. *Animal Behaviour* 48: 479–481.

Hirschleifer, J. 1987. On the emotions as guarantors of threats and promises. In *The Latest on the Best: Essays in Evolution and Optimality*, ed. J. Dupre. MIT Press.

Horner, V., Carter, J. D., Suchak, M., and de Waal, F. B. M. 2011. Spontaneous prosocial choice by chimpanzees. *Proceedings of the National Academy of Sciences* 108: 13847–13851.

Izawa, K. 1980. Social behavior of the wild black-capped capuchin (*Cebus apella*). *Primates* 21: 443–467.

Jacoby, S. 1983. *Wild Justice: The Evolution of Revenge*. Harper and Row.

Jaeggi, A. V., De Groot, E., Stevens, J. M. G., and Van Schaik, C. P. 2013. Mechanisms of reciprocity in primates: Testing for short-term contingency of grooming and food sharing in bonobos and chimpanzees. *Evolution and Human Behavior* 34 (2): 69–77.

Jaeggi, A. V., and van Schaik, C. P. 2011. The evolution of food sharing in primates. *Behavioral Ecology and Sociobiology* 65: 2125–2140.

Janson, C. H. 1988. Food competition in brown capuchin monkeys (*Cebus apella*): Quantitative effects of group size and tree productivity. *Behaviour* 105: 53–76.

Jensen, K., Call, J., and Tomasello, M. 2007. Chimpanzees are rational maximizers in an ultimatum game. *Science* 318: 107–109.

Jensen, K., Hare, B., Call, J., and Tomasello, M. 2006. What's in it for me? Self-regard precludes altruism and spite in chimpanzees. *Proceedings of the Royal Society B* 273: 1013–1021.

Kummer, H. 1991. Evolutionary transformations of possessive behavior. *Journal of Social Behavior and Personality* 6 (6): 75–83.

Melis, A. P., Hare, B., and Tomasello, M. 2008. Do chimpanzees reciprocate received favours? *Animal Behaviour* 76: 951–962.

Mendres, K. A., and de Waal, F. B. M. 2000. Capuchins do cooperate: The advantage of an intuitive task. *Animal Behaviour* 60: 523–529.

Mitani, J. C. 2005. Reciprocal exchange in chimpanzees and other primates. In *Cooperation in Primates and Humans: Evolution and Mechanisms*, ed. P. Kapeller and C. van Schaik. Springer.

Newcomer, D. M., and de Farcy, D. D. 1985. White-faced capuchin (*Cebus capucinus*) predation on a nestling coati (*Nasua narica*). *Journal of Mammalogy* 66: 185–186.

Noë, R., and Hammerstein, P. 1994. Biological markets: Supply and demand determine the effect of partner choice in cooperation, mutualism and mating. *Behavioral Ecology and Sociobiology* 35: 1–11.

Perry, S., and Rose, L. 1994. Begging and transfer of coati meat by white-faced capuchin monkeys, *Cebus capucinus*. *Primates* 35: 409–415.

Price, S. A., and Brosnan, S. F. 2012. To each according to his need? Variability in the responses to inequity in non-human primates. *Social Justice Research* 25 (2): 140–169.

Proctor, D., Williamson, R. A., de Waal, F. B. M., and Brosnan, S. F. 2013. Chimpanzees play the ultimatum game. *Proceedings of the National Academy of Sciences* 110 (6): 2070–2075.

Rose, L. 1997. Vertebrate predation and food-sharing in *Cebus* and *Pan*. *International Journal of Primatology* 18: 727–765.

Sanfey, A. G., Rilling, J. K., Aronson, J. A., Nystrom, L. E., and Cohen, J. D. 2003. The neural basis of economic decision-making in the ultimatum game. *Science* 300: 1755–1758.

Seyfarth, R. M. 1980. The distribution of grooming and related behaviours among adult female vervet monkeys. *Animal Behaviour* 28: 798–813.

Seyfarth, R. M., and Cheney, D. L. 1984. Grooming, alliances, and reciprocal altruism in vervet monkeys. *Nature* 308: 541–543.

Silk, J. B. 1992. The patterning of intervention among male bonnet macaques: Reciprocity, revenge, and loyalty. *Current Anthropology* 33: 318–325.

Silk, J. B., Brosnan, S. F., Vonk, J., Henrich, Joseph, Povinelli, D. J., Richardson, A. S., Lambeth, S.P., Mascaro, J., and Schapiro, S. 2005. Chimpanzees are indifferent to the welfare of unrelated group members. *Nature* 437: 1357–1359.

Stevens, J. R. 2004. The selfish nature of generosity: Harassment and food sharing in primates. *Proceedings of the Royal Society B* 271 (1538): 451–456.

Stevens, J. R., and Hauser, M. D. 2004. Why be nice? Psychological constraints on the evolution of cooperation. *Trends in Cognitive Sciences* 8: 60–65.

Suchak, M., and de Waal, F. B. M. 2012. Monkeys benefit from reciprocity without the cognitive burden. *Proceedings of the National Academy of Sciences* 109: 15191–15196.

Thierry, B., Wunderlich, D., and Gueth, C. 1989. Possession and transfer of objects in a group of brown capuchins (*Cebus apella*). *Behaviour* 110: 294–305.

Trivers, R. L. 1971. The evolution of reciprocal altruism. *Quarterly Review of Biology* 46: 35–57.

van Wolkenten, M., Brosnan, S. F., and de Waal, F. B. 2007. Inequity responses of monkeys modified by effort. *Proceedings of the National Academy of Sciences* 104 (47): 18854–18859.

Visalberghi, E., Quarantotti, B. P., and Tranchida, F. 2000. Solving a cooperation task without taking into account the partner's behavior: The case of capuchin monkeys (*Cebus apella*). *Journal of Comparative Psychology* 114: 297–301.

Watts, D. P. 2002. Reciprocity and interchange in the social relationships of wild male chimpanzees. *Behaviour* 139: 343–370.

Wilkinson, G. S. 1984. Reciprocal food sharing in the vampire bat. *Nature* 308: 181–184.

Wrangham, R. W. 1975. The Behavioral Ecology of Chimpanzees in Gombe National Park, Tanzania. PhD dissertation, Cambridge University.

2 The Fundamental Motives for Why We Buy

Vladas Griskevicius, Joseph P. Redden, and Joshua M. Ackerman

People spend much of their monthly income on housing, transportation, and clothing (source: How the Average U.S. Consumer Spends Their Paycheck, retrieved from http://www.visualeconomics.com in 2010). What motivates people to buy these things? At the most basic level, the answer is straightforward: We seek housing for shelter, transportation to get from point A to point B, and clothing to protect us from the elements. Yet people typically do not purchase the first or the cheapest house, car, or outfit that can provide these essentials.

The more pertinent question about consumers' behavior, then, is "Why would a person choose to purchase one house rather than another, one car rather than another, or one pair of shoes rather than another?" The answer is rarely that the house purchased provides superior shelter, that the car is more effective at getting a person from point A to point B, or that the shoes are superior at protecting the person's feet from the elements. In fact, some people are willing to pay $150 for shoes that cost only $15 to produce, even when such consumers are fully aware that the more expensive pair is materially identical to another pair half its price.

Here we examine the underlying motives for why we buy. We consider motivation from an evolutionary perspective, which is centrally concerned with the deeper reasons for behavior. In the last few decades, evolutionary considerations of human behavior have produced many theoretical and empirical insights in psychology (Buss 1995; Tooby and Cosmides 2005), anthropology (Kaplan et al. 2000), and consumer behavior (Griskevicius et al. 2009a; Miller 2009; Saad 2007; see also the chapter by Frank, the chapter by Preston and Vickers, and the chapter by Saad in this volume). This body of work highlights how our choices are driven by ancestral motives that continue to influence behavior, though not always in obvious or conscious ways. We discuss how, why, and when these motives shape consumer behavior.

Distinguishing Proximate and Ultimate Motives

An evolutionary approach to examining behavior is based on foundational theories within modern biology. This approach suggests that the same forces of natural selection that have shaped such morphological features as our hands and our hearts have also shaped our brains and our behaviors. Evolutionary biologists assert that all living organisms, including humans, evolved to behave in ways that were favored by natural selection—that gave those organisms an evolutionary advantage. This means that we modern humans are endowed with a psychology that inclines us to make decisions in ways that enabled our ancestors to continually survive, thrive, and replicate (Buss 1995; Kenrick et al. 2010a; Tooby and Cosmides 1992).

An evolutionary perspective is central to understanding human motivation. It draws attention to a distinction that biologists have long made between two fundamentally different types of reasons for behavior: *proximate* reasons and *ultimate* reasons (Confer et al. 2010; Tinbergen 1963; see also the chapter by Preston and Vickers, the chapter by Brosnan et al., and the chapter by Saad in this volume). To understand this important distinction, consider a simple example. Suppose that you have a friend who just donated to a charity, and you ask her why she did so. She may simply respond "I wanted to help!" If your generous friend is feeling more analytical, she may mention that she felt a desire to help when she saw a person in need, and that helping made her feel good. This is a proximate explanation of behavior. The reason the word *proximate* is used is that the cause is relatively "up close" and immediately present.

Proximate reasons are important, but they tell only part of the story. Proximate reasons don't address the deeper question of *why* humans feel the need to help others or *why* helping others makes humans feel good. Understanding these deeper reasons for behavior requires an *ultimate* explanation. Unlike proximate causes, ultimate causes focus on the evolutionary function of a behavior—the reason why a behavior has persisted across many generations. Because we have inherited brain mechanisms that are wired to light up when we see people suffering and needing help, this suggests that helping behavior must have been associated with some evolutionary benefit in our ancestral past. If it hadn't been, humans would not have evolved to be helpful.

Sometimes the ultimate and proximate reason for a behavior are closely connected. For example, if you ask a friend why he just ate a brownie, he may say "I was starving!" In this case, the proximate explanation (feeling hunger) is directly connected to the ultimate goal of obtaining calories to survive. But usually the connection between proximate and ultimate reasons is not that clear. Consider, for example, why birds migrate each year. The proximate reason is that the days get shorter—day length is the proximate cue that triggers the bird's motivation to begin its journey. But the ultimate reason for birds' migration has nothing to do with day length. The ultimate reason birds migrate is that the locations of the best food-gathering sites and the best mating sites change with the seasons.

Like most animals, humans do not need to consciously know the connection between the proximate triggers of their behavior and the ultimate reasons behind those behaviors. People are sometimes not at all aware of the proximate reasons for their behavior (Nisbett and Wilson 1977), and people are especially poor at knowing the ultimate reasons for their behavior (Barrett and Kurzban 2006; Tooby and Cosmides 2005; Kenrick et al. 2010a). But because behavior has both ultimate and proximate reasons, this means that people often have multiple motives for a behavior, even if they are not always aware of the ultimate reasons for their choices. For example, a person can be consciously motivated to engage in helping behavior to make herself or someone else feel better (a proximate reason), *and at the same time* be subconsciously motivated to help because doing so can enhance her desirability to a potential mate and thereby enhance her reproductive fitness (an ultimate reason). Proximate and ultimate reasons are not competing explanations; reasons of both kinds are useful for understanding any given behavior.

Consumer researchers, like most social scientists, have typically been concerned with proximate reasons for behavior. In Paco Underhill's popular book *Why We Buy*, for example, all the reasons given for why people buy are proximate reasons. Companies, likewise, use focus groups to try to get at the common proximate reasons for behavior, which include preferences, values, feelings, incentives, and social norms. When asking why people behave in a certain way, consumer researchers often focus on proximate goals—that is, what people want to feel or to avoid feeling. For example, people might seek to feel pleasure, happiness, or satisfaction, while avoiding pain, sadness, or frustration. Commonly studied motivations—including promotion, prevention, approach, avoidance, and the managing of existential terror—all reflect proximate motivation that is not concerned with the evolutionary function of behavior.

An evolutionary perspective highlights a separate, universal level of motivation rooted in the ultimate evolutionary functions of behavior. This is a useful way to look at motivation. Though there could be innumerable proximate reasons for behavior, there is a much smaller set of ultimate, evolutionary reasons. One strength of an evolutionary approach is that it focuses on a single level of analysis—the ultimate level—and attempts to produce a taxonomy of evolutionary motives for human behavior. What are the most common ultimate motives for behavior?

The Fundamental-Motives Framework

When people think about evolutionary "success," they may picture only survival and reproduction. Although they are certainly important, survival and reproduction are only two of the evolutionary challenges that our ancestors had to surmount in order to achieve evolutionary success. Like all other animals, our ancestors needed nourishment and shelter. But because humans are intensely social animals, they also faced a significant and recurrent set of *fundamental social challenges* (Ackerman and Kenrick 2008; Kenrick, Li, and Butner 2003; Kenrick et al. 2010a): evading physical harm, avoiding disease, making friends, attaining status, acquiring a mate, keeping a mate, and caring for offspring.

The individuals who became our ancestors were the ones who protected themselves from enemies and predators, avoided infection and disease, and got along with and gained the respect of the others in their tribe. They also acquired a reproductive partner, probably established some type of bond with that person (perhaps for the rest of their lives), and, if all went well, cared for their needy and relatively helpless offspring. Those who were less successful in dealing with the aforementioned challenges did not become our ancestors. In view of the important implications that these challenges have had for reproductive fitness and human evolution, they can be considered "fundamental" (Kenrick et al. 2010b).

An evolutionary perspective assumes that the brain did not evolve as a general-purpose problem solver. This means that the brain comes with instructions more complex than simply "behave adaptively" or "make choices that maximize the chances of eventually reproducing." Instead, empirical findings suggest that we possess different psychological systems for managing different evolutionary challenges (Bugental 2000; Delton et al. 2012; Griskevicius, Tybur et al. 2009; Lieberman et al. 2007; Saad 2007; see also the chapter by Saad in this volume). We have a specialized psychological system for attracting mates, a different system for avoiding infectious disease, and yet different systems for solving other evolutionary challenges. Each of these challenges maps onto a fundamental motivational system, which is activated by real or imagined perceptual cues indicating that the current situation pertains to a specific evolutionary problem (Kenrick et al. 2010a). For example, the mate-acquisition system can be activated by interacting with a desirable member of the opposite sex, or by merely seeing or imagining an image of such a person. When a fundamental motivational system has been activated, it produces a specific set of consequences for attention, perception, cognition, and behavior (Kenrick et al. 2010b; Neuberg, Kenrick, and Schaller 2010). This coordinated response serves to further the ultimate objective of the currently active system. For example, the activation of the mate-acquisition system will lead a person to make choices in ways that facilitate the ultimate objective of acquiring a mate while suppressing the ultimate objectives of other systems.

An important implication of this framework is that a person's preferences and choices can change depending upon which motivational system is currently active. For example, what house, car, or outfit a person chooses will depend on which system is currently active. That is because what constitutes adaptive behavior to further one ultimate objective may be very different from what is adaptive to further another ultimate objective. Accordingly, the activation of one system often produces unique downstream outcomes compared to the activation of a different system (Maner et al. 2005; Griskevicius et al. 2009a). For example, whereas activating the self-protection system leads people to consciously or subconsciously conform and follow the masses, activating the mate-acquisition system leads people to anti-conform and to try to stand out from the crowd (Griskevicius et al. 2009b).

The Evolutionary Motives Driving Consumer Behavior

Table 2.1 presents the fundamental motivational systems, their environmental triggers, and examples of their behavioral consequences. In the remainder of the chapter, we discuss each fundamental motive in more detail, review the key findings, and discuss the implications of fundamental motives for consumer behavior. (For a breakdown of consumers' motives divided into four Darwinian modules—survival, mating, kin selection, and reciprocity—see the chapter by Saad.)

Self-protection

Although humans have faced many dangerous predators, fellow humans have been their main and most dangerous threat. Criminologists examining skull fragments from earlier human societies, and anthropologists studying other human groups, have found that homicide is not a modern invention (Pinker 2011). Our ancestors lived in groups with homicide rates that would make today's inner-city Detroit or Los Angeles look tame. And even when bad guys weren't out to kill our ancestors, they often tried to steal their belongings, carry off their wives, or burn down their villages.

Table 2.1

Fundamental evolutionary motives, their triggers, and consumers' tendencies.

Motivational system	Ultimate objective	Cues triggering system	Examples of consumers' tendencies and biases
Self-protection	Evade physical danger and remain safe	Possibility of physical danger: Angry faces, outgroup males Darkness, loud noises Interacting with threatening person	Increased paranoia Increased aversion to losses Increased tendency to conform Decreased risk seeking
Disease avoidance	Avoid infections and remain healthy	Potential presence of pathogens: Coughing, sneezing, foul smells Dirtiness, deformity, foreignness Interacting with sick person	Become more introverted Become more xenophobic Seek "clean" and familiar products Avoid used products

Table 2.1
(Continued)

Motivational system	Ultimate objective	Cues triggering system	Examples of consumers' tendencies and biases
Affiliation	Form and maintain cooperative alliances	Friendship threat or opportunity: Social rejection, loneliness Concerns about fairness Interacting with friends or co-workers	Seek products to enhance connection with others Identify with and seek anthropomorphic products Increased susceptibility to word-of-mouth Seek online reviews to know what others think
Status	Gain and maintain respect and prestige	Status threat or opportunity: Competition, success Prestigious objects, successful others Interacting with boss or underlings	Seek products that signal power and prestige Seek exclusive and most up-to-date features Increased prosocial behavior Increased aggression, dominance
Mate acquisition	Acquire a desirable romantic partner	Desirable members of opposite sex: Sexy images, products Romantic stories Interacting with potential date	Increased conspicuous consumption Decreased tendency to conform and more creativity Decreased loss aversion Increased impulsivity and risk taking
Mate retention	Foster long-term mating bond	Relationship threat or celebration: Anniversary, reminisce good times Interloper, wandering eye Interacting with spouse/partner	Seek gifts to foster committed relationship Joint purchases Increased attention to same-sex people
Kin care	Invest in and care for family and kin	Family or vulnerable others: Babies Struggling or suffering person Interacting with family members	Increased trust of others Increased nurturance Increased giving

Our ancestors had to be successful at avoiding and overcoming threats, and similar challenges remain today. Our self-protection system can be activated by a variety of cues indicating physical danger, including angry expressions, unfamiliar men, scary movies or news reports, or just being in the dark (Ackerman et al. 2006; Becker et al. 2007; Schaller, Park, and Mueller 2003; Ohman and Mineka 2001). Activation of this fundamental system makes people more vigilant and paranoid, attuning them to information suggesting that they may be in danger.

A self-protection motive spurs people to seek safety. Activating this motive leads people to take fewer risks (Lerner and Keltner 2001), to be particularly averse to losses (Li et al. 2012), and to prefer the status quo (Jost and Hunyady 2005). It also promotes a "strength in numbers" response, leading people to conform more and to band together with similar others (Griskevicius et al. 2006b; Kugihara 2005; Van Vugt, De Cremer, and Janssen 2007). For example, advertising messages appealing to the behaviors of the masses (e.g., "purchased by over a million people") are more persuasive when a self-protection motive is active, while messages emphasizing uniqueness (e.g., "be different") become less persuasive (Griskevicius, Goldstein et al. 2009).

Although self-protection is usually associated with more cautious behavior, in some instances it can lead to increased risk taking. For example, some studies have found that people from poor and resource-deprived backgrounds respond to physical danger by taking more risks to obtain rewards because they have little to lose (Griskevicius et al. 2012a,b). Nevertheless, the self-protection system will usually tend to produce cautious choices that prioritize safety.

Let's consider which house, car, and outfit a person with an active self-protection motive might purchase. In view of the priority for safety, the house is likely to be inconspicuous (so as to not draw too much attention), to be bright and roomy inside, and to be located in a safe neighborhood but still to have a fence and a security system. The car is likely to have a high crash-safety rating, side-curtain airbags, the latest driver safety features, and an instant connection to an emergency roadside assistance service. The outfit is likely to be conservative (so the wearer will blend in with others) and to make the wearer feel safe and not exposed.

Disease avoidance

Biologists estimate that infectious diseases carried by other humans were an important selection pressure on the human species (Gangestad and Buss 1993). Although modern humans have developed technologies to control many diseases and to limit their spread, virulent and contagious microorganisms still lurk on and within the people we encounter every day, awaiting any moment of contact that might provide an opportunity for them to jump onto us.

One result of this ever-present threat has been the evolution of a sophisticated biological immune system. Another has been the evolution of a psychological behavioral immune system (Schaller and Park 2011), which helps us to avoid infection in the first place. This disease-avoidance system is activated when we contract actual illnesses, such as influenza (Miller and Maner 2011), but is also engaged by cues that heuristically indicate the presence of pathogens, such as people sneezing and coughing, skin lesions, and foul smells (Ackerman et al. 2009; Miller and Maner 2011). The system is also triggered when we taste sour milk, smell rotting food, or merely think about people from places that seem exotic and far away to Westerners, such as Sri Lanka and Ethiopia. Merely seeing someone who might be sick can even trigger our biological immune system and increase inflammation (Schaller, Miller, Gervais, Yager, and Chen 2010).

A disease-avoidance motive spurs people to seek protection from anything associated with pathogens. People exposed to a liquid with a bacteria-laden smell increase their intentions to purchase and use condoms to avoid sexually transmitted disease (Tybur et al. 2011). Similarly, hearing people cough or seeing people wearing face masks increases handwashing behavior (Fleischman et al. 2011). When the disease-avoidance system has been primed, people exhibit a number of socially avoidant behaviors, such as becoming more introverted and feeling less tolerant of foreigners (Mortensen et al. 2010; Schaller and Park 2011). The disease-avoidance system can also be activated by internal cues to vulnerability. During the first trimester of pregnancy, for example, when the developing fetus is particularly susceptible to serious developmental problems if the mother gets sick, women avoid novel foods that might contain pathogens, and they become more xenophobic (Navarrete, Fessler, and Eng 2007).

People worried about disease seek familiar foods and avoid foods of foreign origin (unless the foods are sealed in airtight packaging) (Li, Ackerman, White, Neuberg, and Kenrick, manuscript under review). Merely seeing an advertisement for a pharmacy can activate disease avoidance, and can increase a person's willingness to buy new items rather than used ones (Huang and Ackerman 2012). And products that are in some way associated with disease can "contaminate" nearby goods, leading consumers to avoid nearby products on store shelves or in shopping carts (Morales and Fitzsimons 2007).

Which house, car, and outfit might a person with an active disease-avoidance motive purchase? In view of the priority for cleanliness and avoiding pathogens, the house should be new or at least recently refurbished and well-maintained, should have good air filters, and should be in a familiar area with neighbors who look similar to the owner. The car probably will be basic and not fancy, but it should be clean. It will help the person avoid public transportation. The outfit will probably be made of natural fibers, to minimize allergies, and the person may pay a premium for clothing made in his or her home country.

Affiliation

Although some animals spend most of their lives as veritable hermits, most humans have always lived in groups. To survive and reproduce, our ancestors needed to form coalitions and get along with others (Hill and Hurtado 1996). Having allies and friends provided a natural insurance policy against starvation, enabling people to pool their risk to make it through tough times. Friends also taught one another valuable skills, could team up to achieve tasks too big for an individual, and could provide safety in numbers when the bad guys come around.

Today we continue to invest heavily in building and maintaining our friendships, as is witnessed by the fundamental motive for affiliation (Baumeister and Leary 1995). The affiliation system is activated by existing or potential cues of friendship and coalition membership (e.g., being part of a group), as when your old college roommate sends a Christmas card, when you're thinking about inviting a neighbor for dinner, or when your co-worker picks up the tab for lunch. The system is also triggered when friendships are threatened or exploited, or when a person is socially rejected. This system attunes us to information about acquaintances who might make good friends, whether we are being accepted or rejected by those people, and whether we are getting along with the friends we have.

An affiliation motive promotes the reinforcement of existing friendships and spurs behaviors to make new friends (Maner et al. 2007a). In contrast to a disease-avoidance motive that leads people to become more introverted and treat social contact as a cost, an affiliation motive leads people to become more outgoing and to treat social contact as a benefit. For example, people will spend more money on products that can be enjoyed in the company of others than on products that usually are consumed alone (Mead et al. 2011). An affiliation motive may also promote gift giving, and may lead people to purchase gifts that might run counter to their own identities in order to fulfill the desires of the intended recipient (Ward and Broniarczyk 2011; see also the chapter by Brosnan, de Waal, and Proctor in this volume).

People's relationships with products and brands sometimes mimic their relationships with friends. People often purchase things because they are lonely (Lastovicka and Sirianni 2011), and they sometimes treat those possessions as though they were people (Epley, Waytz, Akalis, and Cacioppo 2008). Just as with friends, people are more likely to engage with brands they perceive as sincere (Aaker, Fournier, and Brasel 2004), and consumers feel the sting of brand transgressions much as they feel the slights of friends (Aaker, Fournier, and Brasel 2004).

What sort of house, car, and outfit might a person with an active affiliation motive purchase? The house will have to be inviting, with plenty of space for entertaining, and ideally it shouldn't be too far from where others live. The car should have enough passenger room, and it should be ready for road trips. The choice of an outfit depends on what your friends are wearing. Your clothes should be just slightly different from theirs, but generally the same brands and style.

Status

As a group-living species, humans not only desire to affiliate; they also seek to gain status in their groups. Being respected by others has always brought a host of benefits, and this did not start with human beings. Dominant baboons get the first crack at food and the best spot at the watering hole, and dominant male chimpanzees get to mate with the most desirable females (Sapolsky 2002). The benefits of status clearly apply to people in the modern world, too. People with higher status have greater interpersonal influence (Miller, Collins, and Brief 1995), more material resources (Cummins 1998), higher self-esteem (Tesser 1988), and better health (Marmot 2004).

Nonhuman animals sometimes gain status mainly by force. But although people can sometimes attain status through dominance (e.g., overpowering others and forcing deference), people often attain and maintain status through prestige (e.g., freely conferred deference) (Henrich and Gil-White 2001; Cheng et al. 2013). Think of Bill Gates or Stephen Hawking, each of whom might lose a fight with the guy who mows his grass but nevertheless has enough status to make the world turn at the snap of a finger.

The status system is triggered by cues of dominance, prestige, or competition, such as accomplishments, rivalries, or highly regarded products or people. It is also activated when people are deprived of status and power (Rucker and Galinsky 2009). It attunes people to where they stand in the hierarchy. When this motive is active, we are prone to place special value on being associated with successful people and objects, to cut off associations with lower-ranked others, and to regard others' disrespect as especially costly.

A status motive spurs people to behave in ways that will lead them to be respected and admired. Sometimes this can increase dominance, such as when activating a status motive increases aggressive behavior (Griskevicius, Tybur, et al. 2009) or leads people to value physically larger and more imposing products (Dubois, Rucker, and Galinsky 2012). But most often, a desire for status leads people to seek prestige, for example by motivating them to acquire high-status products. A status motive leads people to pay more for luxury and reputational goods (Ivanic, Overbeck, and Nunes 2011; Rucker and Galinsky 2008) and to favor flashy brands that are more visible to others (Han, Nunes, and Drèze 2010). Of course, status is primarily relevant only within the group a person is a part of (or wishes to be a part of); in groups in which flashy products aren't prized, status-seeking consumers prefer high-value but subtly branded products (Berger and Ward 2010). When status goods are unattainable, a status motive can lead people to purchase counterfeit products (Wilcox, Kim, and Sen 2009). And once status has been obtained, people exhibit behavior designed to preserve their status (Maner, Gailliot, Butz, and Peruche 2007), such as by prioritizing personal goals over group goals (Maner and Mead 2010).

The desire for status is not all about selfishness and indulgence, though. A person's status in a group can also be enhanced through self-sacrifice (Hardy and Van Vugt 2006). Across cultures, individuals compete for status through prosocial behaviors—a tactic known as *competitive altruism* (Roberts 1998; Van Vugt et al. 2007b; see also the chapter by Brosnan et al. in this volume). Among the indigenous communities of Pacific Northwest America, for example, tribal chiefs compete to see who can give away the most resources, and the most benevolent chief gains status (Cole and Chaikin 1990). Accordingly, activating a status motive can lead people to spend more money on others than on themselves (Rucker, Dubois, and Galinsky 2011). Likewise, a status motive can lead people to choose inferior but environmentally beneficial "green" products because doing so may enhance their prosocial reputations (Griskevicius, Tybur, and Van den Bergh 2010).

What sort of house, car, and outfit might a person with an active status motive purchase? Your house should be in an exclusive part of town and should be impressive (especially the parts that guests can see), highlighting your refined taste and ample cash reserves. (A photo showing you with the president of a prestigious charity organization may be subtly displayed.) Your car, too, should stand out, and should have exclusive or difficult-to-acquire features that demonstrate your superior access to scarce goods. And you should dress to impress, standing out by being a step above and a step ahead in brand names and in fashion.

Mate acquisition

Even if you manage to avoid danger and disease and to get others to like and respect you, it will count for naught (at least in evolutionary terms) if you don't manage to find someone willing to help you transport your genes into the next generation. However, for any social animal, including *Homo sapiens*, the challenge of mating involves a great deal more than just sex. Mate acquisition involves a variety of behaviors that at first glance may appear not to be related to mating at all.

The mate-acquisition system (for heterosexuals, at least) is triggered by the presence of real or imagined members of the opposite sex. This motive is stimulated by sexy ads, by a romantic story, or by touching lingerie. When this motive is activated, people are attuned to information about the desirability of others as sexual partners and their own allure.

A mate-acquisition motive spurs people to boost their attractiveness to the opposite sex. In contrast to a self-protection motive that leads people to want to blend in, a mate-acquisition motive leads people to want to be noticed. When this motive is activated, men and women find products advertised as unique and scarce more appealing than products marketed as popular and best-selling (Griskevicius, Goldstein, et al. 2009).

But although both men and women want to stand out in order to acquire a mate, they often seek to draw attention to themselves in different ways. Men become more creative (Griskevicius, Cialdini, and Kenrick 2006), more manipulative (Ackerman, Griskevicius, and Li 2011), more independent (Griskevicius, Goldstein, et al. 2006), and more heroic (Griskevicius et al. 2007). Men also become less loss averse (Li et al. 2012), seek more risks (Baker and Maner 2008; Knutson, Wimmer, Kuhnen, and Winkielman 2008), become more impulsive (Van den Bergh, Dewitte, and Warlop 2008; Wilson and Daly 2004), and acquire conspicuous luxury products (Griskevicius et al. 2007; Sundie et al. 2011).

Women, too, want to stand out. But instead of showing off their wealth and bravado, as men do, women advertise kindness. Women motivated to acquire a mate become more agreeable and helpful (Griskevicius et al. 2007). Activating a mate-acquisition motive doesn't lead women to become brazenly risky, except for one telling exception: women take more risks if it enhances their appearance (Hill and Durante 2011). Women primed with a mate-acquisition motive are more willing to take diet pills and to tan their bodies, even when they know that tanning can cause cancer.

Women's mate-acquisition system can also be triggered internally during the week-long ovulatory phase of the monthly menstrual cycle (Gangestad and Thornhill 2008). During this period of peak fertility, women seek sexier and more alluring clothes (Durante et al. 2011; Durante, Li, and Haselton 2008); they also become more generous (Durante et al., in press).

What sort of house, car, and outfit might a person with an active mate-acquisition motive purchase? The house should be upscale, distinctive, and inviting, showing men's independence and women's nurturance. For cars, safety is not an issue, since danger can be attractive, and extra room isn't important as long as the car will accommodate two. The clothing should be designed with one goal in mind: signaling desirability. Often this means stylish and expensive, with some elements of flashiness for men and exposed skin for women.

Mate retention

For 95 percent of mammalian species, mating is a short-term affair, the females choosing the most dominant or the most attractive local male. Among humans, gibbons, and members of a few other furry warm-blooded species, however, females and males pick one another, and then often join forces for the long term (Kenrick et al. 2010a). Human mating therefore involves another set of problems beyond acquiring a mate: those entailed in getting along with that mate for years and sometimes decades. The problems associated with keeping a mate are very different from those involved in finding a mate. For example, spending a lot of money on a large party may impress a date, but to a spouse the same behavior may indicate a lack of commitment.

The mate-retention system is activated by cues that celebrate or threaten a long-term relationship, such as reminiscing about the relationship, noticing that an anniversary is coming up, or catching a person of the opposite sex eyeing one's partner. The mate-retention system involves both maintaining current relationship bonds and managing the threat of potential romantic competitors (Campbell and Ellis 2005). When this motive is active, people are attuned to whether their partner seems to be content or miserable. They also scan the social horizon for potential interlopers.

A mate-retention motive spurs people to behave in ways that ensure the solidarity and functioning of their long-term romantic relationships. For example, such a motive leads people to seek to preserve their current relationships by showing increased love and care for their current partner and by purchasing gifts for that partner (Buss and Shackelford 1997; Saad and Gill 2003). Committed people also tend to devalue alternative potential romantic partners (Lydon, Fitzsimons, and Naidoo 2003; Simpson, Gangestad, and Lerma 1990). A mate-retention motive also leads people to be more attentive to attractive members of the same sex, who may represent a threat to the relationship (Maner, Miller, Rouby, and Gailliot 2009). The increases in jealousy and mate-guarding behaviors that result are intended to interfere with the beginning of any potential infidelity.

What sort of house, car, and outfit might a person with an active mate-retention motive purchase? In contrast with the choices made under a mate-acquisition motive, the decisions should prioritize sensibility and relationship stability over uniqueness and flair. The house should be practical, with space that both partners can customize for future use. The cars probably should prioritize safety and multi-use capabilities. The clothes may be somewhat more conservative than those worn before the relationship began, but in settings where attractive threats to the relationship are frequently present people need to continue to impress their current partner.

Kin care

The ultimate reason that parents bond with one another is because it is good for their offspring. Studies of traditional societies show that children without both parents are less likely to survive, and that if they do survive they don't fare as well as those with two investing parents (Hill and Hurtado 1996). Today people still expend huge amounts of time, energy, and financial resources to raise their children. In the United States, it costs $205,960 to raise just one child (and that's without college tuition) (Lino 2010).

The kin-care system is activated around children or family members, especially when they are vulnerable or in need. It can also be triggered by cues of similarity, living together, common goals, and even fictive kinship phrases such as "our company is one big family" (Lieberman, Tooby, and Cosmides 2007; Park, Schaller, and Van Vugt 2008).

Note that the kin-care system is not the system that leads people to have children (the mate-acquisition system takes care of that by motivating us to have sex). Instead, a kin-care motive spurs people to behave in ways that ensure that individuals in need receive proper care and attention. This motive fosters willingness to sacrifice oneself to help others (Burnstein, Crandall, and Kitayama 1994), to provide social support (Kivett 1985), to provide physical protection (Daly and Wilson 1988), and to provide financial support (Smith, Kish, and Crawford 1987). In fact, if your photo is morphed with that of a stranger, you will be more trusting of the stranger and even more willing to give him money (DeBruine 2002).

What sort of house, car, and outfit might a person whose kin-care system has been activated purchase? The school district will be an important factor. The house will have to accommodate children and perhaps members of the extended family, and the emphasis should be on comfort and security rather than on impressing guests. The car should communicate inclusiveness and well-being, and it should have enough space and the latest safety features. The clothes may be directly tied to child care (e.g., baby clothes), but they also may signal value and reliability without needing to stand out.

Conclusion

People everywhere have the same ultimate motives. From Afghanistan to Zimbabwe, all humans have ancestral motives to evade physical harm, avoid disease, make friends, attain status, acquire a mate, keep that mate, and care for kin. These deep-seated ancestral motives continue to shape modern consumers' preferences and decision making, though not always in obvious or conscious ways. One implication of this is that the same person might make different—and sometimes entirely inconsistent—choices depending on which fundamental motive is currently active.

Although the fundamental motives framework has been empirically fruitful in generating many novel hypotheses about basic psychological processes and social cognition, the overwhelming majority of empirical implications for consumers' behavior and their decision making have yet to be tested. Future research is poised to investigate the many ways in which fundamental motives influence preferences, choices, biases, errors, and many other phenomena central to consumers' behavior. Future research is also poised to examine how the strength and workings of each motive might differ across individuals as a function of several factors, including current life stage, biological sex, individual differences in life-history strategy, and culture.

Just as studying consumers' behavior presents an ideal avenue for gaining insight into underlying human motivations, an understanding of evolutionary needs can provide insight into consumers' preferences and their decision processes. An evolutionary perspective offers a powerful framework with a host of implications for theory and research in consumer behavior.

References

Aaker, J., Fournier, S., and Brasel, S. A. 2004. When good brands do bad. *Journal of Consumer Research* 31: 1–16.

Ackerman, J. A., Griskevicius, V., and Li, N. P. 2011. Let's get serious: Communicating commitment in romantic relationships. *Journal of Personality and Social Psychology* 100: 1015–1026.

Ackerman, J. M., Shapiro, J. R., Neuberg, S. L., Kenrick, D. K., Becker, D. V., Griskevicius, V., et al. 2006. They all look the same to me (unless they're angry): From out-group homogeneity to out-group heterogeneity. *Psychological Science* 17: 836–840.

Ackerman, J. M., and Kenrick, D. T. 2008. The costs of benefits: Help-refusals highlight key trade-offs of social life. *Personality and Social Psychology Review* 12 (2): 118–140.

Ackerman, J. M., Becker, D. V., Mortensen, C. R., Sasaki, T., Neuberg, S. L., and Kenrick, D. T. 2009. A pox on the mind: Disjunction of attention and memory in the processing of physical disfigurement. *Journal of Experimental Social Psychology* 45: 478–485.

Baker, M., and Maner, J. K. 2008. Risk-taking as a situationally sensitive male mating strategy. *Evolution and Human Behavior* 29: 391–395.

Barrett, H. C., and Kurzban, R. 2006. Modularity in cognition: Framing the debate. *Psychological Review* 113: 628–647.

Baumeister, R. R., and Leary, M. R. 1995. The need to belong: Desire for interpersonal attachments as a fundamental human motivation. *Psychological Bulletin* 117: 497–529.

Becker, D. V., Kenrick, D. T., Neuberg, S. L., Blackwell, K. C., and Smith, D. 2007. The confounded nature of angry men and happy women. *Journal of Personality and Social Psychology* 92: 179–190.

Berger, J., and Ward, M. K. 2010. Subtle signals of inconspicuous consumption. *Journal of Consumer Research* 37 (4): 555–569.

Bugental, D. B. 2000. Acquisition of the algorithms of social life: A domain-based approach. *Psychological Bulletin* 126: 187–219.

Burnstein, E., Crandall, C., and Kitayama, S. 1994. Some neo-Darwinian decision rules for altruism: Weighing the cues for inclusive fitness as a function of the biological importance of the decision. *Journal of Personality and Social Psychology* 67: 773–789.

Buss, D. M. 1995. Evolutionary psychology: A new paradigm for psychological science. *Psychological Inquiry* 6: 1–30.

Buss, D. M., and Shackelford, T. K. 1997. From vigilance to violence: Mate retention tactics in married couples. *Journal of Personality and Social Psychology* 72: 346–361.

Campbell, L., and Ellis, B. J. 2005. Commitment, love, and mate retention. In *The Handbook of Evolutionary Psychology*, ed. D. Buss. Wiley.

Cheng, J. T., Tracy, J. L., Foulsham, T., Kingstone, A., and Henrich, J. 2013. Two ways to the top: Evidence that dominance and prestige and distinct yet viable avenues to social rank and influence. *Journal of Personality and Social Psychology* 104 (1): 103–125.

Cole, D., & Chaikin, I. (1990). *An Iron Hand upon the People: The Law against the Potlatch on the Northwest Coast.* University of Washington Press.

Confer, J. C., Easton, J. A., Fleischman, D. S., Goetz, C. D., Lewis, D. M., Perilloux, C., et al. 2010. Evolutionary psychology: Controversies, questions, prospects, and limitations. *American Psychologist* 65: 110–126.

Cummins, R. A. 1998. The second approximation to an international standard for life satisfaction. *Social Indicators Research* 43: 307–334.

Daly, M., and Wilson, M. 1988. *Homicide.* Aldine de Gruyter.

DeBruine, L. M. 2002. Facial resemblance enhances trust. *Proceedings of the Royal Society B* 269 (1498): 1307–1312.

Delton, A. W., Cosmides, L., Robertson, T. E., Guemo, M., and Tooby, J. 2012. The psychosemantics of free riding: Dissecting the architecture of a moral concept. *Journal of Personality and Social Psychology* 102: 1252–1270.

Dubois, D. D., Rucker, D., and Galinsky, A. D. 2012. Super size me: Product size as a signal of status. *Journal of Consumer Research* 38 (6): 1047–1062.

Durante, K. M., Griskevicius, V., Hill, S. E., Perilloux, C., and Li, N. P. 2011. Ovulation, female competition, and product choice: Hormonal influences on consumer behavior. *Journal of Consumer Research* 37: 921–934.

Durante, K. M., Li, N. P., and Haselton, M. G. 2008. Changes in women's choice of dress across the ovulatory cycle: Naturalistic and laboratory task-based evidence. *Personality and Social Psychology Bulletin* 34: 1451–1460.

Durante, K. M., Griskevicius, V., Cantu, S., and Simpson, J. A. In press. Money and the monthly ovulation cycle: Hidden hormonal influences on women's decision making. *Journal of Marketing Research.*

Epley, N., Waytz, A., Akalis, S., and Cacioppo, J. T. 2008. When we need a human: Motivational determinants of anthropomorphism. *Social Cognition* 26: 143–155.

Fleischman, D. S., Webster, G. D., Judah, G., de Barra, M., Aunger, R., and Curtis, V. A. 2011. Sensor recorded changes in rates of hand washing with soap in response to the media reports of the H1N1 pandemic in Britain. *British Medical Journal Open* 1: e000127.

Gangestad, S. W., and Buss, D. M. 1993. Pathogen prevalence and human mate preferences. *Ethology and Sociobiology* 14: 89–96.

Gangestad, S. W., and Thornhill, R. 2008. Human oestrus. *Proceedings of the Royal Society B* 275: 991–1000.

Griskevicius, V., Cialdini, R. B., and Kenrick, D. T. 2006a. Peacocks, Picasso, and parental investment: The effects of romantic motives on creativity. *Journal of Personality and Social Psychology* 91: 63–76.

Griskevicius, V., Goldstein, N. J., Mortensen, C. R., Cialdini, R. B., and Kenrick, D. T. 2006b. Going along versus going alone: When fundamental motives facilitate strategic (non)conformity. *Journal of Personality and Social Psychology* 91: 281–294.

Griskevicius, V., Tybur, J. M., Sundie, J. M., Cialdini, R. B., Miller, G. F., and Kenrick, D. T. 2007. Blatant benevolence and conspicuous consumption: When romantic motives elicit costly displays. *Journal of Personality and Social Psychology* 93: 85–102.

Griskevicius, V., Goldstein, N. J., Mortensen, C. R., Sundie, J. M., Cialdini, R. B., and Kenrick, D. T. 2009. Fear and loving in Las Vegas: Evolution, emotion, and persuasion. *Journal of Marketing Research* 46: 385–395.

Griskevicius, V., Tybur, J. M., and Van den Bergh, B. 2010. Going green to be seen: Status, reputation, and conspicuous conservation. *Journal of Personality and Social Psychology* 98: 392–404.

Griskevicius, V., Tybur, J. M., Gangestad, S. W., Perea, E. F., Shapiro, J. R., and Kenrick, D. T. 2009. Aggress to impress: Hostility as an evolved context-dependent strategy. *Journal of Personality and Social Psychology* 96: 980–994.

Griskevicius, V., Tybur, J. M., Delton, A. W., and Robertson, T. E. 2011. The influence of mortality and socioeconomic status on risk and delayed rewards: A life history theory approach. *Journal of Personality and Social Psychology* 100: 1015–1026.

Griskevicius, V., Delton, A. W., Robertson, T. E., and Tybur, J. M. 2011. The environmental contingency of life history strategies: Influences of mortality and socioeconomic status on reproductive timing. *Journal of Personality and Social Psychology* 100: 241–254.

Han, Y. J., Nunes, J. C., and Drèze, X. 2010. Signaling status with luxury goods: The impact of brand prominence. *Journal of Marketing* 74 (July): 14–30.

Hardy, C. L., and Van Vugt, M. 2006. Nice guys finish first: The competitive altruism hypothesis. *Personality and Social Psychology Bulletin* 32: 1402.

Henrich, J., and Gil-White, F. J. 2001. The evolution of prestige: Freely conferred status as a mechanism for enhancing the benefits of cultural transmission. *Evolution and Human Behavior* 22: 165–196.

Hill, S. E., and Durante, K. M. 2011. Courtship, competition, and the pursuit of attractiveness: Mating goals facilitate health-related risk-taking and strategic risk suppression in women. *Personality and Social Psychology Bulletin* 37: 383–394.

Hill, K., and Hurtado, A. M. 1996. *Ache Life History: The Ecology and Demography of a Foraging People*. Aldine de Gruyter.

Huang, J. Y., and Ackerman, J. M. 2012. Preferences for previously owned products: The roles of contagion threat and protection. Manuscript submitted for publication.

Ivanic, A., Overbeck, J. R., and Nunes, J. 2011. Status, race, and money. *Psychological Science* 22: 1557–1566.

Jost, J. T., and Hunyady, O. 2005. Antecedents and consequences of system-justifying ideologies. *Current Directions in Psychological Science* 14: 260–265.

Kaplan, H., Hill, K., Lancaster, J., and Hurtado, A. M. 2000. A theory of human life history evolution: Diet, intelligence, and longevity. *Evolutionary Anthropology* 9: 156–185.

Kenrick, D. T., Griskevicius, V., Neuberg, S. L., and Schaller, M. 2010a. Renovating the pyramid of needs: Contemporary extensions built upon ancient foundations. *Perspectives on Psychological Science* 5: 292–314.

Kenrick, D. T., Li, N. L., and Butner, J. 2003. Dynamical evolutionary psychology: Individual decision rules and emergent social norms. *Psychological Review* 110: 3–28.

Kenrick, D. T., Neuberg, S. L., Griskevicius, V., Schaller, M., and Becker, D. V. 2010b Goal-driven cognition and functional behavior: The fundamental-motives framework. *Current Directions in Psychological Science* 19: 63–67.

Kivett, V. R. 1985. Consanguinity and kin level: Their relative importance to the helping network of older adults. *Journal of Gerontology* 40: 228–234.

Knutson, B., Wimmer, G. E., Kuhnen, C. M., and Winkielman, P. 2008. Nucleus accumbens activation mediates the influence of reward cues on financial risk taking. *Neuroreport* 19: 509–513.

Kugihara, N. 2005. Effects of physical threat and collective identity on prosocial behaviors in an emergency. In *Psychology of Aggression*, ed. J. Morgan. Nova Science.

Lastovicka, J. L., and Sirianni, N. J. 2011. Madly, truly, deeply: Consumers in the throes of material possession love. *Journal of Consumer Research* 37 (2): 323–342.

Lerner, J. S., and Keltner, D. 2001. Fear, anger, and risk. *Journal of Personality and Social Psychology* 81: 146–159.

Li, Y. J., Kenrick, D. T., Griskevicius, V., and Neuberg, S. L. 2012. Economic decision biases and fundamental motivations: How mating and self-protection alter loss aversion. *Journal of Personality and Social Psychology* 102: 550–561.

Li, Y. J., White, A. E., Ackerman, J. M., Neuberg, S. L., and Kenrick, D. T. Manuscript under review. We eat what we are: Disease concerns shift preferences for (un) familiar foods.

Lieberman, D., Tooby, J., and Cosmides, L. 2007. The architecture of human kin detection. *Nature* 445: 727–731.

Lino, M. 2010. Expenditures on children by families, 2009. Retrieved from http://www.cnpp.usda.gov.

Lydon, J. E., Fitzsimons, G. M., and Naidoo, L. 2003. Devaluation versus enhancement of attractive alternatives: A critical test using the calibration paradigm. *Personality and Social Psychology Bulletin* 29: 349–359.

Maner, J. K., DeWall, C. N., Baumeister, R. F., and Schaller, M. 2007a. Does social exclusion motivate interpersonal reconnection? Resolving the "porcupine problem." *Journal of Personality and Social Psychology* 92: 42–55.

Maner, J. K., Gailliot, M. T., Rouby, D. A., and Miller, S. L. 2007b. Can't take my eyes off you: Attentional adhesion to mates and rivals. *Journal of Personality and Social Psychology* 93: 389–401.

Maner, J. K., Gailliot, M. T., Butz, D., and Peruche, B. M. 2007c. Power, risk, and the status quo: Does power promote riskier or more conservative decision-making? *Personality and Social Psychology Bulletin* 33: 451–462.

Maner, J. K., Kenrick, D. T., Neuberg, S. L., Becker, D. V., Robertson, T., Hofer, B., et al. 2005. Functional projection: How fundamental social motives can bias interpersonal perception. *Journal of Personality and Social Psychology* 88: 63–78.

Maner, J. K., and Mead, N. 2010. The essential tension between leadership and power: When leaders sacrifice group goals for the sake of self-interest. *Journal of Personality and Social Psychology* 99 (3): 482–497.

Maner, J. K., Miller, S. L., Rouby, D. A., and Gailliot, M. T. 2009. Intrasexual vigilance: The implicit cognition of romantic rivalry. *Journal of Personality and Social Psychology* 97: 74–87.

Marmot, M. 2004. *Status Syndrome: How Your Social Standing Directly Affects Your Health and Life Expectancy*. Bloomsbury.

Mead, N. L., Baumeister, R. F., Stillman, T. F., Rawn, C. D., & Vohs, K. D. 2011. Social exclusion causes people to spend and consume in the service of affiliation. *Journal of Consumer Research* 37 (5): 902–919.

Miller, A. G., Collins, B. E., and Brief, D. E. 1995. Perspectives on obedience to authority: The legacy of the Milgram experiments. *Journal of Social Issues* 51: 1–19.

Miller, G. F. 2009. *Spent: Sex, Evolution, and Consumer Behavior*. Penguin/Putnam.

Miller, S. L., and Maner, J. K. 2011. Sick body, vigilant mind: The biological immune system activates the behavioral immune system. *Psychological Science* 22: 1467–1471.

Morales, A. C., and Fitzsimons, G. J. 2007. Product contagion: Changing consumer evaluations through physical contact with "disgusting" products. *Journal of Marketing Research* 44: 272–283.

Mortensen, C. R., Becker, D. V., Ackerman, J. M., Neuberg, S. L., and Kenrick, D. T. 2010. Infection breeds reticence: The effects of disease salience on self-perceptions of personality and behavioral avoidance tendencies. *Psychological Science* 21: 440–447.

Navarrete, C. D., Fessler, D. M. T., and Eng, S. J. 2007. Elevated ethnocentrism in the first trimester of pregnancy. *Evolution and Human Behavior* 28 (1): 60–65.

Neuberg, S. L., Kenrick, D. T., and Schaller, M. 2010. Evolutionary social psychology. In *Handbook of Social Psychology*, fifth edition, ed. S. Fiske, D. Gilbert, and G. Lindzey. Wiley.

Nisbett, R., and Wilson, T. 1977. Telling more than we can know: Verbal reports on mental processes. *Psychological Review* 84: 231–259.

Ohman, A., and Mineka, S. 2001. Fears, phobias, and preparedness: Toward an evolved module of fear and fear learning. *Psychological Review* 108: 483–522.

Park, J. H., Schaller, M., and Van Vugt, M. 2008. Psychology of human kin recognition: Heuristic cues, erroneous inferences, and their implications. *Review of General Psychology* 12: 215–235.

Pinker, S. 2011. *The Better Angels of Our Nature: Why Violence Has Declined*. Penguin.

Roberts, G. 1998. Competitive altruism: From reciprocity to the handicap principle. *Proceedings of the Royal Society B* 265: 427–431.

Rucker, D. D., Dubois, D., and Galinsky, A. D. 2011. Generous paupers and stingy princes: Power drives consumer spending on self and others. *Journal of Consumer Research*, 37 (6): 1015–1029.

Rucker, D. D., and Galinsky, A. D. 2008. Desire to acquire: Powerlessness and compensatory consumption. *Journal of Consumer Research* 35: 257–267.

Rucker, D. D., and Galinsky, A. D. 2009. Conspicuous consumption versus utilitarian ideals: How different levels of power shape consumer consumption. *Journal of Experimental Social Psychology* 45: 549–555.

Saad, G. 2007. *The Evolutionary Bases of Consumption*. Erlbaum.

Saad, G., and Gill, T. 2003. An evolutionary psychology perspective on gift giving among young adults. *Psychology and Marketing* 20: 765–784.

Sapolsky, R. M. 2002. *A Primate's Memoir: A Neuroscientist's Unconventional Life among the Baboons*. Scribner.

Schaller, M., Miller, G. E., Gervais, W. M., Yager, S., and Chen, E. 2010. Mere visual perception of other people's disease symptoms facilitates a more aggressive immune response. *Psychological Science* 21: 649–652.

Schaller, M., and Park, J. H. 2011. The behavioral immune system (and why it matters). *Current Directions in Psychological Science* 20: 99–103.

Schaller, M., Park, J. H., and Mueller, A. 2003. Fear of the dark: Interactive effects of beliefs about danger and ambient darkness on ethnic stereotypes. *Personality and Social Psychology Bulletin* 29: 637–649.

Simpson, J. A., Gangestad, S. W., and Lerma, M. 1990. Perception of physical attractiveness: Mechanisms involved in the maintenance of romantic relationships. *Journal of Personality and Social Psychology* 59: 1192–1201.

Smith, M., Kish, B., and Crawford, C. 1987. Inheritance of wealth as human kin investment. *Ethology and Sociobiology* 8 (3): 171–182.

Sundie, J. M., Kenrick, D. T., Griskevicius, V., Tybur, J. M., Vohs, K. D., and Beal, D. J. 2011. Peacocks, Porsches, and Thorstein Veblen: Conspicuous consumption as a sexual signaling system. *Journal of Personality and Social Psychology* 100: 664–680.

Tesser, A. 1988. Toward a self-evaluation maintenance model of social behavior. In *Advances in Experimental Social Psychology*, volume 21, ed. L. Berkowitz. Academic Press.

Tinbergen, N. 1963. On the aims and methods of ethology. *Zeitschrift für Tierpsychologie* 20: 410–433.

Tooby, J., and Cosmides, L. 1992. The psychological foundations of culture. In *The Adapted Mind: Evolutionary Psychology and the Generation of Culture*, ed. J. Barkow, L. Cosmides, and J. Tooby. Oxford University Press.

Tooby, J., and Cosmides, L. 2005. Conceptual foundations of evolutionary psychology. In *Handbook of Evolutionary Psychology*, ed. D. Buss. Wiley.

Tybur, J. M., Bryan, A. D., Magnan, R. E., and Caldwell Hooper, A. E. 2011. Smells like safe sex: Olfactory pathogen primes increase intentions to use condoms. *Psychological Science* 22: 478–480.

Underhill, P. 2000. *Why We Buy: The Science of Shopping*. Simon and Schuster.

Van den Bergh, B., Dewitte, S., and Warlop, L. 2008. Bikinis instigate generalized impatience in intertemporal choice. *Journal of Consumer Research* 35: 85–97.

Van Vugt, M., De Cremer, D., and Janssen, D. P. 2007a. Gender differences in cooperation and competition: The male-warrior hypothesis. *Psychological Science* 18: 19–23.

Van Vugt, M., Roberts, G., and Hardy, C. 2007b. Competitive altruism: Development of reputation-based cooperation in groups. In *Handbook of Evolutionary Psychology*, ed. R. Dunbar and L. Barrett. Oxford University Press.

Ward, M. K., and Broniarczyk, S. M. 2011. It's not me, it's you: How gift giving creates giver identity threat as a function of social closeness. *Journal of Consumer Research* 38: 164–181.

Wilcox, K., Kim, H., and Sen, S. 2009. Why do consumers buy counterfeit luxury brands? *Journal of Marketing Research* 46: 247–259.

Wilson, M., and Daly, M. 2004. Do pretty women inspire men to discount the future? *Proceedings of the Royal Society B* 271 (Suppl. 4): 177–179.

3 The Evolutionary Instincts of *Homo consumericus*

Gad Saad

In the past two decades, evolutionary psychology has established itself as a vibrant discipline and has grown in stature. On March 5, 2012, using "evolutionary psychology" as a search string, I conducted a Google Scholar search to determine the total number of hits per each year in the period 1988–2011. I chose 1988 because that is arguably the year in which evolutionary psychology was founded as a distinct approach for studying human behavior from an evolutionary perspective. (See Daly and Wilson 1988.) Figure 3.1 illustrates the exponential growth of evolutionary psychology from 31 hits in 1988 to 5,030 in 2011. The average yearly increase in Google Scholar hits in the period 1988–2011 was 26 percent. No year received fewer hits than its immediate predecessor.

Despite the infusion of evolutionary psychology across a large number of behavioral fields, scholars of consumption have largely ignored the biological and evolutionary roots of *Homo consumericus* (but see Colarelli and Dettmann 2003; Griskevicius et al. 2009; Griskevicius, Ackerman, and Redden 2012; Miller 2009; Saad 2006a, 2007, 2008, 2010, 2011a, 2013; Saad and Gill 2000; Saad, Gill, and Nataraajan 2005; also see the chapter by Griskevicius, Redden, and Ackerman, the chapter by Preston and Vickers, and the chapter by Frank).

Evolutionary psychologists recognize that human minds are products of evolution. Specifically, in the same way that human kidneys, lungs, and pancreases all evolved to solve specific evolutionary challenges, the human mind too consists of numerous computational systems, each of which serves as an adaptation to a particular problem of evolutionary import (for example, finding a mate, avoiding predators, food foraging, investing in kin, and building non-kin coalitions). Viewed from this perspective, the human mind is an amalgamation of domain-specific algorithms that are

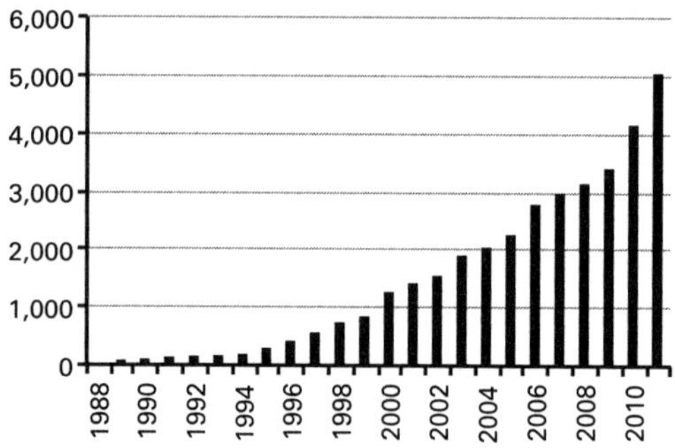

Figure 3.1
The growth of evolutionary psychology as indicated by number of hits obtained via Google Scholar with "evolutionary psychology" as the search term for each of the years specified on the horizontal axis.

triggered by ecologically relevant environmental inputs. (For a similar summary of this argument, see the chapter by Griskevicius, Redden, and Ackerman.) Evolutionary psychology also posits that humans are not born with minds that are empty slates to be subsequently filled by a host of socialization agents be it advertising, parents, or peers. (See Pinker 2002 for a refutation of the blank-slate premise.) Rather, humans are endowed with evolved cognitive blueprints that require no environmental learning—for example, infants display a visual penchant for facial symmetry while in the pre-socialization stage of cognitive development. Whereas the standard social science model overtly relies upon socialization, learning, and culture as satisfactory explanations for an endless number of human phenomena, evolutionary psychology considers such explanations to be incomplete at best (Tooby and Cosmides 1992). Specifically, to the extent that humans are socialized in ways that are consistent across time and space, it is incumbent upon those who offer such explanations to elucidate the genesis of these universal forms of socialization (e.g., in no culture are women taught to be less sexually restrained than men).

Toy preferences offer a telling example of the weakness of the socialization premise. Social constructivists propose that parental socialization shapes our eventual gender roles, and that this process manifests itself in the sex-specific ways in which parents encourage children to interact with toys. Apparently, little boys and girls learn about their expected gender roles by interacting with tough-looking G. I. Joe action figures and pretty

Barbie dolls, respectively. To the extent that this supposed form of socialization happens in exactly the same way across highly disparate cultures, the question that must be asked is "What drives such a universal commonality?" (For an excellent review of the evolutionary roots of toy preferences, see Alexander 2003.) The falsity of the social constructivists' oft-repeated position has been documented across several independent research streams. Sex-specific toy preferences appear very early in infants, in some instances when they don't yet possess the cognitive capacity to be socialized (Alexander, Wilcox, and Woods 2009; Jadva, Hines, and Golombok 2010). Infant vervet and rhesus monkeys display the same sex-specific toy preferences as human infants (Alexander and Hines 2002; Hassett, Siebert, and Wallen 2008). Little girls with congenital adrenal hyperplasia, a masculinizing endocrinological disorder, exhibit a greater preference than a group of control girls for toys traditionally favored by boys, such as helicopters, cars, fire engines, and building blocks (Berenbaum and Hines 1992). The latter findings do not refute the likely role that differential parental socialization plays in shaping sex-specific toy preferences, but they remind us that universal patterns of socialization are rooted in biological realities.

Another important tenet of evolutionary psychology (but more generally of evolutionary theory) is that scientific explanations involving biological organisms could be offered at two levels: that of proximate and that of ultimate causation. Proximate-level analyses explain how a phenomenon operates, whereas ultimate-level analyses elucidate the adaptive forces that would have led to its evolution. (For more on proximate and ultimate arguments, see the chapter by Griskevicius, Redden, and Ackerman and the chapter by Preston and Vickers.) Scott-Phillips, Dickins, and West (2011) provide several examples of proximate and ultimate explanations for phenomena as varied as cooperation, infant crying, and human reasoning. (See also O'Brien and Gallup 2011.) Pregnancy sickness provides a vivid demonstration of the two levels of analyses. How do changing hormonal levels affect a woman's likelihood of experiencing the symptoms of pregnancy sickness? This question is a proximate one in that it seeks to understand the hormonal underpinnings of the condition. An ultimate analysis establishes the adaptive benefits of this malady. Pregnancy sickness is considered a means by which mothers avoid or expel food pathogens during the crucial gestational period of organogenesis, when the baby's organs are forming (Flaxman and Sherman 2000; Pepper and Roberts 2006; Profet 1992).

Accordingly, when physicians prescribe drugs to attenuate the symptoms of pregnancy sickness, they are suppressing an adaptive process that otherwise decreases the likelihood of miscarriages.

In the remainder of this chapter, I demonstrate how acts of consumption can be mapped onto four Darwinian modules (survival, reproduction, kin selection, and reciprocity), briefly address the evolutionary roots of a wide range of cultural products (e.g., song lyrics), and offer several epistemological benefits associated with the infusion of evolutionary psychology within the field of consumer behavior. (For a similar breakdown of consumer behavior into evolutionary psychology modules, see the chapter by Griskevicius, Redden, and Ackerman.)

Consumer Behavior Maps onto Four Darwinian Modules

Consumer behavior and the survival module

Natural selection is the evolutionary process by which adaptations arise because they yield a survival advantage (e.g., camouflage coloring to avoid predation). There are numerous consumer choices and preferences that are vestiges of natural selection, perhaps none more ubiquitous than food-related phenomena. In 2008, the ten most successful global restaurant chains were, in decreasing order, McDonald's, KFC, Burger King, Starbucks, Subway, Pizza Hut, Wendy's, Taco Bell, Domino's Pizza, and Dunkin' Donuts (*Restaurants & Institutions* 2008). These restaurants share one common feature: they offer tasty, highly caloric foods and beverages that are congruent with our evolved gustatory preferences. Humans evolved in an environment of caloric scarcity and uncertainty. Our taste buds evolved as a solution to this evolutionarily recurring challenge. Our ancestors did not prefer to consume raw vegetables more often than fatty game. Thus, it is not surprising that present-day consumers exhibit a universal preference for fat (Drewnowski 1997; Saad 2006b). Different consumers may display heterogeneous preferences in the specific fatty foods they prefer, but on average most people prefer rich and tasty foods (for example, ice cream or a t-bone steak) to uncooked tofu with raw carrots.

Contrary to a common misconception held by marketing scholars, evolutionary scientists do not solely explore human universals (e.g., a universal preference for fat). Cross-cultural differences are also within the purview of evolutionary theory. Darwinian gastronomy is one such field, as it provides compelling biology-based explanations for cross-cultural differences in culinary traditions. Specifically, the extent to which a culture's dishes are meat-based versus vegetable-based, the amount of spices used in dishes, and the prevalence of various food preparation techniques (e.g., food pickling) are all cultural adaptations to one biological problem: exposure to food pathogens (antimicrobial hypothesis; Ohtsubo 2009; Sherman and Billing 1999; Sherman and Hash 2001). The prevalence of food pathogens is correlated to ambient temperature, which depends on a region's latitude. Thus, greater use of spices occurs in hotter climates. Culinary customs are cultural solutions to a biological problem. (See Henrich and Henrich 2010 for an investigation of how Fijian food taboos serve as protection against hazardous marine toxins.) To conjure up E. O. Wilson's famous aphorism (with a slight rephrasing), biology does indeed hold culture on a leash. (For other evolution-based accounts of cooking and/or cuisine, see Katz 1990, Nabhan 2004, Wrangham and Conklin-Brittain 2003, and Wrangham 2009.)

In addition to our own food consumption, our desire to avoid becoming another animal's food source is also a survival instinct (i.e., predator avoidance). Landscape preferences constitute one evolutionary manifestation of this evolved objective. Humans possess a universal preference for landscape topographies that permit a wide visual prospect from the safety of a refuge. (See Falk and Balling 2010 and references therein.) These evolved preferences, along with our biophilic instinct (innate love of nature), can be used to create optimal interior designs (Scott 1993), retail environments (Joye, Poels, and Willems 2011; Joye, Willems, Brengman, and Wolf 2010), "green" advertising (Hartmann and Apaolaza-Ibáñez 2010), and architectural structures (Tsui 1999; Kellert, Heerwagen, and Mador 2008).

Consumer behavior and the mating module

Countless animals (including humans) exhibit traits and behaviors that could not have evolved via natural selection, as they appear to decrease one's likelihood of survival. The prototypical example of such a trait is the peacock's tail. Heavy, burdensome, and conspicuous, it increases the peacock's likelihood of being caught by a predator. Because it is a costly signal to bear, hens are drawn to males who possess such elaborate ornamentation precisely because it serves as an honest indicator of a peacock's genetic and phenotypic qualities (Zahavi and Zahavi 1997). Sexual selection is the parallel evolutionary process that yields such traits—adaptations that confer reproductive advantage on an organism, typically through repeated female mate choice. Not surprisingly, men and women have evolved a repertoire of behavioral strategies to improve their chances in the mating market, and these strategies are ultimately rooted in the process of sexual selection. One such strategy is to use sex-specific products as sexual signals. Among these products are cars (Dunn and Searle 2010; Shuler and McCord 2010), clothes (Barber 1999; Hill, Donovan, and Koyama 2005; Townsend and Levy 1990), high-heel shoes (Smith 1999), hairstyles (Hinsz, Matz, and Patience 2001; Mesko and Bereczkei 2004), cosmetics (Russell 2009; Samson, Fink, and Matts 2010), perfumes (Milinski and Wedekind 2001; Wedekind, Escher, Van de Waal, and Frei 2007), engagement and wedding rings (Cronk and Dunham 2007; Uller and Johansson 2003), cell phones (Lycett and Dunbar 2000), and sun tanning products/services (Saad and Peng 2006). Many of these products constitute forms of conspicuous consumption, which in many instances is an instantiation of sexual signaling (Griskevicius et al. 2007; Saad and Vongas 2009; Sundie et al. 2011).

There is growing evidence that sex-specific hormones are influential across a wide range of consumer phenomena. Several researchers have shown that women's patterns of beautification (e.g., clothing styles) are intimately linked to their menstrual cycles (Durante et al. 2011; Durante, Li, and Haselton 2008; Grammer, Renninger, and Fischer 2004; Haselton et al. 2007; Saad and Stenstrom 2012). Proximate explanations of this phenomenon typically focus on the hormonal shifts that take place across the ovulatory cycle, while the ultimate cause lies in a woman's desire to self-advertise with greater alacrity in the mating market when maximally fertile. In addition to consumers, service providers receive different financial outcomes across the menstrual cycle. Miller, Tybur, and Jordan (2007) found that exotic dancers received larger tips when in the fertile phase of their menstrual cycle. There are two possible causes of this effect: that the dancers exhibited more solicitous and sexual behaviors when maximally fertile and/or that male patrons were able to identify dancers who were in the fertile phase of their menstrual cycles, were more likely to ask them for lap dances, and subsequently gave them larger tips.

Hormones also affect male consumers. Saad and Vongas (2009) investigated the links between conspicuous consumption and men's testosterone levels. Participants drove an expensive new Porsche sports car and an old

Toyota sedan in a public setting (downtown Montreal) or a sparsely populated highway. Salivary assays were collected after each of the four driving conditions, and these were compared against basal levels collected at the start and the end of the experiment. Across both environments, men's testosterone levels increased when they were driving the Porsche. Driving an expensive sports car imbues men with an immediate sense of high social status, and this new reality manifests itself via an endocrinological response associated with social wins or losses. On a related note, the extent to which men have been exposed to testosterone *in utero* has also been shown to affect their risk-taking proclivities, some of which are relevant in the consumer domain (Stenstrom, Saad, Nepomuceno, and Mendenhall 2011).

Consumer behavior and the kin selection and reciprocity modules

Altruistic acts toward kin and non-kin have been documented across numerous species originating from different taxa. Kin selection (Hamilton 1964) and reciprocal altruism (Trivers 1971) are the evolutionary processes by which such acts have evolved. The consumer setting is replete with rituals rooted in these two mechanisms, perhaps none as ubiquitously as the universal act of gift giving. Most scholars who have investigated gift giving have not looked at it from an evolutionary perspective, but some have—see Jonason, Cetrulo, Madrid, and Morrison 2009; Mysterud, Drevon, and Slagsvold 2006; also see the chapter by Brosnan, de Waal, and Proctor). Saad and Gill (2003) studied young adults' allocation of their gift-giving budgets across recipients and, as would be expected from an evolutionary perspective, found a positive correlation between the size of the gift and the genetic relatedness of the giver and the recipient. More recently, Tifferet, Saad, Meiri, and Ido (2012) replicated the genetic relatedness effect using monetary gifts at Israeli weddings and furthermore found that the maternal sides of the families of the bride and the groom offered larger gifts than their paternal counterparts. (Only the maternal sides are genetically certain of their biological links to the newlyweds.) This is in line with several evolution-based studies that have uncovered greater differential solicitude stemming from maternal family members—e.g., maternal grandmothers and maternal uncles and aunts (Euler and Weitzel 1996; Pashos and McBurney 2008).

Many instances of gift giving take place between people who are not kin (e.g., close friends). (For evolution-based accounts of friendship, see

DeScioli and Kurzban 2009 and Vigil 2007.) Many pairs of close friends invite each other to dinner on their respective birthdays. Bachelor and bachelorette parties constitute another example of a consumer ritual in which gifts are exchanged between non-kin. From a classical economic perspective, these rituals are perhaps unnecessary. From an evolutionary perspective, however, such rituals constitute a powerful means of strengthening the bonds of reciprocity. Saad and Gill (2003) found that a larger portion of the gift-giving budgets of their subjects was allocated to their closest friends than to stepfamily members, moderately close kin, or more distant kin (though a smaller portion than was allocated to romantic partners and close kin). In other words, gift-giving practices seem to engender differential solicitude to recipients as a function of the evolutionary import of a particular relationship (romantic partner first, close kin second, close friends third, and various other parties last).

Cultural Products as Fossils of the Human Mind

Evolutionary scientists typically study culture in one of several ways. A cultural form (e.g., religion) can be construed as an adaptation, in which case one has to demonstrate the survival benefits reaped by engaging in the cultural ritual or act. Wilson (2002), using the contentious process of group selection, has argued that a shared faith offers survival advantages to religious groups via greater cohesion and communality. Alternatively, one might propose that a cultural form is an exaptation (that is, an evolutionary by-product). Boyer (2001) proposed that religion utilizes cognitive systems that evolved for other purposes—for example, agency detection or coalitional thinking. Viewed from this perspective, religion parasitizes our minds in its service. (For a review of the adaptation-versus-exaptation debate as it relates to religion, see Pyysiäinen and Hauser 2010.) Other Darwinian-based approaches for studying culture include memetics (Aunger 2002; Blackmore 1999; Dawkins 1976) and gene-culture coevolution (Boyd and Richerson 1985; Richerson and Boyd 2005). In my own work, I take yet another approach to exploring culture from an evolutionary perspective: I propose that, although human minds do not fossilize, the cultural products that they create are vestiges of a universal biology-based human nature.

At the 2012 World Shakespeare Festival, 37 Shakespearean plays were presented in 37 languages associated with highly disparate cultures, including South African dialects, Gujarati, Turkish, Georgian, Dari Persian, Japanese, Arabic (Juba and Palestinian), Lithuanian, Spanish (Mexican, Argentine, and Castilian), English, Serbian, Albanian, Macedonian, Italian, Armenian, Belarusian, British Sign Language, Polish, Russian, Hebrew, Swahili, Korean, French, Hip Hop, Greek, Mandarin, Brazilian Portuguese, Urdu, Bangla, German, Cantonese, Madri, Hindi, Shona, and Yoruba. Shakespearean storylines are easily accessible to people originating from highly diverse cultures because they consist of universal themes that transcend time and place, including sibling rivalry, status competition, unrequited romantic love, romantic jealousy, cuckoldry, parental love, and friendships among non-kin. Our shared biology-based human nature is on display in the cultural products that we create, and subsequently consume, in advertising (Saad 2004), in song lyrics (Saad 2011b, 2012), in collective wisdom (Saad 2012), in religious narratives, in movie plotlines, in romance novels, and in self-help books (Saad 2007, 2011a).

Epistemological Benefits of Darwinizing the Study of Consumer Behavior

Many universities strive for greater interdisciplinarity. Awareness that many of the most important scientific problems and associated solutions occur at the nexus of multiple disciplines is probably driving the zeal to eradicate disciplinary barriers. And few meta-theoretical frameworks could engender interdisciplinary inquiries to the extent that evolutionary theory does. Table 1 on page 726 of Saad 2011c lists a broad range of disciplines that have been infused with evolutionary theory across all university faculties, including disciplines in the humanities (art, dance, literature), in the social sciences (anthropology, psychology, sociology, political science), in the natural sciences (biology, immunology, neurosciences, physiology), and in professional fields (business, medicine, law, architecture). Garcia et al. (2011) compared the departmental affiliations of the first authors of 1,000 articles in ten major psychology journals covering five topical areas: *Evolutionary Psychology*; *Evolution and Human Behavior*; *Annual Review of Neuroscience*; *Neuron*; *Cognition*; *Cognitive Psychology*; *American Journal of Psychoanalysis*; *Journal of the American Psychoanalytic Association*; *Journal of Experimental Psychology: Learning, Memory, and Cognition*; and *Learning and Memory*. *Evolutionary Psychology* and *Evolution and Human Behavior* had a greater number of first authors not housed in psychology departments, and originating from a broader and more diversified number of disciplines. The promise of a truly interdisciplinary science of consumption can best be achieved through the appropriate infusion of evolutionary psychology into the theoretical toolboxes of consumption scholars.

Consilience (unified knowledge—see Wilson 1998) is a hallmark of the natural sciences. The fields of physics, chemistry, and biology possess core knowledge that is integrated within an organized set of meta-frameworks. On the other hand, the social sciences are generally sorely lacking in consilience, yielding disciplines that are rich in methodological sophistication but poor in universally accepted core knowledge. The infusion of evolutionary theory into the study of consumer behavior is the means by which the field might achieve greater consilience (Saad 2007, 2008). Scholars are deeply divided in terms of the foundational principles that guide their research streams. Many radical feminists reject the possibility that innate sex differences exist, and thus any sexual dimorphisms that arise in the consumer arena are construed as manifestations of social construction. Postmodernists deny the existence of human universals, as apparently all knowledge is subjective (and hence no universal truths could exist). Clearly, then, postmodernists would view any proclamations of human universals in the consumer arena with much derision. Many other schools of thought, including deconstructionism, cultural relativism, and Marxist theory, similarly yield foundational principles that are in staunch opposition with evolutionary psychology. Consilience cannot be achieved when scholars of consumption are proponents of such disconnected and disjointed paradigms. Chemists cannot be divided into those who believe in the periodic table and those who reject it. Cosmologists cannot be divided into those who belong and those who do not belong to the Flat Earth Society. Professional biologists cannot be divided into those who accept evolution and those who reject it in favor of Intelligent Design. Consumption scholars, on the other hand, belong to various paradigmatic traditions that are at times perfectly contradictory with one another, and incongruent with the natural sciences. It is in this general sense that the study of consumer behavior might benefit from the consilience afforded by evolutionary psychology.

A third benefit of evolutionary psychology is that it permits consumption scholars to identify novel hypotheses and research questions that would otherwise have remained hidden (Saad and Gill 2000). In other words, evolution-based theorizing opens up new avenues of research that are inaccessible to those who are unaware of ultimate causation. It is difficult to imagine how researchers would have investigated the link between the major histocompatibility complex (genes associated with an individual's immunological profile) and preferences for perfumes (Milinski and Wedekind 2001), the effect of conspicuous consumption on men's testosterone levels (Saad and Vongas 2009), the effects of the ovulatory cycle on women's consumption (Saad and Stenstrom 2012), or the differential efficacy of various advertising strategies when primed either for survival or mating (Griskevicius et al. 2009) if not from an evolutionary/biological perspective. Evolutionary psychology does not threaten the capacity of non-evolution-minded scholars of consumer behavior to do their work. Rather, it offers them new epistemological avenues from which to expand their intellectual explorations.

Conclusion

Having spent nearly fifteen years Darwinizing the field of consumer behavior, I have been exposed on many occasions to consumer researchers' resistance and hostility toward this endeavor. Some marketing scholars are perfectly happy to concede that "basal" phenomena, such as perfume and gustatory preferences, may be rooted in biological processes, but reject the possibility that higher-order cognition is shaped by Darwinian forces. In other words, they succumb to the "evolution stops at the head" bias. Sure, evolution may explain the morphology of the salamander, the social behaviors of canines, or the evolution of our opposable thumbs. But it cannot explain the complexity of human cognition, according to such marketing scholars. ("Consumers are not animals, Professor Saad!") A reviewer from one of the leading consumer journals went so far as to castigate me for confusing biology with psychology. Somehow, according to the reviewer in question, our psychology lies outside of the realm of our biology! Many marketing scholars are also of the opinion that evolutionary theory in general, and evolutionary psychology in particular, consists of nothing more than fanciful and unfalsifiable *post hoc* explanations. A few years ago, a colleague who was working at one of the leading marketing departments in the world "explained" to me in his office that evolution does not meet important canons of the scientific method (e.g., predictability). An esteemed marketing scholar had outright dismissed as non-science perhaps the singularly greatest idea ever proposed by a human brain—evolution, which is the most coherent and parsimonious theory for explaining the evolution of all biological diversity on Earth. (For rebuttals to many of these erroneous concerns, see chapter 1 of Saad 2011a.)

Most consumption scholars will continue to work at the proximate level. This is perfectly fine, as the great majority of scientific pursuits occur at this explanatory level. However, to ignore if not reject the biological and evolutionary roots of our consummatory nature is detrimental to the field, as it generates at best incomplete accounts and at worst incorrect ones. Consumers possess human minds and bodies that were selected via evolution. As such, consumer behavior does not take place in a parallel universe that is somehow "free" of our biological heritage. To recognize the evolutionary instincts of *Homo consumericus* can only yield epistemological benefits.

References

Alexander, G. M. 2003. An evolutionary perspective of sex-typed toy preferences: Pink, blue, and the brain. *Archives of Sexual Behavior* 32: 7–14.

Alexander, G. M., and Hines, M. 2002. Sex differences in response to children's toys in nonhuman primates (*Cercopithecus aethiops sabaeus*). *Evolution and Human Behavior* 23: 467–479.

Alexander, G. M., Wilcox, T., and Woods, R. 2009. Sex differences in infants' visual interest in toys. *Archives of Sexual Behavior* 38: 427–433.

Aunger, R. 2002. *The Electric Meme: A New Theory of How We Think*. Free Press.

Barber, N. 1999. Women's dress fashions as a function of reproductive strategy. *Sex Roles* 40: 459–471.

Berenbaum, S. A., and Hines, M. 1992. Early androgens are related to childhood sex-typed toy preferences. *Psychological Science* 3: 203–206.

Blackmore, S. 1999. *The Meme Machine*. Oxford University Press.

Boyd, R., and Richerson, P. 1985. *Culture and the Evolutionary Process*. University of Chicago Press.

Boyer, P. 2001. *Religion Explained: The Evolutionary Origins of Religious Thought*. Basic Books.

Colarelli, S. M., and Dettmann, J. R. 2003. Intuitive evolutionary perspectives in marketing practices. *Psychology & Marketing* 20: 837–865.

Cronk, L., and Dunham, B. 2007. Amounts spent on engagement rings reflect aspects of male and female mate quality. *Human Nature* 18: 329–333.

Daly, M., and Wilson, M. 1988. *Homicide*. Aldine de Gruyter.

Dawkins, R. 1976. *The Selfish Gene*. Oxford University Press.

DeScioli, P., and Kurzban, R. 2009. The alliance hypothesis for human friendship. *PLOS ONE* 4: e5802.

Drewnowski, A. 1997. Why do we like fat? *Journal of the American Dietetic Association* 97: S58–S62.

Dunn, M. J., and Searle, R. 2010. Effect of manipulated prestige-car ownership on both sex attractiveness ratings. *British Journal of Psychology* 101: 69–80.

Durante, K. M., Griskevicius, V., Hill, S. E., Perilloux, C., and Li, N. P. 2011. Ovulation, female competition, and product choice: Hormonal influences on consumer behavior. *Journal of Consumer Research* 37: 921–934.

Durante, K. M., Li, N. P., and Haselton, M. G. 2008. Changes in women's choice of dress across the ovulatory cycle: Naturalistic and laboratory task-based evidence. *Personality and Social Psychology Bulletin* 34: 1451–1460.

Euler, H. A., and Weitzel, B. 1996. Discriminative grandparental solicitude as reproductive strategy. *Human Nature* 7: 39–59.

Falk, J. H., and Balling, J. D. 2010. Evolutionary influence on human landscape preference. *Environment and Behavior* 42: 479–493.

Flaxman, S. M., and Sherman, P. W. 2000. Morning sickness: A mechanism for protecting mother and embryo. *Quarterly Review of Biology* 75: 113–148.

Garcia, J. R., Geher, G., Crosier, B., Saad, G., Gambacorta, D., Johnsen, L., et al. 2011. The interdisciplinarity of evolutionary approaches to human behavior: A key to survival in the Ivory Archipelago. *Futures* 43: 749–761.

Grammer, K., Renninger, L., and Fischer, B. 2004. Disco clothing, female sexual motivation, and relationship status: Is she dressed to impress? *Journal of Sex Research* 41: 66–74.

Griskevicius, V., Ackerman, J. M., and Redden, J. P. 2012. Why we buy: Evolution, marketing, and consumer behavior. In *Applied Evolutionary Psychology*, ed. S. Craig Roberts. Oxford University Press.

Griskevicius, V., Goldstein, N. J., Mortensen, C. R., Sundie, J. M., Cialdini, R. B., and Kenrick, D. T. 2009. Fear and loving in Las Vegas: Evolution, emotion, and persuasion. *Journal of Marketing Research* 46: 384–395.

Griskevicius, V., Tybur, J. M., Sundie, J. M., Cialdini, R. B., Miller, G. F., and Kenrick, D. T. 2007. Blatant benevolence and conspicuous consumption: When romantic motives elicit strategic costly signals. *Journal of Personality and Social Psychology* 93: 85–102.

Hamilton, W. D. 1964. The genetical evolution of social behaviour (I and II). *Journal of Theoretical Biology* 7: 1–52.

Hartmann, P., and Apaolaza-Ibáñez, V. 2010. Beyond savanna: An evolutionary and environmental psychology approach to behavioral effects of nature scenery in green advertising. *Journal of Environmental Psychology* 30: 119–128.

Haselton, M. G., Mortezaie, M., Pillsworth, E. G., Bleske-Rechek, A., and Frederick, D. A. 2007. Ovulatory shifts in human female ornamentation: Near ovulation, women dress to impress. *Hormones and Behavior* 51: 40–45.

Hassett, J. M., Siebert, E. R., and Wallen, K. 2008. Sex differences in rhesus monkey toy preferences parallel those of children. *Hormones and Behavior* 54: 359–364.

Henrich, J., and Henrich, N. 2010. The evolution of cultural adaptations: Fijian food taboos protect against dangerous marine toxins. *Proceedings of the Royal Society B* 1701: 3715–3724.

Hill, R. A., Donovan, S., and Koyama, N. F. 2005. Female sexual advertisement reflects resource availability in twentieth-century UK society. *Human Nature* 16: 266–277.

Hinsz, V. B., Matz, D. C., and Patience, R. A. 2001. Does women's hair signal reproductive potential? *Journal of Experimental Social Psychology* 37: 166–172.

Jadva, V., Hines, M., and Golombok, S. 2010. Infants' preferences for toys, colors, and shapes: Sex differences and similarities. *Archives of Sexual Behavior* 39: 1261–1273.

Jonason, P. K., Cetrulo, J. F., Madrid, J. M., and Morrison, C. 2009. Gift-giving as a courtship or mate-retention tactic?: Insights from non-human models. *Evolutionary Psychology* 7: 89–103.

Joye, Y., Poels, K., and Willems, K. 2011. "Evolutionary Store Atmospherics"—Designing with evolution in mind. In *Evolutionary Psychology in the Business Sciences*, ed. G. Saad. Springer.

Joye, Y., Willems, K., Brengman, M., and Wolf, K. 2010. The effects of urban retail greenery on consumer experience: Reviewing the evidence from a restorative perspective. *Urban Forestry & Urban Greening* 9: 57–64.

Katz, S. H. 1990. An evolutionary theory of cuisine. *Human Nature* 1: 233–259.

Kellert, S. R., Heerwagen, J., and Mador, M., eds. 2008. *Biophilic Design: The Theory, Science and Practice of Bringing Buildings to Life*. Wiley.

Lycett, J. E., and Dunbar, R. I. M. 2000. Mobile phones as lekking devices among human males. *Human Nature* 11: 93–104.

Mesko, N., and Bereczkei, T. 2004. Hairstyle as an adaptive means of displaying phenotypic quality. *Human Nature* 15: 251–270.

Milinski, M., and Wedekind, C. 2001. Evidence for MHC-correlated perfume preferences in humans. *Behavioral Ecology* 12: 140–149.

Miller, G. 2009. *Spent: Sex, Evolution, and Consumer Behavior*. Viking.

Miller, G., Tybur, J. M., and Jordan, B. D. 2007. Ovulatory cycle effects on tip earnings by lap dancers: Economic evidence for human estrus? *Evolution and Human Behavior* 28: 375–381.

Mysterud, I., Drevon, T., and Slagsvold, T. 2006. An evolutionary interpretation of gift-giving behavior in modern Norwegian society. *Evolutionary Psychology* 4: 406–425.

Nabhan, G. P. 2004. *Why Some Like It Hot: Food, Genes, and Cultural Diversity*. Island.

Ohtsubo, Y. 2009. Adaptive ingredients against food spoilage in Japanese cuisine. *International Journal of Food Sciences and Nutrition* 60: 677–687.

O'Brien, D. T., and Gallup, A. C. 2011. Using Tinbergen's four questions (plus one) to facilitate evolution education for human oriented disciplines. *Evolution: Education and Outreach* 4: 107–113.

Pashos, A., and McBurney, D. H. 2008. Kin relationships and the caregiving biases of grandparents, aunts, and uncles: A two-generational questionnaire study. *Human Nature* 19:311–330.

Pepper, G. V., and Roberts, S. C. 2006. Rates of nausea and vomiting in pregnancy and dietary characteristics across populations. *Proceedings of the Royal Society B* 273: 2675–2679.

Pinker, S. 2002. *The Blank Slate: The Modern Denial of Human Nature*. Viking.

Profet, M. 1992. Pregnancy sickness as adaptation: A deterrent to maternal ingestion of teratogens. In *The Adapted Mind*, ed. J. H. Barkow, L. Cosmides, and J. Tooby. Oxford University Press.

Pyysiäinen, I., and Hauser, M. 2010. The origins of religion: Evolved adaptation or by-product? *Trends in Cognitive Sciences* 14: 104–109.

Restaurants & Institutions. 2008. Top 400 restaurant chains. *Restaurants & Institutions* 118 (10).

Richerson, P. J., and Boyd, R. 2005. *Not by Genes Alone: How Culture Transformed Human Evolution*. University of Chicago Press.

Russell, R. 2009. A sex difference in facial contrast and its exaggeration by cosmetics. *Perception* 38: 1211–1219.

Saad, G. 2004. Applying evolutionary psychology in understanding the representation of women in advertisements. *Psychology & Marketing* 21: 593–612.

Saad, G. 2006a. Applying evolutionary psychology in understanding the Darwinian roots of consumption phenomena. *Managerial and Decision Economics* 27: 189–201.

Saad, G. 2006b. Blame our evolved gustatory preferences. *Young Consumers* 7: 72–75.

Saad, G. 2007. *The Evolutionary Bases of Consumption*. Erlbaum.

Saad, G. 2008. The collective amnesia of marketing scholars regarding consumers' biological and evolutionary roots. *Marketing Theory* 8: 425–448.

Saad, G. 2010. The Darwinian underpinnings of consumption. In *The Handbook of Marketing Theory*, ed. P. Maclaran, M. Saren, B. Stern, and M. Tadajewski. Sage.

Saad, G. 2011a. *The Consuming Instinct: What Juicy Burgers, Ferraris, Pornography, and Gift Giving Reveal About Human Nature*. Prometheus Books.

Saad, G. 2011b. Song lyrics as windows to our evolved human nature. *Evolutionary Review* 2: 127–133.

Saad, G. 2011c. Futures of evolutionary psychology. *Futures* 43: 725–728.

Saad, G. 2012. Nothing in popular culture makes sense except in the light of evolution. *Review of General Psychology* 16: 109–120.

Saad, G. 2013. Evolutionary consumption. *Journal of Consumer Psychology* 23: 351–371.

Saad, G., and Gill, T. 2000. Applications of evolutionary psychology in marketing. *Psychology & Marketing* 17: 1005–1034.

Saad, G., and Gill, T. 2003. An evolutionary psychology perspective on gift giving among young adults. *Psychology & Marketing* 20: 765–784.

Saad, G., Gill, T., and Nataraajan, R. 2005. Are laterborns more innovative and non-conforming consumers than firstborns? A Darwinian perspective. *Journal of Business Research* 58: 902–909.

Saad, G., and Peng, A. 2006. Applying Darwinian principles in designing effective intervention strategies: The case of sun tanning. *Psychology & Marketing* 23: 617–638.

Saad, G., and Stenstrom, E. 2012. Calories, beauty, and ovulation: The effects of the menstrual cycle on food and appearance-related consumption. *Journal of Consumer Psychology* 22: 102–113.

Saad, G., and Vongas, J. G. 2009. The effect of conspicuous consumption on men's testosterone levels. *Organizational Behavior and Human Decision Processes* 110: 80–92.

Samson, N., Fink, B., and Matts, P. J. 2010. Visible skin condition and perception of human facial appearance. *International Journal of Cosmetic Science* 32: 167–184.

Scott, S. C. 1993. Visual attributes related to preference in interior environments. *Journal of Interior Design* 18: 7–16.

Scott-Phillips, T. C., Dickins, T. E., and West, S. A. 2011. Evolutionary theory and the ultimate-proximate distinction in the human behavioral sciences. *Perspectives on Psychological Science* 6: 38–47.

Sherman, P. W., and Billing, J. 1999. Darwinian gastronomy: Why we use spices. *Bioscience* 49: 453–463.

Sherman, P. W., and Hash, G. A. 2001. Why vegetable recipes are not very spicy. *Evolution and Human Behavior* 22: 147–163.

Shuler, G. A., and McCord, D. M. 2010. Determinants of male attractiveness: "Hotness" ratings as a function of perceived resources. *American Journal of Psychological Research* 6: 10–23.

Smith, E. O. 1999. High heels and evolution: Natural selection, sexual selection and high heels. *Psychology, Evolution & Gender* 1: 245–277.

Stenstrom, E., Saad, G., Nepomuceno, M., and Mendenhall, Z. 2011. Testosterone and domain-specific risk: Digit ratios (2D:4D and *rel2*) as predictors of recreational, financial, and social risk-taking behaviors. *Personality and Individual Differences* 51: 412–416.

Sundie, J. M., Kenrick, D. T., Griskevicius, V., Tybur, J. M., Vohs, K. D., and Beal, D. J. 2011. Peacocks, Porsches, and Thorstein Veblen: Conspicuous consumption as a sexual signaling system. *Journal of Personality and Social Psychology* 100: 664–680.

Tifferet, S., Saad, G., Meiri, M., and Ido, N. 2012. Gift-giving at Israeli weddings as a function of genetic relatedness and maternal lineage. Presented at NorthEastern Evolutionary Psychology Society Conference, Plymouth, New Hampshire, 2012.

Tooby, J., and Cosmides, L. 1992. Psychological foundations of culture. In *The Adapted Mind*, ed. J. H. Barkow, L. Cosmides, and J. Tooby. Oxford University Press.

Townsend, J. M., and Levy, G. D. 1990. Effects of potential partners' costume and physical attractiveness on sexuality and partner selection. *Journal of Psychology* 124: 371–389.

Trivers, R. L. 1971. The evolution of reciprocal altruism. *Quarterly Review of Biology* 46: 35–57.

Tsui, E. 1999. *Evolutionary Architecture: Nature as a Basis for Design*. Wiley.

Uller, T., and Johansson, L. C. 2003. Human mate choice and the wedding ring effect: Are married men more attractive? *Human Nature* 14: 267–276.

Vigil, J. M. 2007. Asymmetries in the friendship preferences and social styles of men and women. *Human Nature* 18: 143–161.

Wedekind, C., Escher, S., Van de Waal, M., and Frei, E. 2007. The major histocompatibility complex and perfumers' descriptions of human body odors. *Evolutionary Psychology* 5: 330–343.

Wilson, D. S. 2002. *Darwin's Cathedral: Evolution, Religion, and the Nature of Society.* University of Chicago Press.

Wilson, E. O. 1998. *Consilience: The Unity of Knowledge.* Abacus.

Wrangham, R. 2009. *Catching Fire: How Cooking Made Us Human.* Basic Books.

Wrangham, R., and Conklin-Brittain, N. 2003. Cooking as a biological trait. *Comparative Biochemistry and Physiology A* 136: 35–46.

Zahavi, A., and Zahavi, A. 1997. *The Handicap Principle: A Missing Piece of Darwin's Puzzle.* Oxford University Press.

4 Myopia, Hyperbolic Discounting, and Mental Time Travel: Evolutionary Accounts of Lifetime Decisions

Stephen E. G. Lea

My aim in this chapter is to propose an account of the key facts about human intertemporal choice within a framework of an evolutionary approach to psychology. Intertemporal choice is one of the areas (the area *par excellence*, I would argue) in which the neoclassical rational-choice approach to economic theory—that is, predicting economic behavior by assuming that people make choices that are in their individual best interests—produces predictions that are in flagrant disagreement with the empirical facts. (See Loewenstein and Thaler 1989 and the chapter by Rick in this volume.) Intertemporal choices determine major lifetime outcomes, such as house purchases, credit use, and pension provision. The research on consumer debt that my colleagues and I have carried out over many years (e.g., Lea et al. 1993, 1995; Mewse et al. 2010) reveals a chronic and miserable pattern of people making such choices that harm them in the long run, and this pattern is repeated in many other spheres of intertemporal choice. (See Thaler and Sunstein 2008.) Partly for this reason, intertemporal choice is one of the areas in which behavioral economics has obtained the most purchase both on thinking about economic reality and on economic policy. (See also the chapter by Frank, the chapter by Rick, the chapter by Preston and Vickers, and the chapter by Webley.)

There is, however, another reason why behavioral approaches have found a ready audience in relation to intertemporal choice. Theories can survive quite a considerable weight of contrary evidence; what really moves things along scientifically is the availability of an alternative theory, allowing what Kuhn (1962) called a paradigm shift. In the case of intertemporal choice, the challenge to neoclassical orthodoxy has been supported by an alternative theoretical view rooted in laboratory work in behavioral psychology and brought together by Ainslie (1975, 1992)—an alternative that provided not just a different way of thinking about intertemporal choice, but a way of making quantitative predictions about it.

The purpose of this chapter is not to reiterate the well-established empirical critique of the neoclassical approach to intertemporal choice. Instead, it is to reflect on the basis of the behaviorist alternative that I and others have proposed in the past, and to suggest some ways in which it may not be adequate, particularly when it comes to accounting for lifetime choices and formulating policies that we hope might improve them. I will be seeking to do so from an evolutionary standpoint. (For evolutionary perspectives on consumption, see also the chapter by Griskevicius, Redden, and Ackerman and the chapter by Saad.) However, I do not mean evolutionary psychology in the narrow sense of assuming a massive modularity in human cognition. (See, e.g., Barkow et al. 1992; Gigerenzer and Todd 1999; Pinker 1997.) I simply mean that I want to place the inquiry within an evolutionary context, and to articulate it with the concepts of evolutionary theory—in other words, to see human behavior as a product of an evolutionary process and as continuous with the behavior of other animals. (See also the introductory chapter and the chapter by Preston and Vickers.) As Buller (2005) puts it, I am interested in "evolutionary psychology" rather than "Evolutionary Psychology"—that is, in a field of inquiry rather than a paradigm for making that inquiry.

The Stylized Facts about Human Intertemporal Choice

What everyone now knows about intertemporal choice is that humans are simply terrible at making choices between outcomes that appear at different times in the future. It does not matter whether it is a child faced with a choice between getting a small piece of candy now or a much larger piece in a week's time (Mischel 1958), a commuter choosing between having a little extra sleep now and getting to work punctually in an hour's time, a hard-pressed single parent in South Wales choosing between getting the washing machine repaired now and being free of debt next year (Walker 1997), a company employee choosing between having a little luxury expenditure now and having the income he or she considers adequate in retirement (Laibson 1998), or a smoker choosing between the stress relief from having another cigarette now and decades of improved health in the future (Sjöberg and Johnson 1978). In any of these situations, we have a depressing tendency to choose the short-term advantage. The examples listed here suggest that the tendency applies over a wide range of sizes of outcome and a wide range of delays.

So general is the phenomenon that it has acquired multiple names, including impatience (Fisher 1930), failure to delay gratification (Mischel 1958), lack of self control (Logue 1988), weakness of will (Sjöberg and Johnson 1978), impulsiveness (Navarick 1987), myopia (Strotz 1956), shortened time horizon (Malkoc and Zauberman 2006), inability to consider future consequences (Strathman et al. 1994), excessive delay discounting (Loewenstein and Thaler 1989), and failure of self-regulation (Muraven and Baumeister 2000). Each of these terms has slightly different implications, and they certainly come from different theoretical traditions and carry different theoretical baggage. But all are attempts to grapple with the same broad human tendency.

However, we should not lose sight of a second stylized fact about human intertemporal choice: that although we are terrible at it, we can get better at it. There are some well-understood ways to ensure that we make better choices in specific intertemporal contexts. The classic example is the dozy commuter who puts his alarm clock in a place that requires him to get out bed to shut the alarm off; but almost all of the "nudges" discussed by Thaler and Sunstein (2008) fall into the same class. We are capable of making choices that improve our long-term outcomes by removing or reconfiguring choices that we will face at some time in the future and that we tend to make badly. This is often referred to as "commitment" or "impulse-controlling" behavior, because it commits us to a course of action in which a future opportunity to make an impulsive choice is forgone.

The fact that people can and commonly do make commitment choices might seem to rescue the neoclassical position that people make choices in their own best interests. In reality, however, it undermines that position further, because according to neoclassical theory such choices ought not to be possible. Neoclassical theories of intertemporal choice such as that of Friedman (1957) have to assume that future outcomes are discounted according to an exponential function. The kind of preference reversal that allows impulse-controlling behavior requires discount rates to vary across the discounting period—that is, it requires a discounting function that is non-exponential, the form that is most commonly advocated being the hyperbola, for reasons that will be explained shortly.

The Behaviorist Alternative

The facts about intertemporal choice have been known for decades—centuries even—but within a broadly rational approach the problems they pose are intractable. What made the difference was the proposal, first expounded by Ainslie (1975), of a positive alternative theory of intertemporal (and other) choice: the theory of hyperbolic discounting. Proposing that the subjective discount curve has a hyperbolic rather than an exponential form immediately solves the problem of the inconsistency of intertemporal choices, because it generates a subjective discount rate that is higher for outcomes further in the future than for outcomes near at hand. But many functional forms would do that, so why do we pick on the hyperbolic form in particular?

The answer is that Ainslie (1974), Rachlin and Green (1972), and others had been carrying out experiments and formulating theory on choice under the influence of the so-called matching law that Herrnstein (1961, 1970) formulated to describe the behavior of pigeons working on concurrent variable-interval schedules of reinforcement in operant chambers ("Skinner boxes"). This is why this section is titled "The Behaviorist Alternative" rather than "The Behavioral Alternative"—hyperbolic discounting does not have its origins in behavioral economics, but in the laboratories of operant psychologists working with pigeons and rats. Mazur (1984) showed that animals' choices between rewards varying in both amount and delay can be described by the following hyperbolic equation:

$$V_i = A_i/(1 + KD_i),$$

where V_i is "subjective value," A_i is reward size, D_i is delay, and K is a fitting constant. The V_i values can be used to make quantitative predictions about choice. In particular, this equation successfully predicts behavioral commitment, a phenomenon that Rachlin and Green (1972) and Ainslie (1974) demonstrated in pigeons in a discrete-trial choice situation. Faced with a choice between a small immediate reward and a larger reward delayed by a few seconds, the pigeons almost invariably made the impulsive choice of the small immediate reward; however, if a sufficient time before that choice was made available they had the option to prevent selection of the small immediate reward, they typically made that "commitment" response and so forced themselves to accept the larger, delayed reward later.

First Steps toward an Evolutionary Analysis

The world of the Skinnerian experimental analysis of behavior is far from that of evolutionary biology, despite attempts to unite the two (e.g., Skinner 1984). Furthermore, evolutionary theory in biology, like rational-choice theory in economics, tends to make use of optimality models, and I argued above that the value of introducing the behaviorist approach to choice was precisely that it provides a positive alternative to such models.

However, in practice operant psychology and behavioral ecology are not so far apart in their approaches to choice. (See Lea 1985.) A core topic in behavioral ecology is foraging (also discussed in this volume by Sherry), and a core category of foraging theory, the optimal diet model, lends itself readily to simulation in the operant laboratory (Collier and Rovee-Collier 1981; Lea 1979; Abarca and Fantino 1982). The major qualitative predictions of the optimal diet model are sustained in such simulations, but the behavior observed is also consistent with predictions from the matching law. According to the matching law, animals respond at a rate that is correlated with the amount or duration of reinforcement, particularly when the reinforcement is given in a concurrent variable interval. So although matching is not an optimizing theory, it predicts "good enough" optimization under plausibly natural contingencies.

Matching is a consequence of basic laws of operant conditioning, which is one form of associative learning. Such learning has been demonstrated in all vertebrates that have been tested, and in quite a range of invertebrates, including many arthropods and a number of mollusks; and if it is sufficient to produce nearly optimal foraging, we need look no further for an evolutionary explanation for its prevalence. Indeed, it should be no surprise if the laws of operant conditioning are evolutionarily conservative, since almost all animals need to forage. (See the chapter by Sherry.) Thus, we have a mechanism (operant conditioning) whose effects can be described with reasonable accuracy by an equation (the matching law) that on the one hand predicts a "near enough" optimal outcome in an evolutionarily crucial context (foraging) but on the other hand predicts the massive irrationality that we observe in animals' intertemporal choices; indeed, impulsiveness has been specifically demonstrated in an operant simulation of diet choice (Lea 1979). Humans should be no exception to any of this. Here we appear to have an evolutionarily rooted behaviorist account of our weaknesses in intertemporal choice.

Three Problems with the Initial Analysis

Unfortunately, things are not so simple, and there are a number of problems in applying the analysis above to the kinds of intertemporal choice that most interest us.

First, operant-conditioning analyses of choice have been tested experimentally only over the time and quantity scales that are relevant to natural foraging, and in particular to the kinds of choices that might arise from minute to minute within a foraging bout. We certainly expect animals to learn and remember from day to day or even year to year where to find food and what foods are good to eat. But we have no empirical or theoretical grounds for expecting the matching law to apply to choices that an animal might make only once in a day, or even only once in a year or once in a lifetime. Many interesting human choices involve just such long time scales.

Second, operant-conditioning explanations require the organism to experience the outcomes. When we study animals, we have no choice but to expose them to the contingencies we want them to know about. When we study humans, we can either give them direct exposure or describe the contingencies to them, and in many cases we know that there are major differences between description-based and experience-based choices (Barron and Erev 2003). And in both experiments and real life, choices involving lifetime-scale delays have to be made hypothetically. We cannot spend 40 years paying into a pension scheme, note what the outcome feels like at retirement age, then spend 40 more years not paying into one and see whether its retirement-age outcome feels better.

Third, there are serious questions about whether the matching law applies to humans. There are situations in which matching does seem to describe human choice reasonably accurately. In one early experiment, Conger and Killeen (1974) used a group-conversation situation in which two stooges of the experimenter agreed with statements made by the participant on variable-interval schedules; they found quite good matching of the relative rates at which the participant addressed remarks to the two stooges to their rates of agreement with the participant. In a more formal situation, in which human participants performed on concurrent schedules of button-pressing for rewards of points that were later exchanged for cash, Bradshaw et al. (1979) found that the matching law was generally upheld. However, this result is far from universal. For example, in an experiment quite similar to those of Bradshaw et al., Horne and Lowe (1993) found that only a minority of their participants showed matching. Furthermore, whether or not the participants matched was closely correlated with their understanding of the experimental situation, as gleaned from post-experimental questionnaires. What mattered was not what the contingencies of reinforcement were, but what theory of them the participants had constructed.

It seems, therefore, that although the laws of operant conditioning offer a sufficient and evolutionarily grounded explanation for hyperbolic discounting and myopic choice in short-range choices when animals experience contingencies directly, we cannot rely on them to account for the same phenomena in human lifetime choices. They may well account for some human myopic choices, particularly those whose consequences are fairly short term, are experienced directly and are made without much thought. We should not underestimate the amount of real economic behavior that fits that description, particularly in routine shopping and working. But these are not the choices that are of most concern to policy makers. How else, in evolutionary terms, might we get hyperbolic discounting (or something like it)? There are two basic kinds of possibility. First, humans may have some instinctive mechanism, arising from our evolutionary past, that deals with very long time delays, and turns out to do so myopically and hyperbolically. Second, very long time delays may be outside our evolutionary experience (in the sense that our ancestors never had to make them, so the mechanism for doing so were not subjected to selection), meaning that we have to we use general-purpose cognitive mechanisms to deal with them as best we can. I will consider each of these possibilities in turn.

Instincts for Long-Term Choices

There are animals that have instincts that enable them to make choices with very long-term consequences. For example, birds that migrate must gain weight as spring or autumn approaches, feeding well beyond their immediate metabolic needs. Similarly, hibernators must gain weight in the autumn in order to survive the winter. Animals that survive a food-lean period by hoarding spend much time and energy creating caches during the food-rich season. (See the chapter by Sherry.) Such behaviors appear to be subserved by specific physiological, instinctual, or cognitive mechanisms; for example, some migratory animals show a seasonal change in stomach size (see Piersma et al. 1999), and some scatter hoarders show a seasonal change in the size of the hippocampus (Sherry and Hoshooley 2010; Sherry, this volume), a part of the brain that is associated with the ability to remember the thousands of different locations that the animal must revisit in order to profit from its caching behavior.

Might we humans have instincts that enable us to make long-term choices? It is quite possible that our ancestors had to cope with seasonal variations in food availability, as the animals discussed above do. There have been seasonal migrations of ungulates in Africa involving tens and perhaps hundreds of thousands of animals down to modern times (Grzimek and Grzimek 1960), and if human ancestors were exploiting such species it would have been advantageous for them to be able to respond adaptively to their seasonal variations in availability. If our mechanisms for making long-term choices evolved to cope with seasonal variations in food supplies, it would not be very surprising that they perform badly when pushed to handle choices extending well beyond their natural one-year limitation.

However, many animals also make "choices" between patterns of behavior that affect the entire course of their lives. In evolutionary theory these patterns are referred to as life-history strategies. (See the chapter by Mittal, Griskevicius, and Ellis.) A typical life-history choice is the timing of reproduction—should an animal start reproducing early in life, or later? Obviously species differ greatly in their timing and rate of reproduction. But individuals within a species may also make different "choices" depending on their circumstances. As long-lived, slowly reproducing animals occupying many different ecological niches, humans are good candidates for having multiple evolutionarily stable life-history strategies. In present-day hunter-gatherer societies, the birth rate is well below the maximum achievable rate, implying that some kind of tradeoff is being made to maximize fitness (Kaplan 1996). Furthermore, since the late eighteenth century the birth rate has crashed in one modern society after another, a process termed the "demographic transition"; this further implies that the choice about how many children to have is labile (Newson et al. 2005). Within modern societies, there are undoubted differences between human groups in their reproductive strategies as a function of social class, economic status, and other indicators of environmental harshness and unpredictability (Quinlan 2008; Ellis et al. 2009; Nettle 2010).

So it may be that there are human instincts that tell us, as a function of life circumstances, which life-history strategy it would be better to adopt. Those same instincts may then guide us in other lifetime choices, including economic choices of the sort that are of interest to us in this chapter. Indeed, increased use of credit and reduced saving are typical consequences of economic disadvantage, and they also tend to be associated with an early-reproduction strategy—though of course there are many reasons why that is likely to be so quite apart from any evolved tendency to make shorter-term choices in harsher conditions.

Using General Cognitive Mechanisms to Make Long-Term Choices

When we ask people to make intertemporal choices, whether the contingencies are hypothetical or real, we are asking them to imagine the future. Our capacity to do this is closely linked to our capacity to recall specific events in the past, which we refer to as episodic memory. Suddendorf and Corballis (1997, 2007) call these two processes the capacity for "mental time travel"; Tulving (1985) called them "autonoetic consciousness." Just as traveling backward in time mentally is called episodic memory, traveling forward in time mentally can be called episodic future thought (Szpunar 2010), or, more mundanely, anticipation (Atance and O'Neill 2001).

Suddendorf and Corballis (1997) argue that mental time travel is a uniquely human cognitive capacity; Roberts (2002) similarly argues that animals are largely "stuck in time." Not everyone agrees—see, for example, Clayton et al. 2003. There is now evidence for at least episodic-like memory in quite a range of species, from scrub jays (e.g., Clayton and Dickinson 1998) to rats (e.g., Babb and Crystal 2005). (Also see the chapter by Sherry in this volume.) Planning for the future in animals is much harder to demonstrate, despite interesting claims for scrub jays by Correia et al. (2007) and for great apes by Mulcahy and Call (2006). At the moment I would conclude that we do not yet have enough comparative data to support any particular theory about the evolutionary origin of human mental time travel, and in particular why it might give rise to irrationalities in intertemporal choice.

We may, however, be able to say something about the cognitive mechanisms responsible for those irrationalities. Stewart et al. (2006) have proposed a mechanism they call Decision by Sampling theory. According to Stewart et al., when we have to consider the value of a delayed outcome we compare the proposed delay against a sample of delays drawn from memory. Because long delays are experienced less often than short delays, the distribution in the sample follows a power law. (The same reasoning supports the well-known Zipf's law in linguistics.) Stewart et al. show that this process will yield approximately hyperbolic discounting even with random sampling from memory, without any underlying psychoeconomic scaling process. In other words, if evolution has given us a process that stores the delays to past events, myopic choice about future events is a likely consequence.

Second Steps toward an Evolutionary Analysis

An alternative evolutionary analysis of intertemporal choice, and its vicissitudes, might therefore run as follows: In response to specific niche demands, some species have evolved specific mechanisms that enable them to make adaptive long-term choices. In humans, the most likely candidate for such a niche demand is the need to make choices between life-history strategies, chiefly in the area of the timing and extent of reproduction. We might reasonably expect there will be an evolved mechanism for such choices. At least on the broad, less modular view of the evolution of human cognition, we would expect the same mechanism to be available to subserve choices of other kinds—for example, the long-term economic choices that seem so problematic. The obvious candidate for an evolved human mechanism for long-term choices is our enhanced (or at least more easily demonstrated) capacity for mental time travel. Since there is no suggestion that mental time travel evolved to deal with choices of this kind, there is no reason to expect evolution to have shaped it make them optimally, or even reasonably well; theories such as that of Stewart et al. (2006) offer at least the possibility of explaining how such a capacity might produce bad intertemporal choices in the economic sphere.

The Human Difference

Mental time travel may or may not be unique to humans. Undoubtedly, however, there are human cognitive capacities that are unique to our species. In particular, humans have two ways of responding in situations requiring choice. We saw an example in our consideration of whether humans obey the matching law. In conditions favoring "mindless" performance, such as Conger and Killeen's (1974) group-conversation experiment, the laws of operant conditioning will hold, just as they will for other species. But when people approach a task with a verbalized, problem-solving mindset, as they apparently did in Horne and Lowe's (1993) experiment, quite different results, with no known parallel in animal studies, were seen. Operant psychologists describe such behavior as "rule governed" rather than "contingency governed": the participants generate rules and use them to govern their future behavior. Clearly this requires a capacity for mental time travel: you have to imagine yourself in a future situation in order to construct a rule to tell you what to do when you get there.

Of course there is nothing new about recognizing that humans have multiple ways of making choices, or that this fact may account for some of our problems with intertemporal choice. Similar ideas include the opposition of reason to emotion and motivation as determinants of human behavior, which can be found in philosophy going back to classical times, in work by William James, and in Freud's opposition of the id to the ego and superego. Coming closer to economic behavior, we have Katona's (1975) distinction between habitual buying and problem solving and Thaler and Shefrin's (1981) suggestion that we each contain both a "planner" and a "doer," and that they pull our economic choices in different directions. (For a similar discussion, see the chapter by Robinson, Robinson, and Berridge.) However, the current analysis is not quite the same as these. Many such schemes suppose that we have, as it were, a better and a worse self, and that if only decisions could be left to our better self (our reason, our ego, our planner) they would be made well. In my view, there is no evidence for this. It is true that if we were to allow the laws of operant conditioning to govern our behavior as they govern the behavior of pigeons we would make truly terrible economic decisions, which would imply subjective discount rates of not just thousands but millions of percent per annum. It is also true that under very closely controlled, completely informed conditions, people do sometimes make short-run intertemporal choices in very much the way a neoclassical economist would hope (e.g., Andersen et al. 2011). But my current view is that, on a lifetime scale, even our better selves cannot be relied upon to make very good intertemporal choices, because they did not evolve to fulfill that function.

Final Steps toward an Evolutionary Analysis

So what might an evolutionary analysis that takes human uniqueness into account look like? It must start from the position that, for whatever reason (and there are many hypotheses), humans have evolved the capacity for reflective thought. This gives us a consciousness of the self, and thereby makes mental time travel over long periods possible, in a new way. But although this provides a mechanism we can use for comparing an imagined future with a present reality, there is no reason to suppose we will do it accurately, and the factors that influence it may not be relevant to the finance-based options we now have to choose between.

In addition, the fact that we have two mechanisms available for making many kinds of decisions means that they will sometimes push us in opposite directions. Animals can avoid impulsive choices by making commitment responses, but such responses will occur only insofar as the laws of operant conditioning allow them to. We humans are often trying to improve on the outcomes we could get from those laws. When we use reflective thought to override the response that would be made on the basis of the laws of conditioning, we call that self-control or self-regulation (though it would better be called control by the self). This "mental tool" is used in many situations, including intertemporal choice. Unfortunately, however, it appears that our capacity for self-regulation is a limited resource (Baumeister et al. 1998) that is easily reduced by use, by fatigue, or by frustration. If this analysis is right, the less of this resource we have available the more likely we are to make the seriously maladaptive impulsive choices that result from giving free rein to the laws of operant conditioning, which are useful over periods of seconds but useless over periods of decades.

But even in reasonably self-controlled economic choices, humans show myopia in general and hyperbolic discounting in particular. Why? If anything in human evolution adapts us to make accurate value comparisons over periods of years and decades, it seems to the fact that we have to choose between different life-history strategies concerning reproduction. Beyond that, we can only fall back on general cognitive mechanisms, such as mental time travel. There is no reason to expect either to produce optimal behavior in economic-choice situations.

And what, if anything, can be done about that, either personally or at a policy level? The first step must surely be, as Thaler and Sunstein (2008) argue, to abandon the assumption that people, unaided, will make good intertemporal decisions. That applies to those people for whom we are responsible, whether as parents, as managers, or as members of government; it is hard not to sympathize with Thaler and Sunstein's appeal for at least a libertarian paternalism. But it also applies to ourselves. We need, it seems, to find ways of becoming better mental time travelers.

Acknowledgments

I am grateful to Paul Webley, Lesley Newson, Avril Mewse, Wendy Wrapson, Gordon Brown, Peter Fischer, and David Crelley for discussion of the ideas behind this chapter, and to Detlef Fetchenhauer, Erik Hölzl, and their students at the University of Cologne for discussion of an earlier version.

References

Abarca, N., and Fantino, E. 1982. Choice and foraging. *Journal of the Experimental Analysis of Behavior* 38: 117–123.

Ainslie, G. 1974. Impulse control in pigeons. *Journal of the Experimental Analysis of Behavior* 21: 485–489.

Ainslie, G. 1975. Specious reward: A behavioral theory of impulsiveness and impulse controls. *Psychological Bulletin* 82: 463–496.

Ainslie, G. 1992. *Picoeconomics*. Cambridge University Press.

Andersen, S., Harrison, G. W., Lau, M., and Rutström, E. E. 2011. Discounting behavior: A reconsideration. Available at http://www.dur.ac.uk.

Atance, C. M., and O'Neill, D. K. 2001. Episodic future thinking. *Trends in Cognitive Sciences* 5: 533–539.

Babb, S. J., and Crystal, J. D. 2005. Discrimination of what, when, and where: Implications for episodic-like memory in rats. *Learning and Motivation* 36: 177–189.

Barkow, J., Cosmides, L., and Tooby, J. 1992. *The Adapted Mind: Evolutionary Psychology and the Generation of Culture*. Oxford University Press.

Barron, G., and Erev, I. 2003. Small feedback-based decisions and their limited correspondence to description-based decisions. *Journal of Behavioral Decision Making* 16: 215–233.

Baumeister, R. F., Bratslavsky, E., Muraven, M., and Tice, D. M. 1998. Ego depletion: Is the active self a limited resource? *Journal of Personality and Social Psychology* 74: 1252–1265.

Bradshaw, C. M., Szabadi, E., Bevan, P., and Ruddle, H. V. 1979. The effects of signaled reinforcement availability on concurrent performances in humans. *Journal of the Experimental Analysis of Behavior* 32: 65–74.

Buller, D. J. 2005. *Adapting Minds*. MIT Press.

Clayton, N. S., Bussey, T. J., and Dickinson, A. 2003. Can animals recall the past and plan for the future? *Nature Reviews Neuroscience* 4: 685–691.

Clayton, N. S., and Dickinson, A. 1998. Episodic-like memory during cache recovery by scrub jays. *Nature* 395: 272–274.

Collier, G. H., and Rovee-Collier, C. K. 1981. A comparative analysis of optimal foraging behavior: laboratory simulations. In *Foraging Behavior*, ed. A. Kamil and T. Sargent. Garland.

Conger, R., and Killeen, P. 1974. Use of concurrent operants in small group research: A demonstration. *Pacific Sociological Review* 17: 399–416.

Correia, S. P. C., Dickinson, A., and Clayton, N. S. 2007. Western scrub-jays anticipate future needs independently of their current motivational state. *Current Biology* 17: 856–861.

Ellis, B. J., Figueredo, A. J., Brumbach, B. H., and Schlomer, G. L. 2009. Fundamental dimensions of environmental risk. *Human Nature* 20: 204–268.

Fisher, I. 1930. *The Theory of Interest*. Macmillan.

Friedman, M. 1957. *A Theory of the Consumption Function*. Princeton University Press.

Gigerenzer, G., and Todd, P. M. 1999. Fast and frugal heuristics: The adaptive toolbox. In *Simple Heuristics That Make Us Smart*, ed. G. Gigerenzer, P. Todd, and the ABC Research Group. Oxford University Press.

Grzimek, M., and Grzimek, B. 1960. A study of the game of the Serengeti plains. *Zeitschrift für Saugetierkunde* 24: 1–61.

Herrnstein, R. J. 1961. Relative and absolute strengths of response as a function of frequency of reinforcement. *Journal of the Experimental Analysis of Behavior* 4: 267–272.

Herrnstein, R. J. 1970. On the law of effect. *Journal of the Experimental Analysis of Behavior* 13: 243–266.

Horne, P. J., and Lowe, C. F. 1993. Determinants of human performance on concurrent schedules. *Journal of the Experimental Analysis of Behavior* 59: 29–60.

Kaplan, H. 1996. A theory of fertility and parental investment in traditional and modern human societies. *Yearbook of Physical Anthropology* 39: 91–135.

Katona, G. 1975. *Psychological Economics*. Elsevier.

Kuhn, T. S. 1962. *The Structure of Scientific Revolutions*. University of Chicago Press.

Laibson, D. 1998. Life-cycle consumption and hyperbolic discount functions. *European Economic Review* 42: 861–871.

Lea, S. E. G. 1979. Foraging and reinforcement schedules in the pigeon: Optimal and non-optimal aspects of choice. *Animal Behaviour* 27: 875–886.

Lea, S. E. G. 1985. Operant psychology and ethology: Failures and successes in interdisciplinary interaction. In *Behaviour Analysis and Contemporary Psychology*, ed. C. Lowe, M. Richelle, D. Blackman, and C. Bradshaw. Erlbaum.

Lea, S. E. G., Webley, P., and Levine, R. M. 1993. The economic psychology of consumer debt. *Journal of Economic Psychology* 14: 85–119.

Lea, S. E. G., Webley, P., and Walker, C. M. 1995. Psychological factors in consumer debt: Money management, economic socialization, and credit use. *Journal of Economic Psychology* 16: 681–701.

Loewenstein, G., and Thaler, R. H. 1989. Anomalies: Intertemporal choice. *Journal of Economic Perspectives* 3: 181–193.

Logue, A. W. 1988. Research on self-control: An integrating framework. *Behavioral and Brain Sciences* 11: 665–678.

Malkoc, S. A., and Zauberman, G. 2006. Deferring versus expediting consumption: The effect of outcome concreteness on sensitivity to time horizon. *Journal of Marketing Research* 43: 618–627.

Mazur, J. E. 1984. Tests of an equivalence rule for fixed and variable reinforcer delays. *Journal of Experimental Psychology: Animal Behavior Processes* 10: 426–436.

Mewse, A. J., Lea, S. E. G., and Wrapson, W. 2010. First steps out of debt: Attitudes and social identity as predictors of contact by debtors with creditors. *Journal of Economic Psychology* 31: 1021–1034.

Mischel, W. 1958. Preference for delayed reinforcement: An experimental study of a cultural observation. *Journal of Abnormal and Social Psychology* 56: 57–61.

Mulcahy, N. J., and Call, J. 2006. Apes save tools for future use. *Science* 312: 1038–1040.

Muraven, M., and Baumeister, R. F. 2000. Self-regulation and depletion of limited resources: Does self-control resemble a muscle? *Psychological Bulletin* 126: 247–259.

Navarick, D. J. 1987. Reinforcement probability and delay as determinants of human impulsiveness. *Psychological Record* 37: 219–225.

Nettle, D. 2010. Dying young and living fast: Variation in life history across English neighborhoods. *Behavioral Ecology* 21: 387–395.

Newson, L., Postmes, T., Lea, S. E. G., and Webley, P. 2005. Why are modern families small? Toward an evolutionary and cultural explanation for the demographic transition. *Personality and Social Psychology Review* 9: 360–375.

Piersma, T., Dietz, M. W., Dekinga, A., Nebel, S., van Gils, J. A., Battley, P. F., et al. 1999. Reversible size-changes in stomachs of shorebirds: When, to what extent, and why? *Acta Ornithologia* 34: 175–181.

Pinker, S. 1997. *How the Mind Works*. Norton.

Quinlan, R. J. 2008. Human pair-bonds: Evolutionary functions, ecological variation, and adaptive development. *Evolutionary Anthropology* 17: 227–238.

Rachlin, H., and Green, L. 1972. Commitment, choice, and self-control. *Journal of the Experimental Analysis of Behavior* 17: 15–22.

Roberts, W. A. 2002. Are animals stuck in time? *Psychological Bulletin* 128: 473–489.

Sherry, D. F., and Hoshooley, J. S. 2010. Seasonal hippocampal plasticity in food-storing birds. *Philosophical Transactions of the Royal Society of London B* 365: 933–943.

Sjöberg, L., and Johnson, T. 1978. Trying to give up smoking: A study of volitional breakdowns. *Addictive Behaviors* 3: 149–164.

Skinner, B. F. 1984. Selection by consequences. *Behavioral and Brain Sciences* 7: 477–481.

Stewart, N., Chater, N., and Brown, G. D. A. 2006. Decision by sampling. *Cognitive Psychology* 53: 1–26.

Strathman, A., Gleicher, F., Boninger, D. S., and Edwards, C. S. 1994. The consideration of future consequences: Weighing immediate and distant outcomes of behavior. *Journal of Personality and Social Psychology* 66: 742–752.

Strotz, R. H. 1956. Myopia and inconsistency in dynamic utility maximization. *Review of Economic Studies* 23: 165–180.

Suddendorf, T., and Corballis, M. C. 1997. Mental time travel and the evolution of the human mind. *Genetic, Social, and General Psychology Monographs* 123: 133–167.

Suddendorf, T., and Corballis, M. C. 2007. The evolution of foresight: What is mental time travel, and is it unique to humans? *Behavioral and Brain Sciences* 30: 299–351.

Szpunar, K. K. 2010. Episodic future thought: An emerging concept. *Perspectives on Psychological Science* 5: 142–162.

Thaler, R. H., and Shefrin, H. M. 1981. An economic theory of self-control. *Journal of Political Economy* 89: 392–406.

Thaler, R. H., and Sunstein, C. R. 2008. *Nudge*. Yale University Press.

Tulving, E. 1985. Memory and consciousness. *Canadian Psychology* 26: 1–12.

Walker, C. M. 1997. The Psychology of Debt in the 1990s. Ph.D. thesis, University of Exeter.

Food, Foraging, and Saving

5 Simple Heuristics for Deciding What to Eat

Peter M. Todd and Sara L. Minard

Singapore is a food lover's playground. Combining culinary traditions from more than a half-dozen mingling cultures, the small island nation boasts a vast array of dishes to try, and an even wider range of food stalls and restaurants to try them at. The local guide to eating places, the *Makansutra*, lists 152 types of meals and snacks and evaluates more than 1,200 purveyors in detail, down to the method used to make their sambal sauce. Reading it and absorbing the information it contains might take several days, but poring over its 488 pages would allow the hungry visitor to determine exactly the best spot to go for chili crabs and where to grab the most superlative salted egg yolk custard buns afterwards.

Yet few of us engage in such extensive gathering and pondering of data before deciding what to have for our next meal (though the first author did so, in the name of research). Deep thought is usually out of the question when one is standing before a collection of food stalls in a bustling market and trying to decide which one to favor, or standing in front of one's open refrigerator at the end of a long day and trying to decide what to prepare. Instead, we typically make our food choices rapidly and without much contemplation of options and consequences—something that often leads to "mindless eating" (Wansink 2006). Many of our daily food-consumption decisions are made using simple heuristics or rules of thumb that guide what we eat, when and where, how much, and when we stop. Clearly, preferences and hunger will be factors, but other things may determine our ultimate choices. For instance, we may decide to eat what we see most of the people before us in a line at a stall choose, or what will be easiest to grab from our own fridge and prepare. Such simple rules—for example, "eat what others are eating" or "eat what is most convenient"—are often all we have time for, especially insofar as we make many such decisions each day (more than 200 food-related choices daily, by one estimate—see Wansink 2006). These heuristics do not meet the traditional requirements for rational decision making, which involves gathering all the available information, weighing it appropriately and combining it, and choosing the alternative indicated as being best by the combined weighted data. Nonetheless, deciding in such a "quick and dirty" manner can still lead to effective choices in situations for which it is appropriate (Gigerenzer, Todd, and ABC Research Group 1999; Todd, Gigerenzer, and ABC Research Group 2012).

In this chapter we explore some of the simple rules or heuristics that people use to guide their food-consumption choices, focusing on choosing what to eat. We look at how people decide what to eat when they are alone and when they are in social settings (where they can be influenced by the choices of others). Some of the same sorts of rules are used to guide consumption in domains other than food (e.g., consumer goods), so studying these rules can also give us insights into consumption behavior more broadly, but understanding people's food-choice rules is also important in itself because of the profound consequences our food-consumption behavior has for our health (as in the costly ongoing obesity epidemic—Hammond and Levine 2010) and for our use, and waste, of resources. Furthermore, discovering the rules we use in food decisions can help us shape our own environments with respect to food so that the daily choices we make better align with our long-term health and environmental goals.

Deciding What to Eat

Ways to make decisions

We are interested here in characterizing the rules people use to select what to eat—whether from a menu, from a table, or from a kitchen cabinet or a refrigerator—when faced with a set of food options. What information about the available options do people consider, and how do they process it to come up with a choice? The information taken into account may include previous experiences with a food (including preferences developed in the past), information about a food's ingredients and nutritional aspects, and knowledge of a food's origin, popularity, and cost. We will also consider in a later section where that information comes from, as much research has explored the origins of food preferences and the influence of culture, peers, parents, and media. (See, for example, Logue 2004.)

Given the various pieces of information that could be used in making a choice, that information can be processed in a variety of ways to make a food choice. Prescriptions for rational decision making usually involve gathering and considering all the available information. Specifically, the weighted-additive (WADD) rule, considered a "gold standard" for preferential choice (Payne, Bettman, and Johnson 1993), stipulates collecting information on multiple factors (positive or negative) associated with each alternative, weighting each factor according to its subjective importance for the choice at hand, adding the weighted factors together for each alternative, and choosing the alternative with the greatest sum of factors. Such an approach would guide a visitor to Singapore to the food stall that had the best combination of price, location, popularity, speed, spiciness, cleanliness, fresh ingredients, and so on, all weighted by how important the visitor judged each of those dimensions to be. However, using the WADD rule can require considerable time to gather and assess factors and considerable effort to combine them into an overall judgment of each alternative. Consequently, earlier research on judgment and decision making questioned whether rational rules such as WADD are reasonable descriptions of real human decision making in many common settings. (See, for example, Dawes 1979.)

However, many researchers have proposed that people often make decisions in faster, less effortful ways by using heuristics or shortcuts—employing what Herbert Simon (1955) called "bounded rationality." (See, for example, Kahneman, Slovic, and Tversky 1982; Payne, Bettman, and Johnson 1993; Gigerenzer, Todd, and ABC Research Group 1999.) These simple decision rules typically use a minimal amount of information and processing, for instance basing choices just on what comes most easily to mind or what is recognized. Although some research (e.g., the heuristics and biases program of Kahneman and Tversky) focuses on how heuristics can lead to erroneous decisions or judgments, heuristics also typically yield good choices when they are used in appropriate environments (as studied in the ecological rationality program of Todd, Gigerenzer, and ABC Research Group 2012). Rather than striving for the best or optimal choice, which can be impossible to determine in our uncertain world, simple heuristics operate quickly and without seeking much information to produce decisions that are "good enough."

Previous food-choice research has seldom investigated the mechanisms by which individuals' choices are made, but it has nonetheless often embodied implicit assumptions about how these mechanisms operate. (For a review, see Scheibehenne, Miesler, and Todd 2007.) Much of this research measures how important multiple factors are in food choices, with the underlying assumption that all the factors matter at least somewhat and that people differ in how much importance they assign to each. For instance, the commonly used Food Choice Questionnaire (Steptoe, Pollard, and Wardle 1995) captures an individual's rating of the importance of nine food-related factors: health, price, convenience, mood improvement, sensory appeal, natural content, weight control, familiarity, and ethical concerns about origin and packaging. Sensory appeal, health, convenience, and price are typically rated as most important. In their model of food cognition, Rappoport, Peters, Downey, McCann, and Huff-Corzine (1993) state that "the decision to eat a particular food will depend upon how that food scales on each of the three criteria (pleasure, health, and convenience)," again suggesting the use of a WADD choice rule. Eertmans et al. (2005) explicitly assume that daily food intake is influenced "through the weighting of various food choice motives," such as sensory appeal, health, price, and convenience. Glanz et al. (1998) predicted individuals' consumption of fruits, fast foods, cheese, and breakfast cereals by incorporating their importance ratings of taste, nutritional value, cost, convenience, and weight control into a general linear model implementing a WADD rule.

But these assumed "rational" mechanisms such as WADD have not been tested explicitly in this previous research, despite contentions that "consumers employ heuristics (empirical rules of thumb) to facilitate making a satisfactory choice with minimum effort" (Roering, Boush, and Shipp 1986). What is needed are studies that directly pit these rational full-information choice mechanisms against simple "fast and frugal" heuristics to compare which can better account for people's actual food choices. In the next section, we describe one such study that focuses on the comparison between a "one-reason" heuristic and the WADD rule. We then proceed to describe a variety of other heuristics that may be used in food choice, but for which similar detailed comparative studies must still be done.

Choices made individually

To test empirically how well a simple heuristic is able to account for individual food decisions relative to the rational WADD strategy, Scheibehenne, Miesler, and Todd (2007) showed participants many pairs of lunch dishes and asked them to choose which of the two dishes they preferred in each case. The pairs were created from twenty lunches sampled from a local food court. Photos of the pairs were presented on a computer screen. Each participant then filled out a questionnaire assessing how important they thought each of the Food Choice Questionnaire's nine factors were to them in making their daily food choices (e.g., "The importance of convenience in my daily food choices is 3 out of 5."). They also evaluated each of the twenty dishes on those nine factors (e.g., "I rate the convenience of this bagel sandwich as 4 out of 5"). Given this data on each individual's choices, factor importance weights, and factor values, it is straightforward to test how well various choice mechanisms can produce the former (individual's choices) from the latter (individual factor importance and values).

The WADD strategy uses all the available information to make a choice. It takes each factor value, multiplies it by the associated factor weight, adds all the products up to produce a total weighted sum of factors for each of the two dishes, and then predicts that the individual will choose the dish with the higher sum. In contrast, the simple heuristic used in this case, called LEX, is a lexicographic strategy that uses as little information as it can to distinguish and choose between the two dishes. (LEX is named after the related lexicographic process of alphabetizing using the first letter position where two words being compared have different letters; for example, "squids" and "squidgy" are alphabetized using the sixth letter position). LEX merely looks at the factor that the individual rated as most important and checks to see whether that factor differs for the two dishes (e.g., if price was most important for a given person, then did the price differ for dishes A and B?)—if so, then it stops and chooses the dish with the better value on that factor (e.g., the cheaper dish). If this most important factor did not distinguish between the two dishes (e.g., if their prices are the same), then the next-most-important factor (e.g., convenience) is checked; if that differs, then that factor alone is used to make the choice (e.g., the more convenient dish). If that factor did not distinguish, the third-most-important factor is considered, and so on, until a choice can be made. Thus, LEX only uses one reason in making its choice—the most important reason that allows a definite choice to be made. (Another well-studied lexicographic strategy is the take-the-best heuristic—see Gigerenzer and Goldstein 1996.)

Comparing how many of the participants' food choices were correctly predicted by WADD versus LEX, Scheibehenne et al. found that the much simpler LEX heuristic, using only a single reason, performed as well on average as the information-hungry WADD strategy. For many particular individual participants, LEX described their choices much better. These results indicate that, in view of the extra time and effort using a WADD rule requires to assess the available information, many people are likely to use simple heuristics instead when making food choices. (The results also suggest that there can be individual variation in which choice strategy is used.)

Note, though, that the LEX heuristic could still draw on a number of different pieces of information to determine a choice. In many contexts, people will have very limited information available at the time they must decide what to eat. Consider, for example, someone deciding between a dish that he recognizes and another that is unknown to him—in that case, he cannot compare taste, ethical origin, and mood effects, because he knows nothing about the second dish. In such a situation, the decision maker can do little better than rely on his partial ignorance, choosing recognized options over unrecognized ones. This kind of "ignorance-based reasoning" is embodied in the recognition heuristic (Goldstein and Gigerenzer 2002): When choosing between two objects (based on some criterion), if one is recognized and the other is not, then select the former. For instance, if an individual were choosing between familiar-looking chili crabs and never-before-seen gluey gray squiggles in a bowl based on what may be good to eat, this heuristic would lead her to choose the recognized crabs over the unrecognized mystery bowl. Norway rats follow a similar rule, preferring to eat things they recognize from experience (e.g., items they have smelled on the breath of other rats) over novel items (Galef 2009). The recognition heuristic will be ecologically rational, yielding good choices more often than would random choice, in decision environments where recognition of an option is positively correlated with its value on the criterion being used. This is probably often the case for deciding what is good to eat, if it can be assumed that the person has already found most of the things he enjoys eating through personal experience or by hearing about them from other people. A particularly adventurous individual, however, might use an anti-recognition heuristic to choose dishes that are *not* recognized and thereby further explore the range of options.

In other situations, the chooser may recognize most or all of the available options (and so not be able to distinguish a single choice with the recognition heuristic) but still not know much about each one. If one has encountered these options often, a simple shortcut is to go with habit and choose what one has chosen in the past, which only requires recalling that information from memory. If the options are less familiar, as in the case of dishes listed on the menu of a new restaurant, recognition and habit will not suffice, but a simple "satisficing" strategy (Simon 1955; Gigerenzer 2014) will enable one to make a quick choice: search through the list of options until the first item that is good enough (as determined by one's current goals) is encountered, then choose that item without looking at any of the other possibilities. Satisficers who make such quick choices are often happier with their selections than are maximizers who try to consider all the available options (Schwartz 2004).

Choices made socially

When an individual deciding what to eat also has input from others—not just from his or her own experience and memory—the additional social information greatly expands the range of choice rules that can be used. First, recognition-based decisions can now be made on the basis of what one recognizes as having heard about from others, rather than just on the basis of what one recognizes from having seen it or eaten it before. And if people choose to eat what they recognize from others' accounts, this can result in some items' gaining runaway popularity and ever-increasing recognition (Todd and Heuvelink 2007), something that food companies and restaurant chains clearly hope to capitalize on.

Many more social decision rules depend not on what others have mentioned but on knowledge of what others have chosen and eaten. This is the difference between "Tom mentioned seeing a Red Mango place the other day—maybe I'll try their frozen yogurt now" and "There's Susan eating at Pinkberry—I have to get some, too!" Learning what others have chosen (even without learning about the success of their choices) opens up the possibilities of using decision strategies based on copying particular individuals, copying the majority, and even choosing something different from what others have chosen.

Copying the behavior of others can be a beneficial decision strategy because it can provide "a shortcut to acquiring adaptive information, saving [the individual] the costs of asocial learning," with "the advantage that individuals do not need to . . . sample all potential foods . . . for themselves" (Laland 2004). But copying is not always appropriate—it must be done selectively. The particular social model or models chosen to be copied must provide useful information. Copying the food choices of inexperienced or sick individuals, for instance, could guide one to choose exactly the wrong sorts of things to eat. Laland (ibid.) catalogs several copying decision rules designed to use information from appropriately selected models. Copying the choices of successful individuals can be advantageous when the basis for their success is reflected in their choices—for instance, if fit individuals are healthy in part because of their diet, then other individuals who copy what the fit ones eat may also become healthier. (This copying strategy can also go wrong, as when people copy the fad diet of a celebrity who is fit and successful despite a grapefruit-and-water regimen.) Duncker (1938) observed that children copied heroic characters' described preferences for somewhat unpalatable foods. Advertisers often rely on consumers' use of prestige-based copying rules by showing media and sports stars choosing their products, as in the well-known "Got milk?" ad campaign. Copying kin and other close social partners is beneficial when the copier and the model share similar environments and similar reactions to that environment. For instance, if children see their parents avoiding eating a particular local plant that is eaten elsewhere, this may be because the local plants are not palatable, or because family members react badly to it—both good reasons to copy the parents' choices. (However, it has been argued that children's food choices often differ to a surprising extent from those of their parents, pointing to the influence of peers' choices instead; see Rozin 1991.) Copying older individuals with greater knowledge of the local environment can also be adaptive. Consistent with this, Birch (1980) found that children around 3 to 5 years old copied the food choices of (on average older) peers significantly more than the reverse (mirroring earlier findings by Duncker), and Addessi et al. (2005) found that young children copied the specific novel food choices of familiar adults (although Duncker found contrary evidence in this adult case).

Groups rather than individuals can also be copied. The copy-the-majority rule can spread favorable preferences and behaviors through a population. When consumers follow this rule, the resulting conformity can be seen in "herding" effects toward popular brands (Janssen and Jager 2001; Banerjee 1992). However, there can also be advantages in going against the majority's choice—for instance, choosing rare or expensive items (caviar, foie gras) may signal one's wealth and prestige, and ordering a different dish than everyone else at the table may demonstrate one's individuality (Ariely and Levav 2000). (But see Quester and Steyer 2010 for evidence of conformity when groups at a table are intermediate in size.) Such an avoid-choices-of-others rule could also be used when someone is faced with an undesirable social model, as McFerran, Dahl, Fitzsimons, and Morales (2010a) showed for different portion sizes chosen after observing what an obese model chose.

Interestingly, although rats are influenced in their food preferences by the choices of others, there is considerable evidence (reviewed in Galef 2009) that rats follow few if any of these rules for what specific individual to copy, even ignoring the fact that the model is sick. This may be because in the rats' ecological niche determining *when* to copy is more important than *whom* to copy. A similar distinction may apply in humans: Pliner and Mann (2004) present evidence that people are more strongly influenced by others in how much they eat than in what they choose to eat, perhaps because amounts eaten are under strong pressure from social norms (and hence can be "right" or "wrong") whereas what to eat is more a matter of personal preference (with which there is no arguing—*de gustibus non est disputandum*). This may break down, though, in novel environments where the eater does not have prior preferences and so will be more likely to rely on the choices made by others, particularly those with local knowledge.

Of course, we usually learn more about the food choices of others than the mere fact of what they have eaten—people usually also indicate whether or not they liked what they ate, how much it cost, what it had in it, and so on. Gigerenzer (2014) recommends using social information of this kind in a fast and frugal manner—for instance, by asking a waiter what he would eat (in essence, copying the choice of a local expert) rather than what he would recommend (which might bring conflicting motivations into play). The other copying heuristics described above (copying particular individuals or groups) also can be applied to the copying of individual or group preferences (not just choices): one may take into account how happy the people being copied were with their choices. People clearly consider recommendations when deciding what to eat, and also use subtler cues such as the positive facial expressions of someone enjoying a dish to guide their own choices (Rousset, Schlich, Chatonnier, Barthomeuf, and Droit-Volet 2008). (Diners may also be swayed by less subtle expressions of delight during a meal, as in the "I'll have what she's having" heuristic used in the deli scene in the 1989 film *When Harry Met Sally. . . .*) People may also use an anti-recommendation heuristic—"I'll have something different from what she's having"—when they dislike, distrust, or want to distance themselves from the recommender (similar to the anti-copying avoid-choices-of-others heuristic; see McFerran, Dahl, Fitzsimons, and Morales 2010b for evidence of the use of this rule). Further work is needed to characterize what situations and environments lead people making food choices to rely solely on such social information in a heuristic manner, or to combine it with other information in a more traditionally rational weight-and-add fashion. (For an example of combining social and non-social information, see Barthomeuf, Rousset, and Droit-Volet 2009.)

Deciding What Not to Eat

Decisions regarding "what to eat" are made throughout a meal. Should we wolf down all the fried cheese we took from the buffet, or decide not to do so in an attempt to avoid further arterial damage? Should we finish the overcooked cauliflower, or push it around our plate in the hopes that the host will not notice? These micro-decisions structure our meal, determining what we consume or leave behind, influencing the choices of others we eat with, and ultimately affecting our health and our use and waste of resources. Though it is often overlooked, food waste—the flip-side of food consumption—is a mounting concern for food and health researchers (Cuellar and Webber 2010; Evans 2012; Hall et al. 2009), and it is a growing economic and environmental problem. Recent estimates indicate that about one-third of the food produced for human consumption is lost or wasted at some point in the chain stretching from agriculture to consumers, around 1.3 billion tons per year worldwide (Gustavsson et al. 2011). Understanding our food-choice rules could be useful in combating this extensive, costly waste.

Ethnographic research on household food waste by Evans (2012) suggests that food waste, rather than an instance of human profligacy, is the result of household behavioral patterning, which can be described in terms of food-choice rules. For example, many grocery shoppers often purchase the same foods habitually, week after week, regardless of whether they already have the same items in their refrigerators. Often new produce just brought home from the market will be much more appealing than the withered produce already at home, prompting the householder to discard withered items rather than use them. Similarly, "plate waste" can occur when people simply select their habitual dishes and portions rather than selecting what would suffice to alleviate their hunger. In both cases, simple rules of habitual choice that ignore further information can lead to waste. Further, applying food-choice copying rules at the table may result in waste if the copier turns out not to like the food the model chose.

A closer examination of food waste may reveal different choice rules at work. In a field study of food waste that we conducted in sororities and fraternities, we came across puzzling patterns: whole yolks of hard-boiled eggs languishing on plates, piles of sandwich crusts, entire servings of macaroni and cheese left uneaten. In the absence of detailed interviews of participants, we can only hypothesize about their dietary rules: for example, "Eggs have protein, which I need, but egg yolks are high in fat, which I am trying to avoid; therefore I will eat the white and avoid the yolk," or "My mother always cut the crusts off my sandwiches when she prepared my lunch, so I don't eat crusts." In many cases we saw otherwise familiar foods being wasted, sometimes with an unprompted explanation along the lines of "This doesn't taste like the mac and cheese I am used to." These comments suggest that rigid expectations as to how everyday foods are "supposed" to be prepared or taste may influence consumption and waste decisions. They also point out that the factors used in food-choice decisions made once eating has begun may differ from those guiding the initial choices made regarding what to put on one's plate (e.g., taste for the former, familiarity and mood for the latter).

This shift in decision rules is also seen in purchasing behavior. Evans (2012) found that householders purchased foods with the intention of eating healthily or adventurously, but then consumed familiar and favored foods instead and wasted the healthy or exotic items they had purchased. Dining environments designed to appeal to our curiosity and adventurousness, such as buffets, also result in considerable waste. Having dozens of options is tempting, but it results in high levels of waste after people take a bite of their big helping of (say) lukewarm Waldorf salad and discover that other options are more appealing.

Conclusion

Most people, most of the time, choose what they will eat without much thought —if they even get to choose at all. Instead of considering all the options and weighing the pros and cons, we typically appear to reduce our time and effort by using some simple rules or heuristics (consciously or not) to make a choice based on one or two factors that are important to us, or on our past habits or the choices of others around us. Identifying these possible rules and when they are applied is an important research goal for furthering our understanding of how people decide what to eat, and for enabling us to change our eating environments in ways that can lead to choices promoting health and reducing waste.

References

Addessi, E., Galloway, A. T., Visalberghi, E., and Birch, L. L. 2005. Specific social influences on the acceptance of novel foods in 2–5-year-old children. *Appetite* 45 (3): 264–271.

Ariely, D., and Levav, J. 2000. Sequential choice in group settings: Taking the road less traveled and less enjoyed. *Journal of Consumer Research* 27 (December): 279–290.

Banerjee, A. V. 1992. A simple model of herd behavior. *Quarterly Journal of Economics* 107 (3): 797–817.

Barthomeuf, L., Rousset, S., and Droit-Volet, S. 2009. The desire to eat in front of obese or normal-weight eaters as a function of their emotional facial expression. *Obesity* 18: 719–724.

Birch, L. L. 1980. Effects of peer models' food choices and eating behaviors on preschoolers' food preferences. *Child Development* 51: 489–496.

Cuellar, A. D., and Webber, M. E. 2010. Wasted food, wasted energy: The embedded energy in food waste in the United States. *Environmental Science and Technology* 44 (16): 6464–6469.

Dawes, R. M. 1979. The robust beauty of improper linear models in decision making. *American Psychologist* 34: 571–582.

Duncker, K. 1938. Experimental modification of children's food preferences through social suggestion. *Journal of Abnormal and Social Psychology* 33: 489–507.

Eertmans, A., Victoir, A., Vansant, G., and Van den Bergh, O. 2005. Food-related personality traits, food choice motives and food intake: Mediator and moderator relationships. *Food Quality and Preferences* 16: 714–726.

Evans, D. 2012. Beyond the throwaway society: Ordinary domestic practice and a sociological approach to household food waste. *Sociology* 6 (1): 41–56.

Galef, B. G. 2009. Strategies for social learning: Tests of predictions from formal theory. *Advances in the Study of Behavior* 39: 117–151.

Gigerenzer, G. 2014. *Risk Savvy: How to Make Good Decisions*. Viking.

Gigerenzer, G., and Goldstein, D. G. 1996. Reasoning the fast and frugal way: Models of bounded rationality. *Psychological Review* 103: 650–669.

Gigerenzer, G., Todd, P. M., and the ABC Research Group. 1999. *Simple Heuristics That Make Us Smart*. Oxford University Press.

Glanz, K., Basil, M., Maibach, E., Goldberg, J., and Snyder, D. A. N. 1998. Why Americans eat what they do: Taste, nutrition, cost, convenience, and weight control concerns as influences on food consumption. *Journal of the American Dietetic Association* 98: 1118–1126.

Goldstein, D. G., and Gigerenzer, G. 2002. Models of ecological rationality: The recognition heuristic. *Psychological Review* 109: 75–90.

Gustavsson, J., Cederberg, C., Sonesson, U., Van Otterdijk, R., and Meybeck, A. 2011. *Global Food Losses and Food Waste*. Food and Agriculture Organization.

Hall, K. D., Guo, J., Dore, M., and Chow, C. C. 2009. The progressive increase of food waste in America and its environmental impact. *PLOS ONE* 4 (11): e7940.

Hammond, R. A., and Levine, R. 2010. The economic impact of obesity in the United States. *Diabetes, Metabolic Syndrome and Obesity* 3: 285–295.

Janssen, M. A., and Jager, W. 2001. Fashions, habits and changing preferences: Simulation of psychological factors affecting market dynamics. *Journal of Economic Psychology* 22: 745–772.

Kahneman, D., Slovic, P., and Tversky, A., eds. 1982. *Judgment under Uncertainty: Heuristics and Biases*. Cambridge University Press.

Laland, K. N. 2004. Social learning strategies. *Learning & Behavior* 32: 4–14.

Logue, A. W. 2004. *The Psychology of Eating and Drinking*, third edition. Brunner-Routledge.

McFerran, B., Dahl, D. W., Fitzsimons, G. J., and Morales, A. C. 2010a. I'll have what she's having: Effects of social influence and body type on the food choices of others. *Journal of Consumer Research* 36: 915–929.

McFerran, B., Dahl, D. W., Fitzsimons, G. J., and Morales, A. C. 2010b. Might an overweight waitress make you eat more? How the body type of others is sufficient to alter our food consumption. *Journal of Consumer Psychology* 20: 146–151.

Payne, J. W., Bettman, J. R., and Johnson, E. J. 1993. *The Adaptive Decision Maker*. Cambridge University Press.

Pliner, P., and Mann, N. 2004. Influence of social norms and palatability on amount consumed and food choice. *Appetite* 42: 227–237.

Quester, P., and Steyer, A. 2010. Revisiting individual choices in group settings: The long and winding (less traveled) road? *Journal of Consumer Research* 36 (6): 1050–1057.

Rappoport, L. H., Peters, G. R., Downey, R. G., McCann, T., and Huff-Corzine, L. 1993. Gender and age differences in food cognition. *Appetite* 20: 33–52.

Roering, K. J., Boush, D. M., and Shipp, S. H. 1986. Factors that shape eating patterns: A consumer behavior perspective. In *What Is America Eating? Proceedings of a Symposium*. National Academy Press.

Rousset, S., Schlich, P., Chatonnier, A., Barthomeuf, L., and Droit-Volet, S. 2008. Is the desire to eat familiar and unfamiliar meat products influenced by the emotions expressed on eaters' faces? *Appetite* 50: 110–119.

Rozin, P. 1991. Family resemblance in food and other domains: The family paradox and the role of parental congruence. *Appetite* 16: 93–102.

Scheibehenne, B., Miesler, L., and Todd, P. M. 2007. Fast and frugal food choices: Uncovering individual decision heuristics. *Appetite* 49: 578–589.

Schwartz, B. 2004. *The Paradox of Choice: Why More Is Less*. HarperCollins.

Simon, H. A. 1955. A behavioral model of rational choice. *Quarterly Journal of Economics* 69: 99–118.

Steptoe, A., Pollard, T. M., and Wardle, J. 1995. Development of a measure of the motives underlying the selection of food: The Food Choice Questionnaire. *Appetite* 25: 267–284.

Todd, P. M., Gigerenzer, G., and the ABC Research Group 2012. *Ecological Rationality: Intelligence in the World*. Oxford University Press.

Todd, P. M., and Heuvelink, A. 2007. Shaping social environments with simple recognition heuristics. In *The Innate Mind*, volume 2: *Culture and Cognition*, ed. P. Carruthers, S. Laurence, and S. Stich. Oxford University Press.

Wansink, B. 2006. *Mindless Eating: Why We Eat More Than We Think*. Bantam Books.

6 Decisions, Memory, and the Neuroecology of Food-Storing Birds

David F. Sherry

The interdisciplinary science of consumption seeks to explain familiar human behavior and the social and individual problems that consumption can give rise to by examining, in an integrative fashion, the function, the evolution, and the neural basis of consumption. Elsewhere in this volume, Preston and Vickers describe humans' ability to save material goods, Webley, Rick, Frank, and Lea discuss the ability to save money, and Robinson et al., Plassman and Wager, and Todd and Minard discuss human consumption of food and drugs of abuse. But humans are not the only species that bank resources for later use. Just as we save material goods and money for later use, quite a few animals collect food in excess of what they immediately consume and use their caches to buffer fluctuations in food availability (Vander Wall 1990). This buffering can be long-term, such as storing food in fall to survive winter scarcity, or short-term, such as storing food early in the day to consume later the same day when food availability may be less predictable. There is a great deal of research, especially with birds, on food storing as an adaptation and on the proximate mechanisms of food storing. This research can help us understand how organisms have evolved to set aside resources for later use, and it has revealed changes in the nervous system that have accompanied the evolution of food storing. By examining food-storing behavior in a well-studied animal system, we may be able to shed light on why humans use their stores, hoards, and savings in the way they do and why accumulation and consumption of resources sometimes goes wrong.

In this chapter I will describe the natural history of two species of birds that differ in how they sequester and later use cached food. I will then describe models of the economics of food storing and how food storing interacts with other aspects of energy management. Finally, I will describe how a food-storing way of life has produced a variety of morphological and cognitive adaptations in birds that are specialized to store food.

Acorn Woodpeckers

Acorn woodpeckers are group-living birds that store acorns and sometimes other nuts in large communal granaries. Their granaries are trees, fences, or other wooden structures in which the birds have drilled thousands of small holes, each made to hold a single acorn. Granaries are the result of the efforts of generations of birds and are vigorously defended by the group. Despite the effort invested in preparing granaries and harvesting acorns, stored acorns make up a relatively small part of the acorn woodpecker diet. Full granaries contain only about 16 percent of the birds' total energy requirements (Koenig 1991). Acorn woodpeckers do not maximize the energy they obtain from stored acorns. Instead, they select acorns that best fit the size of existing storage holes in the granary. They receive a nutritional benefit from the mixed diet that acorn storage provides (Koenig and Benedict 2002). They collect 90 percent of the acorns they store from oaks within 150 meters of their communal granary (Koenig, McEntee, and Walters 2008), although there can be exceptions. Scofield et al. (2010) found one granary, among sixteen they observed, in which acorns were harvested from oaks more than 1.3 kilometers away. They suggest that this may have been the result of the loss of a granary by this social group, after which the birds established a new granary in a new territory but continued to harvest acorns from their original territory.

It may seem puzzling that so much effort on the part of the woodpeckers is devoted to collecting acorns and preparing and defending granaries when full granaries contain only a small fraction of the energy they need (Koenig 1991). The value of the hoard, however, may be greater than the energy it contains. Hitchcock and Houston (1994) modeled over-winter survival of acorn woodpeckers at varying levels of foraging success and stored acorn supply. They found that when the probability of successful foraging was relatively high, at 0.7, increasing the size of the hoard from zero to 100 acorns raised the probability of over-winter survival from around 50 percent to over 80 percent. When the probability of foraging success was low, at 0.3, increasing the hoard size from 100 to 200 acorns raised the probability of over winter survival from around

20 percent to over 80 percent. Hitchcock and Houston suggest that variability in foraging success might select for more hoarding because relatively small hoards allow the woodpeckers to invade environments in which foraging success is variable. Indeed, acorn storage is practically universal in coastal California, irregular in the American southwest, Mexico, and Central America, and only occasional in Colombia (Koenig et al. 1995).

Chickadees and Tits

Birds in the family *Paridae*—chickadees, titmice, and Eurasian tits—store food in a different way. These birds store single food items scattered widely within their fall and winter home range. A single bird can store several hundred food items in a single day and over the course of fall and winter may store many thousands. Each food item is usually placed in a separate site, which can include crevices in bark, hollow stems, moss, and leaf litter. Birds store any of the foods they eat, including seeds, parts of nuts, insects and their eggs, spiders, and other invertebrate prey. Food storing can be a long-term or a short-term strategy. Experiments in which stored food was located and monitored show that many caches are recovered within a day or two of hoarding, often within the same day (Cowie, Krebs, and Sherry 1981; Stevens and Krebs 1986). Some of this food may be moved to new storage sites rather than consumed, however, because other studies using radioactively labeled food showed that birds retrieved some food as long as 50 days after storing it, detected because the label left a radioactive trace on the bird's growing feathers (Brodin and Ekman 1994).

Because many chickadees and tits form social groups in fall and winter, in contrast to the individual breeding territories they defend in spring and summer, much food storing takes place in a social context. There is no evidence, however, that caches are shared. Some caches may be lost to pilfering by flock members, but in general the bird that stored the food is the one that recovers it (Sherry, Krebs, and Cowie 1981). This is because birds remember the spatial locations of their caches. Experiments have shown that memory for the locations of caches is quite accurate, can persist for several weeks, and can include the kind of food cached and when it was cached (Feeney, Roberts, and Sherry 2009, 2011). Food-storing chickadees can also remember whether or not they have already harvested food from a site and, if they have, avoid returning to that location (Sherry 1984).

Models of Food Storing

What benefits, then, does storing food provide? How does investing time and energy in storing food, and forgoing immediate consumption, benefit animals that store food? A variety of models have addressed this question (Brodin 2007). These models examine ecological and behavioral factors that might influence food storing and make predictions about what behavior is likely to maximize fitness (McNamara, Houston, and Krebs 1990; Lucas and Walter 1991; Brodin 2007, 2000; Pravosudov and Lucas 2001). Lucas and Walter (1991), for example, used stochastic dynamic programming to model the expected energy gain or loss from the various alternate activities a food-storing bird could engage in, such as searching for food, eating, caching, retrieving food, and perching.

There is remarkable similarity in the predictions of the models, and a number of general conclusions that emerge. The two major causes of over-winter mortality for small food-storing birds are starvation and predation, and predation is likely to be the greater risk despite the relative scarcity of food in winter. This is because storing energy on the body as fat provides a guaranteed energy reserve but at the cost of mass-dependent metabolic costs of carrying this fat, in addition to mass-dependent predation costs. Fat birds have higher metabolic costs, especially in flight. It may therefore benefit a small bird to carry less fat than it could. And to accumulate fat reserves a bird must spend more time foraging and thus exposed to predation. The mass-dependent predation costs are thus attributable to more exposure to predators and a reduced ability to avoid them. Heavy birds accelerate more slowly, climb less steeply, and maneuver less well than light birds. Storing food in food caches incurs none of these costs (though it may incur others) and is therefore combined in some birds with fat storage to minimize both starvation and predation risk, especially in winter. Pravosudov and Lucas (2001) predicted that non-caching birds should maintain greater fat reserves as overnight temperature decreased from –5°C to –15°C and food-caching birds should not. Observations showed that, as predicted, food-storing birds did not increase their fat reserves as overnight temperature decreased, probably because they had a dependable reserve of stored food they could turn to when fat reserves ran low.

Adaptations for Food Storing

Morphology

Because food storing plays such an important role in the lives of some birds, it is not surprising that they possess specializations for the behavior. The most striking morphological adaptation for food storing occurs in the nutcrackers, *Nucifraga* (Lanner 1996). Clark's nutcracker *N. columbiana* in North America and the Eurasian nutcracker *N. caryocatactes* possess a sublingual pouch for carrying seeds—usually pine seeds—from the trees where they are collected to storage sites that may be several kilometers away. Clark's nutcrackers breed at relatively high altitudes in western North America and prefer to store seeds on south-facing slopes. Snow melts earlier on these slopes than on other exposures, and Clark's nutcrackers use their caches when they return to high elevations in spring to breed. Stored pine seed is the primary food used by the birds to sustain themselves during nest building and incubation and is also the main food fed to nestlings. (There are young birds in the nest well before insects have emerged.) Nutcrackers are the primary means of dispersal of several western pines including the whitebark and pinyon pines. These pines possess a number of unusual adaptations for dispersal by food-storing nutcrackers that are not found in other pines (Tomback and Linhart 1990). Cones are located at the tops of trees, with the point of attachment of the cone down and the tip of the cone up. The scales open when seeds are ripe, and the seeds are thus held in place, because the cone is inverted, until the seeds are taken by birds. Seeds also undergo a color change at ripening. The seeds of whitebark and pinyon pine are larger and richer in energy than the seeds of other pines—so much so that they are collected and eaten by people as well as by food-storing birds. All these traits make the seeds of the pines an attractive food source for nutcrackers. Nutcrackers, like chickadees, remember where they have cached food (Balda, Kamil, and Bednekoff 1997), but they retrieve only a portion of the seeds they store and so a great many pine seeds are planted in the ground in ideal conditions for germination.

Coevolution between pines and nutcrackers has resulted in the geographic ranges of these pines being restricted almost exclusively to the geographic range of Clark's nutcracker.

Memory

As was mentioned above, chickadees, tits, and nutcrackers retrieve stored food by remembering where they put their caches. Because the birds depend on stored food, and because memory plays such an important role in cache retrieval, a great deal of research has addressed the question of whether or not memory itself is adaptively specialized in these birds. Remembering the locations of hundreds or even thousands of caches, perhaps for several weeks or more, seems a remarkable feat. The brains of food-storing birds certainly differ from the brains of non-storing birds. In this section I will discuss some of the things that food-storing birds can remember about cache sites.

The basic experimental design in memory research on food-storing birds is to allow them to store food in captivity and then, after an interval of time, allow them to search for their caches. As long ago as 1720, Baron von Pernau noted that marsh tits (*Parus palustris*) held in captivity would store food indoors and recommended watching them do so as an entertainment for the amateur naturalist (Stresemann 1947). In most experiments we have done with black-capped chickadees, birds enter a room in which six to eight tree branches have been placed upright in stands. Each branch has a dozen or so holes drilled in it for storage sites. Birds spend a few minutes searching this empty room and then are given seeds to store. After storing about ten seeds, the bird is let out of the room and allowed to go back into its home cage. The experimenter then takes all the stored seeds out of the room, and the bird is allowed back several hours or several days later to search for its caches. We block all the sites so that birds must clearly indicate by opening the site where they are searching. Their recovery accuracy is compared against the accuracy that would be expected to be achieved by chance or the accuracy that would be expected from the birds' preference to spend time in certain trees or near certain holes (calculated from their initial behavior in the room at the beginning of the trial, before they were given any seeds). These experiments consistently show much greater accuracy in cache retrieval than would be expected to be achieved by chance or on the basis of initial preferences. Cache sites are empty of seeds when the birds are searching, so they cannot use visual, olfactory, or other methods of detecting cached seeds directly (Sherry, Krebs, and Cowie 1981; Sherry 1984; Hitchcock and Sherry 1990; Hampton and Sherry 1994; Petersen and Sherry 1996).

A number of studies have looked at what is remembered about cache sites. Clayton and Dickinson (1998) devised a test to determine whether food-storing scrub jays could remember what kind of food they had stored, where they had stored it, and how long ago. They proposed that behavior of this kind—memory for "what, where, and when"—could be used to determine whether or not the jays had episodic memory, a form of memory that the psychologist Endel Tulving, who first described episodic memory, regarded as a uniquely human trait (Tulving 1983). There continues to be debate over whether the ability to remember "what, where, and when" resembles human episodic memory. Tulving described episodic memory as autobiographical memory for personally experienced past events as distinct from semantic memory for the meaning of words and concepts and from procedural memory for skills and habits. A person might, for example, have both episodic memory of personally visiting the Statue of Liberty and semantic memory of when it was completed (1886) and who designed it (Frédéric Bartholdi). These two kinds of memory are quite different, Tulving argued. The crux of the debate over episodic-like memory is that "what, where, and when," although they are elements of episodic memory, do not fully capture the essence of episodic memory. We may know the "what, where, and when" of an event (an enormous statue, on Liberty Island in New York Harbor, completed in 1886) without having any episodic memory of ever having seen it. Similarly, vivid episodic memories can sometimes lack detail on exactly when or where the event occurred (Zentall et al. 2001).

Nevertheless, memory for what, where, and when is an interesting phenomenon in animal memory, and a number of experiments have shown that animals are capable of forming such memories (Zinkivskay, Nazir, and Smulders 2009; Babb and Crystal 2005; Naqshabandi et al. 2007; Zentall et al. 2001).

Black-capped chickadees can form "what, where, and when" memories (Feeney, Roberts, and Sherry 2009). The most difficult feature of what, where, and when memory to observe is the "when" component—observing it can require quite a complex experimental design. The usual procedure is to train birds that things change with the passage of time. For example, a chickadee may find sunflower seeds and mealworms (which are preferred to sunflower seeds) at hidden sites and learn that after 3 hours both will be replenished at the same sites but after 123 hours only the sunflower seeds will be replenished and the mealworms will not. The palatable mealworms will instead be replaced with unpalatable ones adulterated with quinine or other unpleasant-tasting compounds. If birds can remember when their original discovery of these sites occurred, they will search for preferred mealworms after 3 hours but will search for their less preferred food, sunflower seeds, after 123 hours because they have learned that the mealworms will have "gone bad" by this time (Feeney, Roberts, and Sherry 2009). We found that chickadees could do this and seemed to be genuinely remembering "when." We were able to confirm by control procedures they were not simply relying on memory strength for the food found most recently or using other tricks to solve the "when" problem. But what kind of "when" do these birds remember? There are at least two different ways they could remember "when": they could remember elapsed time (that is, how long ago they found the two food types—12 hours ago for example), or they could remember the point in time at which they found food (around midday yesterday, for example). A clever experimental design first used by Bill Roberts and his students (Roberts et al. 2008) disentangles these two kinds of "when." Experimental trials were designed so that chickadees learned, in only five trials, that whether their preferred food had gone bad or not depended on how long ago they had found it (Feeney, Roberts, and Sherry 2011). The time of day they had found food was varied but had no predictive power. Another group of birds learned that whether their preferred food had gone bad or not depended on the time of day they had found it. How long ago that occurred was varied but had no predictive power. The results showed that chickadees could use both kinds of "when": a point in time and how long ago (Feeney, Roberts, and Sherry 2011). Birds were better at remembering shorter elapsed times than longer elapsed times but seemed equally good at remembering various past points in time. Subsequent studies have also shown that chickadees are able to anticipate events in the future, specifically modifying current foraging choices to make preferred food available later (Feeney, Roberts, and Sherry 2011).

The Neurobiology of Memory

Cache retrieval in black-capped chickadees is dependent on the hippocampus, as is performance of other spatial tasks (Sherry and Vaccarino 1989). A bird whose hippocampus has been removed continues to search for and store food, but its retrieval accuracy is no better than would expected to be achieved by chance. Food-storing birds also have a larger hippocampus than non-storing birds (Krebs et al. 1989; Sherry et al. 1989; Lucas et al. 2004). This latter finding suggests that natural selection for effective cache retrieval has modified one of the brain areas involved in remembering spatial locations.

In addition to differing from the hippocampus of other birds, the hippocampus of food-storing birds shows an interesting pattern of seasonal variation, first described by Smulders et al. (1995) and Barnea and Nottebohm (1994). Food storing itself is seasonal, increasing in frequency in the fall and continuing through the winter. Usually, little food storing occurs in the spring or in the summer, although there may be a second late winter wave of storing (Pravosudov 2006). New neurons are added to the hippocampus in a seasonal cycle that shows a peak that corresponds roughly to the time when most food storing occurs. Seasonal change in hippocampal size has also been described, although this pattern occurs in some studies but not others. Smulders et al. (1995) found a peak in hippocampal size in black-capped chickadees in October at about the time food storing is beginning. Subsequent studies found either no seasonal change in hippocampal size (Hoshooley and Sherry 2004; Hoshooley et al. 2007) or a peak in hippocampal size in spring (Hoshooley and Sherry 2007). Similarly, Barnea and Nottebohm (1994) found a peak in the recruitment of new neurons into the hippocampus in chickadees in October. Our own studies consistently find a seasonal peak in hippocampal recruitment, but later in the season, from January to April (Hoshooley et al. 2007; Hoshooley and Sherry 2007). The most likely explanation for this variation in the seasonality of the hippocampus is that, unlike seasonal change in the song-control circuitry of the avian brain (Dawson et al. 2001), it is not under photoperiodic control (MacDougall-Shackleton et al. 2003) but instead is influenced by experience. Food availability and predictability, dominance, and flock demography can all influence food-storing behavior.

If hippocampal neuroanatomy and neurogenesis respond (probably with a delay) to variation in food-storing behavior caused by these factors, variation in the seasonal timing of hippocampal change would be the likely result (Sherry and Hoshooley 2010). Pravosudov and colleagues have found remarkable variation in hippocampal size and neurogenesis along latitudinal and altitudinal gradients in environmental harshness, probably for similar reasons (Roth and Pravosudov 2009). Hippocampal plasticity is, by its nature, responsive to experience, and variation in the seasonal timing of hippocampal change is the likely outcome of seasonal variation in food-storing behavior.

Consolidation and reconsolidation of memory

Memory requires time to become permanently established. Whereas short-term memory is maintained by ongoing neuronal activity, long-term memory involves more permanent modification of synaptic connections. This latter process depends on protein synthesis and is referred to as memory consolidation (McGaugh 2000; Barrientos, O'Reilly, and Rudy 2002). The reconsolidation hypothesis proposes that information retrieved from memory becomes labile and must be reconsolidated into long-term memory (Nader, Schafe, and LeDoux 2000a,b). Both consolidation and reconsolidation require protein synthesis. The reconsolidation hypothesis offers an attractive model for the modification of information in long-term memory because information that was initially consolidated into long-term memory may be altered at reconsolidation.

Food-storing birds' memory for caches is flexible. Chickadees, for example, collect and consume stored food at the same time of year and even on the same day that they make new food caches. Experiments show that chickadees can distinguish, within a batch of caches created at the same time, which ones they have already harvested and which they have left in place (Sherry 1984). If remembered caches are retrieved as a batch during the search for caches, it is possible that memory for all caches created at about the same time becomes labile, and that memory for the ones not actually retrieved must be reconsolidated into long-term memory. We used the protein synthesis inhibitor anisomycin to test the consolidation and reconsolidation hypotheses in black-capped chickadees (Barrett and Sherry 2012) and found that inhibition of protein synthesis during two time windows (0–2 hours after caching and 4–6 hours after caching) reduced the accuracy of search for caches, which indicated that protein-synthesis-dependent consolidation is indeed a component of long-term memory for caches.

If memory for caches is activated in a batch during the search for caches, the reconsolidation hypothesis predicts that reconsolidation would be necessary in order for caches not actually harvested to be remembered. We found, however, that administration of anisomycin either from 0 to 2 hours or from 4 to 6 hours after search for caches did not disrupt memory for caches not actually collected. Either cache sites are not retrieved from memory as a batch or reconsolidation is not required after search and partial cache retrieval. We did find, interestingly, that anisomycin disrupted birds' later ability to distinguish sites they had emptied from sites they had left intact. Birds given anisomycin later searched for both kinds of caches; control birds did not. This is in keeping with the basic idea of memory consolidation. Whatever process is involved in distinguishing empty from intact sites—either tagging empty sites in memory or deleting them from memory altogether—this process depends on protein synthesis, and so disrupting protein synthesis has the effect that birds continue to search for caches they have already emptied.

Conclusions

Food-storing birds are unusual consumers. They defer consumption of some of the food they have encountered in order to consume it later, presumably at greater benefit to themselves than they would obtain by consuming it immediately. As the models of food storing described in this chapter show, the birds are in effect raising the value of some encountered food by deferring its consumption to a time when it will make a greater contribution to survival than if consumed immediately.

Food storing by birds occurs in two forms: larder hoarding (practiced by acorn woodpeckers) and scatter hoarding (practiced by chickadees, tits, jays, and nutcrackers). Scatter hoarding has been investigated extensively because memory for the spatial locations of caches is a crucial part of cache retrieval by birds that practice it. Many laboratory experiments and field experiments have examined memory in scatter hoarders, and a good deal is known about the involvement of the hippocampus in memory for cache sites. Among the most notable findings is that chickadees and other food storers can recall not only where they placed their caches but also when they were made and what they contain. In addition, one part of avian brain, the hippocampus, has been modified as a result of this reliance on memory by food storers. Food-storing birds provide a unique insight into the action of ecological selection pressures on behavior and the evolutionary responsiveness of both cognition and the neural mechanisms of cognition to these pressures.

References

Babb, S., and Crystal, J. 2005. Discrimination of what, when, and where: Implications for episodic-like memory in rats. *Learning and Memory* 36: 177–189.

Balda, R. P., Kamil, A. C., and Bednekoff, P. A. 1997. Predicting cognitive capacities from natural history. *Current Ornithology* 13: 333–366.

Barnea, A., and Nottebohm, F. 1994. Seasonal recruitment of hippocampal neurons in adult free-ranging black-capped chickadees. *Proceedings of the National Academy of Science* 91: 11217–11221.

Barrett, M. C., and Sherry, D. F. 2012. Consolidation and reconsolidation of memory in black-capped chickadees (*Poecile atricapillus*). *Behavioral Neuroscience* 126 (6): 809–818.

Barrientos, R. M., O'Reilly, R. C., and Rudy, J. W. 2002. Memory for context is impaired by injecting anisomycin into dorsal hippocampus following context exploration. *Behavioural Brain Research* 134: 299–306.

Brodin, A. 2000. Why do hoarding birds gain fat in winter in the wrong way? Suggestions from a dynamic model. *Behavioral Ecology* 11: 27–39.

Brodin, A. 2007. Theoretical models of adaptive energy management in small wintering birds. *Philosophical Transactions of the Royal Society B* 362: 1857–1871.

Brodin, A., and Ekman, J. 1994. Benefits of food hoarding. *Nature* 372: 510.

Clayton, N. S., and Dickinson, A. 1998. Episodic-like memory during cache recovery by scrub jays. *Nature* 395: 272–274.

Cowie, R. J., Krebs, J. R., and Sherry, D. F. 1981. Food storing by marsh tits. *Animal Behaviour* 29: 1252–1259.

Dawson, A., King, V. M., Bently, G. E., and Ball, G. F. 2001. Photoperiodic control of seasonality in birds. *Journal of Biological Rhythms* 16: 365–380.

Feeney, M. C., Roberts, W. A., and Sherry, D. F. 2009. Memory for what, where, and when in the black-capped chickadee (*Poecile atricapillus*). *Animal Cognition* 12: 767–777.

Feeney, M. C., Roberts, W. A., and Sherry, D. F. 2011. Mechanisms of what-where-when memory in black-capped chickadees (*Poecile atricapillus*): Do chickadees remember "when"? *Journal of Comparative Psychology* 125: 308–316.

Hampton, R. R., and Sherry, D. F. 1994. The effects of cache loss on choice of cache sites in black-capped chickadees. *Behavioral Ecology* 5: 44–50.

Hitchcock, C. L., and Houston, A. L. 1994. The value of a hoard: Not just energy. *Behavioral Ecology* 5: 202–205.

Hitchcock, C. L., and Sherry, D. F. 1990. Long-term memory for cache sites in the black-capped chickadee. *Animal Behaviour* 40: 701–712.

Hoshooley, J. S., Phillmore, L. S., Sherry, D. F., and MacDougall-Shackleton, S. A. 2007. Annual cycle of the black-capped chickadee: Seasonality of food-storing and the hippocampus. *Brain, Behavior and Evolution* 69: 161–168.

Hoshooley, J. S., and Sherry, D. F. 2004. Neuron production, neuron number, and structure size are seasonally stable in the hippocampus of the food-storing black-capped chickadee (*Poecile atricapillus*). *Behavioral Neuroscience* 118: 345–355.

Hoshooley, J. S., and Sherry, D. F. 2007. Greater hippocampal neuronal recruitment in food-storing than in non-food-storing birds. *Developmental Neurobiology* 67: 406–414.

Koenig, W. D. 1991. The effects of tannins and lipids on digestion of acorns by acorn woodpeckers. *Auk* 108: 79–88.

Koenig, W. D., and Benedict, L. S. 2002. Size, insect parasitism, and energetic value of acorns stored by acorn woodpeckers. *Condor* 104: 539–547.

Koenig, W. D., Stacey, P. B., Stanback, M. T., and Mumme, R. L. 1995. Acorn woodpecker (*Melanerpes formicivorus*). In *The Birds of North America Online*, ed. A. Poole. Cornell Lab of Ornithology.

Koenig, W. D., McEntee, J. P., and Walters, E. L. 2008. Acorn harvesting by acorn woodpeckers: Annual variation and comparison with genetic estimates. *Evolutionary Ecology Research* 10: 811–822.

Krebs, J. R., Sherry, D. F., Healy, S. D., Perry, V. H., and Vaccarino, A. L. 1989. Hippocampal specialization of food-storing birds. *Proceedings of the National Academy of Sciences* 86: 1388–1392.

Lanner, R. M. 1996. *Made for Each Other: A Symbiosis of Birds and Pines*. Oxford University Press.

Lucas, J. R., Brodin, A., de Kort, S. R., and Clayton, N. S. 2004. Does hippocampal size correlate with the degree of caching specialization? *Proceedings of the Royal Society B* 271: 2423–2429.

Lucas, J. R., and Walter, L. R. 1991. When should chickadees hoard? Theory and experimental results. *Animal Behaviour* 41: 579–601.

MacDougall-Shackleton, S.A., Sherry, D.F., Clark, A.P., Pinkus, R., and Hernandez, A. M. 2003. Photoperiodic regulation of food storing and hippocampus volume in black-capped chickadees, *Poecile atricapillus*. *Animal Behaviour* 65: 805–812.

McGaugh, J. L. 2000. Memory—a century of consolidation. *Science* 287: 248–251.

McNamara, J. M., Houston, A. I., and Krebs, J. R. 1990. Why hoard? The economics of food storing in tits, *Parus* spp. *Behavioral Ecology* 1: 12–23.

Nader, K., Schafe, G. E., and LeDoux, J. E. 2000a. The labile nature of consolidation theory. *Nature Reviews Neuroscience* 1: 216–219.

Nader, K., Schafe, G. E., and LeDoux, J. E. 2000b. Fear memories require protein synthesis in the amygdala for reconsolidation after retrieval. *Nature* 406: 722–726.

Naqshabandi, M., Feeney, M. C., McKenzie, T. L. B., and Roberts, W. A. 2007. Testing for episodic-like memory in rats in the absence of time of day cues: Replication of Babb and Crystal. *Behavioural Processes* 74: 217–225.

Petersen, K., and Sherry, D. F. 1996. No sex difference occurs in hippocampus, food-storing, or memory for food caches in black-capped chickadees. *Behavioural Brain Research* 79: 15–22.

Pravosudov, V. V. 2006. On seasonality in food-storing behaviour in parids: Do we know the whole story? *Animal Behaviour* 71: 1455–1460.

Pravosudov, V. V., and Lucas, J. R. 2001. A dynamic model of short-term energy management in small food-caching and non-caching birds. *Behavioral Ecology* 12: 207–218.

Roberts, W. A., Feeney, M. C., Macpherson, K., Petter, M., McMillan, N., and Musolino, E. 2008. Episodic-like memory in rats: Is it based on when or how long ago? *Science* 320: 113–115.

Roth, T. C., and Pravosudov, V. V. 2009. Hippocampal volumes and neuron numbers increase along a gradient of environmental harshness: A large-scale comparison. *Proceedings of the Royal Society B* 276 (1656): 401–405.

Scofield, D. G., Sork, V. L., and Smouse, P. E. 2010. Influence of acorn woodpecker social behaviour on transport of coast live oak (*Quercus agrifolia*) acorns in a southern California oak savanna. *Journal of Ecology* 98: 561–572.

Sherry, D. F. 1984. Food storage by black-capped chickadees: Memory for the location and contents of caches. *Animal Behaviour* 32: 451–464.

Sherry, D. F., and Hoshooley, J. S. 2010. Seasonal hippocampal plasticity in food-storing birds. *Philosophical Transactions of the Royal Society B* 365: 933–943.

Sherry, D. F., Krebs, J. R., and Cowie, R. J. 1981. Memory for the location of stored food in marsh tits. *Animal Behaviour* 29: 1260–1266.

Sherry, D. F., and Vaccarino, A. L. 1989. Hippocampus and memory for food caches in black-capped chickadees. *Behavioral Neuroscience* 103: 308–318.

Sherry, D. F., Vaccarino, A. L., Buckenham, K., and Herz, R. S. 1989. The hippocampal complex of food-storing birds. *Brain, Behavior and Evolution* 34: 308–317.

Smulders, T. V., Sasson, A. D., and DeVoogd, T. J. 1995. Seasonal variation in hippocampal volume in a food-storing bird, the black-capped chickadee. *Journal of Neurobiology* 27: 15–25.

Stevens, T. A., and Krebs, J. R. 1986. Retrieval of stored seeds by marsh tits *Parus palustris* in the field. *Ibis* 128: 513–525.

Stresemann, E. 1947. Baron von Pernau, pioneer student of bird behavior. *Auk* 64: 35–52.

Tomback, D. F., and Linhart, Y. B. 1990. The evolution of bird-dispersed pines. *Evolutionary Ecology* 4: 185–219.

Tulving, E. 1983. *Elements of Episodic Memory*. Clarendon.

Vander Wall, S. B. 1990. *Food Hoarding in Animals*. University of Chicago Press.

Zentall, T. R., Clement, T. S., Bhatt, R. S., and Allen, J. 2001. Episodic-like memory in pigeons. *Psychonomic Bulletin and Review* 8: 685–690.

Zinkivskay, A., Nazir, F., and Smulders, T. V. 2009. What-where-when memory in magpies. *Animal Cognition* 12: 119–125.

7 The Psychology of Acquisitiveness

Stephanie D. Preston and Brian D. Vickers

Modern humans are obsessed with their possessions. People spend inordinate amounts of time and income—even borrowing against their own uncertain futures—to acquire houses, cars, clothing, and any manner of goods deemed necessary to fill the spaces of their lives. Though many of these goods are surely useful and necessary, our material excesses have grown in recent decades to a point of backlash. Countless books, blogs, and magazine articles are now dedicated to teaching people how to reduce, organize, and practice extreme forms of voluntary simplicity, such as the "zero footprint" lifestyle. (See, for example, Gabbert and Schein 2010; Zero Emission People, n.d.) Why are we driven to acquire and keep so many goods, most of which we don't even use or enjoy in any given month or year? This chapter is dedicated to addressing this question by focusing on a heretofore understudied aspect of human behavior: acquisitiveness, defined as the desire to acquire and keep goods *per se*, above and beyond what appears necessary for one's own basic comfort, survival, and success. After framing our view of acquisitiveness as an adaptive and normally distributed behavior, we will describe the underlying proximate and ultimate factors that support the behavior. We will then elaborate on the influence of emotions on related economic choices and the neural underpinnings of acquisitiveness before ending with some promising future directions for the field.

The Framework: Acquisitiveness as a Normally Distributed Trait

Our work seeks to understand acquisitiveness as a normal, adaptive behavior that exists to varying degrees across individuals and reflects multiple, underlying instincts that are shared across mammalian species. The word *adaptive* as it is used in this context assumes that the behavior, when exhibited in normative, directed, and context-dependent ways, contributes positively to an individual's reproductive success. (On the adaptiveness of consumption, see also the chapter by Saad, the chapter by Mittal, Griskevicius, and Ellis, and the chapter by Griskevicius, Redden, and Ackerman.) Rather than assessing whether a person is acquisitive or not, we assume that all people are somewhere on a continuum from low to high acquisitiveness. At the low end are "Spartans"—people who appear to avoid acquisitiveness. They acquire and keep only a small amount of goods, avoid clutter, and perhaps focus on their most valued items (Preston, Muroff, and Wengrovitz 2009). Spartans are an interesting phenotype that should be studied to examine the traits and motives of those who do not fall victim to typical overconsumption. At present we know less about these individuals than we know about more acquisitive people, and more work is needed before any specific claims can be made about their motivations.

Most people are at an intermediate level of acquisitiveness. They spend time acquiring and accumulating goods and suffer some degree of clutter or overspending. (See also the chapter by Whybrow and the chapter by Frank.) However, these habits are usually monitored and kept in check. At the high end of the acquisitiveness spectrum are what we call "Acquirers"—people who acquire and fail to discard a large quantity of goods, which then become hard to manage or problematic for multiple reasons. (For a related but distinct discussion of "spendthrifts," see the chapter by Rick.) For example, once acquisitiveness reaches a certain level, people usually experience financial problems, relationship conflicts, trouble locating goods, and disinclination to invite people to visit who might witness the disorder in their homes. Acquirers should not be equated with individuals with hoarding disorder, because people can be highly acquisitive in the absence of a problem severe enough to be considered a psychiatric disorder and in the absence of any comorbid diagnosable mental illness. We also do not have direct evidence that Acquirers have significant personal or mental health problems associated with their performance on our experiments, apart from elevated scores on self-report questionnaires of hoarding and psychopathology. However, individuals with hoarding disorder, which is usually comorbid with anxiety, depression, and obsessive-compulsive disorder (Frost, Steketee, and Tolin 2011), are assumed to be at the high extreme of the acquisitive continuum. Being acquisitive and having a hoarding disorder may represent distinct underlying problems, but our research suggests that they do not. Acquirers and individuals with hoarding disorder share trait tendencies, motivations, and neural correlates with one another, and with nonhuman mammals who store and amass resources (Preston 2014; Vickers and Preston 2014). Based upon this framework, we conduct studies of self-described "packrats"—who are not clinically interviewed but must score at appropriate levels on validated hoarding disorder instruments—in order to test our hypothesis that hoarding disorder is an extreme form of normally varying acquisitiveness.

We view humans' hoarding of goods—including food, money, and material items—through an ethological lens as a normal and typically adaptive behavior that is also observed in food-storing animals such as squirrels and birds and in decorating species such as bowerbirds and packrats (Preston 2014; Vander Wall 1990; see also the chapters in this volume by Sherry, Lea, Kringelbach, and Knutson and Karmarkar). These behaviors are not considered abnormal or problematic when exhibited in ways that are responsive to the environmental context. For example, squirrels, kangaroo rats, hamsters, and caching birds collect nuts and seeds in the autumn (when they proliferate), or after a heavy rainfall, and cache them in scatterhoards over the home range or in larderhoards in the home burrow, to be retrieved when the source is less available (Vander Wall 1990, Sherry, this volume). This is analogous and perhaps even homologous to human aggregation and saving. For example, the hoarding of food to eat and materials to keep one warm in winter helps humans and nonhumans alike to survive cold and snowy conditions in places where resources are in great demand for large parts of the year. In addition, modern families save cuts of meat, cans of tomato sauce, or jars of jam in pantries and extra freezers after a large purchase or harvest, which adaptively saves not only the resources acquired over the year but also time, money, and gasoline. Distinct from what is observable in nonhuman animals, people also save money when they are working for use when they are unemployed or retired (see also the chapters by Webley and Lea), and maintain domestic goods, such as furniture, clothes, and appliances, that are required for the modern lifestyle. People also save holiday decorations, craft supplies, and clothes for other seasons in attics or garages for use in the following year.

Thus, like nonhuman foragers, humans keep and save items when it is less costly or more beneficial to do so than it would be to have to find or acquire the items again when they are needed. Unless the tendency goes beyond what is adaptive or necessary, such acquisitiveness is not necessarily problematic or in need of intervention. However, human acquisitiveness should be studied empirically, not only because it is a fundamental human behavior, but also because at its extremes, which are increasing in prevalence, it is associated with excessive environmental waste, financial problems, and reduced quality of life—negative characteristics that could be ameliorated if they were better understood. (See the chapters by Whybrow and Frank.)

Experimental Support for the Framework

In order to demonstrate that acquisitiveness is a normally distributed and adaptive behavior that is continuous with mechanisms of animal food storing and human hoarding disorder, we have performed four types of studies. We have developed an experimental task that elicits and measures degrees of acquisitiveness in the lab, which can then be predicted by variables associated with excessive human hoarding (e.g., anxiety, depression, obsessive-compulsive disorder, indecisiveness). We have also directly manipulated the relevant basic emotions (e.g., anxiety, uncertainty, sadness) in healthy control populations to show that acquisitiveness can be increased in the presence of these states. In addition, we have studied a few well-characterized decision-making processes to determine if they underlie acquisitiveness, and we have studied the neural bases of decisions about goods to examine potential overlap with regions known to subserve animal food storing and human hoarding disorder.

The Object Decision Task

Most of our early studies on acquisitiveness utilized a novel computerized decision-making paradigm, the Object Decision Task (ODT), which was designed to be sensitive to varying degrees of acquisitiveness, to confirm that acquisitiveness is a normally distributed trait that is continuous with hoarding disorder, and to measure phases of information processing that may contribute to acquisitiveness, such as excessive acquisition, inability to discard, insensitivity to cost, and the overvaluation of goods (Preston et al. 2009; Wang et al. 2012).

In the first block of the traditional ODT, participants can acquire as many objects as they want from a pool of more than 100 objects that they view in serial, randomized order. In subsequent blocks, participants can discard as many items from their collection as they would like without pressure. Next, there is unenforced pressure to discard some acquired items so that the whole collection fits into a standard shopping cart. Finally, there is additional unenforced pressure to discard items so that everything fits into a paper grocery bag. Each participant also rates the monetary value, desirability, and beauty of each item, to determine whether acquired items are viewed as more valuable.

A few features of this task are unusual but intentional. This is done to allow us to study the full variation of acquisitiveness, from taking only new and desirable items to keeping essentially useless items even when doing so is not practical. For example, items in the ODT vary widely in multiple characteristics, such as desirability, usefulness, and cost. Some of the items are low-price, used, broken, or undesirable objects that people may have at home that are not usually included in similar studies in marketing or economics but are included here because they are the types of goods that distinguish unimpaired individuals from those with hoarding disorder. In addition, participants do not pay for items, as they do in marketing and economics. They are told to imagine, in an explicitly hypothetical task, that "all of the items are in the lab today and you can take home as many of them as you would like for free." (Incentivized versions of the task in which participants know they will receive some selected items at the end produce similar results.) Items are always offered for free, for three reasons: (1) it is impractical to actually give people as many items as they could acquire in a task that measures acquisitiveness, (2) we do not want to confound acquisitiveness with spending tendencies (see Rick, Cryder, and Loewenstein 2008 and the chapter by Rick in this volume), and (3) we want to study the types of objects that highly acquisitive individuals really do obtain (Frost et al. 1998; Frost, Tolin, Steketee, Fitch, and Selbo-Bruns 2009). Moreover, the constraint to fit items into the cart or the bag is not enforced, because taking more than fits is characteristic of hoarding disorder, which we want to measure.

Supporting our hypothesis that acquisitiveness and hoarding disorder are continuous, the number of objects that typical, non-clinical individuals acquire and keep is significantly correlated with trait scores associated with hoarding disorder, including multiple hoarding inventories such as the Savings Inventory-Revised (Frost, Steketee, and Grisham 2004), the Savings and Cognitions Inventory (Steketee, Frost, and Kyrios 2003), the Obsessive-Compulsive Inventory (Foa et al. 2002), and measures of indecisiveness such as the Frost Indecisiveness Scale (Frost and Shows 1993), the Decisional Procrastination Scale (Mann 1982), and the Melbourne Decision Making Questionnaire (Mann, Burnett, Radford, and Ford 1997). Our college and community participants who take more also overestimate the usefulness, desirability, and price of items, indicating that more acquisitive individuals view items more favorably than their peers (Preston et al. 2009). Self-described "hoarders" or "packrats" also take more on the ODT, overrate the qualities of items, and score at clinical levels on hoarding inventories (e.g., the Savings Inventory-Revised and Hoarding Rating Scale; see Tolin, Frost, and Steketee 2010), further confirming that the ODT is sensitive to pathologies of acquisitiveness (Preston, unpublished data). Thus, across multiple early experimental studies, we have confirmed that acquisitiveness is a normally distributed phenomenon that exists to varying degrees across people and is correlated with underlying traits that support clinical hoarding at the extremes.

Emotions as Proximate Cues to Acquire

If we assume an affect-driven mechanism for acquisitiveness, then, just as chronic anxiety, depression, and life stress foster excessive acquisitiveness (Frost et al. 2011; Hartl, Duffany, Allen, Steketee, and Frost 2005; Timpano, Keough, Traeger, and Schmidt 2011a), tonic anxiety, sadness, and stress should temporarily increase acquisitiveness in typical populations. Anxiety and stress are theoretically viewed as proximate cues that the environment or situation is uncertain, which can be adaptively addressed by acquiring or stockpiling needed items that may not always be available. Thus, as food-storing animals begin to hoard food when deprived or stressed (Keen-Rhinehart, Dailey, and Bartness 2010), and kangaroo rats larderhoard after their caches are stolen (Preston and Jacobs 2001, 2005), people eat more when they are stressed and stockpile goods when a predicting a large storm (Preston 2014). Thus, an evolved mechanism to adaptively respond to uncertainty and need can become maladaptive when resources are overabundant and stress is chronic (Preston 2006, 2011).

Some data support this mechanism in typical populations. For example, anxiety increases preference for goods that convey safety or control (Raghunathan, Pham, and Corfman 2006), and mortality salience increases materialism (Rindfleisch, Burroughs, and Wong 2009). Sadness also motivates consumption, but usually for more hedonic goods that may alleviate a negative state, such as those that enhance self-esteem or status (Raghunathan et al. 2006). Sad people also pay more for goods when the sadness causes them to be inwardly focused (Cryder, Lerner, Gross, and Dahl 2008). Sadness is also associated with compulsive shopping (Roberts 1998), which is motivated by an expectation that it will alleviate their negative mood (Atalay and Meloy 2011). Social rejection similarly increases consumption, particularly of goods that re-ingratiate victims with their with peers (Mead, Baumeister, Stillman, Rawn, and Vohs 2011). Sadness in humans (Evers, Marijn Stok, and de Ridder 2010; Macht 2008) and stress and anxiety across species (Epel, Lapidus, McEwen, and Brownell 2001; Greeno and Wing 1994; Morley, Levine, and Rowland 1983; Strongman 1965; Tataranni et al. 1996) increase food consumption, particularly in some individuals. Additionally, individuals with hoarding disorder have higher body-mass indices (Timpano, Schmidt, Wheaton, Wendland, and Murphy 2011b). Such common effects of affect on consumption across species and domains suggest similar underlying mechanisms that need to be investigated further (Preston 2011; Preston 2014).

While the aforementioned publications suggest that negative states can increase the motivation to consume, they do not address our main interest in the sheer *quantity* of items people want to acquire and keep—in acquisitiveness *per se*. To test this, we induced anxiety, sadness, or a neutral control state in non-clinical participants and measured the quantity of items they wanted to acquire on a modified ODT. As expected, anxiety and an uncertain form of sadness increased the quantity of objects people acquired, particularly useful objects (Vickers and Preston 2012). However, sadness *per se* did not change consumption, perhaps because of a higher level of certainty and/or because of the types of items offered. Thus, especially for anxiety, we have demonstrated that affective states that chronically produce extreme acquisitiveness can also temporarily change acquisitiveness in non-clinical individuals.

Economic Decision Processes and Acquisitiveness

The "endowment effect"

In the classic "endowment effect," people overvalue objects they own relative to objects they do not own (Thaler 1980). By definition, individuals with hoarding disorder struggle to discard possessions, but they are not impaired when discarding the goods of other people (Preston, unpublished data; Preston et al. 2009; Tolin, Kiehl, Worhunsky, Book, and Maltby 2009). Despite this seemingly strong evidence that hoarders suffer from an endowment problem, the experimental evidence to date is quite mixed. Grisham and colleagues found that obsessive-compulsive individuals with hoarding tendencies were initially more attached to a keychain that the experimenters gave them, but they did not grow any more attached to the item over time (Grisham et al. 2009). We have also not been able to find convincing evidence that endowment problems correlate with acquisitiveness or hoarding using either the classic mug task (Kahneman, Knetsch, and Thaler 1990) or the status quo bias task (Samuelson and Zeckhauser 1988; Boffi, Preston, Rick, and Stansfield 2012). These limited effects may reflect the fact that endowment is already very high in typical populations or that there are limitations in these common tasks, particularly when they require a monetary exchange.

Intertemporal choice

Another possible decision-making phenomenon that could predict acquisitiveness is intertemporal choice (also known as intertemporal or delay discounting—see Loewenstein 1988 and the chapters by Rick and Lea in this volume). In typical intertemporal choice trials, participants choose between a smaller reward delivered sooner (e.g., "$15 today") or a larger one delivered later (e.g., "$20 in two weeks"). At a general behavioral level, individuals with hoarding disorder do exhibit some impulsivity (McElroy, Keck, and Phillips 1995; Preston et al. 2009) and appear to disregard the effect of hoarding on their quality of life as a whole. However, they are phenomenologically risk averse, explicitly keeping items because they believe they will be useful some day (Frost and Gross 1993). We compared intertemporal discounting for money, material goods, and snack foods across individuals with high and low acquisitiveness (Vickers, Gonzalez, Angott, and Preston 2012). More acquisitive individuals did discount goods and food more steeply, accepting smaller quantities if they could have them sooner; however, they discounted money *less* steeply—they were willing to wait longer to obtain more. Thus, acquisitiveness appears to reflect an impulse-control problem specifically directed at concrete items rather than a general impulse-control problem (Hayward and Coles 2009).

The Neural Bases of Acquisitiveness

Across species, decision and reward processes are generally associated with the mesolimbocortical system, including the frontal cortex, the ventral striatum (particularly the nucleus accumbens), the amygdala, the insula, the hippocampus, and the cingulate cortex (Naqvi, Shiv, and Bechara 2006; O'Doherty 2004; Schultz, Tremblay, and Hollerman 2000; see also the chapter by Robinson, Robinson and Berridge, the chapter by Plassmann and Wager, the chapter by Knutson and Karmarkar, and the chapter by Kringelbach in this volume). In prefrontal regions, the ventral medial prefrontal cortex and the orbital frontal cortex (OFC) are thought to integrate inputs from other regions that indicate the most desired and advantageous choice during conscious deliberation (Bechara, Damasio, and Damasio 2000). The dorsolateral prefrontal cortex (DLPFC) is thought to act in concert with the OFC to apply explicit processes that allow decision makers to maintain and compare important cost–benefit information while monitoring choice (Bechara, Damasio, Tranel, and Anderson 1998; Duncan 2001; Fellows and Farah 2005). The ACC is generally associated with negative affectivity in response to decision conflict or error (Allman, Hakeem, Erwin, Nimchinsky, and Hof 2001; Gehring and Fencsik 2001). In the medial temporal lobe, the dopaminergic nucleus accumbens responds to a range of hedonically rewarding substances including foods, juices, social rewards, monetary rewards, drugs of abuse, and material goods—even in the absence of choice (Clithero, Reeck, Carter, Smith, and Huettel 2011; Hare, O'Doherty, Camerer, Schultz, and Rangel 2008; Knutson, Rick, Wimmer, Prelec, and Loewenstein 2007; Preston 2011; Trezza, Damsteegt, Achterberg, and Vanderschuren 2011; Volkow, Fowler, and Wang 2003; Wang et al. 2012). Moreover, activation in this region is dynamically sensitive to the uncertainty of the rewards (Berns, McClure, Pagnoni, and Montague 2001), the individual's homeostatic state and transitory subjective interest in the item (Small, Zatorre, Dagher, Evans, and Jones-Gotman 2001), and the extrinsic value of the item (Plassmann, O'Doherty, Shiv, and Rangel 2008). Assigning these regions to functions in deciding to purchase a material good, activity in the nucleus accumbens is usually associated with the hedonic appraisal of the item, insula activity with the excessive price of goods or the risks associated with a choice, and the OFC with the integration of this information into a choice (Knutson and Karmarkar, this volume; Knutson et al. 2007; Knutson et al. 2008). Insular activity also reflects expected risk (Knutson and Bossaerts 2007) and susceptibility to the endowment effect (Knutson et al. 2008).

Work on hoarding disorder has partially implicated this decision and reward system in acquisitiveness, particularly for the OFC (Preston 2011, 2014; Wang et al. 2012). Tasks in which individuals must discard or imagine discarding goods often implicate the OFC, but sometimes activation is higher and sometimes lower than in comparison groups (An et al. 2008; Mataix-Cols et al. 2004; Tolin et al. 2009). Activity in ventral prefrontal regions (and other areas in the mesolimbic system) also increases with individuals' subjective anxiety during discarding tasks (e.g., An et al. 2008; Mataix-Cols et al. 2003). The anterior cingulate cortex (ACC) (Tolin et al. 2009; Tolin et al. 2012), and sometimes the insula (Tolin et al. 2012), are overactive in individuals with hoarding disorder during symptom provocation relative to healthy controls; however, dorsal ACC activity decreases with anxiety during discarding (An et al. 2008) and is lower at rest in hoarders than in non-hoarders (Saxena et al. 2004). An underactive DLPFC was also associated with increased anxiety during a discarding task (An et al. 2008).

To examine a role for the mesolimbocortical system in typical, non-clinical decisions to acquire and discard objects, we used a modified Object Decision Task with healthy control participants deciding whether to acquire goods for personal preference or for monetary profit (Wang et al. 2012). As in other work, the OFC was implicated across decision types (i.e., acquiring or discarding, for preference or money). The nucleus accumbens was activated during acquisition only to the extent that individuals had trouble with acquisitiveness in daily life. This is the first study to find a relationship between the nucleus accumbens and hoarding. Perhaps because the task didn't focus exclusively on discarding, the relationship that we found suggests that even common goods can produce drug-like incentive salience responses in more acquisitive individuals. More personal decisions activated midline, self-referential areas, including the ACC, in keeping with the activation of these regions when people with hoarding disorder in prior studies made decisions about their own personal items (Tolin et al. 2009; Tolin et al. 2012). Monetary decisions activated the DLPFC, which is associated with the executive control system, even though the personal decisions took longer to make. Thus, even personal preferences may require fairly difficult integrative functions to balance current and future needs and hedonic desires. The most rapid decisions were made for more immediately rewarding items, such as snack foods and petty cash, again implicating the subcortical reward system in impulsive decisions to acquire items with little monetary value but high hedonic importance. (See also the chapter by Kringelbach.)

Taken together, there is consistent evidence that the OFC and the ACC are involved during decisions to acquire and discard goods; however, even in these areas there is contradictory evidence, with the locus and direction of effects changing across studies (Preston 2014). On the other hand, the nucleus accumbens is typically involved in studies of decision and reward processing, and it was active in our task, but the region is normally not associated with hoarding disorder. Future work needs to more carefully parse the contribution of different subregions of the medial frontal and temporal cortex, while including both the drive to acquire and the fear of discarding in the same task and de-confounding acquisition and purchasing.

Outstanding Issues

There is compelling evidence that acquisitiveness is a real human phenomenon that exists to degrees across individuals and is continuous with hoarding behavior in nonhuman animals and human hoarding disorder. However, significant issues need to be addressed. For example, it is not clear why our own attempts to reproduce relationships between sadness or endowment and acquisitiveness have been so limited. In addition, our current understanding of resource-allocation processes cannot explain why some people appear highly impulsive when it comes to money (Rick et al. 2008; Rick, this volume) and others focus on material goods (Vickers et al. 2012). The mesolimbocortical system clearly is involved in resource-allocation decisions across species; however, the role of each region and subregion in evaluating, acquiring, and choosing to discard goods requires further study. Integrative research is needed that directly compares preferences for money and material goods across individuals with varying trait tendencies for chronic affective states, risk aversion, acquisitiveness, and materialism.

There are also questions about the underlying motivations for acquisitiveness. The current framework emphasizes acquisition and retention as a form of resource allocation—to maintain access to goods that are important for survival. However, there are at least two strong alternative possible motivations to acquire that are commonly observed in nonhuman animals: social signaling and a form of nesting behavior. For example, the feathers of the peacock are considered signals to peahens of the male's health status and overall quality (Zahavi and Zahavi 1999), and a man's flashy sports car is a similar signal to women (Miller 2009; Saad, this volume; Saad 2007). In addition, Griskevicius and colleagues have examined people's purchasing preferences after being primed with attractive mates, which causes males to want more conspicuous goods (e.g., luxury cars and watches) and females to be more conspicuously generous (Griskevicius et al. 2007; Griskevicius, this volume). Thus, people could acquire goods as a signal of their identity and their belongingness to social partners and potential friends. For example, university students acquire more "university spirit wear" after being socially rejected in the lab (Mead et al. 2011). People purchase many more items than they strictly need or could use—an excess that could derive from the need to signal one's financial or stylish largess through continually new and more lavish purchases (see Frank, this volume). Signaling motives are probably prominent any time the level of acquisition is very high; in adaptive cases of signaling through acquisition, however, discarding must also be high to maintain a high-quality collection and the appearance of order. The signaling motives in hoarding disorder may also be prominent, in view of their attachment to items with special historical or artistic meaning.

Even more speculatively, humans may amass goods as a form of "nesting," as when nonhuman animals prepare burrows or nests to keep themselves warm and protected from predators. There is little, if any, empirical research on this, but the affective feelings of comfort and discomfort that people feel when surrounded by too few or too many goods indicates some nonconscious comfort derived from their presence, regardless of their utility. Moreover, hoarding disorder often begins after a major life stressor that leaves the individual feeling anxious and insecure (Frost, Hartl, Christian, and Williams 1995; Timpano et al. 2011a). Hoarders also often have social phobia (Frost et al. 2011) and seem to want to be surrounded by goods more than they care about the identity of the items *per se*, particularly in extreme forms of hoarding (Frost et al. 2009). For example, when the accumulated possessions of hoarders are removed, the items are usually replaced very quickly (Tolin, Frost, Steketee, Gray, and Fitch 2008). Moderate levels of acquisitiveness probably reflect a combination of future use and social signaling that is not properly regulated, while the excessive retention of apparent trash reflects a more protective instinct.

Conclusions

We have summarized the evidence that acquisitiveness is a normal, adaptive human behavior that varies continuously across the population and shares features with animal food storing and with human hoarding disorder. These responses are largely mediated by the mesolimbocortical system, which evolved to respond adaptively to uncertainty with the acquisition and retention of key resources—a response that can become maladaptive in the presence of chronic negative affect and superabundant goods. There are still many gaps in this nascent field of research, but the fact that so many disciplines can contribute to the topic demonstrates an interest in the nature of consumption. If we create a genuinely coherent body of research on consumption across disciplines—including work on sustainability—we will be able to generate practical and effective solutions to the externalities of modern consumption, as outlined by Peter Whybrow in the preface to this volume.

References

Allman, J. M., Hakeem, A., Erwin, J. M., Nimchinsky, E., and Hof, P. 2001. The anterior cingulate cortex. *Annals of the New York Academy of Sciences* 935 (1): 107–117.

An, S. K., Mataix-Cols, D., Lawrence, N. S., Wooderson, S., Giampietro, V., Speckens, A., et al. 2008. To discard or not to discard: The neural basis of hoarding symptoms in obsessive-compulsive disorder. *Molecular Psychiatry* 14 (3): 318–331.

Atalay, A. S., and Meloy, M. G. 2011. Retail therapy: A strategic effort to improve mood. *Psychology and Marketing* 28 (6): 638–659.

Bechara, A., Damasio, H., and Damasio, A. R. 2000. Emotion, decision making and the orbitofrontal cortex. *Cerebral Cortex* 10 (3): 295–307.

Bechara, A., Damasio, H., Tranel, D., and Anderson, S. W. 1998. Dissociation of working memory from decision making within the human prefrontal cortex. *Journal of Neuroscience* 18 (1): 428–437.

Berns, G. S., McClure, S. M., Pagnoni, G., and Montague, P. R. 2001. Predictability modulates human brain response to reward. *Journal of Neuroscience* 21 (8): 2793–2798.

Boffi, C., Preston, S. D., Rick, S. I., and Stansfield, R. B. 2012. *Hoarding and the endowment effect: Empirical tests of valuation and ownership*. B. S., University of Michigan, Ann Arbor, unpublished senior thesis.

Clithero, J. A., Reeck, C., Carter, R. M. K., Smith, D. V., and Huettel, S. A. 2011. Nucleus accumbens mediates relative motivation for rewards in the absence of choice. *Frontiers in Human Neuroscience* 5: 87.

Cryder, C. E., Lerner, J. S., Gross, J. J., and Dahl, R. E. 2008. Misery is not miserly: Sad and self-focused individuals spend more. *Psychological Science* 19 (6): 525–530.

Duncan, J. 2001. An adaptive coding model of neural function in prefrontal cortex. *Nature Reviews Neuroscience* 2 (11): 820–829.

Epel, E., Lapidus, R., McEwen, B., and Brownell, K. 2001. Stress may add bite to appetite in women: A laboratory study of stress-induced cortisol and eating behavior. *Psychoneuroendocrinology* 26 (1): 37–49.

Evers, C., Marijn Stok, F., and de Ridder, D. T. D. 2010. Feeding your feelings: Emotion regulation strategies and emotional eating. *Personality and Social Psychology Bulletin* 36 (6): 792–804.

Fellows, L. K., and Farah, M. J. 2005. Dissociable elements of human foresight: A role for the ventromedial frontal lobes in framing the future, but not in discounting future rewards. *Neuropsychologia* 43 (8): 1214–1221.

Foa, E. B., Huppert, J. D., Leiberg, S., Langner, R., Kichic, R., Hajcak, G., et al. 2002. The Obsessive-Compulsive Inventory: Development and validation of a short version. *Psychological Assessment* 14 (4): 485–496.

Frost, R. O., and Gross, R. C. 1993. The hoarding of possessions. *Behaviour Research and Therapy* 31 (4): 367–381.

Frost, R. O., Hartl, T. L., Christian, R., and Williams, N. 1995. The value of possessions in compulsive hoarding: Patterns of use and attachment. *Behaviour Research and Therapy* 33 (8): 897–902.

Frost, R. O., Kim, H.-J., Morris, C., Bloss, C., Murray-Close, M., and Steketee, G. 1998. Hoarding, compulsive buying and reasons for saving. *Behaviour Research and Therapy* 36 (7–8): 657–664.

Frost, R. O., and Shows, D. L. 1993. The nature and measurement of compulsive indecisiveness. *Behaviour Research and Therapy* 31 (7): 683–692.

Frost, R. O., Steketee, G., and Grisham, J. 2004. Measurement of compulsive hoarding: Saving inventory-revised. *Behaviour Research and Therapy* 42 (10): 1163–1182.

Frost, R. O., Steketee, G., and Tolin, D. F. 2011. Comorbidity in hoarding disorder. *Depression and Anxiety* 28 (10): 876–884.

Frost, R. O., Tolin, D. F., Steketee, G., Fitch, K. E., and Selbo-Bruns, A. 2009. Excessive acquisition in hoarding. *Journal of Anxiety Disorders* 23 (5): 632–639.

Gabbert, L., and Schein, J., directors. 2010. *No Impact Man: The Documentary*. Eden Wurmfeld Films.

Gehring, W. J., and Fencsik, D. E. 2001. Functions of the medial frontal cortex in the processing of conflict and errors. *Journal of Neuroscience* 21 (23): 9430–9437.

Greeno, C. G., and Wing, R. R. 1994. Stress-induced eating. *Psychological Bulletin* 115 (3): 444–464.

Grisham, J. R., Frost, R. O., Steketee, G., Kim, H.-J., Tarkoff, A., and Hood, S. 2009. Formation of attachment to possessions in compulsive hoarding. *Journal of Anxiety Disorders* 23 (3): 357–361.

Griskevicius, V., Tybur, J. M., Sundie, J. M., Cialdini, R. B., Miller, G. F., and Kenrick, D. T. 2007. Blatant benevolence and conspicuous consumption: When romantic motives elicit strategic costly signals. *Journal of Personality and Social Psychology* 93 (1): 85–102.

Hare, T. A., O'Doherty, J., Camerer, C. F., Schultz, W., and Rangel, A. 2008. Dissociating the role of the orbitofrontal cortex and the striatum in the computation of goal values and prediction errors. *Journal of Neuroscience* 28 (22): 5623–5630.

Hartl, T. L., Duffany, S. R., Allen, G. J., Steketee, G., and Frost, R. O. 2005. Relationships among compulsive hoarding, trauma, and attention-deficit/hyperactivity disorder. *Behaviour Research and Therapy* 43 (2): 269–276.

Hayward, L. C., and Coles, M. E. 2009. Elucidating the relation of hoarding to obsessive compulsive disorder and impulse control disorders. *Journal of Psychopathology and Behavioral Assessment* 31 (3): 220–227.

Kahneman, D., Knetsch, J. L., and Thaler, R. H. 1990. Experimental tests of the endowment effect and the Coase theorem. *Journal of Political Economy* 98 (6): 1325–1348.

Keen-Rhinehart, E., Dailey, M. J., and Bartness, T. 2010. Physiological mechanisms for food-hoarding motivation in animals. *Philosophical Transactions of the Royal Society B* 365 (1542): 961–975.

Knutson, B., and Bossaerts, P. 2007. Neural antecedents of financial decisions. *Journal of Neuroscience* 27 (31): 8174–8177.

Knutson, B., Rick, S., Wimmer, G. E., Prelec, D., and Loewenstein, G. 2007. Neural predictors of purchases. *Neuron* 53: 147–156.

Knutson, B., Wimmer, G. E., Rick, S., Hollon, N. G., Prelec, D., and Loewenstein, G. 2008. Neural antecedents of the endowment effect. *Neuron* 58 (5): 814–822.

Loewenstein, G. F. 1988. Frames of mind in intertemporal choice. *Management Science* 34 (2): 200–214.

Macht, M. 2008. How emotions affect eating: A five-way model. *Appetite* 50 (1): 1–11.

Mann, L. 1982. *The Decisional Procrastination Scale*. Flinders University of South Australia.

Mann, L., Burnett, P., Radford, M., and Ford, S. 1997. The Melbourne Decision Making Questionnaire: An instrument for measuring patterns for coping with decisional conflict. *Journal of Behavioral Decision Making* 10: 1–19.

Mataix-Cols, D., Cullen, S., Lange, K., Zelaya, F., Andrew, C., Amaro, E., et al. 2003. Neural correlates of anxiety associated with obsessive-compulsive symptom dimensions in normal volunteers. *Biological Psychiatry* 53 (6): 482–493.

Mataix-Cols, D., Wooderson, S., Lawrence, N., Brammer, M. J., Speckens, A., and Phillips, M. L. 2004. Distinct neural correlates of washing, checking, and hoarding symptom dimensions in obsessive-compulsive disorder. *Archives of General Psychiatry* 61 (6): 564–576.

McElroy, S. L., Keck, P. E., Jr., and Phillips, K. A. 1995. Kleptomania, compulsive buying, and binge-eating disorder. *Journal of Clinical Psychiatry* 56 (4): 14–26.

Mead, N. L., Baumeister, R. F., Stillman, T. F., Rawn, C. D., and Vohs, K. D. 2011. Social exclusion causes people to spend and consume strategically in the service of affiliation. *Journal of Consumer Research* 37 (5): 902–919.

Miller, G. 2009. *Spent: Sex, Evolution, and Consumer Behavior*. Viking.

Morley, J. E., Levine, A. S., and Rowland, N. E. 1983. Stress induced eating. *Life Sciences* 32 (19): 2169–2182.

Naqvi, N., Shiv, B., and Bechara, A. 2006. The role of emotion in decision making: A cognitive neuroscience perspective. *Current Directions in Psychological Science* 15 (5): 260–264.

O'Doherty, J. P. 2004. Reward representations and reward-related learning in the human brain: Insights from neuroimaging. *Current Opinion in Neurobiology* 14 (6): 769–776.

Plassmann, H., O'Doherty, J., Shiv, B., and Rangel, A. 2008. Marketing actions can modulate neural representations of experienced pleasantness. *Proceedings of the National Academy of Sciences* 105 (3): 1050–1054.

Preston, S. D. 2006. Averting the tragedy of the commons: An ecological and psychological perspective. *Shift* 13: 25–28.

Preston, S. D. 2011. Toward an interdisciplinary science of consumption. *Annals of the New York Academy of Sciences* 1236: 1–16.

Preston, S. D., and Jacobs, L. F. 2001. Conspecific pilferage but not presence affects Merriam's kangaroo rat cache strategy. *Behavioral Ecology* 12 (5): 517–523.

Preston, S. D., and Jacobs, L. F. 2005. Cache decision making: The effects of competition on cache decisions in Merriam's kangaroo rat. *Journal of Comparative Psychology* 119: 187–196.

Preston, S. D., Muroff, J. R., and Wengrovitz, S. M. 2009. Investigating the mechanisms of hoarding from an experimental perspective. *Depression and Anxiety* 26 (5): 425–437.

Preston, S. D. 2014. Hoarding in animals: The argument for a homology. In *The Oxford Handbook of Hoarding and Acquiring*, ed. R. Frost and G. Steketee. Oxford University Press.

Raghunathan, R., Pham, M. T., and Corfman, K. P. 2006. Informational properties of anxiety and sadness, and displaced coping. *Journal of Consumer Research* 32 (4): 596–601.

Rick, S. I., Cryder, C. E., and Loewenstein, G. 2008. Tightwads and spendthrifts. *Journal of Consumer Research* 34 (6): 767–782.

Rindfleisch, A., Burroughs, James E., and Wong, N. 2009. The safety of objects: Materialism, existential insecurity, and brand connection. *Journal of Consumer Research* 36 (1): 1–16.

Roberts, J. A. 1998. Compulsive buying among college students: An investigation of its antecedents, consequences, and implications for public policy. *Journal of Consumer Affairs* 32 (2): 295–319.

Saad, G. 2007. *The Evolutionary Bases of Consumption*. Erlbaum.

Samuelson, W., and Zeckhauser, R. 1988. Status quo bias in decision making. *Journal of Risk and Uncertainty* 1 (1): 7–59.

Saxena, S., Brody, A. L., Maidment, K. M., Smith, E. C., Zohrabi, N., Katz, E., et al. 2004. Cerebral glucose metabolism in obsessive-compulsive hoarding. *American Journal of Psychiatry* 161 (6): 1038–1048.

Schultz, W., Tremblay, L., and Hollerman, J. R. 2000. Reward processing in primate orbitofrontal cortex and basal ganglia. *Cerebral Cortex* 10 (3): 272–283.

Small, D. M., Zatorre, R. J., Dagher, A., Evans, A. C., and Jones-Gotman, M. 2001. Changes in brain activity related to eating chocolate from pleasure to aversion. *Brain* 124 (9): 1720–1733.

Steketee, G., Frost, R., and Kyrios, M. 2003. Cognitive aspects of compulsive hoarding. *Cognitive Therapy and Research* 27 (4): 463–479.

Strongman, K. T. 1965. The effect of anxiety on food intake in the rat. *Quarterly Journal of Experimental Psychology* 17 (3): 255–260.

Tataranni, P. A., Larson, D. E., Snitker, S., Young, J. B., Flatt, J. P., and Ravussin, E. 1996. Effects of glucocorticoids on energy metabolism and food intake in humans. *American Journal of Physiology—Endocrinology and Metabolism* 271 (2): E317–E325.

Thaler, R. 1980. Towards a positive theory of consumer choice. *Journal of Economic Behavior and Organization* 1: 39–60.

Timpano, K. R., Keough, M. E., Traeger, L., and Schmidt, N. B. 2011a. General life stress and hoarding: Examining the role of emotional tolerance. *International Journal of Cognitive Therapy* 4 (3): 263–279.

Timpano, K. R., Schmidt, N. B., Wheaton, M. G., Wendland, J. R., and Murphy, D. L. 2011b. Consideration of the BDNF gene in relation to two phenotypes: Hoarding and obesity. *Journal of Abnormal Psychology* 120 (3): 700–707.

Tolin, D. F., Frost, R. O., and Steketee, G. 2010. A brief interview for assessing compulsive hoarding: The Hoarding Rating Scale-Interview. *Psychiatry Research* 178 (1): 147–152.

Tolin, D. F., Frost, R. O., Steketee, G., Gray, K. D., and Fitch, K. E. 2008. The economic and social burden of compulsive hoarding. *Psychiatry Research* 160 (2): 200–211.

Tolin, D. F., Kiehl, K. A., Worhunsky, P., Book, G. A., and Maltby, N. 2009. An exploratory study of the neural mechanisms of decision making in compulsive hoarding. *Psychological Medicine* 39 (2): 325–336.

Tolin, D. F., Stevens, M. C., Villvicencio, A. L., Norberg, M. M., Calhoun, V. D., Frost, R. O., et al. 2012. Neural mechanisms of decision-making in hoarding disorder. *Archives of General Psychiatry* 1: 180–188.

Trezza, V., Damsteegt, R., Achterberg, E. J. M., and Vanderschuren, L. J. M. J. 2011. Nucleus accumbens μ-opioid receptors mediate social reward. *Journal of Neuroscience* 31 (17): 6362–6370.

Vander Wall, S. B. 1990. *Food Hoarding in Animals*. University of Chicago Press.

Vickers, B. D., Gonzalez, R., Angott, A. M., and Preston, S. D. 2012. Show me the money or show me the yummy? Population and domain interactions in temporal discounting. Presented at annual meeting of Society for Personality and Social Psychology, San Diego.

Vickers, B. R., and Preston, S. D. 2012. I took it, but why? Presented at biennial meeting of Interdisciplinary Science of Consumption, Ann Arbor.

Vickers, B. D., and Preston, S. D. 2014. The economics of hoarding. In *The Oxford Handbook of Hoarding and Acquiring*, ed. R. Frost and G. Steketee. Oxford University Press.

Volkow, N. D., Fowler, J. S., and Wang, G. J. 2003. The addicted human brain: Insights from imaging studies. *Journal of Clinical Investigation* 111 (10): 1444–1452.

Wang, J. M., Seidler, R. D., Hall, J. L., and Preston, S. D. 2012. The neural bases of acquisitiveness: Decisions to acquire and discard everyday goods differ across frames, items, and individuals. *Neuropsychologia* 50 (5): 939–948.

Zahavi, A., and Zahavi, A. 1999. *The Handicap Principle: A Missing Piece of Darwin's Puzzle*. Oxford University Press.

Zero Emission People. n.d. My Zero Emission Lifestyle Calculator. Retrieved from http://www.zeroemissionpeople.com.

8 Tightwads, Spendthrifts, and the Pain of Paying: New Insights and Open Questions

Scott I. Rick

Many decisions in life, from the mundane to the monumental, involve tradeoffs among costs and benefits occurring at different times. Enjoying a piece of chocolate cake today, for example, can take a toll in the future in the form of slightly increased weight, among other added health risks. Choosing not to indulge is difficult because the costs of immediate indulgence are not only delayed but often intangible. The amount of weight one gains after consuming one piece of cake may be imperceptible, especially if the consumer is not closely monitoring his or her weight. Such delayed and intangible costs often serve as an insufficient deterrent when people are tempted by the immediate and tangible benefits of indulging (Rick and Loewenstein 2008). (For a comparative perspective on discounting the future, see the chapter by Lea in this volume.)

From the standard economic perspective, the decision should not be so tilted in favor of immediate indulgence. When faced with the decision to buy a $15 DVD, for example, the decision maker should consider the next-best use of the $15 (the good's opportunity cost) and compare the pleasure of buying and consuming the DVD to the pleasure of the next-best use of the money (or at least behave *as if* he is performing such informed comparisons). Becker, Ronen, and Sorter (1974) nicely captured the traditional perspective by proposing that "decision makers confronted with a showcase full of beluga caviar consider how much hamburger they could buy with the money [that] a pound of caviar costs" and that "people intuitively take opportunity costs into account."

Unfortunately, it is difficult to consider opportunity costs spontaneously. For example, when Frederick et al. (2009) asked participants if they would be willing to pay $15 for a desirable DVD, the option of not buying was either framed as "not buy this entertaining video" or "keep the $15 for other purchases." Objectively, the decision is equivalent across conditions. The participants should, of course, have understood that not buying the video implied that they would be keeping the money for other uses. However, they were significantly less likely to buy when they were reminded of opportunity costs, which suggests that many people do not spontaneously think about prices in terms of opportunity costs.

Although opportunity costs are probably not the deterrents they should be according to the standard economic perspective, many people are able to control their spending. Recent research suggests they may do so by relying on negative affect as a deterrent, in place of a more deliberate consideration of opportunity costs. Emotions help to "shift the relevant future payoffs into the current moment" (Frank 1988), and negative affect may be how the brain "immediatizes" delayed and intangible opportunity costs. Indeed, Prelec and Loewenstein (1998) proposed that the existence of a "pain of paying" can help explain a variety of phenomena that are anomalous from the standard economic perspective. For example, the pain associated with repeatedly incurring charges can help explain the common and costly preference for flat-rate telephone-usage plans over metered plans (Kridel, Lehman, and Weisman 1993; Lambrecht and Skiera 2006).

Researchers have asked whether the pain of paying actually exists, or whether people simply behave as if they suffer from it. In other words, is the pain of paying real, or simply a helpful metaphor? Because the pain of paying may be subtle and difficult to report, Knutson et al. (2007) bypassed self-reporting and used functional magnetic resonance imaging (fMRI) to examine the pain of paying. Participants in their study were given money and presented with a series of discounted products. In each of several trials, participants viewed a product, considered its price, and then decided whether or not to buy it, all while having their brains scanned by means of fMRI. Knutson et al. found insula activation in response to prices to be negatively correlated with purchase decisions made seconds later. The insula commonly generates feelings that help to guide behavior (Paulus et al. 2003). It is active when people experience distressing events—for example, social exclusion (Eisenberger, Lieberman, and Williams 2003) or unfairness (Sanfey et al. 2003)—and it correlates with subjective ratings of distress (Masten et al. 2009). Although the insula is also involved in other processes, including taste perception, the results appear to be most consistent with the hypothesis that the pain of paying exists and helps to deter spending. (For another description of the aforementioned study, see the chapter by Knutson and Karmarkar.)

Tightwads and Spendthrifts

The pain of paying may be a useful but noisy proxy for opportunity costs. In many cases, relying on feelings may lead to the same spending decision as considering opportunity costs, while saving on costly cognitive effort. But some people may experience too much pain for their own good (e.g., because they have been over-trained to associate spending with pain or because they are more chronically prone to experience any kind of pain), and may spend less than they would have spent had they carefully considered the opportunity costs. Other people may experience too little pain for their own good, and may spend more than they would like to spend.

Rick, Cryder, and Loewenstein (2008) proposed that a chronic tendency to experience the pain of paying is likely to influence the extent to which an individual's typical spending behavior diverges from his or her ideal spending behavior. Rick et al. referred to people who tend to experience a great deal of pain of paying and thus spend less than they would like to spend as "tightwads," to people who tend to experience minimal pain of paying and thus spend more than they would like to spend as "spendthrifts," and to people who tend to experience a moderate amount of pain of paying and thus tend to spend close to what they would like to spend as "unconflicted consumers."

Rick et al. developed a simple tightwad-spendthrift scale to assess individual differences in the tendency to experience the pain of paying. They proposed score cutoffs for identifying tightwads, unconflicted consumers, and spendthrifts, though the scale can also be used as a continuous measure of an individual's tendency to experience the pain of paying. When establishing the discriminant validity of the scale, Rick et al. found that tightwaddism was most closely related to frugality (Lastovicka et al. 1999). Follow-up analyses revealed that tightwaddism was driven primarily by the pain of paying, whereas frugality was driven primarily by a pleasure of saving. Thus, tightwaddism and frugality both promote saving, but for different reasons. (For a discussion of other factors that encourage saving, see the chapter by Lea and the chapter by Webley.) Indeed, tightwad-spendthrift scores significantly predicted both savings-account balances and amounts of credit card debt, but were not related to income. Thus, tightwaddism does not appear to be constrained by one's actual ability to spend, but it may be constrained by one's perceived ability to spend. Subsequent research has also revealed the tightwad-spendthrift construct to be distinct from chronic hyperopia, defined as a stable aversion to indulgence (Haws and Poynor 2008), and from a chronic propensity to plan for the short run or the long run (Lynch, Netemeyer, Spiller, and Zammit 2010).

Rick et al. hypothesized that if tightwads are the people most likely to experience the pain of paying, they should be the ones most sensitive to situational factors that reduce the pain of paying. By the same logic, spendthrifts should be the people least sensitive to such factors. Rick et al. speculated that the pain of paying might be due in part to the psychological magnitude of prices. For example, a price of \$5 may feel like \$10 to a tightwad, but may feel closer to \$5 to a spendthrift. To examine this possibility, Rick et al. asked participants to imagine that they would receive a DVD for free in four weeks, but that by paying \$5 they could receive it the next day. Rick et al. manipulated whether the overnight shipping charge was described as a "\$5 fee" or a "small \$5 fee." The \$5 fee may already feel small to spendthrifts, but framing it as "small" may cause tightwads to behave more like spendthrifts. Consistent with this reasoning, tightwads were significantly more likely to pay the fee when it was described as "small." Spendthrifts, by contrast, were almost completely insensitive to how the fee was described. Thus, spendthrifts were significantly more likely than tightwads to pay the fee when it was described as a "\$5 fee," but they behaved similarly to tightwads when it was described as a "small \$5 fee."

Thomas et al. (2011) similarly examined whether paying with credit, rather than cash, reduced differences in spending between tightwads and spendthrifts. Previous research had found that people generally tend to spend more when using credit than when using cash. (See, e.g., Prelec and Simester 2001.) Aside from the simple fact that people often have more available credit than they have available cash, a variety of psychological explanations have been offered for this phenomenon, including craving induced by credit card logos (Feinberg 1986) and the fact that prices appear smaller when compared with a person's credit limit than when compared with the amount of money in a person's wallet (Morewedge, Holtzman, and Epley 2007). Another factor that probably helps to explain this effect is that cash purchases are more concrete (involving the immediate departure of money from one's possession) than credit purchases (which involve the swiping of a card and the accumulation of debt that can be dealt with later). The reduced vividness of credit transactions may help reduce the pain of paying (Raghubir and Srivastava 2008). As a result, the use of credit should reduce differences in spending between tightwads and spendthrifts. And indeed, in study conducted in a simulated grocery store in which participants paid for products with either cash or credit, Thomas et al. (2011) found that tightwads spent significantly more when using credit than when using cash. Spendthrifts, by contrast, were almost completely insensitive to payment method. Those results provide further support for the notion that situational reductions in the pain of paying reduce tightwad-spendthrift differences in spending.

Outside of the lab, of course, payment mechanisms have the potential to reduce tightwad-spendthrift spending differences only if tightwads choose to utilize mechanisms that reduce the pain of paying—something they may not do. Consider, for example, what Raghubir and Srivastava (2009) termed the "denomination effect." (see also Mishra, Mishra, and Nayakankuppam 2006.) They found that people generally spend less when carrying a single large bill (e.g., one $20 bill) than when carrying the same amount of money in smaller denominations (e.g., twenty $1 bills). Thus, choosing to carry a large bill may partly be an act of self-control, whereas choosing to carry smaller bills exposes one to greater risk of spending. In one experiment, Raghubir and Srivastava manipulated whether or not participants thought they were about to enter an environment that would be likely to tempt them to spend. They asked participants how they would like to receive $100 in study compensation before entering this environment: whether as one $100 bill or as five $20 bills. They found that spendthrifts were insensitive to the manipulation—they chose the large bill about half of the time, perhaps reflecting some chronic vigilance toward controlling their spending. Tightwads, by contrast, rarely chose the large bill when entering the low-temptation environment (20 percent), but were much more likely to do so in the high-temptation environment (58 percent). In other words, when tightwads expected to be tempted by opportunities to spend, they were slightly more likely than spendthrifts to carry money in a way that discourages spending. This raises the possibility that, outside of the lab, payment mechanisms that reduce the pain of paying may actually do little to reduce spending differences between tightwads and spendthrifts.

Weemaes, Dewitte, and Warlop (2011) recently uncovered another way in which the division of money can moderate tightwad-spendthrift spending differences. They found that people were generally more reluctant to spend when spending would deplete the balance in a checking account to zero than when it would not, holding total wealth constant. For example, someone with $50 in his checking account and $50 in his saving account is less likely to buy a $50 watch than someone with $100 in his checking account and $0 in his saving account. (See also Morewedge, Holtzman, and Epley 2007.) Weemaes et al. found that spendthrifts were particularly likely to display this pattern. When spending would not deplete an account to zero, spendthrifts were significantly more likely to buy than tightwads. However, when spending would deplete an account to zero, spendthrifts behaved like tightwads. Tightwads, by contrast, were insensitive to whether or not spending would deplete an account to zero. Perhaps because tightwads distort the perceived magnitude of prices (cf. Rick et al. 2008), tightwads always behaved as if spending money would deplete an account to zero.

Taken together, the research done to date suggests that tightwads may be especially likely to misperceive the magnitude of prices, causing them to behave as if spending will reduce their funds to zero (Weemaes et al. 2011), and to be susceptible to simple manipulations such as framing a price as "small" (Rick et al. 2008). There is some evidence that less concrete and less vivid payment mechanisms, such as credit, can make spending less painful, reducing tightwad-spendthrift spending differences (Thomas et al. 2011), but the results presented by Raghubir and Srivastava (2009) raise questions about whether tightwads would actually desire a payment mechanism that encourages spending.

Broader Implications

Does a person's location on the tightwad-spendthrift dimension have implications beyond spending and saving? Built into the construct is an assumption that tightwads and spendthrifts do not like being tightwads and spendthrifts. Tightwads are chronically spending less than they would like to spend, and spendthrifts are chronically spending more than they would like to spend. Both, then, should be unhappy with that aspect of themselves.

Rick, Small, and Finkel (2011) examined whether this had implications for the choice of a spouse and for the quality of the marriage. Previous data on mate selection "overwhelmingly supported the existence of positive assortment" (Watson et al. 2004). In other words, it is generally the case that birds of a feather flock together. We tend to marry people with similar attitudes, behavioral tendencies, and demographic characteristics. Indeed, this generally seems to be a rational strategy: spousal dissimilarity predicts increased marital conflict, which in turn predicts diminished marital well-being (Luo and Klohnen 2005).

However, whether the common pattern of positive assortment would generalize to disliked aspects of the self was questioned in previous work. Klohnen and Mendelsohn (1998), in particular, argued that complementarity (an "opposites attract" pattern) was likely to be observed for characteristics people dislike in themselves. This was consistent with Ogilvie's (1987) finding that people were more motivated to avoid becoming their "undesired self" than to become their "ideal self." If the undesired self is so objectionable, then presumably a potential mate who resembles one's undesired self would not be appealing. This line of reasoning is highly relevant to the tightwad-spendthrift construct, since presumably both tightwads and spendthrifts are unhappy with that aspect of themselves.

Rick et al. (2011) therefore examined whether tightwads and spendthrifts tended to marry one another. They began by examining whether tightwads and spendthrifts were indeed unhappy with those aspects of themselves, administering the tightwad-spendthrift scale and then asking "How happy are you with yourself regarding the spending issues raised above?" and "Do you wish that you could change yourself with respect to the spending issues raised above?" As predicted, there was an inverted-U-shaped relationship between tightwad-spendthrift scores and both satisfaction items: tightwads and spendthrifts were least satisfied with their location on the tightwad-spendthrift dimension. People in the middle of the scale (unconflicted consumers) were most satisfied with their location on the tightwad-spendthrift dimension.

In a subsequent study, Rick et al. asked married participants to evaluate themselves and their spouse on one of three spending scales: the tightwad-spendthrift scale, a price-consciousness scale, or a sale-proneness scale. These other scales, developed by Lichtenstein, Ridgway, and Netemeyer (1993), were used to address the possibility that one's location on a subjectively defined spending dimension is difficult to assess, leading one to utilize one's spouse as a reference point and thereby creating the appearance of more spousal difference than actually exists. If that is the case, complementarity (a negative correlation between self and spouse) should be observed on all three scales. However, if participants are not contrasting themselves with their spouse, complementarity should be observed only on the tightwad-spendthrift dimension, as it is the only dimension in which the extremes are unhappy with that aspect of themselves. (The price-consciousness and sale-proneness scales were also pre-tested, and did not demonstrate an inverted-U-shaped relationship with the satisfaction items discussed above.) As predicted, Rick et al. found a negative and significant correlation between self and spouse on the tightwad-spendthrift dimension, suggesting that opposites tend to attract on that dimension. Positive and significant correlations between self and spouse were observed on the price-consciousness and sale-proneness dimensions, which was consistent with the standard positive assortment pattern. A subsequent study in which each spouse evaluated only himself or herself also revealed complementary attraction on the tightwad-spendthrift dimension.

Rick et al. then examined the potential effects of complementary attraction on the tightwad-spendthrift dimension on marital quality. They found that the more spouses differed on the tightwad-spendthrift dimension, the more likely they were to argue over money and the less satisfied they were with the marriage. These relationships held when actual financial outcomes in the marriage (savings and debt) were controlled for. Financial outcomes correlated with the tightwad-spendthrift status of spouses in the expected direction: tightwad-tightwad couples saved more and had less debt than tightwad-spendthrift couples, who were financially better off than spendthrift-spendthrift couples. The results suggest that a tightwad may be psychologically and financially better off if he or she marries another tightwad. The recommendations are mixed for spendthrifts: they may be financially better off by marrying a tightwad, but psychologically better off by marrying a spendthrift. Of course, the experiment that must be run so as to give firm recommendations about who to marry—randomly assigning spouses to one another and following the marriages over time—would not be well received by most institutional review boards.

Open Questions

Several questions regarding the pain of paying and the tightwad-spendthrift construct remain open. For example, it isn't clear whether the pain of paying is closer to psychological distress or to physical pain. Previous research has found significant overlap between psychological pain (e.g., the pain of rejection) and physical pain. For example, DeWall et al. (2010) found that acetaminophen (which suppresses physical pain) reduced self-reported and neural evidence of psychological pain after social rejection—including reduced activity in the insula, a region of the brain that Knutson et al. (2007) identified as playing a role in the pain of paying. However, preliminary evidence from Plassmann, Mazar, and Rangel (2011) and from Mazar, Plassmann, Robitaille, and Linder (2011) suggests that the pain of paying is unlike a physical pain. If the pain of paying is ultimately found to be closer to psychological distress, future research should examine which discrete negative emotion(s) constitute(s) what might best be called the "psychological pain of paying."

Evidence from Knutson et al. (2007), Rick et al. (2008), and others suggests that the pain of paying influences spending, but many questions about situational factors that influence the pain of paying remain open. For example, is the pain of paying a simple function of prices? Intuitively, a positive relationship seems plausible, but Knutson et al. (2007) observed no correlation between insula activation and prices. One important moderator of the price-pain relationship may be the familiarity of products. When a product is familiar, and people have a good feel for its value, a strongly positive relationship between price and pain seems likely. When a product is unfamiliar, novel, or otherwise difficult to evaluate, its price is likely to convey important information about its quality (e.g., Rao and Monroe 1989), and a high price may elicit feelings of anticipatory pleasure that serve to buffer the pain of paying (Prelec and Loewenstein 1998), attenuating the price-pain relationship.

It is also worth considering whether the pain of paying is a substitute for thinking about opportunity costs or a function of thinking about opportunity costs. Frederick et al. (2009) conducted a study in which participants chose between a good $700 stereo system and a better one priced at $1,000. For half of the participants, choosing the cheaper stereo was framed as "leaving you $300 in cash," which helped to remind participants that spending money on the stereo entailed forgoing something else in the future. Frederick et al. found that tightwads were slightly more likely to buy the cheaper stereo when opportunity costs were highlighted (80 percent vs. 65 percent). Spendthrifts, by contrast, were much more likely to buy the cheaper stereo when opportunity costs were highlighted (87 percent vs. 41 percent). The results suggest that tightwads may be more naturally inclined to construe prices in terms of opportunity costs, which raises the possibility that their greater pain of paying is a function of their greater consideration of opportunity costs. However, one cannot draw that conclusion definitively, since tightwads were more likely to buy the cheaper stereo when opportunity costs were not highlighted. (That is, highlighting opportunity costs could have increased the proportion of tightwads choosing the cheaper stereo by 35 percent at most, whereas highlighting opportunity costs increased the proportion of spendthrifts choosing the cheaper stereo by 46 percent.) A cleaner test of whether tightwads are more likely to spontaneously consider opportunity costs might involve asking participants to describe what goes through their mind as they make a particular purchase decision and coding their responses for evidence of opportunity cost consideration. (See Spiller 2011.)

Finally, it is important to examine whether other factors can help explain differences in spending between tightwads and spendthrifts. Rick et al. (2008) established that tightwads are more likely to experience the pain of paying, and this helps to explain why they are less likely to spend money. But do tightwads differ from spendthrifts in other important ways? For example, are tightwads less likely than spendthrifts to find products attractive? If they are, that may help to explain why tightwads are less likely to spend.

Clearly, much has been learned about the pain of paying and about tightwaddism within the past 15 years. However, much more remains to be understood about the nature, the causes, and the consequences of the pain of paying and of tightwaddism, and this promises to be an exciting area for future research.

References

Becker, S. W., Ronen, J., and Sorter, G. H. 1974. Opportunity costs: An experimental approach. *Journal of Accounting Research* 12 (2): 317–329.

DeWall, C. N., MacDonald, G., Webster, G. D., Masten, C. L., Baumeister, R. F., Powell, C., et al. 2010. Acetaminophen reduces social pain: Behavioral and neural evidence. *Psychological Science* 21 (7): 931–937.

Eisenberger, N. I., Lieberman, M. D., and Williams, K. D. 2003. Does rejection hurt? An fMRI study of social exclusion. *Science* 302 (5643): 290–292.

Feinberg, R. A. 1986. Credit cards as spending facilitation stimuli: A conditioning interpretation. *Journal of Consumer Research* 13: 348–356.

Frank, R. H. 1988. *Passions Within Reason: The Strategic Role of the Emotions*. Norton.

Frederick, S., Novemsky, N., Wang, J., Dhar, R., and Nowlis, S. 2009. Opportunity cost neglect. *Journal of Consumer Research* 36 (4): 553–561.

Haws, K. L., and Poynor, C. 2008. Seize the day! Encouraging indulgence for the hyperopic consumer. *Journal of Consumer Research* 35 (4): 680–691.

Klohnen, E. C., and Mendelsohn, G. A. 1998. Partner selection for personality characteristics: A couple-centered approach. *Personality and Social Psychology Bulletin* 24 (3): 268–278.

Knutson, B., Rick, S. I., Wimmer, E., Prelec, D., and Loewenstein, G. 2007. Neural predictors of purchases. *Neuron* 53 (1): 147–156.

Kridel, D. J., Lehman, D. E., and Weisman, D. L. 1993. Option value, telecommunications demand, and policy. *Information Economics and Policy* 5 (2): 125–144.

Lambrecht, A., and Skiera, B. 2006. Paying too much and being happy about it: Existence, causes, and consequences of tariff-choice biases. *Journal of Marketing Research* 43 (2): 212–223.

Lastovicka, J. L., Bettencourt, L. A., Hughner, R. S., and Kuntze, R. J. 1999. Lifestyle of the tight and frugal: Theory and measurement. *Journal of Consumer Research* 26 (1): 85–98.

Lichtenstein, D. R., Ridgway, N. M., and Netemeyer, R. G. 1993. Price perceptions and consumer shopping behavior: A field study. *Journal of Marketing Research* 30 (2): 234–245.

Luo, S., and Klohnen, E. C. 2005. Assortative mating and marital quality in newlyweds: A couple-centered approach. *Journal of Personality and Social Psychology* 88 (2): 304–326.

Lynch, J. G., Netemeyer, R. G., Spiller, S. A., and Zammit, A. 2010. A generalizable scale of propensity to plan: The long and the short of planning for time and money. *Journal of Consumer Research* 37 (1): 108–128.

Masten, C. L., Eisenberger, N. I., Borofsky, L. A., Pfeifer, J. H., McNealy, K., Mazziotta, J. C., et al. 2009. Neural correlates of social exclusion during adolescence: Understanding the distress of peer rejection. *Social Cognitive and Affective Neuroscience* 4 (2): 143–157.

Mazar, N., Plassmann, H., Robitaille, N., and Linder, A. 2011. The origin of the pain of paying. Presented at North American Conference of the Association for Consumer Research, St. Louis.

Mishra, H., Mishra, A., and Nayakankuppam, D. 2006. Money: A bias for the whole. *Journal of Consumer Research* 32 (4): 541–549.

Morewedge, C. K., Holtzman, L., and Epley, N. 2007. Unfixed resources: Perceived costs, consumption, and the accessible account effect. *Journal of Consumer Research* 34 (4): 459–467.

Ogilvie, D. M. 1987. The undesired self: A neglected variable in personality research. *Journal of Personality and Social Psychology* 52 (2): 379–385.

Paulus, M. P., Rogalsky, C., Simmons, A., Feinstein, J. S., and Stein, M. B. 2003. Increased activation in the right insula during risk-taking decision making is related to harm avoidance and neuroticism. *NeuroImage* 19 (4): 1439–1448.

Plassmann, H., Mazar, N., and Rangel, A. 2011. Is paying painful? Neuropsychological underpinnings of abstract and somatosensory costs during consumer decision making. Presented at North American Conference of the Association for Consumer Research, St. Louis.

Prelec, D., and Loewenstein, G. 1998. The red and the black: Mental accounting of savings and debt. *Marketing Science* 17 (1): 4–28.

Prelec, D., and Simester, D. 2001. Always leave home without it: A further investigation of the credit-card effect on willingness to pay. *Marketing Letters* 12 (1): 5–12.

Raghubir, P., and Srivastava, J. 2008. Monopoly money: The effect of payment coupling and form on spending behavior. *Journal of Experimental Psychology: Applied* 14 (3): 213–225.

Raghubir, P., and Srivastava, J. 2009. The denomination effect. *Journal of Consumer Research* 36 (4): 701–713.

Rao, A. R., and Monroe, K. B. 1989. The effect of price, brand name, and store name on buyers' perceptions of product quality: An integrative review. *Journal of Marketing Research* 26 (3): 351–357.

Rick, S. I., Cryder, C. E., and Loewenstein, G. 2008. Tightwads and spendthrifts. *Journal of Consumer Research* 34 (6): 767–782.

Rick, S. I., and Loewenstein, G. 2008. Intangibility in intertemporal choice. *Philosophical Transactions of the Royal Society B* 363 (1511): 3813–3824.

Rick, S. I., Small, D. A., and Finkel, E. J. 2011. Fatal (fiscal) attraction: Spendthrifts and tightwads in marriage. *Journal of Marketing Research* 48 (2): 228–237.

Sanfey, A. G., Rilling, J. K., Aronson, J. A., Nystrom, L. E., and Cohen, J. D. 2003. The neural basis of economic decision-making in the ultimatum game. *Science* 300 (5626): 1755–1758.

Spiller, S. A. 2011. Opportunity cost consideration. *Journal of Consumer Research* 38 (4): 595–610.

Thomas, M., Desai, K. K., and Seenivasan, S. 2011. How credit card payments increase unhealthy food purchases: Visceral regulation of vices. *Journal of Consumer Research* 38 (1): 126–139.

Watson, D., Klohnen, E. C., Casillas, A., Simms, E. N., Haig, J., and Berry, D. S. 2004. Match makers and deal breakers: Analyses of assortative mating in newlywed couples. *Journal of Personality* 72 (5): 1029–1068.

Weemaes, B., Dewitte, S., and Warlop, L. 2011. Resources running out: How arbitrary resource fragmentation decreases consumer spending. Presented at North American Conference of Association for Consumer Research, St. Louis.

Neurobiological Perspectives

9 Appetite, Consumption, and Choice in the Human Brain

Brian Knutson and Uma Karmarkar

According to the Tibetan Buddhist *bhavacakra* (wheel of life), people who have lived less-than-exemplary lives are reborn in lower realms. Those unfortunate enough to be sent to the realm of *pretas* (hungry ghosts) awaken as ravenous beings whose tiny mouths and necks block sustenance from entering their large but empty stomachs. The hungry ghosts thus continually suffer from insatiable appetites (Gyatso 1992). This seemingly exotic fate of the hungry ghosts symbolizes a more common earthly state of affairs: when appetite cannot be sated with consumption, as in the case of addiction, the rhythm of life is permanently disrupted. Without the eventual calming effects of consumption, excessive appetites may drive organisms to ruin. The plight of the hungry ghosts implies that appetite and consumption are different but must eventually connect.

From the perspective of neuroscience, this mythical dilemma raises a number of questions. Can different phases of reward processing be distinguished neurally? How do they interact? Can their coordinated function contribute to optimal choice and well-being? In this chapter, we attempt to define appetite and consumption psychologically, and then to describe human neuroimaging research indicating that these phases of reward processing can be visualized in the human brain. We then survey emerging research suggesting that neural study of these processes may help scientists to better predict choice and understand processes that promote decision making.

Definitions

More than 100 years ago, the ethologist Wallace Craig defined appetitive and consummatory behavior as follows (Craig 1918): "An appetite . . . is a state of agitation which continues so long as a certain stimulus . . . is absent. When the appeted stimulus is at length received it stimulates a consummatory reaction, after which the appetitive behavior ceases and is succeeded by a state of relative rest." Craig's prescient definition has a number of implications. First, the cycle of appetite and consumption has distinct behavioral components that occur sequentially. Second, although both appetite and consumption evoke arousal, appetite involves higher arousal than consumption. Third, consumption forms a negative feedback loop that can eventually reduce appetite. Fourth, although the terms *appetitive behavior* and *consummatory behavior* may have originally referred to eating episodes, they can also extend to a broader range of activities (see the chapter by Plassmann and Wager, the chapter by Preston, Kringelbach, and Knutson, the chapter by Preston and Vickers, the chapter by Kringelbach, and the chapter by Robinson, Robinson, and Berridge).

As with most scientifically useful definitions, Craig also clarified what appetitive and consummatory behavior are not. He argued that appetitive and consummatory behaviors were driven by positive motivation, but not by negative motivation (associated with avoidance behavior). He also specified that appetitive and consummatory behaviors were not reflexive (as might be assumed by later behaviorists), nor were they strictly yoked to goals (as might be assumed by later cognitive theorists). In this chapter, we use Craig's ethological definition as a starting point. We further assume that, although appetitive behavior clearly involves motor processes and consummatory behavior clearly promotes sensory stimulation, the motivational elements of these phases cannot be *reduced* to either primary motor or primary sensory processes.

Beyond outlining the core elements of reward processing, these definitions imply that if one could measure appetitive processes one might use them to predict future consummatory behavior (e.g., eating or drinking). Further, if this predictive framework extends beyond primary (or directly sensed and unlearned) rewards to secondary (or more abstract and learned) rewards, predictions of consumption might extend to a broad range of human activities (e.g., investing and shopping), and into the future. Further, the relative appetitive response to different potential rewards might allow investigators to predict which is eventually chosen and consumed. An underlying theme involves the notion that appetitive processes eventually lead to choice and consumption, and that these sequential processes are critical components of value-based decision making. (For a discussion of anticipatory effects on consumption, see also the chapter by Plassmann and Wager.)

Over the past century, animal research has suggested that evolutionarily conserved neural circuits deep below the cortex can unconditionally elicit positive and negative emotional states that coordinate approach toward opportunities and avoidance of threats (MacLean 1990; Panksepp 1998). Until recently, scientists lacked techniques with adequate resolution to determine whether people also recruit these circuits during appetitive and consummatory phases of reward processing and during processing of primary and secondary rewards. New technology with sufficient spatial and temporal resolution to resolve distinct stages of reward processing, however, has begun to yield coherent answers to these questions.

Localizing Appetite and Consumption

Consistent with early ethological distinctions between appetite and consumption, investigations of animals have implicated different neural circuits and chemistries in different phases of reward processing. (See also the chapter by Kringelbach and the chapter by Robinson, Robinson, and Berridge.) For instance, research on feeding in rats suggests that manipulating dopamine activity in the nucleus accumbens (NAcc), lateral hypothalamus, and midbrain ventral tegmental area (VTA) can induce appetitive behavior (indexed by eventual quantity of food consumed). On the other hand, manipulations of opioid activity in "hotspots" (including the NAcc, ventral pallidum, and brain-stem parabrachial nuclei) instead evoke consummatory behavior, indexed by lip smacking during consumption (Berridge and Kringelbach 2008).

Technological advances at the close of the twentieth century enabled animal researchers to temporally distinguish appetitive from consummatory phases of reward processing. For instance, using electrophysiological recordings of ventral tegmental neurons in monkeys, researchers established that dopamine firing increases in response to cues that signal upcoming delivery of juice rewards (Schultz et al. 1997). Further, using *in vivo* cyclic voltammetry in rats, researchers demonstrated that NAcc dopamine release also occurs when rats anticipate the impending delivery of food and drug rewards (Roitman et al. 2004; Stuber et al. 2004). Though this animal research implicated specific neural circuits in the appetitive phase of primary reward processing, it could not establish whether these findings would generalize to humans, or whether they would extend to more abstract secondary rewards.

At about the time of these animal discoveries, human neuroimaging methods with better resolution emerged. Historically, although electroencephalography had afforded excellent temporal resolution on the order of milliseconds, it could not spatially localize activity, particularly in subcortical circuits. In contrast, positron emission tomography had allowed investigators to visualize changes in subcortical metabolic and chemical activity, but suffered from limited temporal resolution, on the order of minutes or longer. The development of functional magnetic resonance imaging (fMRI) in the early 1990s offered an optimal tradeoff, allowing visualization of activity in smaller subcortical circuits on a second-to-second time scale. This led to the development of novel experimental designs and analyses that could deconstruct different stages of reward processing into appetitive and consummatory phases. Below, therefore, we focus primarily on fMRI studies of reward processing and choice.

Initial human fMRI experiments attempted to "localize" sensory and motor circuits by systematically varying relevant aspects of stimuli (e.g., the size of a flickering circle or the rate of finger tapping) and identifying correlated neural activity. Subsequent studies of reward processing adopted a similar localization strategy by presenting primary and secondary rewards to humans undergoing fMRI. Primary rewards included a variety of pleasant stimuli, including tastes (Berns et al. 2001; O'Doherty et al. 2002), smells (Anderson and Sobel 2003; Gottfried et al. 2002), touch (Rolls et al. 2003), sights (Aharon et al. 2001; Arnow et al. 2002), and sounds (Menon and Levitin 2005). Secondary rewards included monetary gain (Delgado et al. 2000; Elliott et al. 2000; Knutson et al. 2000; O'Doherty et al. 2001) and pleasant social interactions (Rilling et al. 2002). Building from and extending animal research, these early experiments demonstrated reward-correlated activity in regions innervated by mesolimbic dopamine projections—including subcortical regions in the ventral striatum (such as the NAcc, ventral putamen, and ventral caudate), as well as in the medial orbital frontal cortex (MOFC) and medial prefrontal cortex (MPFC). Together, these findings implied that activity in overlapping mesolimbic projection areas responds to both primary and secondary rewards—a conclusion supported by later reviews of the literature (e.g., Haber and Knutson 2010; see also the chapter by Kringelbach, the chapter by Plassmann and Wager, the chapter by Robinson, Robinson, and Berridge, and the chapter by Preston and Vickers).

With enhanced temporal resolution, investigators began to explore not only how the human brain *responded* to rewards (which might occur during the consummatory phase) but also how it *anticipated* rewards (which might occur during the appetitive phase). Answering these questions required temporally precise designs and analyses that could split single trials into anticipation and outcome phases—innovations that also promoted studies of reward learning which are not reviewed here owing to their dynamic nature (O'Doherty 2004). These experiments utilized both primary rewards (e.g., juice) and secondary rewards (e.g., money), and typically presented cues that elicited anticipation of uncertain reward followed by either reward outcomes or nonreward outcomes (sometimes after requiring a response). Initial findings suggested that ventral striatal activity (including activity in the NAcc) increased during anticipation of both monetary and juice rewards (Knutson et al. 2001a; O'Doherty et al. 2002), and further that medial prefrontal cortical (MPFC) activity increased in response to reward outcomes (Knutson et al. 2001b; Knutson et al. 2003; Ramnani and Miall 2003). Other studies, however, did not find such clearly distinct patterns of activity in response to reward anticipation and outcomes (e.g., Breiter et al. 2001).

Recent reviews of the literature unanimously implicate mesolimbic circuitry (including MPFC, the NAcc, and VTA) in reward processing. Not all concur, however, on whether different parts of this circuit respond preferentially to different phases of reward processing. Specifically, some meta-analyses support the notion that NAcc activity primarily increases during reward anticipation, and that MPFC activity increases in response to reward outcomes (Knutson and Greer 2008; Diekhof et al. 2012), but others do not (Liu et al. 2011; Bartra et al. 2013; see also the chapter by Plassmann and Wager). Powerful and efficient methods for inferring the likelihood of functional descriptions from an observed activation (rather than the inverse) have recently been developed (Yarkoni et al. 2011). By controlling for the base rate of activity in different regions, this quantitative "reverse inferential" meta-analytic technique can yield information about the specificity of functional inferences from local activity. Thus, to reevaluate the conclusions of recent reviews, we conducted a reverse inferential meta-analysis of the terms "reward" (203 studies), "anticipation" (74 studies), and "outcome" (114 studies) using the Neurosynth database (Yarkoni et al. 2011; date April 15, 2013; $p < 0.05$; false discovery rate corrected for whole brain; Z ranging from 2 to 9). This meta-analysis confirmed that increased activity in the MPFC, in the NAcc, and in the VTA was clearly associated with the appearance of the word "reward" in a study description. Activity in different subsets of these regions, however, was associated with the words "anticipation" and "outcome." Whereas increased activity in the NAcc and VTA was associated with the word "anticipation," increased activity in the MPFC and NAcc was associated with the word "outcome" (see figure 9.1). Interestingly, forward inference analyses of brain activity given these same terms revealed less selective associations (Bartra et al. 2013).

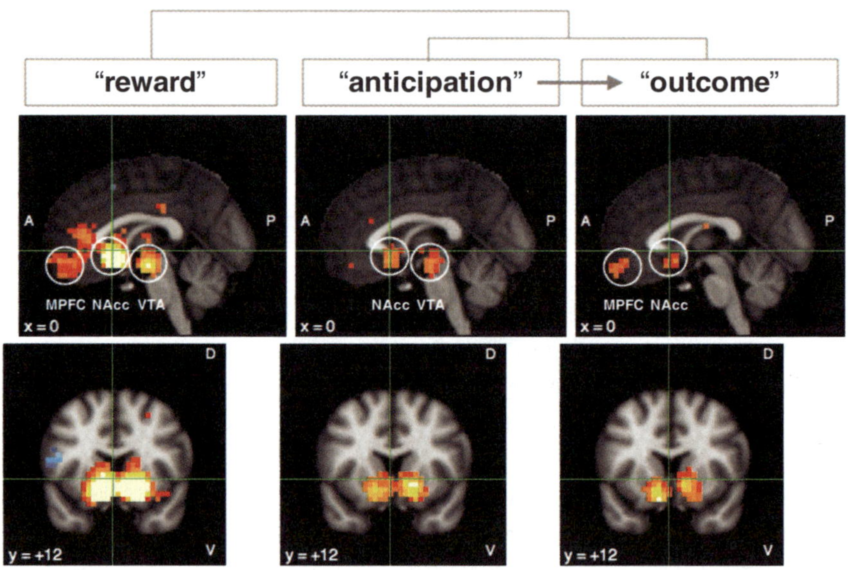

Figure 9.1
Neurosynth reverse-inferential meta-analysis of the probability of incentive processing terms appearing in a report based on localized brain activity (i.e., whole brain tests; FDR corrected at $p < .05$; Z ranging from 2 to 9. "Reward" is associated with MPFC, NAcc, and VTA activity (203 studies). "Anticipation" is associated with NAcc and VTA activity (74 studies). "Outcome" is associated with MPFC and NAcc activity (114 studies).

These reverse inferential findings suggest that increased NAcc activity is associated with both reward anticipation and outcomes, and that increased MPFC activity is preferentially associated with reward outcomes. Even the apparent association of NAcc activity with both reward anticipation and outcomes could be questioned, though, since brain activation contrasts describe the difference between two conditions (reward versus nonreward in this case) but cannot describe the relation of activity to a common standard (e.g., average activity over time). In fact, when NAcc activity time courses are plotted, NAcc activity during reward anticipation increases, whereas NAcc activity during nonreward anticipation stays close to baseline, generating a positive contrast value. On the other hand, NAcc activity in response to reward outcomes typically stays close to baseline, whereas NAcc activity in response to nonreward outcomes dips below baseline, *also* generating a positive contrast value (Knutson et al. 2003). Thus, NAcc activity may differ during reward anticipation and outcomes, even though statistical contrast maps appear similar (Knutson and Wimmer 2007). These differences in activity take on significance when investigators seek to use that activity (rather than contrasts) to predict choice.

The reverse inferential findings also more specifically associate MPFC activity with responses to reward outcomes, which might imply that MPFC is more involved in consummatory processing. Reward outcomes, however, usually involve integration of different values before the act of consumption. For instance, reward outcomes often involve shifts from uncertainty to certainty, even before a reward is physically obtained. Thus, MPFC activity might increase before consumption as a function of value integration. Indeed, localization studies suggest that while manipulating the magnitude of anticipated monetary reward activates the NAcc, manipulating its probability additionally activates the MPFC, even before revelation of outcomes (Knutson et al. 2005). This "value integration" account of MPFC activity has gained popularity in the literature on neuroimaging of choice. (See, e.g., Blair et al. 2006.)

In summary, a substantial literature now implicates NAcc (and VTA) activity in reward anticipation and MPFC (and possibly NAcc) activity in responding to reward outcomes—both primary and secondary. These findings may help investigators to localize reward-related activity in the human brain, and also to predict subsequent choice and consumption. By reversing the typical logic of neuroimaging studies, instead of searching for neural correlates of input into the brain (e.g., an "input" model), one could use brain activity to predict subsequent behavior (e.g., an "output" model). In fact, researchers have pursued exactly this predictive strategy in a growing number of studies, which we survey below.

Predicting Choice and Consumption

Shifting from input studies to output studies raises several new questions, including whether previous appetitive or consummatory neural activity best predicts future choice and consumption and whether relative neural responses to different options might allow investigators to predict which option will ultimately be chosen and consumed. Since evolutionarily conserved mesolimbic circuits process both primary and secondary rewards, their activity might provide a neural "common currency" for evaluating diverse rewards (Montague and Berns 2002; Levy and Glimcher 2012). Specifically, if this activity not only correlates with reactions to the current state of affairs but also implies future action, investigators might then use it to predict consumption and choice. (See also the chapter by Plassmann and Wager.) In the simplest case these predictions might involve the choice of whether or not to approach and consume a single reward, but more complex scenarios might involve predicting the choice of one among many rewards.

Following on the successes of reward localization studies, researchers began to examine neural correlates of consumer preferences. Early fMRI studies of preferences for consumer products found increased MPFC and sometimes increased NAcc activity in response to presentation of images of preferred cars (Erk et al. 2002) and drinks (Paulus and Frank 2003; Deppe et al. 2005), as well as to delivery of preferred drinks (McClure et al. 2004). Though these findings did not involve choice, they suggested similar processing of primary and secondary rewards—not just metaphorically, but also concretely in the form of overlapping brain circuits. (For a similar argument, see the introductory chapter and the chapter by Preston and Vickers.) Thus, as in consumer research, choice may index the intent to consume products.

Subsequent neuroimaging studies have examined consumer choice either by presenting several choice options simultaneously—e.g., a product or multiple products along with an asking price; see, e.g., Plassmann et al.

2007—or by presenting information sequentially—e.g., a product followed by an asking price followed by a choice prompt; see, e.g., Knutson et al. 2007. Each type of design has strengths and limitations. On the one hand, while simultaneous tasks are designed to elicit immediate and integrated evaluations, it is difficult to determine whether correlated neural activity occurs in response to all options or only in response to some subset of those options (e.g., the most valued option, the entire set of options, or a reaction to choice). On the other hand, although sequential tasks are designed to elicit isolated responses to each newly presented piece of information before choice, those responses may or may not eventually influence the final choice.

Consistent with reward localization findings, preferred products typically elicit increased MPFC activity and sometimes NAcc activity in simultaneous designs (Levy and Glimcher 2012). (See also the chapter by Plassmann and Wager.) For this reason, researchers often report having found that mesolimbic activity correlated with product valuation "at the time of" but not before choice. The present ethological framework, however, implies that earlier activity, whether appetitive or consummatory, may drive eventual choice. Since sequential designs can distinguish antecedent neural activity from choice, we will review the collected findings of sequentially designed studies that have used neural activity to predict choice in greater detail below.

Sooner predictions

Encouraged by the demonstration that brain activity could be used to predict financial choices (Kuhnen and Knutson 2005), researchers sought to also predict consumer choice. To elicit typical purchasing behavior in the scanner, Knutson et al. (2007) gave subjects a cash endowment and asked them to consider buying eighty consumer products while undergoing fMRI scanning. During each trial of this "Save Holdings Or Purchase" (SHOP) Task, subjects saw a product (e.g., a box of chocolates), then a discounted price associated with that product (e.g., 25 percent of the retail price), and then a choice prompt. At the prompt, subjects indicated whether or not they wanted to purchase each item at its designated price. After leaving the scanner, subjects rated how much they wanted each product and what they would be willing to pay for it. Finally, two trials were selected at random to count "for real" and evaluated—that is, if subjects had previously indicated they would buy the product, they were sent the product and they kept the remainder of their endowment; otherwise, they retained their entire endowment).

Traditional "input" analyses showed that NAcc activity correlated with wanting during product presentation, and that MPFC activity correlated with perceived worth (what economists call "consumer surplus") during price presentation. New "output" analyses that used volume of interest neural activity from these regions to predict choice indicated that positive NAcc responses to the product and positive MPFC responses and negative anterior insula responses to the price predicted choice on a trial-to-trial basis (i.e., 60 percent versus 50 percent chance, cross-validated across subjects, $p < .001$). (For a discussion of the role of the insula in choice in this task, see the chapter by Rick.) When combined with (correlated) self-report variables, neural predictions remained significant, though adding only slight additional power over self-report. These findings demonstrated that neural activity alone could predict consumer choice, but raised further questions. For instance, could activity in these circuits predict choices that occurred later—after scanning, without purchase intent, and even without attention to the options?

Subsequent research explored potential limits of the neural predictions of consumer choice. One study showed that ventral striatal activity and MFPC activity in response to passively presented images of faces, houses, and paintings could still predict preferences for those images, even when preferences were assessed after scanning (Lebreton et al. 2009). A second study showed that ventral striatal activity and MPFC activity in response to passively presented products predicted product valuation and choice, which were both elicited after scanning (Levy et al. 2011). A third study showed that ventral striatal activity and MPFC (and insular) activity predicted intention to buy products (i.e., cars) elicited after scanning regardless of whether subjects viewed the products while rating how much they liked them or while being distracted by an attentionally demanding symbol identification task (Tusche et al. 2010). These findings indicate that neural responses to an item can predict valuation and choice minutes later—even in the absence of any explicit intention to evaluate the item, and even when explicit attention is directed elsewhere. These automatic neural evaluations, as foreseen by Zajonc (1980), nonetheless allow prediction of later choice.

In most of these studies, both NAcc activity and MPFC activity predicted eventual choice. The ability of NAcc activity to predict future choice is consistent with an appetitive interpretation. The ability of MPFC activity to predict future choice, however, is more consistent with a "value integration" interpretation than with a strict consummatory interpretation, since consumption in these experiments presumably occurred at some point in the future after choice. Further, in some of these experiments (e.g., those reported in Knutson et al. 2007) MPFC activity began to predict choice only after a second attribute (e.g., price) was added to the initial presentation of a product. Since these experiments elicited choices at the end of each experimental session, though, they could not address whether neural activity could predict choices in the more distant future.

Later predictions

Since reviews suggest that rewarding images of pleasing food or attractive people can activate mesolimbic circuits, this activity might then predict individual differences in choice and consumption, both in the near future and in the distant future. In one experiment, individual differences in subjects' MPFC responses to monetary rewards and their responses to faces predicted their willingness to pay to see the same faces at the end of a scanning session (Smith et al. 2010). In a second experiment, though, individual differences in subjects' NAcc responses to appetizing food predicted weight gain, and NAcc responses to erotic pictures predicted sexual activity more than six months after scanning (Demos et al. 2012). The latter findings suggested that activity in mesolimbic circuits can predict individual differences in choice, and presumably in consumption, long after the conclusion of an experiment. But could the brain activity of a few subjects further scale to the aggregate level and predict the choices of many?

Aggregate predictions

If the neural responses of a few could predict the preferences of many, this could increase the relevance of neuroimaging for marketing and policy applications (Ariely and Berns 2010). In line with findings that mesolimbic activity predicts individuals' willingness to pay for consumer goods, a subsequent study indicated that increased NAcc activity during exposure to unfamiliar songs predicted individuals' willingness to pay to download those songs after scanning (Salimpoor et al. 2013). In an ambitious investigation of whether individual neural reactions to novel songs could further predict aggregate demand, Berns and Moore (2011) had adolescent subjects listen to and rate how much they liked novel songs as they were scanned with fMRI. More than three years later, the researchers obtained aggregate song download statistics from Nielsen's SoundScan database. Remarkably, group NAcc activity in response to each song predicted (log-transformed) downloads several years later. Though MPFC activity also predicted downloads, this association could be fully accounted for by including NAcc activity in the model. Interestingly, subjects' group liking ratings of each song did not predict download rates. These findings suggest not only that NAcc activity in response to novel stimuli can predict choice and consumption, but also that predictions can in some cases scale to the aggregate level and far into the future. Additional research will be needed to replicate and extend these findings and to determine whether they will generalize to choices of other consumable goods (e.g., luxury products versus practical products).

Other predictions

Investigators have begun to use neuroimaging data to predict choices that extend beyond the realm of consumer goods, both at the individual level and at the group level. For instance, increased anterior cingulate cortex activity and MPFC activity during peoples' contemplation of their future identities and plans predicts the extent to which they value future monetary rewards (Ersner-Hershfield et al. 2009; Mitchell et al. 2011; Peters and Büchel 2010). Further, increased MPFC activity in response to advertisements and appeals can predict individual differences in future healthy behavior (e.g., increased sunscreen use, reduced smoking; Falk et al. 2010; Chua et al. 2011; Falk et al. 2011), and may even extend to aggregate responses to health-related appeals (Falk et al. 2012). In the context of consumer research, these findings suggest that the neural focus of predictive activity may depend on abstractness of the choice under consideration. Specifically, as individuals increasingly integrate dimensions of value within options, across options, and even across time, predictive neural activity may shift upward along the medial wall of the prefrontal cortex. Thus, integration of more abstract values may recruit increasingly ascending frontostriatal circuits (Haber and Knutson 2009).

Improving predictions

Although neuroimaging designs and analyses had historically been optimized to identify neural activity correlated with input, using neural data to predict output raises new methodological challenges. Continued progress will therefore require innovations in experimental design and analysis. Specifically, investigators might wish not only to predict future behavior but also to interpret which neural circuits predict that behavior. Thus, designs should ideally be structured to elicit temporally specific, strong, and reliable brain activity before behavioral output. Output models also will require investigators to use many correlated neural features to try to predict a few behavioral outcomes; the "$p >> n$ problem" is also prevalent in genetics. Thus, analytic techniques designed to deal with massive correlated predictors of limited outputs must be developed. For instance, a regression technique called GraphNet can induce sparsity, clustering, and structured priors on multivariate data to automatically select neural features that optimally classify associated outcomes (Grosenick et al. 2013).

Applied to neuroimaging data, these models can select out neural activity in space and time that predicts choice. For instance, in the case of fMRI data acquired during purchasing (i.e., in the SHOP task) these techniques increased the prediction of choice from 60 percent observed using volume of interest methods to 74 percent (a level approaching that of self-report variables collected after the scan), but also revealed which features predict purchasing and when they do so (Grosenick et al. 2008, 2013). Consistent with original predictions, these models verified that NAcc responses to products and MPFC responses to prices separately predict purchasing, but additionally implicated the posterior cingulate's response to prices in purchasing. (See figure 9.2.) Although not previously recognized, the predictive power of posterior cingulate activity may reflect greater visuospatial attention to products that would eventually be purchased. Thus, beyond validating and improving predictions, output analyses can identify novel features for future functional characterization. Eventually, as research accumulates, behavioral prediction benchmarks may be established and improved, promoting reliable and incremental scientific advances. Ultimately, mediation models may help investigators to understand not only which neural features predict output, but also which can connect input to output (Wager et al. 2008). All these developments lie on the near horizon for neuroimaging research, but further innovations in multilevel design

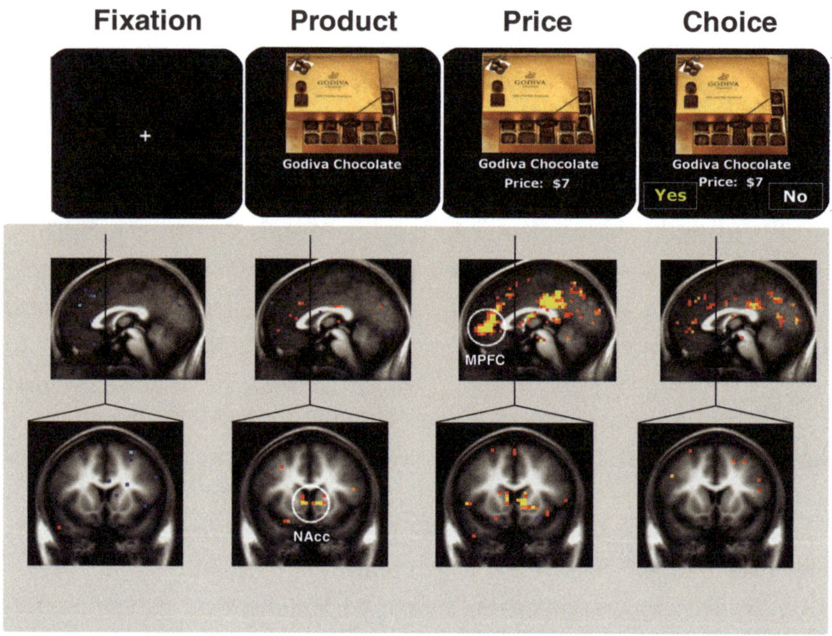

Figure 9.2
Spatiotemporal features that predict consumer choice identified with GraphNet (adapted from Grosenick et al. 2013). When subjects see a product, ventral striatal activity predicts choice; when an associated price appears, MPFC, dorsal striatal, and posterior cingulate activity predict choice. (Note the relative absence of predictive features during the fixation and choice periods.)

and analyses may be necessary to scale from individual to aggregate predictions.

Implications

Since the turn of the twenty-first century, research has consistently and coherently implicated mesolimbic circuitry in human reward processing. Within this circuit, although subcortical NAcc and VTA activity may be more associated with appetitive processes, cortical MFPC and NAcc activity may be more associated with integrative or consummatory processes. Prediction studies further indicate that NAcc activity and sometimes MPFC activity can predict choice and purchasing of consumer products, both in the near future and in the distant future, within and across individuals.

Since NAcc activity specifically increases during reward anticipation, "appetitive" signals from this circuit may best predict choice and subsequent consumption. Remarkably, in only ten years scientists have advanced from asking *whether* brain activity can be used to predict consumption to determining *how well* brain activity can be used to predict consumption. (See also the chapter by Plassmann and Wager.)

Other circuits may also play major roles in predicting choice and consumption, but contexts that evoke their input have not yet been delineated. For instance, anterior insula activity may also predict choice when potential losses are at stake (Knutson and Greer 2008; see also the chapter by Rick), and MFPC activity may also predict choice when multiple dimensions of the same options or different options are under consideration (Haber and Knutson 2010). Dorsal medial frontal activity may play more prominent roles when self-relevance and extended time scales are at stake (Peters and Büchel 2010). Together, these findings fit into and extend a framework for value-based decision making in which primary anticipatory affective responses initially guide choice, which can then be subsequently modulated by more integrative and distal considerations (Knutson and Greer 2008). The current neuroimaging evidence is consistent with the notion that decision making involves a hierarchical multi-component process that unfolds dynamically and flexibly.

The current rate of progress suggests that in the next ten years methods will further improve prediction of behavior from brain signals. Some advances will result from technological enhancements in spatial and especially temporal resolution (e.g., more rapid and homogenous image acquisition due to simultaneous acquisition of multiple slices). Even more significant advances may result from conceptual innovations (e.g., more sophisticated and efficient predictive designs and analyses). Neural prediction of choice and consumption may soon surpass predictions derived from more conventional sources such as self-report, particularly when people are unaware of, unsure of, or reluctant to share their reactions. Though these improved predictions may raise ethical questions related to the neuroimaging of "hidden" information (Ariely and Berns 2010), it is unlikely that anyone will ever be scanned against his or her will, since obtaining interpretable data requires subject cooperation (i.e., minimal motion). Even more promising, some individual predictions may scale to the group level. Investigators will have to clarify the conditions under which this "scaling" can occur (e.g., to which groups, at which time scales, and under which conditions). Most important, neuroimaging findings should feed back on and inform decision theory, clarifying which accounts correctly predict choice at both the individual and the aggregate level and which do not (and therefore deserve revision or retirement).

Epilogue

More than 100 years after its conception, the early ethological ethological distinction between appetitive and consummatory reward processing has held up well. Beyond animal research, human neuroimaging research now indicates that appetitive and consummatory circuits can be distinguished in space and time. Findings also suggest that the appetitive component motivates positive arousal and approach towards both primary and secondary rewards. Additional findings not reviewed here (see, e.g., Knutson and Greer 2008) suggest that appetitive circuits can be distinguished from aversive circuits and that their activity does not depend on sensory input or motor output. Mounting evidence implies that activity in appetitive circuits can predict eventual choice and consumption, both in the near future and in the distant future. These findings thus have implications not only for decision theory but also for applications to predicting choice in the context of consumer preference and product marketing.

As the unfortunate fate of the hungry ghosts suggests, appetitive and consummatory phases of reward processing may be linked. Consistent with the modern notion of a "reward prediction error" (Schultz et al. 1997), consummatory circuits may eventually calm appetites. When the two become disconnected, however, appetitive behavior may grow excessive, disrupting the rhythm of life and threatening mental stability. Brain lesions or excessive drug use may imbalance these circuits, but so might experiential factors that include learning, social influence, and even cultural values (Tsai et al. 2006; see also the chapter by Whybrow, the chapter by Kringelbach, the chapter by Robinson, Robinson and Berridge, and the chapter by Plassmann and Wager). Thus, mapping the appetitive and consummatory circuits that support reward processing may eventually improve the knowledge of how they dynamically interact with and balance each other, with long-term implications for health and well-being.

Table 9.1
Studies using neural (fMRI) activity to predict consumer choice.

Study	Region labels	Consumable good	Targeted, or whole brain?	Sooner, or later?	Individual, or group?
Knutson et al. 2007	NAcc, MPFC, Ains(-)	Products	Targeted*	Sooner (seconds)	Individual
Tusche et al 2010	VStr*, MPFC, Ains(?)	Cars	Whole	Sooner (minutes–hours)	Individual
Lebreton et al. 2009	NAcc, MFPC	Images (faces, houses, paintings)	Targeted?	Sooner (minutes–hours)	Individual
Levy et al. 2011	VStr, MPFC	Products	Targeted	Sooner (minutes–hours)	Individual
Smith et al. 2010	VStr*, MPFC	Images (faces)	Targeted?	Sooner (minutes–hours)	Individual
Demos et al. 2012	NAcc	Food, sex	Targeted	Later (6 months)	Individual
Salimpoor et al. 2013	NAcc	Songs	Targeted	sooner (minutes–hours)	Individual
Berns and Moore 2011	NAcc	Songs	Targeted?	Later (3 years)	Group

*With corrections for small volumes.

Acknowledgments

This research was partially supported by NSF Grant 0748915 to Brian Knutson. We thank Katja Spreckelmeyer and Stephanie Preston for feedback on drafts.

References

Aharon, I., Etcoff, N., Ariely, D., Chabris, C. F., O'Connor, E., and Breiter, H. C. 2001. Beautiful faces have variable reward value: fMRI and behavioral evidence. *Neuron* 32 (3): 537–551.

Anderson, A. K., and Sobel, N. 2003. Dissociating intensity from valence as sensory inputs to emotion. *Neuron* 39 (4): 581–583.

Ariely, D., and Berns, G. S. 2010. Neuromarketing: The hope and hype of neuroimaging in business. *Nature Reviews Neuroscience* 11 (4): 284–292.

Arnow, B. A., Desmond, J. E., Banner, L. L., Glover, G. H., Solomon, A., Polan, M. L., et al. 2002. Brain activation and sexual arousal in healthy, heterosexual males. *Brain* 125 (5): 1014–1023.

Bartra, O., McGuire, J. T., and Kable, J. W. 2013. The valuation system: A coordinate-based meta-analysis of BOLD fMRI experiments examining neural correlates of subjective value. *NeuroImage* 76, 412–427.

Berns, G. S., McClure, S. M., Pagnoni, G., and Montague, P. R. 2001. Predictability modulates human brain response to reward. *Journal of Neuroscience* 21 (8): 2793–2798.

Berns, G. S., and Moore, S. E. 2011. A neural predictor of cultural popularity. *Journal of Consumer Psychology* 22 (1): 154–160.

Berridge, K. C., and Kringelbach, M. L. 2008. Affective neuroscience of pleasure: Reward in humans and animals. *Psychopharmacology* 199 (3): 457–480.

Blair, K., Marsh, A. A., Morton, J., Vythilingam, M., Jones, M., Mondillo, K., et al. 2006. Choosing the lesser of two evils, the better of two goods: Specifying the roles of ventromedial prefrontal cortex and dorsal anterior cingulate in object choice. *Journal of Neuroscience* 26 (44): 11379–11386.

Breiter, H. C., Aharon, I., Kahneman, D., Dale, A., and Shizgal, P. 2001. Functional imaging of neural responses to expectancy and experience of monetary gains and losses. *Neuron* 30 (2): 619–639.

Chua, H. F., Ho, S. S., Jasinska, A. J., Polk, T. A., Welsh, R. C., Liberzon, I., et al. 2011. Self-related neural response to tailored smoking-cessation messages predicts quitting. *Nature Neuroscience* 14 (4): 426–427.

Craig, W. 1918. Appetites and aversions as constituents of instincts. *Biological Bulletin* 34 (2): 91–107.

Delgado, M. R., Nystrom, L. E., Fissell, C., Noll, D. C., and Fiez, J. A. 2000. Tracking the hemodynamic responses to reward and punishment in the striatum. *Journal of Neurophysiology* 84 (6): 3072–3077.

Demos, K. E., Heatherton, T. F., and Kelley, W. M. 2012. Individual differences in nucleus accumbens activity to food and sexual images predict weight gain and sexual behavior. *Journal of Neuroscience* 32: 5549–5552.

Deppe, M., Schwindt, W., Kugel, H., Plassmann, H., and Kenning, P. 2005. Nonlinear responses within the medial prefrontal cortex reveal when specific implicit information influences economic decision making. *Journal of Neuroimaging* 15 (2): 171–182.

Diekhof, E. K., Kaps, L., Falkai, P., and Gruber, O. 2012. The role of the human ventral striatum and the medial orbitofrontal cortex in the representation of reward magnitude: An activation likelihood estimation meta-analysis of neuroimaging studies of passive reward expectancy and outcome processing. *Neuropsychologia* 50 (7): 1252–1266.

Elliott, R., Friston, K. J., and Dolan, R. J. 2000. Dissociable neural responses in human reward systems. *Journal of Neuroscience* 20 (16): 6159–6165.

Erk, S., Spitzer, M., Wunderlich, A. P., Galley, L., and Walter, H. 2002. Cultural objects modulate reward circuitry. *Neuroreport* 13 (18): 2499.

Ersner-Hershfield, H., Wimmer, G. E., and Knutson, B. 2009. Saving for the future self: Neural measures of future self-continuity predict temporal discounting. *Social Cognitive and Affective Neuroscience* 4 (1): 85–92.

Falk, E. B., Berkman, E. T., and Lieberman, M. D. 2012. From neural responses to population behavior: Neural focus group predicts population level media effects. *Psychological Science* 23: 439–445.

Falk, E. B., Berkman, E. T., Mann, T., Harrison, B., and Lieberman, M. D. 2010. Predicting persuasion-induced behavior change from the brain. *Journal of Neuroscience* 30: 8421–8424.

Falk, E. B., Berkman, E. T., Whalen, D., and Lieberman, M. D. 2011. Neural activity during health messaging predicts reductions in smoking above and beyond self-report. *Health Psychology* 30: 177–185.

Gottfried, J. A., O'Doherty, J., and Dolan, R. J. 2002. Appetitive and aversive olfactory learning in humans studied using event-related functional magnetic resonance imaging. *Journal of Neuroscience* 22 (24): 10829–10837.

Grosenick, L., Greer, S., and Knutson, B. 2008. Interpretable classifiers for fMRI improve prediction of purchases. *IEEE Transactions on Neural Systems and Rehabilitation Engineering* 16 (6): 539–548.

Grosenick, L., Klingenberg, B., Katovich, K., Knutson, B., and Taylor, J. E. 2013. Interpretable whole-brain prediction analysis with GraphNet. *NeuroImage* 72: 304–321.

Gyatso, T. 1992. *The Meaning of Life*. Wisdom Publications.

Haber, S. N., and Knutson, B. 2010. The reward circuit: Linking primate anatomy and human imaging. *Neuropsychopharmacology Reviews* 35 (1): 4–26.

Knutson, B., Adams, C. M., Fong, G. W., and Hommer, D. 2001a. Anticipation of increasing monetary reward selectively recruits nucleus accumbens. *Journal of Neuroscience* 21 (16): RC159.

Knutson, B., Fong, G. W., Adams, C. M., Varner, J. L., and Hommer, D. 2001b. Dissociation of reward anticipation and outcome with event-related fMRI. *Neuroreport* 12 (17): 3683–3687.

Knutson, B., Fong, G. W., Bennett, S. M., Adams, C. M., and Hommer, D. 2003. A region of mesial prefrontal cortex tracks monetarily rewarding outcomes: Characterization with rapid event-related fMRI. *NeuroImage* 18 (2): 263–272.

Knutson, B., and Greer, S. M. 2008. Anticipatory affect: Neural correlates and consequences for choice. *Philosophical Transactions of the Royal Society B* 363 (1511): 3771–3786.

Knutson, B., Taylor, J., Kaufman, M., Peterson, R., and Glover, G. 2005. Distributed neural representation of expected value. *Journal of Neuroscience* 25 (19): 4806–4812.

Knutson, B., Westdorp, A., Kaiser, E., and Hommer, D. 2000. FMRI visualization of brain activity during a monetary incentive delay task. *NeuroImage* 12 (1): 20–27.

Knutson, B., and Wimmer, G. E. 2007. Splitting the difference. *Annals of the New York Academy of Sciences* 1104 (1): 54–69.

Knutson, B., Rick, S., Wimmer, G. E., Prelec, D., and Loewenstein, G. 2007. Neural predictors of purchases. *Neuron* 53 (1): 147–156.

Kuhnen, C. M., and Knutson, B. 2005. The neural basis of financial risk taking. *Neuron* 47 (5): 763–770.

Lebreton, M., Jorge, S., Michel, V., Thirion, B., and Pessiglione, M. 2009. An automatic valuation system in the human brain: Evidence from functional neuroimaging. *Neuron* 64 (3): 431–439.

Levy, D. J., and Glimcher, P. W. 2012. The root of all value: A neural common currency for choice. *Current Opinion in Neurobiology* 22: 1–12.

Levy, I., Lazzaro, S. C., Rutledge, R. B., and Glimcher, P. W. 2011. Choice from non-choice: Predicting consumer preferences from blood oxygenation level-dependent signals obtained during passive viewing. *Journal of Neuroscience* 31 (1): 118–125.

Liu, X., Hairston, J., Schrier, M., and Fan, J. 2011. Common and distinct networks underlying reward valence and processing stages: A meta-analysis of functional neuroimaging studies. *Neuroscience and Biobehavioral Reviews* 35 (5): 1219–1236.

MacLean, P. D. 1990. *The Triune Brain in Evolution: Role in Paleocerebral Functions*. Plenum.

McClure, S. M., Li, J., Tomlin, D., Cypert, K. S., Montague, L. M., and Montague, P. R. 2004. Neural correlates of behavioral preference for culturally familiar drinks. *Neuron* 44 (2): 379–387.

Menon, V., and Levitin, D. J. 2005. The rewards of music listening: Response and physiological connectivity of the mesolimbic system. *NeuroImage* 28 (1): 175–184.

Mitchell, J. P., Schirmer, J., Ames, D. L., and Gilbert, D. T. 2011. Medial prefrontal cortex predicts intertemporal choice. *Journal of Cognitive Neuroscience* 23 (4): 857–866.

Montague, P. R., and Berns, G. S. 2002. Neural economics and the biological substrates of valuation. *Neuron* 36 (2): 265–284.

O'Doherty, J. P. 2004. Reward representations and reward-related learning in the human brain: Insights from neuroimaging. *Current Opinion in Neurobiology* 14 (6): 769–776.

O'Doherty, J., Kringelbach, M. L., Rolls, E. T., Hornak, J., and Andrews, C. 2001. Abstract reward and punishment representations in the human orbitofrontal cortex. *Nature Neuroscience* 4 (1): 95–102.

O'Doherty, J. P., Deichmann, R., Critchley, H. D., and Dolan, R. J. 2002. Neural responses during anticipation of a primary taste reward. *Neuron* 33 (5): 815–826.

Panksepp, J. 1998. *Affective Neuroscience: The Foundations of Human and Animal Emotions*. Oxford University Press.

Paulus, M. P., and Frank, L. R. 2003. Ventromedial prefrontal cortex activation is critical for preference judgments. *Neuroreport* 14 (10): 1311–1315.

Peters, J., and Büchel, C. 2010. Episodic future thinking reduces reward delay discounting through an enhancement of prefrontal-mediotemporal interactions. *Neuron* 66 (1): 138.

Plassmann, H., O'Doherty, J., and Rangel, A. 2007. Orbitofrontal cortex encodes willingness to pay in everyday economic transactions. *Journal of Neuroscience* 27 (37): 9984–9988.

Ramnani, N., and Miall, R. C. 2003. Instructed delay activity in the human prefrontal cortex is modulated by monetary reward expectation. *Cerebral Cortex* 13 (3): 318–327.

Rilling, J. K., Gutman, D. A., Zeh, T. R., Pagnoni, G., Berns, G. S., and Kilts, C. D. 2002. A neural basis for social cooperation. *Neuron* 35 (2): 395–405.

Roitman, M. F., Stuber, G. D., Phillips, P. E., Wightman, R. M., and Carelli, R. M. 2004. Dopamine operates as a subsecond modulator of food seeking. *Journal of Neuroscience* 24 (6): 1265–1271.

Rolls, E. T., O'Doherty, J., Kringelbach, M. L., Francis, S., Bowtell, R., and McGlone, F. 2003. Representations of pleasant and painful touch in the human orbitofrontal and cingulate cortices. *Cerebral Cortex* 13 (3): 308–317.

Salimpoor, V. N., van den Bosch, I., Kovacevic, N., McIntosh, A. R., Dagher, A., and Zatorre, R. J. 2013. Interactions between the nucleus accumbens and auditory cortices predict music reward value. *Science* 340 (6129): 216–219.

Schultz, W., Dayan, P., and Montague, P. R. 1997. A neural substrate of prediction and reward. *Science* 275 (5306): 1593–1599.

Smith, D. V., Hayden, B. Y., Truong, T.-K., Song, A. W., Platt, M. L., and Huettel, S. 2010. Distinct value signals in anterior and posterior ventromedial prefrontal cortex. *Neuron* 30 (7): 2490–2495.

Stuber, G. D., Roitman, M. F., Phillips, P. E., Carelli, R. M., and Wightman, R. M. 2004. Rapid dopamine signaling in the nucleus accumbens during contingent and noncontingent cocaine administration. *Neuropsychopharmacology* 30 (5): 853–863.

Tsai, J. L., Knutson, B., and Fung, H. H. 2006. Cultural variation in affect valuation. *Journal of Personality and Social Psychology* 90 (2): 288–307.

Tusche, A., Bode, S., and Haynes, J. D. 2010. Neural responses to unattended products predict later consumer choices. *Journal of Neuroscience* 30 (23): 8024–8031.

Wager, T. D., Davidson, M. L., Hughes, B. L., Lindquist, M. A., and Ochsner, K. N. 2008. Prefrontal-subcortical pathways mediating successful emotion regulation. *Neuron* 59 (6): 1037–1050.

Yarkoni, T., Poldrack, R. A., Nichols, T. E., Van Essen, D. C., and Wager, T. D. 2011. Large-scale automated synthesis of human functional neuroimaging data. *Nature Methods* 8 (8): 665–670.

Zajonc, R. B. 1980. Feeling and thinking: Preferences need no inferences. *American Psychologist* 35 (2): 151–175.

10 Incentive Salience in Addiction and Over-Consumption

Michael J. F. Robinson, Terry E. Robinson, and Kent C. Berridge

Drug Addiction, Recovery, and Relapse

Most adults have used a potentially addictive drug at least once, if caffeine, alcohol, and nicotine are included in addition to illicit drugs. In some cases, contact with a substance is so frequent and socially accepted that many people fail to recognize it as a "drug." However, even among those who have used such potent drugs as cocaine or heroin, relatively few develop formal addiction. Addiction is characterized by compulsive drug seeking, impairment of social and psychological functions, and/or damage to health. Typically it involves overwhelming involvement with the addictive reward, loss of control, and narrowing of interests. According to a 2010 survey, less than 10 percent of the Americans met the criteria for chronic alcohol-abuse or drug-abuse disorder, and an even smaller proportion suffered from chronic addiction (SAMHSA 2011). Yet the worldwide monetary and social costs associated with addiction are enormous.

A chief problem in treating addiction is chronic or repeated relapse among those who are trying to quit. Even after prolonged periods of withdrawal and abstinence, a high percentage of addicted individuals in treatment programs eventually relapse to drug taking. For example, in the case of a study of heroin users, relapse rates after cessation were approximately 60 percent within 3 months and at least 75 percent within 12 months (Hunt, Barnett, and Branch 1971). For this reason, drug addiction is characterized as a chronic relapsing disorder; relapse is the rule rather than the exception, and often occurs repeatedly.

There are three conventional reasons often suggested in addiction neuroscience to explain relapse in drug addiction:

Drug euphoria Addicts resume drug taking to experience the intense pleasure (euphoria) they remember the drug producing.

Over-learning of habits or predictions Drug taking becomes such a well-entrenched habit that relapse is almost inevitable, or learning becomes distorted in other ways to create false predictions about drugs' rewards.

Withdrawal escape The withdrawal syndrome that accompanies the cessation of drug intake is so unpleasant that an addict would do anything to stop it, and so relapse occurs as an escape from withdrawal.

Each of these three explanations certainly plays a role in relapse. However, we believe, for several reasons, that these explanations are insufficient to explain the central problem underlying relapse in addiction.

First, drug pleasure or euphoria certainly accounts for the initial pattern of drug use and abuse, but it may have more difficulty accounting for relapse as tolerance can develop to the pleasure. Even addicts who no longer find their drugs particularly pleasant may experience increases in drug craving that persist for a long time. (See also the chapter by Kringelbach.)

It also has been suggested by some learning-oriented scientists that the repeated use of drugs creates a learning disorder, such as making drug taking an overly ritualized habitual act or creating false expectations of exaggerated reward. Ritualization may be true of the act of drug taking, but cannot explain the preceding flexible acts of drug seeking during craving. And there is little reason to believe that addicts mispredict the reward value of their drugs or the consequences of their actions. Learned habits or mispredictions alone cannot account for the excessive motivational attraction of addiction.

Many addictive drugs surely induce tolerance (when the drug is present) and withdrawal (when the drug is absent). Withdrawal is typically described as an intense negative emotional state accompanied by dysphoria, anxiety, and irritability, and may indeed be a potent reason why many addicts relapse and take drugs, at least while the withdrawal lasts. Yet withdrawal is a relatively short-lived phenomenon; it decays substantially within days to weeks. By contrast, relapse often occurs even after withdrawal is no longer reported, and even in fully "detoxified" addicts months after "recovery."

In contrast to these suggestions, the incentive sensitization theory (Robinson and Berridge 1993) proposes an alternative explanation that can account for the persistence of relapse and the independence of addiction from pleasure, withdrawal, or faulty expectations. It may also have applications to some addictions that extend beyond drugs. The incentive sensitization theory proposes that relapse often occurs as a result of brain changes that lead to intense incentive motivation for drugs. These brain changes generate pulses of incentive salience or "wanting," often triggered by encountering drug cues, which may be experienced as feelings of drug craving or may even control one's behavior implicitly without need of strong conscious feelings. Craving occurs when the process of incentive salience (or core "wanting"), mediated primarily by subcortical mesolimbic brain systems that use dopamine as an important neurotransmitter, is translated into conscious awareness. Prior to any conscious awareness of drug craving, the motivation to take drugs is due to the over-attribution of incentive salience to drug-related stimuli. It is important to note that incentive salience is a distinct psychological process from withdrawal and drug pleasure. In some cases, attribution of incentive salience to reward-predicting cues may make the cues as "wanted" as the reward itself. Such cues become motivational magnets, sometimes prompting irrational behaviors, such as interactions with cues specific to those previously seen only during interactions with the reward itself (Davey and Cleland 1982), as when a person addicted to crack cocaine scans the floor for a white speck (which is more likely to be an ordinary pebble than crack cocaine), picks it up, inspects it, puts it in a pipe, and tries to light it and smoke it—a phenomenon that has been called "chasing ghosts" (Rosse et al. 1993).

Incentive Salience and Utility

In this section we consider the aforementioned explanation of addiction in terms of forms of reward utility that are important to decision making: predicted utility, decision utility, experienced utility, and remembered utility (Kahneman, Wakker, and Sarin 1997; see also the chapter by Knutson and Karmarkar and the chapter by Plassmann and Wager). Predicted utility is an expectation of how much a future drug reward will be liked. Decision utility is the valuation of the drug manifest in choice and pursuit. Experienced utility is how much the pleasant drug is liked when actually taken. Remembered utility is the memory of how pleasant the drug was in the past. Experienced utility is considered the end point of the decision process.

It is the state reached after successful attainment of a particular outcome, pertaining to the hedonic evaluation of that outcome. Experienced utility informs both remembered and predicted utility to some degree. However, other signals are needed in order for decisions to actually be made. The incentive-sensitization theory suggests that only one of these—decision utility, of which incentive salience is one constituent—need be distorted to create a compulsive addiction.

Typically, decision utility is determined by predicted and remembered utility. However, predicted and remembered utility may fail to be perfect representations of experienced utility, because hedonic memories can become distorted, as when peak-end averages of a hedonic experience outweigh in memory the actual amount of pain or pleasure that was experienced (Kahneman, Wakker, and Sarin 1997). Drug addicts are also believed to often fail to accurately translate experienced utility into decisions (Bechara 2005). In general, any distortion in memory or prediction that leads to faulty predictive utility will likewise affect decision utility, producing decisions that fail to maximize the experienced utility of chosen outcomes.

However, addicts may continue to have problems in excessive decision utility even when their remembered utility and predicted utility for a drug's consequence are quite accurate. Incentive salience has a special role in this. Incentive salience, or cue-triggered "wanting," is a specific form of Pavlovian-related motivation for rewards (Berridge and Robinson 1998; Berridge 2012). Incentive salience is mediated by mesocorticolimbic brain systems, and is especially modulated by dopamine levels. (See also the chapter by Kringelbach.) "Wanting" typically coheres with "liking" (hedonic impact) for the same reward, but "wanting" and "liking" can be dissociated in certain circumstances and by some manipulations, especially those that specifically involve dopamine. Finally, "wanting" can also be distinguished from learning about the same reward. For example, "wanting" triggered by a Pavlovian reward cue can dramatically increase motivation for the reward, even if its previously learned value has not changed (e.g., in hunger, satiety, stress, or drug-related states) (Robinson and Berridge 2013). Abstinence from smoking for only 24 hours can dramatically potentiate neural responses to smoking-related cues (McClernon et al. 2009).

In this framework, incentive salience "wanting" is a pure form of decision utility, distinct from other forms of utility, and in some conditions it can decouple from all the others (Berridge and Aldridge 2008). That is, "wanting" an outcome is distinguishable from experienced utility (hedonic impact, or "liking" the outcome), from the remembered utility of how nice the outcome was in the past, and from the anticipated or predicted utility of how nice it will be in the future. For incentive salience, under conditions of dopamine-related stimulation, situations exist in which cue-triggered decision utility exceeds remembered utility from the past and, similarly, decision utility exceeds predicted utility for future reward value. In other words, it is possible to addictively "want" something that is not expected to be liked, or remembered to be liked, as well as something that is not actually liked when obtained.

Such addictive "wants" may be especially triggered on particular encounters with addictive cues but not on other encounters with the same cues. According to the incentive sensitization theory of addiction (Robinson and Berridge 1993), attribution of incentive salience to a reward cue becomes exaggerated in addicts as a result of long-lasting mesolimbic brain changes (Paulson, Camp, and Robinson 1991). Exaggeration can happen because incentive salience, which makes up part of decision utility, always results from the synergy between two sources: previously learned associations about the reward cue and the current brain state at the time the cue is encountered (Berridge 2012; Zhang et al. 2009).

Fluctuations in the temptation power of cues, which illustrate the difference between decision utility and predicted utility, hinge on the current neurobiological state factors related to dopamine at the moment the cue is encountered. In particular, incentive sensitization suggests that craving and relapse are magnified by a sensitized neural system (mesocorticolimbic dopamine and related systems), which can flip into a super-reactive mode under several conditions: when the person is under stress, or when a person tries to "just take one" hit of his or her addictive drug (which primes mesolimbic systems to react more powerfully to cues), or during other emotional states that heighten mesolimbic reactivity. At such moments, ordinary stimuli, such as cues associated with rewards, are transformed into potent incentive stimuli, making such cues attractive and able to trigger an urge to pursue and consume their associated reward.

This type of synergistic modulation of "wanting" is not limited to addicts. Most people have experienced at least moderate pulses of incentive salience generated by similar rules. For example, advertisements that pop up on a Web page may prompt clicking. The smell of food as you walk down the street may make you suddenly feel quite hungry, even if you weren't feeling that way moments earlier. But the smell of food as a cue is not constant in its temptation power: if you really haven't eaten all day you might find the aroma extremely tempting, whereas you won't if you have recently eaten. The essence of incentive sensitization suggests that addicts encounter fluctuations like this in the temptation power of their drug-associated cues, but that, because of the enduring sensitization of their mesolimbic systems, their maximal peaks of temptation are much higher than those that other people are likely to experience in daily life.

The basic mechanisms of the excessive attribution of incentive salience to drugs and drug-related stimuli can even occur as a mostly automatic and unconscious process, creating urges to take drugs whether or not a strong subjective feeling of craving is simultaneously present. Such dissociation between acted-on motivation and confusing subjective feelings is what often renders the compulsive quality of an addict's behavior astonishing even to the addict.

Only "wanting," and not "liking," becomes sensitized, and consequently more intense on its own, as addiction develops. That is because "liking" has separable and more restricted brain mechanisms. In animal studies, sensitization increases neuronal firing in pathways that code incentive salience as well as the behavioral ability of reward cues to trigger frenzied bursts of effort to obtain the reward (Tindell et al. 2005; Wyvell and Berridge 2001). Yet sensitization does not increase "liking" reactions that reflect the hedonic impact of the reward when it actually arrives. Similarly, in humans who are becoming drug-tolerant addicts, incentive motivation to take the drug can grow as they become addicted, so that a single hit of the drug can provoke intense urges to take more even if the person reports the dose of drug no longer gives as much pleasure as initially. Beyond drug addiction, consequent incentive sensitization may also manifest itself in food bingeing, pathological gambling, hypersexuality, and other compulsive motivations.

The neuroadaptations responsible for the sensitization of incentive salience are long lasting if not permanent, potentially persisting for years after the individual stops taking drugs. For example, neurochemically, sensitization leads to an enhanced dopamine elevation produced by an addictive drug in the synapses of the nucleus accumbens in the face of a drug challenge (Vezina 1993; Kalivas and Duffy 1990). Anatomically, there are also persistent changes in the brain cells and circuits of the mesolimbic system that respond to drugs and control incentive salience (Robinson and Kolb 1997). These include structural changes in the morphology of neurons in brain structures of the nucleus accumbens and prefrontal cortex, increased release of dopamine, and increased sensitivity of dopamine D1 receptors. There have also been reports that cocaine causes an increase in the subpopulation of dopamine D2 receptors that are in a high-affinity state, which may occur even in spite of a reduction in overall D2 receptors and which may result in dopamine supersensitivity in addicts (Seeman et al. 2005; Flagel et al. 2010). This, we suggest, is why relapse is prevalent and persistent despite recovery, and regardless of withdrawal, even when strong pleasure is not to be expected from taking a drug.

Liking and Wanting Things Other Than Drugs

Over-eating is a chief cause of obesity. Could exaggerated "wanting" or "liking" play a role in some individuals over-eating? Excessive hedonic reactions to food would magnify both "liking" and "wanting" above that of a regular individual, thus contributing to binge eating and obesity (Berridge, Robinson, and Aldridge 2009; Davis et al. 2009). Alternatively, changes in "wanting" alone could be responsible for over-eating. Sensitization of mesolimbic dopamine systems by exposure to cycles of binging and dieting has been suggested to occur (Avena and Hoebel 2003a,b). Enhanced sensitivity of the mesolimbic reward system could attribute high levels of incentive motivation to the sights and smells related to food, and could drive excessive consumption, without necessarily producing comparable levels of "liking," when the food is consumed. (See also the chapter by Todd and Minard.)

A different set of problems may face individuals who have been suggested to have elevated "liking" as well as elevated "wanting"—individuals who may deserve to be called food addicts (Davis and Carter 2009; Davis et al. 2009). Notably, Davis and colleagues found that certain individuals who are both obese and binge eaters are far more likely to carry both an allele for a gene that codes a gain of function for μ-opioids and an allele for a gene that may be associated with higher binding for the dopamine

D2 receptor. Together these genetic traits have been suggested by Davis and colleagues to combine to simultaneously increase "liking" and "wanting" for foods in a manner that strongly promotes binge eating and gives rise to addiction-like features, including loss of control and relapse. Similarly, it has been suggested that individuals who carry genes promoting elevated dopamine function may experience stronger cue-triggered urges in response to food cues, which may make them more liable to develop obesity (Campbell and Eisenberg 2007).

Conversely, it has been suggested that anorexia nervosa is related to a reward dysfunction that suppresses the "wanting" for food despite leaving the "liking" portion intact (as well as developing an abnormal "wanting" for body perceptions of self as thin) (Keating et al. 2012).

Gambling may also involve special recruitment of incentive salience brain systems. Uncertainty may especially promote incentive salience under conditions that mirror many of the hallmarks of gambling. (For more on the role of uncertainty in material acquisitiveness, see the chapter by Preston and Vickers.) This may produce a further example of the dissociation between experienced or remembered utility and decision utility. Individuals sometimes seem driven by cues to gamble, in all cases at a global monetary loss, for only a moderate experienced utility. Compulsive gamblers may also show other addictions (Zhang et al. 2009).

Other Consumer Behaviors

Even beyond addiction, situations may arise in everyday life in which incentive salience becomes particularly high, inducing moments of strong decision utility for pursuing or consuming an incentive. (See also the chapter by Plassmann and Wager, the chapter by Preston and Vickers, and the chapter by Knutson and Karmarkar.) Consumer goods can similarly be strong incentives influenced by powerful cues. Some situational factors, such as being in a store, may increase how much consumer goods are "wanted" while the extent to which they are "liked" remains unchanged (Litt, Khan, and Shiv 2010). Purchasing a product without actually "liking" the product sufficiently to make the purchase under normal circumstances is likely to induce regret. Accordingly, Litt et al. (2010) suggested that "wanting" and "liking" consumer goods can be driven in opposite directions, almost mimicking reports of drug addiction. When people experienced failure while pursuing a desired outcome (e.g., a $5 gift card), they showed increased willingness to pay for the reward—that is, they "wanted" the reward more. However, these individuals also happened to "like" the reward less in the sense that they were more likely to trade it away for an equivalent but different prize (a $5 gift card for a similar store).

Incentive Salience in Temporal Discounting?

Individuals are often faced with having to make the choice between smaller rewards received sooner and larger ones received later. Such dynamic inconsistencies are central to temporal-discounting models. (See the chapter by Rick, the chapter by Lea, and the chapter by Preston and Vickers.) A recent interpretation of temporal discounting by Leonhard Lades (2011) suggests that incentive salience may be a factor in temporal discounting, particularly by driving up the value of immediate goals and making them "wanted" more than they may be "liked." As described by Lades, drawing on other decision theorists, the incentive-salience model of intertemporal choice originates from intertemporal-discounting models that posit two decision systems, one (System 1) affective, impulsive and "in the now" and the other (System 2) more patient, cognitive, and analytical (Berns, Laibson, and Loewenstein 2007; Hoch and Loewenstein 1991; Kahneman 2003; Strack, Werth, and Deutsch 2006; Loewenstein 1996). Lades suggests that in cases of perfect self-control, or in the absence of cue-triggered "wanting," there is a direct correlation between the expected pleasure of a reward and the motivation to consume it (Lades 2011). In such situations, decisions are products of the reflective System 2. When decisions are influenced by cues that trigger "wanting," however, the relationship breaks down and the impulsive System 1 becomes the prevalent decision maker.

Similar dissociations between "liking" and "wanting" have been applied to social incentives. Dai, Brendl, and Ariely (2010) have suggested that there are two types of impulsive preferences toward identical human faces—face likability and face incentive value—which they believe to correspond to "liking" and "wanting" respectively. Dai et al. find that under certain conditions there may be a disconnection between "wanting" to look at a face and "liking" the face. "Liking" reactions are independent of the viewers' gender, whereas males "want" to visually consume attractive female faces much more than females "want" to look at attractive male faces. (On evolved mate-selection preferences in males, see also the chapter by Saad and the chapter by Griskevicius, Redden, and Ackerman.)

Summary

The incentive-sensitization theory helps explain why the development of addiction is a gradual and incremental process, but also why addiction is a persistent problem once established. Essentially, the magnification of decision utility can create a sense of compulsive motivation without altering the predicted utility, the experienced utility, or the remembered utility of the drug. Exaggerated discounting of other rewards relative to the drug will result, as will a probabilistic form of compulsion in which the addict remains in principle capable of resisting temptation on any single trial but in practice is likely to succumb to relapse if required to encounter a series of repeated temptations.

Powerful "wanting," often in the absence of equivalent "liking," is not restricted to addictive drugs. The incentive-sensitization theory may provide an explanation for why consumer goods and certain foods can also become excessively compelling incentives. In turn, cues such as those contained in advertisements can trigger potent "wanting" peaks that propel susceptible individuals toward over-consumption of material goods and toward addiction-like disorders such as binge eating. However, there is a tremendous amount of individual variation in sensitization and in the functioning of the mesolimbic dopamine system. Some individuals, owing to their genes, their hormones, their life experiences, and other factors, are highly susceptible to sensitization. Other individuals are relatively resistant and less likely to develop the neurobiological changes in brain dopamine systems that underlie sensitization. This may explain why relatively few people who take drugs or over-indulge in other forms of reward actually develop compulsive levels of "wanting," and why certain individuals may be better equipped to resist temptation than others.

References

Avena, N., and B. Hoebel. 2003a. A diet promoting sugar dependency causes behavioral cross-sensitization to a low dose of amphetamine. *Neuroscience* 122 (1): 17–20.

Avena, N., and B. Hoebel. 2003b. Amphetamine-sensitized rats show sugar-induced hyperactivity (cross-sensitization) and sugar hyperphagia. *Pharmacology, Biochemistry, and Behavior* 74 (3): 635–639.

Bechara, A. 2005. Decision making, impulse control and loss of willpower to resist drugs: A neurocognitive perspective. *Nature Neuroscience* 8 (11): 1458–1463.

Berns, G., D. Laibson, and G. Loewenstein. 2007. Intertemporal choice: Toward an integrative framework. *Trends in Cognitive Sciences* 11 (11): 482–488.

Berridge, K. 2012. From prediction error to incentive salience: Mesolimbic computation of reward motivation. *European Journal of Neuroscience* 35 (7): 1124–1143.

Berridge, K., and J. Aldridge. 2008. Decision utility, the brain, and pursuit of hedonic goals. *Social Cognition* 26 (5): 621–646.

Berridge, K., and T. Robinson. 1998. What is the role of dopamine in reward: hedonic impact, reward learning, or incentive salience? *Brain Research Brain Research Reviews* 28 (3): 309–369.

Berridge, K., T. Robinson, and J. Aldridge. 2009. Dissecting components of reward: "Liking," "wanting," and learning. *Current Opinion in Pharmacology* 9 (1): 65–73.

Campbell, B., and D. Eisenberg. 2007. Obesity, attention deficit-hyperactivity disorder and the dopaminergic reward system. *Collegium Antropologicum* 31 (1): 33–38.

Dai, X., C. Brendl, and D. Ariely. 2010. Wanting, liking, and preference construction. *Emotion* 10 (3): 324–334.

Davey, G., and G. Cleland. 1982. Topography of signal-centered behavior in the rat: Effects of deprivation state and reinforcer type. *Journal of the Experimental Analysis of Behavior* 38 (3): 291–304.

Davis, C., and J. Carter. 2009. Compulsive overeating as an addiction disorder: A review of theory and evidence. *Appetite* 53 (1): 1–8.

Davis, C., R. Levitan, C. Reid, J. Carter, A. Kaplan, K. Patte, N. King, C. Curtis, and J. Kennedy. 2009. Dopamine for "wanting" and opioids for "liking": A comparison of obese adults with and without binge eating. *Obesity* 17 (6): 1220–1225.

Flagel, S., T. Robinson, J. Clark, S. Clinton, S. Watson, P. Seeman, P. Phillips, and H. Akil. 2010. An animal model of genetic vulnerability to behavioral disinhibition and responsiveness to reward-related cues: Implications for addiction. *Neuropsychopharmacology* 35 (2): 388–400.

Hoch, S., and G. Loewenstein. 1991. Time-inconsistent preferences and consumer self-control. *Journal of Consumer Research* 17: 492–507.

Hunt, W., L. Barnett, and L. Branch. 1971. Relapse rates in addiction programs. *Journal of Clinical Psychology* 27 (4): 455–456.

Kahneman, D. 2003. Maps of bounded rationality: Psychology for behavioral economics. *American Economic Review* 93 (5): 1449–1475.

Kahneman, D., P. Wakker, and R. Sarin. 1997. Back to Bentham? Explorations of experienced utility. *Quarterly Journal of Economics* 112 (2): 375–406.

Kalivas, P., and P. Duffy. 1990. Effect of acute and daily cocaine treatment on extracellular dopamine in the nucleus accumbens. *Synapse* 5 (1): 48–58.

Keating, C., A. Tilbrook, S. Rossell, P. Enticott, and P. Fitzgerald. 2012. Reward processing in anorexia nervosa. *Neuropsychologia* 50 (5): 567–575.

Lades, L. 2011. Towards an Incentive Salience Model of Intertemporal Choice. Papers on Economics and Evolution no. 118.

Litt, A., U. Khan, and B. Shiv 2010. Lusting while loathing: Parallel counterdriving of wanting and liking. *Psychological Science* 21 (1): 118–125.

Loewenstein, G. 1996. Out of control: Visceral influences on behavior. *Organizational Behavior and Human Decision Processes* 65 (3): 272–292.

McClernon, F., R. Kozink, A. Lutz, and J. Rose. 2009. 24-h smoking abstinence potentiates fMRI-BOLD activation to smoking cues in cerebral cortex and dorsal striatum. *Psychopharmacology* 204 (1): 25–35.

Paulson, P., D. Camp, and T. Robinson. 1991. Time course of transient behavioral depression and persistent behavioral sensitization in relation to regional brain monoamine concentrations during amphetamine withdrawal in rats. *Psychopharmacology* 103 (4): 480–492.

Robinson, M., and K. Berridge. 2013. Instant transformation of learned repulsion into motivational "wanting." *Current Biology* 23 (4): 282–289.

Robinson, T., and K. Berridge. 1993. The neural basis of drug craving: An incentive-sensitization theory of addiction. *Brain Research Reviews* 18 (3): 247–291.

Robinson, T., and B. Kolb. 1997. Persistent structural modifications in nucleus accumbens and prefrontal cortex neurons produced by previous experience with amphetamine. *Journal of Neuroscience* 17 (21): 8491–8497.

Rosse, R., M. Fay-McCarthy, J. Collins,D. Risher-Flowers, T. Alim, and S. Deutsch. 1993. Transient compulsive foraging behavior associated with crack cocaine use. *American Journal of Psychiatry* 150 (1): 155–156.

SAMHSA (Substance Abuse and Mental Health Services Administration). 2011. Results From the 2010 National Survey on Drug Use and Health: Summary of National Findings.

Seeman, P., D. Weinshenker, R. Quirion, L. Srivastava, S. Bhardwaj, D. Grandy, R. Premont, et al. 2005. Dopamine supersensitivity correlates with D2High states, implying many paths to psychosis. *Proceedings of the National Academy of Sciences* 102 (9): 3513–3518.

Strack, F., L. Werth, and R. Deutsch. 2006. Reflective and impulsive determinants of consumer behavior. *Journal of Consumer Psychology* 16 (3): 205–216.

Tindell, A., K. Berridge, J. Zhang, S. Peciña, and J. Aldridge. 2005. Ventral pallidal neurons code incentive motivation: Amplification by mesolimbic sensitization and amphetamine. *European Journal of Neuroscience* 22 (10): 2617–2634.

Vezina, P. 1993. Amphetamine injected into the ventral tegmental area sensitizes the nucleus accumbens dopaminergic response to systemic amphetamine: An in vivo microdialysis study in the rat. *Brain Research* 605 (2): 332–337.

Wyvell, C., and K. Berridge. 2001. Incentive sensitization by previous amphetamine exposure: Increased cue-triggered "wanting" for sucrose reward. *Journal of Neuroscience* 21 (19): 7831–7840.

Zhang, J., K. Berridge, A. Tindell, K. Smith, and J. Aldridge. 2009. A neural computational model of incentive salience. *PLOS Computational Biology* 5 (7): e1000437.

11 Balancing Consumption: Brain Insights from Pleasure Cycles

Morten L. Kringelbach

The past twenty years have seen significant progress in the scientific study of pleasure. One strategy has been to define pleasure as a driving force for ensuring survival and procreation of both individuals and species (Kringelbach 2005; Kringelbach and Berridge 2010). As such, pleasure could be seen as evolution's boldest trick, and neural mechanisms for pleasure have been selected for and conserved only if they ultimately play a key role in fulfilling Darwinian imperatives of gene proliferation via improved survival and procreation, suggesting that the capacity for pleasure must have been fundamentally important in evolutionary fitness (Darwin 1872; Panksepp 1999; Berridge and Kringelbach 2008; also see the preface to this volume).

The main challenge for the brain is to successfully balance resource allocation for survival and procreation (Lou, Joensson, and Kringelbach 2011). In order to achieve this balance in the brain, different rewards compete for resources, and therefore this balancing act typically follows a cyclical time course (figure 11.1). Within this framework, pleasure helps to initiate, sustain, or terminate phases of wanting, liking, and satiety, and thus plays a crucial part in guiding the survival-related decision making involved in optimizing the allocation of the brain's resources.

This chapter briefly reviews the main findings from hedonia research. The word *hedonia* is derived from the ancient Greek word *hedone*, which comes from *hedus*, meaning the sweet taste of honey. Hedonia research has demonstrated that pleasure consists of multiple brain networks and processes relating to incentive salience ('wanting'), hedonic valuation ('liking'), and learning (Berridge and Kringelbach 2008; Berridge 1996; Kringelbach 2005; also see the chapter by Robinson, Robinson, and Berridge and the chapter by Knutson and Karmarkar in this volume). (The

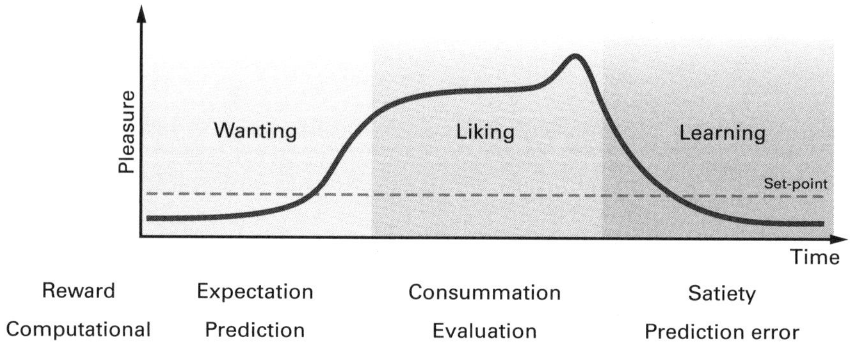

Figure 11.1

Pleasure cycles. Fundamental pleasures are associated with behaviors that are necessary for a species' survival and, together with higher-order pleasures, are associated with a cyclical time course. Typically, rewarding moments go through a phase of expectation or wanting for a reward, which sometimes leads to a phase of consummation or liking of the reward, which can have a peak level of pleasure (e.g., encountering a loved one, a tasty meal, orgasm, a drug rush, winning a gambling bet). This can be followed by a satiety phase, in which one learns and updates predictions for the reward. Note, however, that learning obviously can take place throughout the cycle. These various phases have been identified at many levels of investigation. The recent research on the computational mechanisms underlying prediction, evaluation, and prediction error (Zhang et al. 2009; Friston and Kiebel 2009) is particularly interesting. The few candidates for rewards that may have a brief or missing satiety phase include money, some abstract rewards, and some drug and brain-stimulation rewards that activate dopamine systems rather directly.

single quotation marks around the words 'liking' and 'wanting' are meant to indicate the neural processing linked to overt behavioral changes.)

The discovery of pleasure mechanisms has come primarily from food research (Berridge and Kringelbach 2008; Kringelbach, Stein, and van Hartevelt 2012) and, in turn, has informed the study of other fundamental and higher-order pleasures (Georgiadis and Kringelbach 2012). The evidence suggests that the underlying principles are shared across many different rewards.

Here, the focus is on how general pleasure mechanisms may underlie balanced states of well-being, linking hedonia to eudaimonia, a life experienced as engaging and valuably meaningful. In particular, the reward networks are integral parts of more general resting-state networks in the brain. In fact, balancing the reward networks may help to more generally rebalance the resting-state networks, which can become unbalanced in affective disorders. Balancing 'wanting' and 'liking' processes may help optimize consumption decisions and may ideally help individuals reach states of well-being.

A Science of Pleasure

As was mentioned above, pleasure is central to fulfilling the Darwinian imperatives of survival and procreation, which means that in all animals fundamental pleasure can be evoked by food and sex (Berridge 1996; Kringelbach 2004; Georgiadis and Kringelbach 2012). In social animals, the propagation of genes is linked to the social interactions with conspecifics, which are important for both survival and procreation. Social pleasures are thus part of the human repertoire of fundamental pleasures (Kringelbach and Rolls 2003). In particular, for the development of the social pleasures, the early attachment bonds between parents and infants are likely to be extremely important (Lorenz 1943; Stein et al. 1991). In social species such as humans, it could well be that the social pleasures are at least as pleasurable as the sensory and the sexual ones (Parsons et al. 2010; Aragona et al. 2006; Kringelbach et al. 2008; Britton et al. 2006; Leknes and Tracey 2008; Frith and Frith 2010; King-Casas et al. 2005).

In addition to these fundamental pleasures, there are a large number of higher-order pleasures, including monetary, artistic, musical, altruistic, and transcendent pleasures (Frijda 2010; Leknes and Tracey 2010; Skov 2010; Vuust and Kringelbach 2010; Salimpoor et al. 2011; Kringelbach 2005). Even rewarding drugs of abuse are widely viewed to hijack the hedonic brain systems that evolved to mediate food pleasure, sexual pleasure, and other natural sensory pleasures (Koob and Volkow 2010; Everitt et al. 2008; Kelley and Berridge 2002; Robinson, Robinson, and Berridge, this volume). Thus, brains may be viewed as having conserved and recycled some of the neural mechanisms of hedonic generation for higher pleasures that originated early in evolution for simpler sensory pleasures.

In the last hundred years, a large number of animal experiments have investigated reward processing in the brain. Many people have subsequently defined pleasure as the conscious experience of reward, but it is questionable whether such a narrow definition is meaningful or useful.

Such a definition would limit pleasure to conscious organisms, which is problematic for a number of reasons, not least because we do not have a good definition of consciousness.

Pleasure—even sensory pleasure—is never merely a sensation (Frijda 2010; Ryle 1954; Kringelbach 2010; Kringelbach and Berridge 2010). Instead pleasure always requires the recruitment of specialized brain systems to actively paint an additional "hedonic gloss" onto a sensation. Active recruitment of the brain's pleasure-generating systems is what makes a pleasant experience 'liked.'

The capacity of certain stimuli, such as a sweet taste or a loved one, to reliably elicit pleasure—to nearly always be painted with a hedonic gloss—reflects the privileged ability of such stimuli to activate the hedonic brain systems responsible for manufacturing and applying the gloss. Hedonic brain systems are well developed in the brain, spanning subcortical and cortical levels, and are quite similar across humans and other animals.

Pleasure reactions can be elicited by many stimuli and, in the normal brain, lead to activity in widespread brain networks, some of which are deep in the brain (nucleus accumbens, ventral pallidum, brain stem) and some of which are in the cortex (orbitofrontal, cingulate, medial prefrontal, and insular cortices) (Cardinal et al. 2002; Everitt and Robbins 2005; Kringelbach 2010; Kringelbach et al. 2003; Kringelbach and Rolls 2004; Berridge 1996; Watson, Shepherd, and Platt 2010; Amodio and Frith 2006).

Different regions or nodes in this distributed pleasure network play different roles in terms of controlling the transitions between the various phases of the pleasure cycle. One of the most important distinctions is between regions involved in the 'wanting' and 'liking' phases, where 'wanting' corresponds to the motivational salience and 'liking' corresponds to the hedonic valence of stimuli. (See the chapter by Robinson, Robinson and Berridge and the chapter by Knutson and Karmarkar.) Regions involved in 'liking' can be further subdivided into those that are involved in generating pleasure (hedonic hotspots) and those that are involved in decoding pleasure, although some regions are involved in both. Typically, the former hedonic hotspots are inferred on the basis of a change in pleasure as a consequence of a brain manipulation such as a lesion or stimulation (Smith et al. 2010; Green, Pereira, and Aziz 2010), whereas the pleasure coding regions are inferred by using human neuroimaging to measure brain activity correlated to a pleasant stimulus (De Araujo, Kringelbach, Rolls, and

Hobden 2003; De Araujo, Kringelbach, Rolls, and McGlone 2003; Kringelbach et al. 2003).

'Liking' mechanisms

Only a few brain regions have been identified that are involved in generating increases in 'liking' reactions consequent to brain manipulation. These hedonic hotspots have been found in subcortical structures in the rodent brain. In the rodent brain they are typically only about a cubic millimeter in volume (figure 11.2D). In humans, hedonic hotspots have yet to be identified but would presumably be about a cubic centimeter in volume.

In rodents, hedonic hotspots have been identified in the nucleus accumbens shell, in the ventral pallidum, and in deep brain-stem regions, including the parabrachial nucleus in the pons (Peciña, Smith, and Berridge 2006). The pleasure-generating capacity of these hotspots has been revealed in part by studies in which microinjections of drugs stimulated neurochemical receptors on neurons within a hotspot, and caused a doubling or a tripling of the number of hedonic 'liking' reactions normally elicited by a pleasant sucrose taste (figure 11.2A) (Smith et al. 2010).

Hedonic hotspots are anatomically distributed but closely interact to form a functional integrated circuit. The circuit obeys control rules that are largely hierarchical and organized into brain levels. Top levels function together as a cooperative heterarchy, so that, for example, multiple unanimous "votes in favor," from simultaneously participating hotspots in the nucleus accumbens and in the ventral pallidum are required for opioid stimulation in either forebrain site to enhance 'liking' above normal (Smith and Berridge 2007).

In contrast, regions decoding pleasure are found mostly in the cortex. Hedonic evaluation of pleasure valence is anatomically distinguishable from precursor operations such as sensory computations, suggesting the existence of a hedonic cortex proper (figure 11.2B) (Kringelbach 2004). Hedonic cortex involves the orbitofrontal cortex, the insula, the medial prefrontal cortex, and the cingulate cortex (Amodio and Frith 2006; Kringelbach 2005; Craig 2002; Beckmann, Johansen-Berg, and Rushworth 2009). A wealth of human neuroimaging studies have shown the aforementioned brain regions to code for hedonic evaluations (including anticipation, appraisal, experience, and memory of pleasurable stimuli) and to have close anatomical links to subcortical hedonic hotspots.

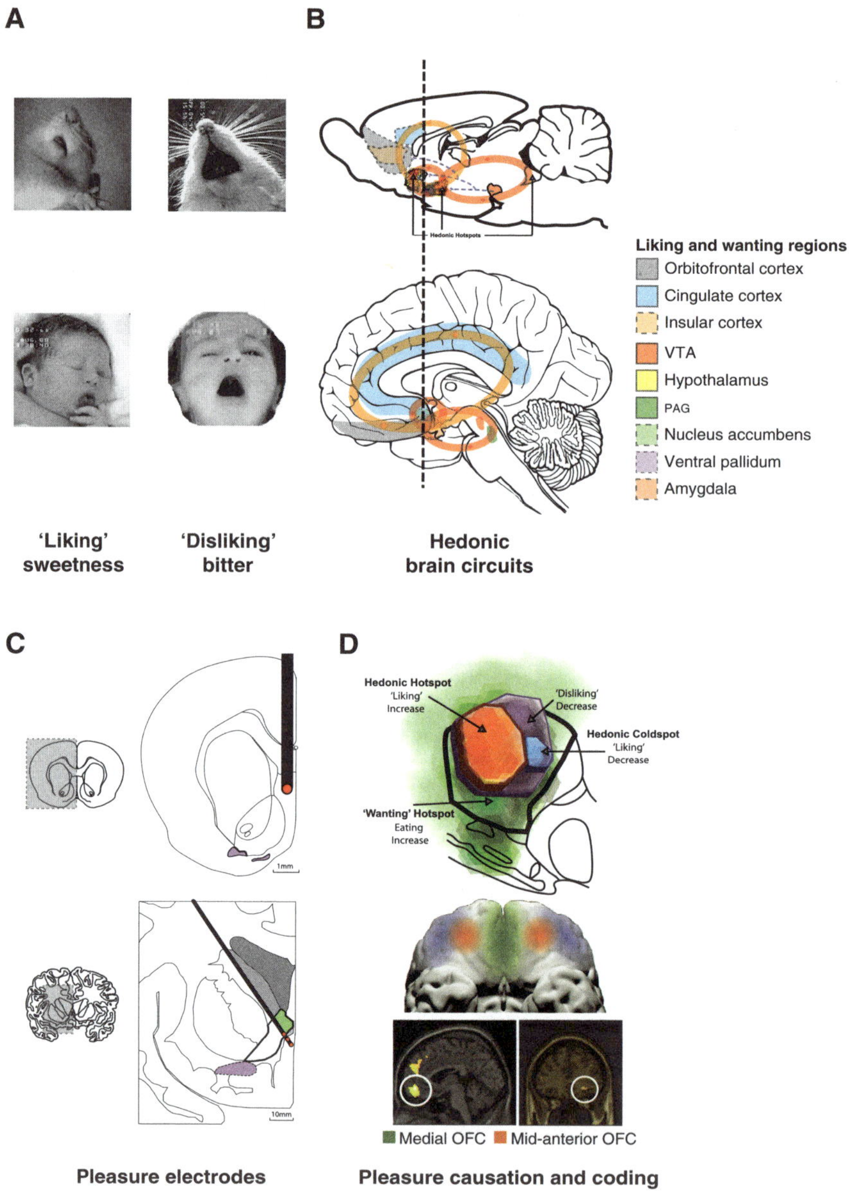

Figure 11.2

Hedonic brain circuitry. The schematic diagram shows the brain regions for causing and coding fundamental pleasures in rodents and humans. (A) Facial 'liking' and 'disliking' expressions elicited by sweet and bitter taste are similar in rodents and human infants. (B, D) Pleasure causation has been identified in rodents as arising

Figure 11.2
(Continued) from interlinked subcortical hedonic hotspots, such as in the nucleus accumbens and the ventral pallidum, where neural activation may increase 'liking' expressions to sweetness. Similar pleasure coding and incentive salience networks have also been identified in humans. (C) The so-called pleasure electrodes in rodents and humans are unlikely to have elicited true pleasure and may have elicited only incentive salience or 'wanting.' (D) The cortical localization of pleasure coding may reach an apex in various regions of the orbitofrontal cortex, which differentiate subjective pleasantness from valence processing of aspects of the same stimulus, such as a pleasant food.

Pleasure encoding may reach an apex of cortical localization in a mid-anterior subregion within the orbitofrontal cortex, where neuroimaging activity correlates strongly to subjective pleasantness ratings of food varieties (Kringelbach et al. 2003)—and to other pleasures, such as orgasm (Georgiadis et al. 2006), drugs (Völlm et al. 2004), chocolate (Small et al. 2001), and music (Blood and Zatorre 2001). (See also the chapter by Plassmann and Wager.) Most important, mid-anterior orbitofrontal activity tracks changes in subjective pleasure, such as a decline in palatability when the reward value of one food is reduced by eating it to satiety while the reward value of another food remains high (Kringelbach 2005; Kringelbach et al. 2003). The mid-anterior subregion of orbitofrontal cortex is thus a prime candidate for the coding of the subjective experience of pleasure (Kringelbach 2005).

Another coding site for positive hedonics in the orbitofrontal cortex is along its medial edge, which has activity related to the valence of positive and negative events (Kringelbach and Rolls 2004) whereas lateral portions have been suggested to code unpleasant events (O'Doherty et al. 2001), although the activity in the lateral part is more likely to reflect a signal to escape the situation rather than displeasure *per se* (Kringelbach and Rolls 2003, 2004; Iversen and Mishkin 1970; Hornak et al. 2004).

The medial-lateral hedonic gradient in the orbitofrontal cortex interacts with an abstraction-concreteness gradient in the posterior-anterior dimension, so that more complex or abstract reinforcers (such as monetary gain and loss—see O'Doherty et al. 2001) are represented more anteriorly in the orbitofrontal cortex than less complex sensory rewards, such as taste (Small et al. 2001). The medial region does not, however, appear to change its activity as the reinforcement is devalued, and so may not reflect the full dynamics of pleasure.

'Wanting' mechanisms

In addition to 'liking' mechanisms, pleasure is translated into motivational processes in part by activating a second component of reward termed 'wanting' or incentive salience, which makes stimuli attractive when attributed to them by mesolimbic brain systems (Berridge and Robinson 2003; Robinson et al., this volume). Incentive salience depends in particular on mesolimbic dopamine neurotransmission between select regions of the pleasure network, although other neurotransmitters and structures also are involved.

Incentive salience is not the same as hedonic impact or pleasure 'liking' (Berridge 2007). This is why an individual can 'want' a reward without necessarily 'liking' the same reward. Irrational 'wanting' without liking can occur in addiction via incentive sensitization of the mesolimbic dopamine system and connected structures (Robinson and Berridge 2003; Robinson, Robinson and Berridge, this volume). At the extreme, the addict may come to 'want' what is neither 'liked' nor expected to be liked, a dissociation that is possible because 'wanting' mechanisms are largely subcortical and separable from cortically mediated declarative expectation and conscious planning. This is one reason why addicts may compulsively 'want' to take drugs even if, at a more cognitive and conscious level, they do not want to do so.

Learning mechanisms

Learning, which is important for linking the 'wanting' and 'liking' components over time, usually, but not exclusively, follows consumption. (For more on the effects of learning and anticipation on consumption, see the chapter by Plassmann and Wager.)

Powerful learning mechanisms are involved when the consumption of a highly liked food causes an adverse effect such as an allergic reaction. Through learning one will be aware to avoid the liked substance in the future in order to avoid the negative outcome. Memories obtained through such Pavlovian learning remain stable until devaluation occurs or until new information becomes available (Zhang et al. 2009; Smith, Berridge, and Aldridge 2011).

'Wanting' is known to exhibit dynamic fluctuation corresponding to, for example, varying states of hunger, but it can also shift from a reward food stimulus to a conditioned stimulus or cue. This cue itself could become highly wanted and thus become a motivational magnet. The immense attractive properties of such a motivational magnet can be seen when it is hard to ignore the cue; for example, rats will try to consume an inedible cue that predicts the arrival of food instead of the food itself (Berridge 2012; Robinson et al., this volume).

'Wanting' and 'liking' are difficult to tease apart in behavioral studies, and there is an ongoing debate about how to best dissociate them (Havermans 2012). Some of the best evidence comes from Berridge (2012), who has demonstrated a phenomenon he calls "persistent 'miswanting.'" In this case, wanting persists even when a food stimulus is disliked. Such wanting is seen in drug addicts after bad drug experiences. Additionally, 'wanting' and 'liking' can be successfully dissociated by various pharmacological manipulations, for example through changing dopamine levels in select brain regions (Smith, Berridge, and Aldridge 2011).

We have introduced a behavioral 'wanting'-'liking' paradigm whereby human participants indicate their subjective liking of a stimulus and also indicate how much effort they are willing to put in to prolong or shorten exposure to the stimulus (Parsons et al. 2011). This paradigm has been used to demonstrate that even though men and women differ in their liking ratings of baby faces, they have similar viewing times (which in the task is a measure of their wanting by exerted effort to influence viewing times).

In humans, neuroimaging offers a way to investigate the partly separable liking, wanting, and learning components in the human brain with spatiotemporal monitoring of activity patterns in the different cortical regions regulating each of these components.

Learning is an important component of eating-related decision making, in which the brain must compare and evaluate the predicted reward values of various behaviors. This processing can be complex, as the estimations will vary in quality depending on the sampling rate of the behavior and the variance of reward distributions. It is difficult to provide a reliable estimate of the reward value of a food that appears to be highly desirable and is high in nutritional value but is only rarely available and varies significantly in quality.

This raises a classic problem in animal learning of how to optimize behavior such that the amount of exploration is balanced with the amount of exploitation, where exploration is the time spent sampling the outcome of different behaviors and exploitation is the time spent performing existing behaviors with known reward values.

Ultimately, pleasure can be thought of as an important tool for controlling this balancing act between exploitation and exploration. As was mentioned above, the evidence from neuroimaging studies has linked regions of the human brain—particularly the orbitofrontal cortex—to various aspects of eating, and especially to the representation of the subjective pleasantness of foods (Kringelbach 2004).

Brain Networks for Resource Allocation

Overall, the data gathered from animal and human studies support the existence of reward networks with important subcomponents of wanting, liking, and learning. Though it is tempting to work out the circuitry of brain regions in these networks in isolation, it is pertinent to take a more global perspective on how to interpret the changes found in brain activity.

In particular, it is important to integrate these reward networks with activity in wide distributed brain networks, often called resting-state networks. We have previously speculated that activity in one of these, the so-called default mode network (Gusnard and Raichle 2001; Raichle et al. 2001), is closely linked to reward processing and may have an important role in shaping our overall well-being (Kringelbach and Berridge 2009).

The last few years have seen a shift in the focus of neuroimaging from studying brain activity caused by external stimuli to studying intrinsic brain activity (Biswal et al. 2010). This change has been brought about by the realization that, although the vast majority of neuroimaging studies have been devoted to studying task-related changes in brain activity, the additional energy associated with this activity is remarkable low, often less than 5 percent (Raichle and Mintun 2006). Instead, the majority of the brain's energy consumption is devoted to intrinsic brain activity.

When such intrinsic brain activity was mapped during rest periods (when participants were not performing the task) in cognitive studies, researchers found a network of brain regions with remarkably high rates of change in such metabolic markers as cerebral blood flow, oxygen extraction, and blood oxygen level dependent fMRI (Lou et al. 1999). This network of brain regions was termed the default mode network. Its main regions showed the largest deactivations or reductions in activity while participants were performing the extrinsic cognitive tasks (Raichle et al. 2001; Gusnard and Raichle 2001).

Subsequently, sophisticated independent component analyses of resting-state patterns have identified at least seven networks that remain coherent over several minutes (Damoiseaux et al. 2006). On the basis of their brain components, these networks have been classified as follows:

primary input-output networks (including sensorimotor, visual, and auditory regions)

higher integrative networks (including attention, language, default mode, and executive regions) (Beckmann et al. 2005)

cortico-subcortical networks (including the thalamus, the basal ganglia, and the cerebellum) (Fox and Raichle 2007).

Regions of the default mode network will remain tightly coherent but tend to show negative correlations with task-positive regions in the other networks.

The intrinsic activity of the human brain must be closely related to the large-scale anatomical connectivity between brain regions. Diffusion spectrum imaging and graph theory have revealed that the human brain exhibits a special kind of topology known as small-world architecture (Watts and Strogatz 1998), which is characterized by high levels of local clustering among neighboring nodes (Bullmore and Sporns 2009; Hagmann et al. 2007). Some nodes have higher connectivity than others and are called hubs (He et al. 2009). The default mode network mostly consists of hubs, and in particular the precuneus and posterior cingulate cortex have been proposed to form the structural core (Hagmann et al. 2008).

Understanding the workings of these resting-state networks is necessary in order to understand the fundamentals of how our brains work, and in particular the role of memory-dependent self-reference in binding these networks together. Lou, Joensson, and Kringelbach (2011) have proposed the existence of a common paralimbic network that serves to regulate and balance the dynamic resource allocation needed to ensure survival. This process, guided by processes linked to awareness, attention, and emotion, supports memory-dependent self-reference, which in narrative self-consciousness is extended into adjacent neocortical regions.

The inputs from the senses of vision, hearing, taste, smell, and touch (which are linked to survival-related rewards such as food and sex) and their subsequent evaluation have the potential to temporarily shift the focus of the brain networks to allow for efficient brain processing and control over behaviors (Berridge and Kringelbach 2008). The paralimbic network helps to ensure that the processing remains balanced over longer time periods across many reward cycles.

Implications for Consumption

Consumption is linked not only to the consummatory phase of the pleasure cycle but to all of that cycle's various phases. Disorders of consummatory behavior can arise from unbalancing of the neural processing underlying the pleasure cycle. Unbalancing of neural processing, in turn, leads to unbalanced resource allocation for the resting-state networks of the brain, which is found in many brain and neuropsychiatric disorders. For example, resting-state networks have been found to undergo changes in Alzheimer's Disease, in Parkinson's Disease, and in depression and some other affective disorders (Greicius 2008; Broyd et al. 2009; van Eimeren et al. 2009).

Anhedonia, the lack of pleasure, is one of the most important symptoms of disorders of consummatory behavior. Kringelbach, Green, and Aziz (2011) and Kringelbach and Berridge (2009) have proposed that anhedonia can be viewed as an acute and sometimes chronic unbalancing of the brain networks supporting the pleasure cycle.

Although anhedonia can be expressed differently across individual patients, and sometimes even across time within the same patient, as in bipolar disorder (Nelson et al. 2009), there are clear differences between the imbalances in affective and those in addictive disorders.

In the normal brain, 'wanting,' 'liking,' and learning are balanced over time. A breakdown of the balancing of these processes can lead to various expressions of anhedonia. An imbalance can lead to a reduced ability to pursue and experience pleasure, as seen in the affective disorders. However, this progressive decrease in 'wanting' and 'liking' is markedly different from the imbalance that leads to addictive and impulse-control disorders, where 'wanting' to take drugs, for example, grows over time independently of 'liking' for drugs, as suggested by the incentive-sensitization model of addiction (Robinson and Berridge 1993; Robinson, Robinson, and Berridge, this volume).

Conclusion

This chapter has put forward the hypothesis that pleasure helps to optimize the survival-related decision making involved in allocating the brain's resources. We have made important progress in understanding the underlying neural processing of reward. In particular, we have begun to investigate mechanisms underlying the full pleasure cycle, and in particular the brain processes that initiate, sustain, and terminate the various phases of wanting, liking, and satiety.

Many brain disorders arise from the unbalancing of these reward mechanisms, and this imbalance can, in turn, have repercussions for the resource allocation among more general resting-state networks. The growing understanding of partly dissociable mechanisms of 'wanting' and 'liking' has led to a better understanding of differences in anhedonia found in affective versus addictive disorders. In affective disorders, such as monopolar depression, anhedonia is usually manifested in decreases in both wanting and liking, whereas addictive disorders often lead to an increase in wanting with a simultaneous decrease in liking. This new understanding may, in time, lead to new and more precisely targeted treatments. Similarly, a fuller understanding of how 'wanting' processes can act as motivational magnets for wanted rewards may also benefit the treatment of patients with consummatory behavior problems.

More generally, however, this new understanding of pleasure may, in the fullness of time, help people to achieve more balanced states of well-being. Hedonic happiness could be conceived of as 'liking' without 'wanting'—that is, a state of pleasure without disruptive desires, a state of contentment (Kringelbach and Berridge 2009).

At the same time, balanced processing of 'wanting' and 'liking' can facilitate engagement with the world. What is important is to avoid too much 'wanting,' because it can readily spiral into maladaptive consummatory patterns, such as those found in addiction, which can provide a direct route to great unhappiness. Maximization of any of the underlying processes at the expense of the others leads to unbalanced states that are unsustainable. (See the chapter by Whybrow and the chapter by Frank.) The way to achieve positive well-being would seem to be to find the best way to balance the many demands on our brain so that we can use our time to engage meaningfully with the fullness of what life has to offer.

Acknowledgments

This research was supported by the TrygFonden Charitable Foundation. I thank Kent Berridge for our many wonderful discussions on the nature of pleasure. Some of the ideas expressed in this chapter have previously been presented in our joint papers.

References

Amodio, D. M., and Frith, C. D. 2006. Meeting of minds: The medial frontal cortex and social cognition. *Nature Reviews Neuroscience* 7 (4): 268–277.

Aragona, B. J., Liu, Y., Yu, Y. J., Curtis, J. T., Detwiler, J. M., Insel, T. R., et al. 2006. Nucleus accumbens dopamine differentially mediates the formation and maintenance of monogamous pair bonds. *Nature Neuroscience* 9 (1): 133–139.

Beckmann, C. F., DeLuca, M., Devlin, J. T., and Smith, S. M. 2005. Investigations into resting-state connectivity using independent component analysis. *Philosophical Transactions of the Royal Society B* 360: 1001–1013.

Beckmann, M., Johansen-Berg, H., and Rushworth, M. F. 2009. Connectivity-based parcellation of human cingulate cortex and its relation to functional specialization. *Journal of Neuroscience* 29 (4): 1175–1190.

Berridge, K. C. 1996. Food reward: Brain substrates of wanting and liking. *Neuroscience and Biobehavioral Reviews* 20 (1): 1–25.

Berridge, K. C. 2007. The debate over dopamine's role in reward: The case for incentive salience. *Psychopharmacology* 191 (3): 391–431.

Berridge, K. C. 2012. From prediction error to incentive salience: Mesolimbic computation of reward motivation. *European Journal of Neuroscience* 35: 1124–1143.

Berridge, K. C., and Kringelbach, M. L. 2008. Affective neuroscience of pleasure: Reward in humans and animals. *Psychopharmacology* 199: 457–480.

Berridge, K. C., and Robinson, T. E. 2003. Parsing reward. *Trends in Neurosciences* 26 (9): 507–513.

Biswal, B. B., Mennes, M., Zuo, X. N., Gohel, S., Kelly, C., Smith, S. M., et al. 2010. Toward discovery science of human brain function. *Proceedings of the National Academy of Sciences* 107 (10): 4734–4739.

Blood, A. J., and Zatorre, R. J. 2001. Intensely pleasurable responses to music correlate with activity in brain regions implicated in reward and emotion. *Proceedings of the National Academy of Sciences* 98 (20): 11818–11823.

Britton, J. C., Phan, K. L., Taylor, S. F., Welsh, R. C., Berridge, K. C., and Liberzon, I. 2006. Neural correlates of social and nonsocial emotions: An fMRI study. *NeuroImage* 31 (1): 397–409.

Broyd, S. J., Demanuele, C., Debener, S., Helps, S. K., James, C. J., and Sonuga-Barke, E. J. 2009. Default-mode brain dysfunction in mental disorders: A systematic review. *Neuroscience and Biobehavioral Reviews* 33 (3): 279–296.

Bullmore, E., and Sporns, O. 2009. Complex brain networks: Graph theoretical analysis of structural and functional systems. *Nature Reviews Neuroscience* 10 (3): 186–198.

Cardinal, R. N., Parkinson, J. A., Hall, J., and Everitt, B. J. 2002. Emotion and motivation: The role of the amygdala, ventral striatum, and prefrontal cortex. *Neuroscience and Biobehavioral Reviews* 26 (3): 321–352.

Craig, A. D. 2002. Opinion: How do you feel? Interoception: The sense of the physiological condition of the body. *Nature Reviews Neuroscience* 3 (8): 655–666.

Damoiseaux, J. S., Rombouts, S. A. R. B., Barkhof, F., Scheltens, P., Stam, C. J., Smith, S. M., et al. 2006. Consistent resting-state networks across healthy subjects. *Proceedings of the National Academy of Sciences* 103: 13848–13853.

Darwin, C. 1872. *The Expression of the Emotions in Man and Animals*, third edition. University of Chicago Press.

De Araujo, I. E. T., Kringelbach, M. L., Rolls, E. T., and Hobden, P. 2003. The representation of umami taste in the human brain. *Journal of Neurophysiology* 90 (1): 313–319.

De Araujo, I. E. T., Kringelbach, M. L., Rolls, E. T., and McGlone, F. 2003. Human cortical responses to water in the mouth, and the effects of thirst. *Journal of Neurophysiology* 90 (3): 1865–1876.

Everitt, B. J., Belin, D., Economidou, D., Pelloux, Y., Dalley, J. W., and Robbins, T. W. 2008. Neural mechanisms underlying the vulnerability to develop compulsive drug-seeking habits and addiction. *Philosophical Transactions of the Royal Society B* 363 (1507): 3125–3135.

Everitt, B. J., and Robbins, T. W. 2005. Neural systems of reinforcement for drug addiction: From actions to habits to compulsion. *Nature Neuroscience* 8 (11): 1481–1489.

Fox, M. D., and Raichle, M. E. 2007. Spontaneous fluctuations in brain activity observed with functional magnetic resonance imaging. *Nature Reviews Neuroscience* 8: 700–711.

Frijda, N. 2010. On the nature and function of pleasure. In *Pleasures of the Brain*, ed. M. Kringelbach and K. Berridge. Oxford University Press.

Friston, K., and Kiebel, S. 2009. Predictive coding under the free-energy principle. *Philosophical Transactions of the Royal Society B* 364 (1521): 1211–1221.

Frith, U., and Frith, C. 2010. The social brain: Allowing humans to boldly go where no other species has been. *Philosophical Transactions of the Royal Society B* 365 (1537): 165–176.

Georgiadis, J. R., Kortekaas, R., Kuipers, R., Nieuwenburg, A., Pruim, J., Reinders, A. A., et al. 2006. Regional cerebral blood flow changes associated with clitorally induced orgasm in healthy women. *European Journal of Neuroscience* 24 (11): 3305–3316.

Georgiadis, J. R., and Kringelbach, M. L. 2012. The human sexual response cycle: Brain imaging evidence linking sex to other pleasures. *Progress in Neurobiology* 98 (1): 49–81.

Green, A. L., Pereira, E. A., and Aziz, T. Z. 2010. Deep brain stimulation and pleasure. In *Pleasures of the Brain*, ed. M. Kringelbach and K. Berridge. Oxford University Press.

Greicius, M. 2008. Resting-state functional connectivity in neuropsychiatric disorders. *Current Opinion in Neurology* 21 (4): 424–430.

Gusnard, D. A., and Raichle, M. E. 2001. Searching for a baseline: Functional imaging and the resting human brain. *Nature Reviews Neuroscience* 2 (10): 685–694.

Hagmann, P., Cammoun, L., Gigandet, X., Meuli, R., Honey, C. J., Wedeen, V. J., et al. 2008. Mapping the structural core of human cerebral cortex. *PLOS Biology* 6 (7): e159.

Hagmann, P., Kurant, M., Gigandet, X., Thiran, P., Wedeen, V. J., Meuli, R., et al. 2007. Mapping human whole-brain structural networks with diffusion MRI. *PLOS ONE* 2 (7): e597.

Havermans, R. C. 2012. How to tell where 'liking' ends and 'wanting' begins. *Appetite* 58 (1): 252–255.

He, Y., Wang, J., Wang, L., Chen, Z. J., Yan, C., Yang, H., et al. 2009. Uncovering intrinsic modular organization of spontaneous brain activity in humans. *PLOS ONE* 4 (4): e5226.

Hornak, J., O'Doherty, J., Bramham, J., Rolls, E. T., Morris, R. G., Bullock, P. R., et al. 2004. Reward-related reversal learning after surgical excisions in orbitofrontal and dorsolateral prefrontal cortex in humans. *Journal of Cognitive Neuroscience* 16 (3): 463–478.

Iversen, S. D., and Mishkin, M. 1970. Perseverative interference in monkeys following selective lesions of the inferior prefrontal convexity. *Experimental Brain Research* 11: 376–386.

Kelley, A. E., and Berridge, K. C. 2002. The neuroscience of natural rewards: Relevance to addictive drugs. *Journal of Neuroscience* 22 (9): 3306–3311.

King-Casas, B., Tomlin, D., Anen, C., Camerer, C. F., Quartz, S. R., and Montague, P. R. 2005. Getting to know you: reputation and trust in a two-person economic exchange. *Science* 308 (5718): 78–83.

Koob, G. F., and Volkow, N. D. 2010. Neurocircuitry of addiction. *Neuropsychopharmacology* 35 (1): 217–238.

Kringelbach, M. L. 2004. Food for thought: Hedonic experience beyond homeostasis in the human brain. *Neuroscience* 126: 807–819.

Kringelbach, M. L. 2005. The orbitofrontal cortex: Linking reward to hedonic experience. *Nature Reviews Neuroscience* 6 (9): 691–702.

Kringelbach, M. L. 2010. The hedonic brain: A functional neuroanatomy of human pleasure. In *Pleasures of the Brain*, ed. M. Kringelbach and K. Berridge. Oxford University Press.

Kringelbach, M. L., and Berridge, K. C. 2009. Towards a functional neuroanatomy of pleasure and happiness. *Trends in Cognitive Sciences* 13 (11): 479–487.

Kringelbach, M. L., and Berridge, K. C. 2010. *Pleasures of the Brain*. Oxford University Press.

Kringelbach, M. L., Green, A. L., and Aziz, T. Z. 2011. Balancing the brain: Resting state networks and deep brain stimulation. *Frontiers in Integrative Neuroscience* 5: 8.

Kringelbach, M. L., Lehtonen, A., Squire, S., Harvey, A. G., Craske, M. G., Holliday, I. E., Green, A. L., Aziz, T. Z., Hansen, P. C., Cornelissen, P. L., and Stein, A. 2008. A specific and rapid neural signature for parental instinct. *PLoS ONE* 3 (2): e1664.

Kringelbach, M. L., O'Doherty, J., Rolls, E. T., and Andrews, C. 2003. Activation of the human orbitofrontal cortex to a liquid food stimulus is correlated with its subjective pleasantness. *Cerebral Cortex* 13 (10): 1064–1071.

Kringelbach, M. L., and Rolls, E. T. 2003. Neural correlates of rapid context-dependent reversal learning in a simple model of human social interaction. *NeuroImage* 20 (2): 1371–1383.

Kringelbach, M. L., and Rolls, E. T. 2004. The functional neuroanatomy of the human orbitofrontal cortex: Evidence from neuroimaging and neuropsychology. *Progress in Neurobiology* 72 (5): 341–372.

Kringelbach, M. L., Stein, A., and van Hartevelt, T. J. 2012. The functional human neuroanatomy of food pleasure cycles. *Physiology and Behavior* 106 (3): 307–316.

Leknes, S., and Tracey, I. 2008. A common neurobiology for pain and pleasure. *Nature Reviews Neuroscience* 9 (4): 314–320.

Leknes, S., and Tracey, I. 2010. Pleasure and pain: masters of mankind. In *Pleasures of the Brain*, ed. M. Kringelbach and K. Berridge. Oxford University Press.

Lorenz, K. 1943. Die angeborenen Formen möglicher Erfahrung. *Zeitschrift für Tierpsychologie* 5: 235–519.

Lou, H. C., Joensson, M., and Kringelbach, M. L. 2011. Yoga lessons for consciousness research: A paralimbic network balancing brain resource allocation. *Frontiers in Psychology* 2: 366.

Lou, H. C., Kjaer, T. W., Friberg, L., Wildschiodtz, G., Holm, S., and Nowak, M. 1999. A 15O-H2O PET study of meditation and the resting state of normal consciousness. *Human Brain Mapping* 7 (2): 98–105.

Nelson, S. E., Gebauer, L., LaBrie, R. A., and Shaffer, H. J. 2009. Gambling problem symptom patterns and stability across individual and timeframe. *Psychology of Addictive Behaviors* 23 (3): 523–533.

O'Doherty, J., Kringelbach, M. L., Rolls, E. T., Hornak, J., and Andrews, C. 2001. Abstract reward and punishment representations in the human orbitofrontal cortex. *Nature Neuroscience* 4 (1): 95–102.

Panksepp, J. 1999. *Affective Neuroscience*. Oxford University Press.

Parsons, C. E., Young, K. S., Murray, L., Stein, A., and Kringelbach, M. L. 2010. The functional neuroanatomy of the evolving parent-infant relationship. *Progress in Neurobiology* 91: 220–241.

Parsons, C. E., Young, K. S., Kumari, N., Stein, A., and Kringelbach, M. L. 2011. The motivational salience of infant faces is similar for men and women. *PLOS ONE* 6 (5): e20632.

Peciña, S., Smith, K. S., and Berridge, K. C. 2006. Hedonic hot spots in the brain. *Neuroscientist* 12 (6): 500–511.

Raichle, M. E., MacLeod, A. M., Snyder, A. Z., Powers, W. J., Gusnard, D. A., and Shulman, G. L. 2001. A default mode of brain function. *Proceedings of the National Academy of Sciences* 98 (2): 676–682.

Raichle, M. E., and Mintun, M. A. 2006. Brain work and brain imaging. *Annual Review of Neuroscience* 29: 449–476.

Robinson, T. E., and Berridge, K. C. 1993. The neural basis of drug craving: An incentive-sensitization theory of addiction. *Brain Research Reviews* 18 (3): 247–291.

Robinson, T. E., and Berridge, K. C. 2003. Addiction. *Annual Review of Psychology* 54: 25–53.

Ryle, G. 1954. Pleasure. *Proceedings of the Aristotelian Society* 28: 135–146.

Salimpoor, V. N., Benovoy, M., Larcher, K., Dagher, A., and Zatorre, R. J. 2011. Anatomically distinct dopamine release during anticipation and experience of peak emotion to music. *Nature Neuroscience* 14 (2): 257–262.

Skov, M. 2010. The pleasures of art. In *Pleasures of the Brain*, ed. M. Kringelbach and K. Berridge. Oxford University Press.

Small, D. M., Zatorre, R. J., Dagher, A., Evans, A. C., and Jones-Gotman, M. 2001. Changes in brain activity related to eating chocolate: From pleasure to aversion. *Brain* 124 (9): 1720–1733.

Smith, K. S., and Berridge, K. C. 2007. Opioid limbic circuit for reward: Interaction between hedonic hotspots of nucleus accumbens and ventral pallidum. *Journal of Neuroscience* 27 (7): 1594–1605.

Smith, K. S., Berridge, K. C., and Aldridge, J. W. 2011. Disentangling pleasure from incentive salience and learning signals in brain reward circuitry. *Proceedings of the National Academy of Sciences* 108 (27): E255–E264.

Smith, K. S., Mahler, S. V., Pecina, S., and Berridge, K. C. 2010. Hedonic hotspots: generating sensory pleasure in the brain. In *Pleasures of the Brain*, ed. M. Kringelbach and K. Berridge. Oxford University Press.

Stein, A., Gath, D. H., Bucher, J., Bond, A., Day, A., and Cooper, P. J. 1991. The relationship between post-natal depression and mother-child interaction. *British Journal of Psychiatry* 158: 46–52.

van Eimeren, T., Monchi, O., Ballanger, B., and Strafella, A. P. 2009. Dysfunction of the default mode network in Parkinson disease: A functional magnetic resonance imaging study. *Archives of Neurology* 66 (7): 877–883.

Völlm, B. A., de Araujo, I. E. T., Cowen, P. J., Rolls, E. T., Kringelbach, M. L., Smith, K. A., et al. 2004. Methamphetamine activates reward circuitry in drug naïve human subjects. *Neuropsychopharmacology* 29 (9): 1715–1722.

Vuust, P., and Kringelbach, M. L. 2010. The pleasure of music. In *Pleasures of the Brain*, ed. M. Kringelbach and K. Berridge. Oxford University Press.

Watson, K. K., Shepherd, S. V., and Platt, M. L. 2010. Neuroethology of pleasure. In *Pleasures of the Brain*, ed. M. Kringelbach and K. Berridge. Oxford University Press.

Watts, D. J., and Strogatz, S. H. 1998. Collective dynamics of "small-world" networks. *Nature* 393 (6684): 440–442.

Zhang, J., Berridge, K. C., Tindell, A. J., Smith, K. S., and Aldridge, J. W. 2009. A neural computational model of incentive salience. *PLOS Computational Biology* 5 (7): e1000437.

12 How Expectancies Shape Consumption Experiences

Hilke Plassmann and Tor D. Wager

The act of consumption is a primal and important one, essential for the survival of virtually all species. However, human consumption differs from that of other species in many ways. We consume foods, goods, and experiences. Our consumption goes far beyond products that satisfy basic survival needs, and includes the satisfaction of such higher-order needs as the needs to think, believe, and belong (Cacioppo and Petty 1982; Maslow 1959). Multidisciplinary evidence suggests that important factors influencing the value or enjoyment derived from consumption are also based on psychological associations and cognitive concepts (for example, brand images, beliefs about the quality or efficacy of products and treatments, and nutritional information on food packaging) that can occur independent of, and in extreme cases can even override, mere "physical consumption" (Ariely and Norton 2009).

In this chapter, we focus on one important driver of the effects of cognitive concepts on consumption: expectancies. Expectancies are beliefs and predictions about future feelings, events, or outcomes. Whereas some researchers reserve the term *expectancies* for conscious, reportable experiences, here we use it in a more general sense, and include predictive brain processes that may or may not be reportable. Because predicting future states is a fundamental function of the nervous system, expectancies can play many roles. Among their best-known functions are preparatory processes and learning. For example, in what may be the most famous psychology experiment in history, the Russian physiologist Ivan Pavlov showed that after learning dogs began to salivate upon hearing a bell that predicted food delivery. The prediction and anticipation of food constitutes a kind of expectancy, likely with both conscious and unconscious aspects. More recently, expectancies have been quantitatively modeled in the form of expected value signals that drive learning. Along those lines, Schultz, Dayan, and Montague (1997) showed that after learning, dopaminergic neurons fire not when monkeys are receiving a food reward, but when they see or hear a signal that *predicts* receiving the food reward. Conditioning processes such as these lead to multiple kinds of predictions that appear to be implemented in different brain circuits. How diverse "expectancy" signals are and how conscious, reportable "expectancies" are qualitatively different from other kinds of predictions are open questions in the field. Here we are agnostic on these issues, and we focus mainly on the effects of expectancies on hedonic experience and choice. (Neural anticipation during consumption decisions is also discussed in the chapter by Knutson and Karmarkar, in the chapter by Kringelbach, and in the chapter by Whybrow.)

Human expectancies can be based on a variety of learned cognitive concepts and beliefs. For example, your decision to consume a rewarding food item, such as piece of chocolate, probably would depend on cognitions of several kinds, including the memory of what you ate before, what other options are available, your estimate of the chocolate's quality, how good you anticipate it will taste, how unhealthy you think it is, and what other people would think of you if you were to eat a chocolate of this brand rather than one of a lower-priced brand. For a nonhuman animal, however, the decision to consume a food reward would be a "no-brainer"—it would presumably be based largely on the predicted appetitive value of the chocolate, moderated by hunger and food-specific satiety signals. (See the chapter by Preston and Vickers and the chapter by Lea.)

From an economic perspective, the effect of expectancies on immediate valuation can be traced back to Bentham's concept of utility, which suggests that anticipation, like consumption itself, is an important source of pleasure and pain since it simulates the consumption experience (Kahneman, Wakker, and Sarin 1997; Loewenstein 1987). Indeed, our ability to construct "what if" scenarios and our ability to envision the future have received multidisciplinary attention (Bar 2009; Barrett 2006; Moulton and Kosslyn 2009; Roy, Shohamy, and Wager 2012; Schacter, Addis, and Buckner 2007). The chocolate example shows that expectancies are linked to multiple types of prior experiences, some linked to learning and conditioning (Bar 2011) and others to the context-dependent meaning of the stimulus (Roy et al. 2012), which depends on how we conceptualize the chocolate (Barrett 2006)—for example, perhaps you remember that a certain kind of chocolate tasted very good the last time you had it, or you remember that your spouse liked it and told you about it, but you also remember reading in a medical journal that chocolate in general is unhealthy.

Sometimes we even create false memories of our past consumption experiences. For example, falsely telling you that the last time you ate a certain kind of chocolate you felt sick afterward, or showing you commercials in which people report being overly happy after eating the chocolate, can change your memory and may indeed create the expectation that you will feel sick or happy after eating this chocolate (Braun, Ellis, and Loftus 2002; Laney, Morris, Bernstein, Wakefield, and Loftus 2008). In other words, expectancies can be based on recollection of or association with our own real or false prior consumption experiences or those of others. If we haven't had any previous experiences with a consumable good, generalizations of learned cue-to-value associations can serve as the basis for expectancies. In such cases, expectancies are based on factors such as the price of the good (Plassmann, O'Doherty, Shiv, and Rangel 2008; Shiv, Carmon, and Ariely 2005; Waber, Shiv, Carmon, and Ariely 2008), the information on the packaging (Chandon and Wansink 2007; L. Lee, Frederick, and Ariely 2006; W.-C. J. Lee, Shimizu, Kniffin, and Wansink 2013), and information provided by a salesperson, a medical doctor, or some other trusted authority.

Thus, cognitive concepts and learned values lead to expectancies that, in turn, influence consumption and the value derived from it (Ariely and Norton 2009; Berdik 2012). In this chapter, we outline the effect that expectations have on behavioral aspects of consumption. We then review the neuropsychological underpinnings of these effects. We conclude by proposing an interdisciplinary model of expectancy effects and highlighting open questions for future research.

Expectations and Consumption Behavior

A large body of literature in consumer psychology has been dedicated to studying how people's expectancies shape consumption experiences with the physical properties of consumed goods kept constant. In one study, some consumers were informed about the brand of the beer they were consuming and some were not. Those who had the brand information reported to like the taste of their favorite brand the most, whereas those who did not liked the tastes of all beers about the same (Allison and Uhl 1964). This paper was among the first to show that advertising and branding can create expectations in a consumer's mind that can alter the enjoyment of physical consumption. Converging evidence for this idea has been shown in follow-up studies involving both products and services (Boulding, Kalra, Staelin, and Zeithaml 1993; Kopalle and Lehmann 2001; L. Lee et al. 2006; Raghunathan, Walker Naylor, and Hoyer 2006; Steenhuis et al. 2010; Wansink and Chandon 2006; Wilcox, Roggeveen, and Grewal 2011). In fact, evidence of how expectations shape consumption has been found in a variety of domains. Expectancies about how funny a cartoon will be changed the reported enjoyment of viewing the cartoon (Wilson, Lisle, Kraft, and Wetzel 1989), and the reported enjoyment of a film was influenced by expectations about its quality (Klaaren, Hodges, and Wilson 1994). In these cases, the higher the expectation of enjoyment, the more participants enjoyed the experience. Stereotypes also influence how people are perceived (Darley and Gross 1983; Klein and Snyder 2003). For example, strategically setting low expectations so as to later claim that a candidate for political office did better in a televised debate than had been expected actually results in lower ratings of the performance (Norton and Goethals 2004). In addition, ritualistic behavior potentiates the consumption of indulgent and healthy foods, and enhances their enjoyment (Vohs, Wang, Gino, and Norton 2013), and information about the calorie count of a milkshake alters reported fullness and satiation after consumption of identical milkshakes (Brunstrom, Brown, Hinton, Rogers, and Fay 2011; Brunstrom and Rogers 2009).

Expectancies also have strong influences on pain, providing an aversive counterpart to consumption experiences (e.g., Atlas and Wager 2012; Atlas, Bolger, Lindquist, and Wager 2010; Colloca and Benedetti 2005; Geuter, Eippert, Attar, and Bchel 2013). In one study, information about the price of a painkiller affected ratings of pain elicited by mild electric shocks (Waber et al. 2008). A "discounted" analgesic cream was reported to be less effective than an expensive one, even though the creams were identical. This effect was recently replicated by Geuter et al. (2013), who also showed related reductions in "pain-processing" centers in the brain with the expensive cream.

Interestingly, expectancy effects go beyond reported enjoyment and perception of the consumption experience. Expectations can also change subsequent behavior. Consumers who thought they were drinking a wine from California reported greater enjoyment of the wine than consumers who thought they were drinking a wine from North Dakota; in addition, they consumed more wine and more food (Wansink, Payne, and North 2007). In a study of dieters, calling a food by a "healthy" name (i.e., "salad" vs. "pasta") increased the reported tastiness of the food and the quantity consumed. This effect was not found for non-dieters (Irmak, Vallen, and Robinson 2011). It is possible that in these studies the change in consumption was driven by the change in perceived tastiness or liking of the food. A study by Morewedge et al. (2010), however, showed that people who had imagined eating cheese cubes many times subsequently consumed fewer cubes than did people who had imagined eating the cubes fewer times (Morewedge, Huh, and Vosgerau 2010). Morewedge et al. (2010) suggest that such effects are due to the fact that merely expecting or imagining eating a food results in hedonic satiation to this specific food, decreasing the "wanting" but not the liking of the food item. (For a discussion of this dissociation and its mechanisms in animal models, see the chapter by Robinson, Robinson, and Berridge.)

Other studies have demonstrated effects of expectations on cognitive performance, arousal, and physiological responses. For example, a study by Shiv et al. (2005) showed that expectations about the efficacy of an energy drink, as manipulated by its price tag, influences both the consumption experience and subsequent performance in mental tasks. In the study by Shiv et al., participants who had purchased the drink at a discounted price subsequently performed more poorly on a puzzle-solving task than participants who had purchased the drink at full price.

A growing literature suggests that placebo treatments can influence physiological responses as well (Meissner et al. 2011). In studies of placebo caffeine, participants' beliefs that they had consumed caffeine were found to increase motor performance and heart rate, although the subjects had not in fact consumed caffeine (Kirsch and Sapirstein 1998). Similarly, placebo treatment supported by conditioning has been shown to reduce autonomic responses to painful stimuli (Nakamura et al. 2012). As in other domains discussed here, it is an open question whether physiological effects can be elicited purely by "conceptual" information, or whether they require cues conditioned through experience. For example, Flaten and Blumenthal (1999) found that consumption of decaffeinated coffee increased skin conductance and arousal and reduced heart rate relative to consumption of orange juice. In a subsequent study (Flaten et al. 2004), however, information that participants were receiving either a stimulant or a relaxant (in separate conditions) had no effects on caffeine-induced physiological arousal. A related field study showed that hotel room attendants whose daily work was framed as physical exercise, in conformity with the Surgeon General's recommendations for an active lifestyle, perceived themselves to be getting significantly more exercise than before (Crum and Langer 2007). As a result, they showed a decrease in weight, blood pressure, body fat, waist-to-hip ratio, and body-mass index relative to a control group. In another study, participants who thought they had consumed a high-calorie milkshake rather than a low-calorie one showed elevated levels of the satiety-related gut peptide ghrelin (Crum, Corbin, Brownell, and Salovey 2011). Those who had consumed a milkshake labeled "high-calorie" rather than an identical milkshake labeled "low-calorie" showed both a steeper anticipatory increase in ghrelin and a steeper post-consumption decrease in ghrelin. No effect on hunger ratings was found. These effects are consistent with the notion that conditioned cues can trigger brain processes that regulate metabolism (Woods and Ramsay 2000), but go beyond this to suggest that conceptual information can activate metabolic regulatory circuits.

Taken together, these studies show that expectancies across a variety of different domains can trigger "placebo effects" that change consumption while physical properties of consumed goods are kept constant. They also suggest that expectancies not only change the perception of the consumption experience, but also change subsequent behavior and thus can create "self-fulfilling prophecies" (Merton 1948).

Why are expectations so powerful that they can override physical properties of goods? There are possible explanations at many levels, but theories from social psychology suggest that one reason is that people strive to overcome cognitive dissonance and seek confirmation for their beliefs (Festinger 1962; Lord, Ross, and Lepper 1979). Further findings in consumer psychology and neuroscience, which we review below, are extending this view by shedding light on what is actually happening in the "black box" of the consumer's brain.

A Neuroscience Perspective on How Expectations Shape Consumption

Understanding the brain processes underlying expectancy, value, and learning is critical to understanding why expectations have such a powerful influence on consumption. Are these effects mere "reporting biases" based on post-consumption rationalization and cognitive dissonance, or do expectancies change how the consumption experience is actually encoded in the brain?

Placebo effects in pain are a classical example of how expectancy influences affective experience. A large body of medical and neuroscientific work has begun to increase our understanding of the neural mechanism underlying the effects of placebos on the perception of pain (Atlas and Wager 2012; Benedetti et al. 2003; Colloca and Benedetti 2005; Kirsch and Sapirstein 1998; Wager and Atlas 2013). In this section, we first review findings regarding how expectancy affects brain markers of pain processing and how expectations lead to changes in subjective pain. We then review findings of neural correlates of the effects of expectancy on other, positive, affective experiences that are closer to everyday consumption experiences.

Traditionally, the term "placebo effect" refers to the pain-reducing or analgesic response caused by treatments that a patient believes will reduce pain but that in reality have no active ingredients. For example, if you take a starch pill believing that it is a painkiller, the belief about the efficacy of treatment causes you to lower your subjective ratings of pain (Colloca and Benedetti 2005). An important question is whether these effects truly affect pain-related processing or whether they simply reflect demand characteristics and reporting biases. The studies that provided the first evidence of placebo effects' altering pain processing via active neurochemical processes were conducted by Levine and colleagues. (See, for example, Levine 1978.) They found that placebo analgesia was attenuated when patients were given the opioid antagonist naloxone. Their findings suggest placebo effects depend on the release of opioids within the patient's brain, since the placebo effect was attenuated when opioid receptors were blocked. These initial findings have been complemented by brain imaging studies investigating the effect of placebo treatments (Bingel, Lorenz, Schoell, Weiller, and Büchel 2006; Meissner et al. 2011; Wager et al. 2004) and the effect of pain expectancy cues (Atlas et al. 2010; Koyama 2005) on neural signatures of pain processing.

Wager et al. (2004) used functional magnetic resonance imaging (fMRI) to test whether placebo effects caused reduced responses to painful stimuli in so-called pain-processing regions in the brain. After a placebo cream was administered, subjects' brains were imaged while they received mildly painful shocks or thermal pain. In a first step, we tested which brain regions were sensitive to stimulus intensity; in the second step, we tested whether any of these "pain regions" showed reduced neural activity in response to a placebo cream relative to an identical control cream. (The difference was in the instructions to participants and in their earlier experiences that the placebo was effective.) With placebo treatment, we found reduced responses in pain-responsive portions of the insula, the thalamus, and the anterior cingulate and correlations between the reductions in pain reports and reductions in brain activity, as shown in figure 12.1.

In related studies, Atlas et al. (2010), Koyama (2005), and Lorenz et al. (2005) investigated whether short-term expectations about pain intensity could also alter pain perception and pain-related responses in the brain. Atlas et al. (2010) used conditioning and verbal information to induce expectations about noxious heat intensity cued by auditory tones. They identified regions that predicted trial-by-trial variations in pain (i.e., medial and lateral pain systems), and found that many of these regions showed enhanced activity when cues predicted high rather than low pain, even though the stimulus intensity was identical for both cues. Interestingly, several recent studies (Eippert, Finsterbusch, Bingel, and Büchel 2009; Matre, Casey, and Knardahl 2006) suggest that expectancies can directly alter pain-related responses in the spinal cord. These studies complement the findings reviewed above by providing evidence that expectancies can change pain-related signals before they even reach the level of the brain, suggesting that expectancies have profound effects on stimulus processing that extend far beyond reporting biases.

Complementing research on placebo effects in the pain domain, a few studies also have investigated whether expectancies alter other, positive, affective experiences, such as taste, flavor, and visual pleasantness, in the

Figure 12.1

Pain regions showing correlations between placebo effects in reported pain (control-placebo) and placebo effects in neural pain (control-placebo) in two studies using electric shocks and thermal pain stimulation.

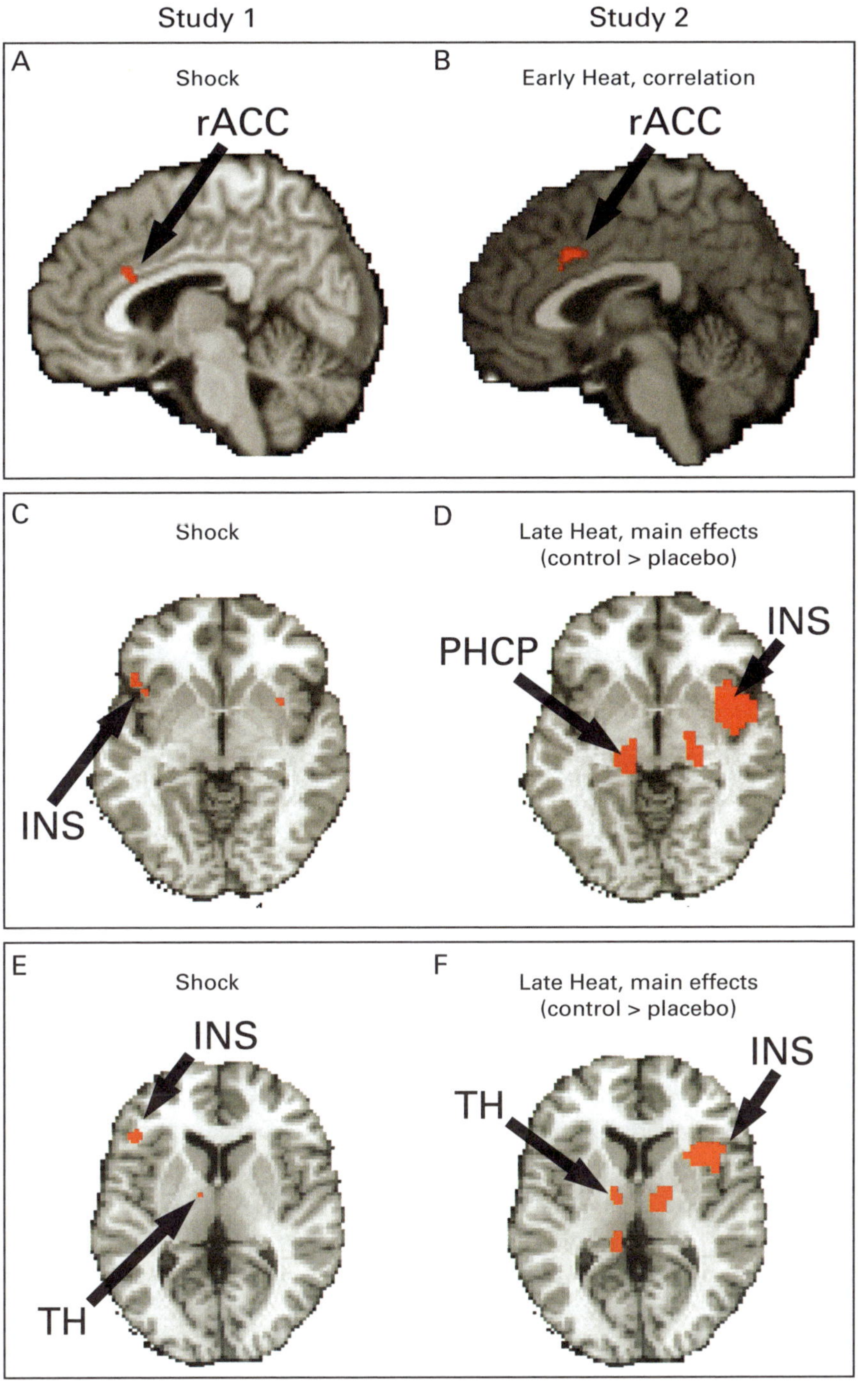

Study 1
Study 2
A
Shock
rACC
B
Early Heat, correlation
rACC
C
Shock
INS
D
Late Heat, main effects
(control > placebo)
PHCP
INS
E
Shock
INS
TH
F
Late Heat, main effects
(control > placebo)
TH
INS

brain. (For an overview, see Plassmann, Ramsøy, and Milosavljevic 2012.) McClure et al. (2004) investigated whether brand labels of colas (Pepsi vs. Coke) altered neural processing during consumption. They found that knowing vs. not knowing the brand name influenced neural activity in brain areas linked to cognitive regulation of affective responses and working memory (i.e., the dorsolateral prefrontal cortex) and also other memory structures (i.e., the bilateral hippocampus). De Araujo, Rolls, Velazco, Margot, and Cayeux (2005) investigated the influence of verbal labels of smells (cheese vs. body odor) on neural signatures of olfactory processing. They found that indeed when subjects were smelling identical odors, a positive or a negative description altered neural activity in ventromedial prefrontal cortex (vmPFC) and also in the bilateral amygdala, which are linked to olfactory processing and value construction more broadly. Nitschke et al. (2006) found that expecting an aversive taste to be less aversive reduces neural activity in regions of the insula associated with primary gustatory processes, although the intensity of the flavor itself was kept constant.

In another study (Plassmann et al. 2008), activity in the mOFC/vmPFC in response to the consumption of wine depended on quality beliefs about its price. Consuming identical wines with high vs. low price tags correlated with changes in neural activity in the mOFC/vmPFC, which has been considered "secondary taste cortex" and also responds to value-related signals and conceptual processes outside the gustatory realm (see, e.g., Plassmann et al. 2007, 2010; Roy, Shohamy, and Wager 2012). No such effects were found for taste-intensity ratings or when subjects did not know the wine's price, indicating that these effects were due to expectations induced by the price and that they were specific to the processing of taste pleasantness. Plassmann et al. also showed that behavioral pleasantness ratings across wines and control liquids correlated with brain activity in the same region of the mOFC/vmPFC. Kirk et al. (2009) found that pleasure derived from viewing art pieces, and accompanying engagement of the vmPFC, depended on whether the subjects believed that the pieces had been created by an expert (i.e., an artist) or by a non-expert (the experimenter).

Together, these findings suggest that, across domains, expectancy manipulations are associated with changes in neural processing linked to consumption-related processing in the brain, ruling out the hypothesis that expectancy effects simply reflect demand characteristics or report biases.

Expectations truly influence neurobiological responses to the experience of different stimuli. But which of these changes in "value-related" processes are related to decision processes that create reporting bias, and which of them influence pre-decision aspects of value? For example, conformity biases have been shown to influence signals in the medial prefrontal cortex (Klucharev, Hytönen, Rijpkema, Smidts, and Fernández 2009). Further studies are needed to identify brain regions and signals with different stages of the perception-decision-learning cycle.

Underlying Neuropsychological Mechanisms of Expectancy Biases

The experiments reviewed above provide evidence that expectancies not only alter reported measures of pleasure or displeasure of consumption but also affect brain responses in consumption-related brain systems. Another crucial question, however, is how expectancies actually shape consumption. To shed light on the underlying neuropsychological mechanisms, we will review studies that have investigated individual differences correlated with the size of expectancy's effects on consumption. We will then review studies that have examined brain mediators of these effects.

Behavioral studies reveal correlations between increased placebo responsiveness and personality traits linked to increased dopaminergic functioning, such as behavioral activation and optimism (Geers, Helfer, Kosbab, Weiland, and Landry 2005; Morton, Watson, El-Deredy, and Jones 2009; Schweinhardt, Seminowicz, Jaeger, Duncan, and Bushnell 2009). Also, subjects who are more suggestible show greater responsiveness to a placebo (De Pascalis, Chiaradia, and Carotenuto 2002). Subjects who showed stronger neural markers of reward responsiveness, lower levels of dopamine and opioid binding during pain stimulation (Scott et al. 2007; Wager, Scott, and Zubieta 2007; Zubieta 2005), and greater gray-matter density in mesolimbic brain regions (e.g., ventral striatum, insula, and prefrontal cortex; see Schweinhardt et al. 2009) also showed stronger expectancy effects.

Another approach to testing for underlying mechanisms of expectancy effects is to test for correlations between such effects on brain *and* behavior. For example, in the study by Plassmann et al. (2008), the extent to which a high vs. a low price tag of an identical wine altered ratings of taste pleasantness correlated significantly with the difference in neural activity in the mOFC/vmPFC during consumption of high-priced wine (see figure 12.2).

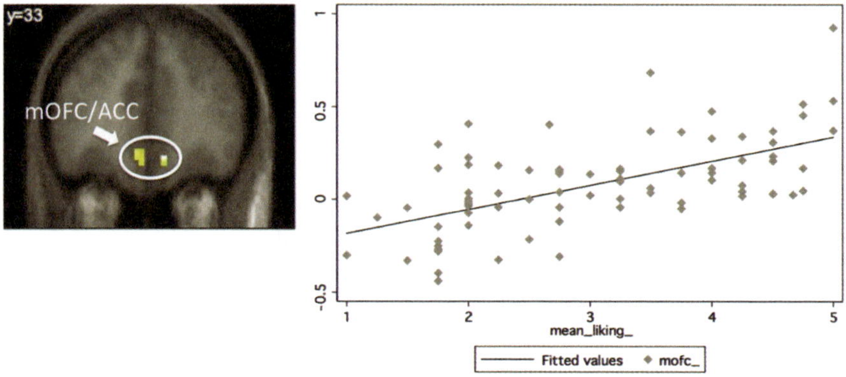

Figure 12.2
The effect of price on the enjoyment of wines. Left: Conjunction analysis. Activity in the medial OFC/rACC was higher in the high-price condition than in the low-price condition for both wine 1 and wine 2. Right: Correlation of behavioral and BOLD responses. Each point denotes an individual wine pair. The horizontal axis measures the change in reported pleasantness between the high-price and the low-price conditions. The vertical axis computes an analogous measure using the betas from the general linear model in a 5-millimeter spherical volume surrounding the area depicted at left. Reprinted from Plassmann et al. 2008.

Wager et al. (2004) found correlations between the magnitude of placebo effects on reported pain and the magnitude of heat-evoked responses in the insula, the thalamus, and the rostral anterior cingulate cortex. However, the brain's pain regions were not the only regions to correlate with placebo effects. During pain anticipation, brain regions that are also involved in cognitive control and in working memory (i.e., the dorsolateral prefrontal cortex) and in predicted value encoding (i.e., the orbitofrontal cortex) showed significant correlations between placebos' effects and reported pain. In fact, a new analysis of data from studies by Wager et al. (2011) in which machine learning and pattern analysis were used showed that anticipatory responses in brain systems involved in emotion regulation and emotional appraisal were more predictive than activity in the brain's pain-processing regions.

Taken together, expectancies might affect consumption-related circuitry not only because they simulate the consumption experience prior to consumption, but also because expectancies influence intervening processes such as emotion and attention. Indeed, although most of the studies reviewed above suggest that expectations modulate responses in consumption-related brain regions, some studies on placebo analgesia (e.g., Kong 2006) found expectancy effects primarily on prefrontal and subcortical regions that are not uniquely associated with pain processing, including the lateral prefrontal cortex, the orbitofrontal cortex, the parahippocampus, and the striatum. It also should be noted that a particular brain region is rarely *specifically* involved in a single mental process, such as encoding painful or pleasurable experiences (Poldrack 2006, 2011). In other words, expectancy effects in these regions may be associated with other intervening processes. Since the regions of the brain that are most frequently influenced by expectancy can be shaped by emotion, attention, and other processes that are likely to be affected by expectations, mediating mechanisms should also be investigated (Atlas et al. 2010; Atlas and Wager 2012).

Atlas et al. (2010) were the first to use multilevel mediation analysis to investigate the underlying neural mechanisms of expectancy's effects on pain experience. They used formal mediation analysis to identify the regions that link expectancy's effects on pain-related responses with its effects on subjective pain reports. In their study, cue-based expectations and pain reports varied from trial to trial, and they tested whether responses in the brain on a particular trial contributed to the link between cue-based expectation for high vs. low pain and changes in the pain experience. Mediation implies that expectancy's effects on a particular brain region explain more variability in pain reports than the expectancy effects themselves. They found that a subset of pain-responsive regions (including the insula, the cingulate, and the thalamus) formally mediated expectancy's effects on pain trial by trial, and that expectancy's effects on these regions were, in turn, mediated by expectancy-induced anticipatory responses in the ventral striatum and the vmPFC. These regions have been widely studied in the context of conditioning and value-based economic decision making in humans and animals (Rangel, Camerer, and Montague 2008), suggesting a link between these fields and expectancy's effects on pain experience. (On the role of these regions in valuation across species, see also the introduction to this volume, the chapter by Knutson and Karmarkar, the chapter by Kringelbach, the chapter by Preston and Vickers, and the chapter by Robinson, Robinson, and Berridge.) These findings are also consistent with the fact that anticipatory responses in emotion networks predict expectancy effects across individuals, as reviewed above. Expectancy's effects on consumption may be mediated by emotional responses during the experience of consumption *and* during anticipation of it.

Conclusions and Open Questions

In this chapter, we have integrated research from different disciplines, including psychology, marketing, neuroscience, and medicine, that all investigate the effects of expectancy on affective experiences. Most of the works in this area find evidence for assimilation effects—that is, influences of a context (such as a high vs. a low price) on a judgment (such as experienced utility derived from consumption of a wine) such that judgments and contextual information are correlated positively, a higher price resulting in a higher experienced utility and a lower price in a lower experienced utility (Sherif, Taub, and Hovland 1958). In the pain domain, most research has focused on placebo (i.e., positive expectations that an inert treatment will relieve pain) and "nocebo" (i.e., negative expectations that an inert treatment will result in more pain) effects (Atlas and Wager 2012; Benedetti, Amanzio, Vighetti, and Asteggiano 2006; Scott et al. 2008; Wager and Atlas 2013). In all of these streams of the literature, however, there is little evidence for contrast effects (i.e., a negative correlation between judgments and contextual information such that a high price tag would lead to a lower experienced utility).

In one prominent paper in the placebo literature, Benedetti et al. (2003) reported evidence for contrast effects on a lower cognitive level measuring hormone secretion, whereas they reported assimilation effects on a higher cognitive level using ratings and motor performance. A group of healthy subjects and a group of Parkinson's patients went through different conditioning phases (i.e., pre-treatment with a painkiller for pain conditioning in the healthy subject group, subthalamic nucleus stimulation for Parkinson's patients), then were treated with sumatriptan for cortisol and growth hormone secretion, and then received verbal information that induced expectations that were either consistent or inconsistent with the conditioned response, i.e., the prior physical experience. Benedetti et al. found that placebo effects on pain ratings and motor performance reversed with different verbal instructions and thus depended upon the conscious belief, whereas effects on biophysical and hormonal responses did not reverse with instructions and thus followed the conditioned response. Gneezy and List (2013) varied the price *and* the quality (physical and perceived) of wines, and found the typical assimilation effect for the high-quality wine but not for the low-quality wine. For the low-quality wine, they found evidence for a contrast effect. It is important to note that Plassmann et al. (2008) also varied the physical quality levels of the wines. They administered one wine that received 80 points and one that received 92 points (on a range from 50 to 100 in an expert quality point system) at a high and a low price level. However, in contrast to the study by Gneezy and List, in a blind tasting no effect of the quality points on subjects' liking ratings (i.e., perceived quality) was found. This suggests possible boundaries for expectancy's effects on consumption. If the affective experience falls within a certain "latitude of acceptance" (Sherif 1963), expectancy effects may result in assimilation; if the affective experience falls outside this range of acceptable experiences, contrast effects may be observed. More research is needed to better understand the role of learning and its effect on physical consumption for contrast vs. assimilation effects of expectancy biases on a behavioral and a neurobiological level.

Research on the relationship between expectations and consumption shows that expectations about specific expectations—for example, verbal suggestions about the efficacy of a drug, a white lab coat, the price of a drug, or the price or brand name of a product—can profoundly influence neural and behavioral measures of consumption. The various types of expectations studied across different domains, from pain to flavor and visual experiences, not only influence reported consumption-related measures; they also influence the known brain markers of consumption experiences. Interestingly, each type of expectation seems to be related not only to sensory specific processing, but also to more general affective processing and regulation: brain mediators of expectancy's effects on pain also involve responses in brain networks encoding more general affective processes that are not specific to pain processing, and individual differences in placebo analgesia are best predicted by responses in such affective brain systems. More systematic research is needed to understand the underlying neuropsychological mechanisms of expectancy's effects not only in the pain domain but also in everyday consumption experiences.

References

Allison, R. I., and Uhl, K. P. 1964. Influence of beer brand identification on taste perception. *Journal of Marketing Research* 1 (3): 36–39.

Ariely, D., and Norton, M. I. 2009. Conceptual consumption. *Annual Review of Psychology* 60 (1): 475–499.

Atlas, L. Y., and Wager, T. D. 2012. How expectations shape pain. *Neuroscience Letters* 520 (2): 140–148.

Atlas, L. Y., Bolger, N., Lindquist, M. A., and Wager, T. D. 2010. Brain mediators of predictive cue effects on perceived pain. *Journal of Neuroscience* 30 (39): 12964–12977.

Bar, M. 2009. Predictions: A universal principle in the operation of the human brain. *Philosophical Transactions of the Royal Society B* 364 (1521): 1181–1182.

Bar, M. 2011. *Predictions in the Brain: Using Our Past to Generate a Future.* Oxford University Press.

Barrett, L. F. 2006. Solving the emotion paradox: Categorization and the experience of emotion. *Personality and Social Psychology Review* 10 (1): 20–46.

Benedetti, F., Amanzio, M., Vighetti, S., and Asteggiano, G. 2006. The biochemical and neuroendocrine bases of the hyperalgesic nocebo effect. *Journal of Neuroscience* 26 (46): 12014–12022.

Benedetti, F., Pollo, A., Lopiano, L., Lanotte, M., Vighetti, S., and Rainero, I. 2003. Conscious expectation and unconscious conditioning in analgesic, motor, and hormonal placebo/nocebo responses. *Journal of Neuroscience* 23 (10): 4315–4323.

Berdik, C. 2012. *Mind over Mind.* Current.

Bingel, U., Lorenz, J., Schoell, E., Weiller, C., and Büchel, C. 2006. Mechanisms of placebo analgesia: rACC recruitment of a subcortical antinociceptive network. *Pain* 120 (1–2): 8–15.

Boulding, W., Kalra, A., Staelin, R., and Zeithaml, V. A. 1993. A dynamic process model of service quality: From expectations to behavioral intentions. *Journal of Marketing Research* 30 (1): 7–27.

Braun, K. A., Ellis, R., and Loftus, E. F. 2002. Make my memory: How advertising can change our memories of the past. *Psychology and Marketing* 19 (1): 1–23.

Brunstrom, J. M. J., Brown, S., Hinton, E. C. E., Rogers, P. J. P., and Fay, S. H. S. 2011. "Expected satiety" changes hunger and fullness in the inter-meal interval. *Appetite* 56 (2): 310–315.

Brunstrom, J. M., and Rogers, P. J. 2009. How many calories are on our plate? Expected fullness, not liking, determines meal-size selection. *Obesity* 17 (10): 1884–1890.

Cacioppo, J. T., and Petty, R. E. 1982. The need for cognition. *Journal of Personality and Social Psychology* 42 (1): 116–131.

Chandon, P., and Wansink, B. 2007. The biasing health halos of fast-food restaurant health claims: Lower calorie estimates and higher side-dish consumption intentions. *Journal of Consumer Research* 34 (3): 301–314.

Colloca, L., and Benedetti, F. 2005. Placebos and painkillers: Is mind as real as matter? *Nature Reviews Neuroscience* 6 (7): 545–552.

Crum, A. J., and Langer, E. J. 2007. Mind-set matters: Exercise and the placebo effect. *Psychological Science* 18 (2): 165–171.

Crum, A. J., Corbin, W. R., Brownell, K. D., and Salovey, P. 2011. Mind over milkshakes: Mindsets, not just nutrients, determine ghrelin response. *Health Psychology* 30 (4): 424–429.

Darley, J. M., and Gross, P. H. 1983. A hypothesis-confirming bias in labeling effects. *Journal of Personality and Social Psychology* 44 (1): 20–33.

de Araujo, I. E., Rolls, E. T., Velazco, M. I., Margot, C., and Cayeux, I. 2005. Cognitive modulation of olfactory processing. *Neuron* 46 (4): 671–679.

De Pascalis, V., Chiaradia, C., and Carotenuto, E. 2002. The contribution of suggestibility and expectation to placebo analgesia phenomenon in an experimental setting. *Pain* 96 (3): 393–402.

Eippert, F., Finsterbusch, J., Bingel, U., and Büchel, C. 2009. Direct evidence for spinal cord involvement in placebo analgesia. *Science* 326 (5951): 404.

Festinger, L. 1962. *A Theory of Cognitive Dissonance*. Stanford University Press.

Flaten, M. A., and Blumenthal, T. D. 1999. Caffeine-associated stimuli elicit conditioned responses: An experimental model of the placebo effect. *Psychopharmacology* 145 (1): 105–112.

Flaten, M. A., Simonsen, T., Zahlsen, K. R., Aamo, T., Sager, G., and Olsen, H. 2004. Stimulant and relaxant drugs combined with stimulant and relaxant information: A study of active placebo. *Psychopharmacology* 176 (3–4): 426–434.

Geers, A. L., Helfer, S. G., Kosbab, K., Weiland, P. E., and Landry, S. J. 2005. Reconsidering the role of personality in placebo effects: Dispositional optimism, situational expectations, and the placebo response. *Journal of Psychosomatic Research* 58 (2): 121–127.

Geuter, S., Eippert, F., Attar, C. H., and Bchel, C. 2013. Cortical and subcortical responses to high and low effective placebo treatments. *NeuroImage* 67: 227–236.

Gneezy, U., and List, J. 2013. *The Why Axis: Hidden Motives and the Undiscovered Economics of Everyday Life*. PublicAffairs.

Irmak, C., Vallen, B., and Robinson, S. R. 2011. The impact of product name on dieters' and nondieters' food evaluations and consumption. *Journal of Consumer Research* 38 (2): 390–405.

Kahneman, D., Wakker, P. P., and Sarin, R. 1997. Back to Bentham? Explorations of experienced utility. *Quarterly Journal of Economics* 112 (2): 375–406.

Kirk, U., Skov, M., Hulme, O., Christensen, M. S., and Zeki, S. 2009. Modulation of aesthetic value by semantic context: An fMRI study. *NeuroImage* 44 (3): 1125–1132.

Kirsch, I., and Sapirstein, G. 1998. Listening to Prozac but hearing placebo: A meta-analysis of antidepressant medication. *Prevention and Treatment* 1 (2).

Klaaren, K. J., Hodges, S. D., and Wilson, T. D. 1994. The role of affective expectations in subjective experience and decision-making. *Social Cognition* 12 (2): 77–101.

Klein, O., and Snyder, M. 2003. Stereotypes and behavioral confirmation: From interpersonal to intergroup perspectives. *Advances in Experimental Social Psychology* 35: 153–234.

Klucharev, V., Hytönen, K., Rijpkema, M., Smidts, A., and Fernández, G. 2009. Reinforcement learning signal predicts social conformity. *Neuron* 61 (1): 140–151.

Kong, J. 2006. Brain activity associated with expectancy-enhanced placebo analgesia as measured by functional magnetic resonance imaging. *Journal of Neuroscience* 26 (2): 381–388.

Kopalle, P. K., and Lehmann, D. R. 2001. Strategic management of expectations: The role of disconfirmation sensitivity and perfectionism. *Journal of Marketing Research* 38 (3): 386–394.

Koyama, T. 2005. The subjective experience of pain: Where expectations become reality. *Proceedings of the National Academy of Sciences* 102 (36): 12950–12955.

Laney, C., Morris, E. K., Bernstein, D. M., Wakefield, B. M., and Loftus, E. F. 2008. Asparagus, a love story: Healthier eating could be just a false memory away. *Experimental Psychology* 55 (5): 291–300.

Lee, L., Frederick, S., and Ariely, D. 2006. Try it, you'll like it: The influence of expectation, consumption, and revelation on preferences for beer. *Psychological Science* 17 (12): 1054–1058.

Lee, W.-C. J., Shimizu, M., Kniffin, K. M., and Wansink, B. 2013. Food quality and preference. *Food Quality and Preference* 29 (1): 33–39.

Levine, J. D. 1978. The mechanism of placebo analgesia. *Lancet* 312 (8091): 654–657.

Loewenstein, G. 1987. Anticipation and the valuation of delayed consumption. *Economic Journal* 97 (387): 666–684.

Lord, C. G., Ross, L., and Lepper, M. R. 1979. Biased assimilation and attitude polarization: The effects of prior theories on subsequently considered evidence. *Journal of Personality and Social Psychology* 37 (11): 2098–2109.

Lorenz, J., Hauck, M., Paur, R. C., Nakamura, Y., Zimmermann, R., Bromm, B., et al. 2005. Cortical correlates of false expectations during pain intensity judgments: A possible manifestation of placebo/nocebo cognitions. *Brain, Behavior, and Immunity* 19 (4): 283–295.

Maslow, A. H. 1959. A theory of human motivation. *Psychological Review* 56: 251–276.

Matre, D., Casey, K. L., and Knardahl, S. 2006. Placebo-induced changes in spinal cord pain processing. *Journal of Neuroscience* 26 (2): 559–563.

McClure, S. M., Li, J., Tomlin, D., Cypert, K. S., Montague, L. M., and Montague, P. R. 2004. Neural correlates of behavioral preference for culturally familiar drinks. *Neuron* 44 (2): 379–387.

Meissner, K., Bingel, U., Colloca, L., Wager, T. D., Watson, A., and Flaten, M. A. 2011. The placebo effect: Advances from different methodological approaches. *Journal of Neuroscience* 31 (45): 16117–16124.

Merton, R. K. 1948. The self-fulfilling prophecy. *Antioch Review* 8: 193–210.

Morewedge, C. K., Huh, Y. E., and Vosgerau, J. 2010. Thought for food: Imagined consumption reduces actual consumption. *Science* 330 (6010): 1530–1533.

Morton, D. L., Watson, A., El-Deredy, W., and Jones, A. K. 2009. Reproducibility of placebo analgesia: Effect of dispositional optimism. *Pain* 146 (1–2): 194–198.

Moulton, S. T., and Kosslyn, S. M. 2009. Imagining predictions: Mental imagery as mental emulation. *Philosophical Transactions of the Royal Society B* 364 (1521): 1273–1280.

Nakamura, Y., Donaldson, G. W., Kuhn, R., Bradshaw, D. H., Jacobson, R. C., and Chapman, C. R. 2012. Investigating dose-dependent effects of placebo analgesia: A psychophysiological approach. *Pain* 153 (1): 227–237.

Nitschke, J. B., Dixon, G. E., Sarinopoulos, I., Short, S. J., Cohen, J. D., Smith, E. E., et al. 2006. Altering expectancy dampens neural response to aversive taste in primary taste cortex. *Nature Neuroscience* 9 (3): 435–442.

Norton, M. I., and Goethals, G. R. 2004. Spin (and pitch) doctors: Campaign strategies in televised political debates. *Political Behavior* 26 (3): 227–248.

Plassmann, H., O'Doherty, J., and Rangel, A. 2007. Orbitofrontal cortex encodes willingness to pay in everyday economic transactions. *Journal of Neuroscience* 27 (37): 9984–9988.

Plassmann, H., O'Doherty, J., and Rangel, A. 2010. Appetitive and aversive goal values are encoded in the medial orbitofrontal cortex at the time of decision making. *Journal of Neuroscience* 30 (32): 10799–10808.

Plassmann, H., O'Doherty, J., Shiv, B., and Rangel, A. 2008. Marketing actions can modulate neural representations of experienced pleasantness. *Proceedings of the National Academy of Sciences* 105 (3): 1050–1054.

Plassmann, H., Ramsøy, T. Z., and Milosavljevic, M. 2012. Branding the brain: A critical review and outlook. *Journal of Consumer Psychology* 22 (1): 18–36.

Poldrack, R. A. 2006. Can cognitive processes be inferred from neuroimaging data? *Trends in Cognitive Sciences* 10 (2): 59–63.

Poldrack, R. A. 2011. Inferring mental states from neuroimaging data: From reverse inference to large-scale decoding. *Neuron* 72 (5): 692–697.

Raghunathan, R., Walker Naylor, R., and Hoyer, W. 2006. The unhealthy = tasty intuition and its effects on taste inferences, enjoyment, and choice of food products. *Journal of Marketing* 70 (4): 170–184.

Rangel, A., Camerer, C., and Montague, P. R. 2008. A framework for studying the neurobiology of value-based decision making. *Nature Reviews Neuroscience* 9 (7): 545–556.

Roy, M., Shohamy, D., and Wager, T. D. 2012. Ventromedial prefrontal-subcortical systems and the generation of affective meaning. *Trends in Cognitive Sciences* 16 (3): 147–156.

Schacter, D. L. D., Addis, D. R. D., and Buckner, R. L. R. 2007. Remembering the past to imagine the future: The prospective brain. *Nature Reviews Neuroscience* 8 (9): 657–661.

Schultz, W., Dayan, P., and Montague, P. R. 1997. A neural substrate of prediction and reward. *Science* 275 (5306): 1593–1599.

Schweinhardt, P., Seminowicz, D. A., Jaeger, E., Duncan, G. H., and Bushnell, M. C. 2009. The anatomy of the mesolimbic reward system: A link between personality and the placebo analgesic response. *Journal of Neuroscience* 29 (15): 4882–4887.

Scott, D. J., Stohler, C. S., Egnatuk, C. M., Wang, H., Koeppe, R. A., and Zubieta, J.-K. 2007. Individual differences in reward responding explain placebo-induced expectations and effects. *Neuron* 55 (2): 325–336.

Scott, D. J., Stohler, C. S., Egnatuk, C. M., Wang, H., Koeppe, R. A., and Zubieta, J.-K. 2008. Placebo and nocebo effects are defined by opposite opioid and dopaminergic responses. *Archives of General Psychiatry* 65 (2): 220–231.

Sherif, C. W. 1963. Social categorization as a function of latitude of acceptance and series range. *Journal of Abnormal and Social Psychology* 67: 148–156.

Sherif, M., Taub, D., and Hovland, C. I. 1958. Assimilation and contrast effects of anchoring stimuli on judgments. *Journal of Experimental Psychology* 55 (2): 150–155.

Shiv, B., Carmon, Z., and Ariely, D. 2005. Placebo effects of marketing actions: Consumers may get what they pay for. *Journal of Marketing Research* 42: 383–393.

Steenhuis, I. H. M., Kroeze, W., Vyth, E. L., Valk, S., Verbauwen, R., and Seidell, J. C. 2010. The effects of using a nutrition logo on consumption and product evaluation of a sweet pastry. *Appetite* 55 (3): 707–709.

Vohs, K. D., Wang, Y., Gino, F., and Norton, M. I. 2013. Rituals enhance consumption. *Psychological Science* 24 (9): 1714–1721.

Waber, R. L., Shiv, B., Carmon, Z., and Ariely, D. 2008. Commercial features of placebo and therapeutic efficacy. *Journal of the American Medical Association* 299 (9): 1016–1017.

Wager, T. D. 2004. Placebo-induced changes in fMRI in the anticipation and experience of pain. *Science* 303 (5661): 1162–1167.

Wager, T. D., and Atlas, L. Y. 2013. How is pain influenced by cognition? Neuroimaging weighs in. *Perspectives on Psychological Science* 8 (1): 91–97.

Wager, T. D., Atlas, L. Y., Leotti, L. A., and Rilling, J. K. 2011. Predicting individual differences in placebo analgesia: Contributions of brain activity during anticipation and pain experience. *Journal of Neuroscience* 31 (2): 439–452.

Wager, T. D., Rilling, J. K., Smith, E. E., Sokolik, A., Casey, K. L., Davidson, R. J., et al. 2004. Placebo-induced changes in FMRI in the anticipation and experience of pain. *Science* 303 (5661): 1162–1167.

Wager, T. D., Scott, D. J., and Zubieta, J. K. 2007. Placebo effects on human μ-opioid activity during pain. *Proceedings of the National Academy of Sciences* 104 (26): 11056–11061.

Wansink, B., and Chandon, P. 2006. Can "low-fat" nutrition labels lead to obesity? *Journal of Marketing Research* 43 (4): 605–617.

Wansink, B., Payne, C. R., and North, J. 2007. Fine as North Dakota wine: Sensory expectations and the intake of companion foods. *Physiology and Behavior* 90 (5): 712–716.

Wilcox, K., Roggeveen, A. L., and Grewal, D. 2011. Shall I tell you now or later? Assimilation and contrast in the evaluation of experiential products. *Journal of Consumer Research* 38 (4): 763–773.

Wilson, T. D., Lisle, D. J., Kraft, D., and Wetzel, C. G. 1989. Preferences as expectation-driven inferences: Effects of affective expectations on affective experience. *Journal of Personality and Social Psychology* 56 (4): 519–530.

Woods, S. C., and Ramsay, D. S. 2000. Pavlovian influences over food and drug intake. *Behavioural Brain Research* 110 (1–2): 175–182.

Zubieta, J. K. 2005. Placebo effects mediated by endogenous opioid activity on μ-opioid receptors. *Journal of Neuroscience* 25 (34): 7754–7762.

Consumption Across the Life Span

13 The Development of Saving

Paul Webley

Saving is usually conceived of as deferred consumption. To buy something you have to have saved money, even if only for the limited time from when you earned it or were given it to arriving at the store or market. Saving for a "rainy day" is just deferred emergency consumption, and saving for one's children is just deferring the consumption of others. So saving is commonly seen as the means through which individuals adjust the flow of their income (or incoming resources) to their spending (or consumption of resources), as money (or other resources) rarely arrives in the right amounts and at the right time. (See the chapter by Preston and Vickers, the chapter by Lea, and the chapter by Rick.)

In this chapter, I argue that there is more to saving than deferred consumption, and that understanding the processes that underpin the development of saving will help us understand a wide range of consumption phenomena, including such major economic life choices as saving and planning for retirement, adult individual differences in behavior, and "pathologies" such as credit abuse and consumer debt. Understanding these processes also helps us to understand the development of behavior that does not necessarily involve money but does involve tradeoffs between the present and the future, such as exercise, dieting, and doing one's homework. I will base this argument largely on the studies of children and adolescent saving that my colleagues and I have carried out over the last twenty years, and which will form the bulk of this chapter.

I don't believe that Tryon Edwards (1866) got it right when he wrote "Most controversies would soon be ended, if those engaged in them would first accurately define their terms," but definitions do matter—especially when we wrongly think that our assumptions are shared. So I will begin by considering the question "What is saving?"

Income must be spent or saved, whether for the individual, for the family, or for the economy as a whole. What is not spent is, by definition, saved, and constitutes savings. But we have to think about the accounting period we are using in talking about saving. A child may spend \$5 of the \$10 weekly allowance she receives on Saturday and the remaining \$5 on the subsequent Tuesday. Alternatively, she may save all her income from her allowance for a month and then spend \$40 on a computer game. Or she may put \$5 aside every week to spend on Christmas gifts at the end of the year. Each of these alternatives involves saving, though they require different amounts of commitment and self-control. In everyday conversation, one might use the word "saving" for only the last of these. Whether something is defined as saving or not depends entirely on the accounting period we use. And insofar as saving is deferred consumption, we should bear in mind that the amount of consumption that is deferred may not be the same as the amount that is possible in the future. Savings may increase (as a result of interest or intelligent investment), or may shrink (if, for example, interest rates are lower than the prevailing rate of inflation), just as sometimes a hamster's hoard of grain may be lost or rot.

There are also crucial distinctions between various forms of saving. Katona (1975) highlights the importance of distinguishing among contractual, discretionary, and involuntary saving. Discretionary saving involves an active decision to save during the current accounting period, whereas contractual saving is the consequence of a decision made in a previous accounting period. Thus, signing up for a pension plan that involves regular payments over many years would be contractual saving, whereas deciding to set aside some money for a few months to buy some furniture would discretionary saving, since one could save more or less and could change one's mind about what to purchase. Involuntary saving is saving that occurs when there is no actual decision to save. This includes the idea of savings as a residual (simply what is left over after one has spent), as well as institutional arrangements that create savings of which the individual is unaware. For a child this might be the automatic deducting of some proportion of his or her allowance by a parent to put in a savings plan; for an adult it might involve over-withholding of taxes by the IRS.

Another important distinction is between recurrent saving (regular saving that goes on in each accounting period) and total savings (the total value of accrued assets) (Lunt and Livingstone 1992). Total savings are the end result of the different forms of saving outlined above, as well as spending and borrowing. Lunt and Livingstone found that total savings were linked to demographic and income variables, whereas recurrent saving was better predicted by psychological variables.

In addition to clear definitions, it is important to have a grasp of previous research. What does the rather limited information on children's saving—information derived from a wide variety of sources, including surveys, interview studies, laboratory experiments, and role playing—tell us?

The clearest and least surprising finding is that there are age-related changes in the level and the forms of saving in childhood. Dickins and Ferguson (1957) found that saving increased with age; that isn't surprising, since income also increases with age. They investigated 7-year-olds and 11-year-olds, and found that most children in both age groups said that they were saving for a particular purpose (Christmas presents being the most common reason). In a larger and broader survey of how children learn to buy, Ward, Wackmann, and Wartella (1977) also found that saving increased with age. More recent studies have confirmed this finding, but have also provided more detail. Furnham and Thomas (1984) reported that older children were more likely to use a savings account, and that, rather than saving for a particular purpose, they saved because they anticipated a generalized need for money in the future. Underlying age changes in both the motivation and the mechanism for saving have also been found by Furnham (1999) and Jundin (1985). Jundin studied Swedish adolescents aged 13–18 and found that two-thirds of the youngest children kept their money at home, but 87 percent of the eldest group used banks. She also found that, like the British adolescents studied by Furnham, her participants saved not for a particular purpose but so as to have money on hand when it was needed. Doss, Marlowe, and Godwin (1995), who investigated how American children aged 10 to 15 years acquired and used money, found that about three-fifths of their subjects saved at least some money over a four-week period, though the average amounts of money saved were relatively small. The amount of money children saved was positively related to their income. Rather surprisingly, Mortimer et al. (1994), who studied American 14- and 15-year-olds, found no evidence that getting an allowance affected their saving behavior—neither receipt of an allowance nor its duration was related to the subjects' reported savings.

This research gives us a broad-brush picture of how saving behavior develops, but it tells us little about the processes that underlie this behavior.

Empirical Studies of Child and Adolescent Saving

Studies (mainly experimental) focusing on the individual

A series of experimental studies of saving on children (Webley, Levine, and Lewis 1991; Sonuga-Barke and Webley 1993; Otto, Schots, Westerman, and Webley 2006) suggest that a number of processes are involved in the development of children's saving. They report results from six studies, five of which involved a savings board game and one of which involved a play economy. In some instances tokens were earned through taking part in an operant task; in others tokens were paid out during the board game, when a child's game piece landed on a particular square; and in the play economy money was paid out in the form of a "daily" allowance. (The "day" was actually ten minutes.) The underlying logic of the situation, and the problem facing the participating child, was the same in all cases. At the outset, the child selected a preferred toy—the long-term target he or she was saving for—from a "toy shop" (an area in the lab that we stocked with desirable items). The child had an income stream, and in some studies an endowment, and in all cases a child who played the game successfully would end up with candies, small toys, or soft drinks in addition to the target toy. Typically, to be successful would involve saving about 70 percent of income over the duration of the game. Each game presented the child with a range of problems that were similar to those she would encounter in the real economy. So she might be tempted by passing a sweet shop full of attractive candies or a toy shop with desirable small toys, or threatened by a robber (an unusually kindly one who took only a single token each time a child passed by). These internal and external threats had the potential of using up enough of a child's money so that she would not reach her saving target. A child could deal with these problems in several ways. There was a bank, in which the child could deposit some or all of his or her money; it provided protection from the external threat and, because it wasn't always available to withdraw, provided protection from temptation. A child could deposit all of the money that had been accumulated so far in the bank, and travel past the robber or sweet shop, safe in the knowledge that no money could be stolen or spent, and she would be able to take her money out when she needed it. A simpler strategy, possible in some versions of the board game, was just to take a detour so that temptations were not encountered.

In a later version, the board unrolled during the game, releasing the information a little at a time, which meant that the future was unknown to the child (including when the game would end). This had the great advantage of increasing both uncertainty and mundane realism (life is like that). In another study, children took part in a play economy where economic problems were presented temporally rather than spatially. Here money was provided in the form of "daily" pocket money, and a child had to save over a "week" to obtain a chosen toy (as has already been noted, a "day" was ten minutes, and the duration of the experiment was more than an hour). The play economy was situated in a suite of four rooms that gave children opportunities to take part in various activities. Some activities (e.g., a video arcade and a café) cost tokens; others were free (a library, drawing materials). A child, having received her ten tokens, would have to spend ten minutes in a room where she could splurge all of that day's money on one activity (e.g., watching a film), spend some of it (e.g., on candy) and retain the rest, or keep it all by taking part in a free activity.

The focus in these studies was mainly on children, but in some studies their parents were interviewed or given a questionnaire. The ages of the children ranged from 4 to 12 years.

These studies do not tell us what children actually do (indeed there was limited correspondence between what parents told us and what we observed their children do during the play economy), but they do tell us what children are capable of, and provide a good basis for analyzing the processes involved in the development of saving strategies and decisions and saving attitudes and beliefs. It is striking that by the age of 6 years children know that saving is a "good thing." They have learned—presumably from their parents, from teachers, from stories that they have read, and from television programs—that self-control, patience, and thrift are virtuous. There seems no doubt that there is a cultural value of thrift, though most parents claim not to be teaching the purpose of saving or explicitly instilling the value of thrift (and some parents definitely try to "shield" their children from the big, bad economic world—see Leiser and Ganin 1996).

Although 6-year-olds have picked up the cultural value of thrift and have learned that saving is a "good thing," they do not like it very much, nor are they very good at it. In our study they often made deposits in the bank when doing so could serve no economic purpose. Some children of this age see money saved as money lost. Sarah (age 6) said "If I put my money in the bank I won't have any left," and Beth (age 6), when asked if she wanted to use a money box, replied "I don't, because I am saving up." What may underlie this belief may be the experience of putting money into a bank account but not being allowed to take any out. In most of the studies, marked improvement both in successful saving and in understanding came between the ages of 6 and 9. Four-year-olds showed no pattern in use of the bank, nor were they able to provide any justification for their actions in the game. When asked why she used the bank, Patty (age 4) simply replied "Because I do; because I did it before."

We can see a good example of the mature understanding of saving by 9-year-olds in one of the board-game studies, in which children were able to deposit money in the bank just before encountering the robber or the candy shop. Putting money in the bank was a sound strategy, since they would then have no cash for the robber to steal (or for themselves to spend on candies). Nine-year-olds understood this very well: Gail commented "I'll put [the money] in [the bank] to make it safe from the robber," and Mary, when she landed on a square just before the toy shop, where she could take money out of the bank if she wished, said "I won't take [money] out of the bank, as I don't want to be tempted."

The findings were similar in the play economy. Six-year-olds were not very good at saving (about half did not save at all). Those who did not save seemed to have no concern about the effect of current spending on their ability to save up for the target toy. Kim (age 6) put it this way: "I might spend half, I might spend all my money. I might spend all of it accidentally because I don't know how much things are." Again we encountered the theme that money put into the bank was money lost. This is nicely illustrated by the following exchange.

Experimenter: Would you put money in the bank?

Sam: No.

Experimenter: Why not?

Sam: Because I want to save it.

Experimenter: When you put money in the bank, what happens to it?

Sam: You lose it, and they give you a tiny bit of money back.

Saving is a skill. In our study, it had been acquired by most of the 9-year-olds and all of the 12-year-olds. The latter understand interest (and cite it as their primary reason for using a bank) and the benefit of the illiquidity of money in a bank account. Chris (age 12) put it this way: "[A bank helps you to save] 'cause you can never get it to take your money out." But saving is only one way of solving the economic problems facing children, and not necessarily the most effective way. The obvious alternative is to get more money out of their parents. Some children have developed a range of techniques for doing this, including requesting an advance on an allowance, straight pleading, and emotional blackmail (for example, claiming to have no money and asking for money with which to buy a birthday present for a sibling). Saving is not seen as good *per se* by children of most ages, but just as one possible way of achieving a goal. We saw this in the play economy, where some of the older participants, having realized that they had failed to save enough for the target toy, deployed considerable negotiating skill to try to persuade the experimenter either to make up the difference between the amount they had saved and the amount needed or to allow them to chose a cheaper target toy.

In some studies of children's understanding of economics (e.g., Webley 2005) researchers have found stages at which economic events and actions are understood primarily in social terms. Such stages also were found in our studies of saving. Not only did the 6-year-olds say that they saved because it was a "good thing"; they also called the robber "that naughty man." A social interpretation was also evident in their behavior. In one study, children could either take a route that involved spending tokens on something that was socially neutral (a ferry) or take a route that meant they would encounter the robber but would cost them less. (Remember, these robbers were kindly.) Faced with these options, the younger children tended to choose the ferry, which was socially better but more expensive. The older children went past the robber (socially worse but economically better).

The findings can be summarized quite simply. First, children learn what saving is, and that is it socially valued, but they do not know what it is for, and are not particularly keen on it. We might term this "functionless" saving. Then they learn to save effectively: they realize what saving is for, and recognize the value of certain saving technologies in protecting them against threats from within (temptation) and from without (other people). Next, they learn about a number of other strategies (e.g., pleading, negotiating, and working) that can also be used to solve the problem of acquiring a large lump sum of money, and they have a nuanced understanding of the pros and cons of these different strategies. The origins of individual differences in approaches to saving were also evident in these cross-sectional developmental studies, although in these studies we didn't focus on learning how such cross-individual differences emerged.

Focusing on the context (panel studies, surveys, secondary data analysis)

For three reasons, saving by children and adolescents should be seen in context. First, just like children, researchers have to recognize that saving is just one strategy of dealing with consumption across time, and we cannot assume that it is the most important. Second, we need to understand the role of parents (and other socializing agents) in fostering saving. We need to go beyond the simple idea that children learn the general social value of saving from them, and to discover exactly what is being passed on. And third, we need to understand continuities and consistencies in behavior across the life span. To explore these issues, saving needs to be investigated within the context of the lifespan; this means a shift from experiments to cross-sectional surveys, panel studies, and one three-generation study.

We begin by looking at how important saving is for children relative to other options for obtaining lump sums of money (not the only function of saving, but a very important one). There are obviously a number of other ways of obtaining lump sums, or the goods that one wishes to buy with the money, apart from saving. A child could ask a parent or another relative to purchase the desired item as a Christmas present or a birthday present, or simply to give the child the requisite sum of money. She could ask to be paid for doing some jobs around the house. She could negotiate and/or plead with her parents. She could borrow the money from her parents or from other relatives. She could sell unwanted possessions. She could steal from her parents or from a store. An older child could get a part-time job or work extra hours in a part-time job she already had. These approaches to getting hold of a lump sum of money obviously differ in a number of ways. Some of them (working under the age of 13, stealing) are illegal. Some may take considerable time and effort. All of them—unlike saving—depend on interactions with others. Not all will be realistic options for all children. To take on a part-time job, one must be old enough. In order for a child to earn money at home, the parents have to be willing and able to provide appropriate opportunities.

We explored the importance of these strategies by carrying out a questionnaire study of 470 British school students from 11 to 18 years old (Otto and Webley 2011). The questionnaire asked the children about their income (in considerable detail), about their saving and spending behavior, and about how likely they would be to use particular options for getting hold of lump sums of money. Options that fell into four different categories were presented: "saving," "relying on parents," "working," and "selling." Each category included at least three possibilities—for example, there were separate questions on selling unwanted possessions at a car boot sale, selling them to friends, and selling them to a secondhand shop. The results showed that age and disposable income were positively related. Whereas parents were the most important source of income for younger adolescents, for older adolescents out-of-school-hours employment was the most significant. In terms of getting hold of lump sums of money, up to the age of 15 "saving" and "relying on parents" were equally important and more important than "selling things" or "earning"—that is, children were just as likely to ask their parents to buy a desired item for them as they were to save up for it. After the age of 15, there was a decline in reliance on parents. For those closer to 18, saving became the most important strategy, followed by working. In view of the notable increase in part-time working across this age group (when adolescents begin to work part-time they experience a huge boost in their disposable income, which might be thought to make saving nugatory), the fact that they employ saving even more than working is a testimony to the importance of saving in adolescence. The changing behavior of the late adolescent participants toward active saving and working suggests that family-linked strategies become less important as children enter the adult economic world, although families still play a role as a lender of last resort for adults.

Not surprisingly, those adolescents who generally tended to save were more likely to save if they needed a lump sum. Being accustomed to economizing and budgeting makes it easier to chose saving as a strategy to solve a particular problem. Children who reported that they enjoyed spending money and who lacked financial self-control were more likely to rely on their parents. In addition to confirming the significance of parents, this provides some hints to the precursors of being a "tightwad" or a "spendthrift." (On "tightwads" and "spendthrifts," see the chapter by Rick.)

A three-generation study of adolescents and their parents and grandparents (Otto 2009; Webley, Nyhus and Otto 2011; Nyhus and Webley 2013; Webley and Nyhus 2011) gives some insight into the role of parents in promoting children's saving. Data were collected from families in two medium-size cities: Kristiansand (in Norway) and Exeter (in the United Kingdom). At schools in both cities, 14-year-olds and 15-year-olds were given a questionnaire that asked questions pertaining to money management, personality (conscientiousness and future orientation), and the perceived parental style of their parents. The questionnaire also asked for information about the composition of a student's family, including the composition of the household and the number of living grandparents. Each child was then given a set of questionnaires for members of his or her family to complete—one for each parent and one for each set of grandparents (maternal and paternal). Each parent's questionnaire solicited general information, information about the child's income and management of pocket money, a rating of the child's attitude toward saving, information about the child's personality, information about the parent's childhood, and general information about money management (household income, savings, and so on). Similarly, the questionnaires for grandparents solicited general information, information about personality and general money management, information about their grandchild's income and how much money the grandparent gave the child, the child's management of pocket money, and various aspects of grandparenting (face-to-face contact, activities done together, intimacy, helping, instrumental assistance, authority, discipline). Grandparents were also asked to answer some questions about what they did with respect to pocket money and economic socialization when their own children were between 11 and 16 years old. These questionnaires yielded a great deal of information about saving and about the roles of parents and grandparents, some contemporaneous (about the teenagers themselves) and some retrospective (for example, about their parents' childhood). Some information (such as that on the income of adolescents) could be cross-checked; some (such as that on parental style) was based on one informant alone. As far as I am aware, this was the first study to look at economic orientation and behavior across three generations. But limitations of the data should be borne in mind. Participants had to be both willing and able to provide accurate reports, and retrospective self-reports are particularly problematic. Though the participation level of the adolescents was good, less than half of the parents and less than a third of the grandparents took part. Presumably the children of the parents and grandparents who did take part were more conscientious and more future oriented than the children of those who didn't. The generalizability of the data was also limited in that data were gathered in two affluent European countries at only one particular point in history, early in the twenty-first century.

With the aforementioned caveats in mind, what do the data tell us? For the Norwegian adolescents, conscientiousness and future time perspective were both positively associated with a preference for saving over spending and with a self-reported ability to control spending. Present hedonistic orientation, on the other hand, was associated with a preference for spending over saving and a relative inability to control spending. These economic orientations of adolescents were linked to parenting. Adolescents who saw their parents as psychologically controlling (that is, using guilt induction, shaming, and making acceptance contingent on good behavior) were less future oriented and conscientious and more present oriented and hedonistic than others. Parents who were seen as warm and responsive, and as granting their children autonomy and independence, had children who were more future oriented and conscientious than others. The UK sample yielded two notable findings. First, and perhaps not very surprising, mothers matter more than fathers. It is predominantly mothers who are involved in pocket money, and where there are significant differences in parental practices with respect to money and saving (for example, talking to their child about ways to limit spending) it is virtually always the mother who reports using a particular practice more often. Overall, there are many more relationships between the saving behavior of adolescents and the measures obtained from their mothers than there are with measures obtained from their fathers. It seems as if mothers influence the saving behavior of their child through modeling, and that a mother's influence depends more on the quality of her own money management than on particular economic socialization practices.

Second, the relationship between parenting style and a child's approach to economic life was strong, whereas relationships between specific parenting practices (e.g., providing pocket money, paying children for doing work) and a child's economic behavior and approach were weak or nonexistent. The model presented by Otto (2009) implicates two parental variables: an authoritative parenting style (which affects the child's preference for saving over spending through its effect on the child's conscientiousness and attitude toward saving) and the mother's educational attitude toward adolescent saving. Authoritative parents, who demand maturity and self-control from their children while displaying sensitivity, emotional warmth, and involvement themselves, have a generally positive effect on their children's behavior in a wide variety of domains (Steinberg and Silk 2002), so this finding is predictable. More surprising is the irrelevance of specific parenting practices. A secondary data analysis of Dutch panel data that include retrospective data on economic socialization as well as detailed information about economic behavior provides some support for this finding, in that parental encouragement of saving (which is likely to be associated with parental style) is a significant predictor of adult saving, whereas specific economic socialization practices are not (Webley, Nyhus, and Otto 2011).

The direct effect of grandparents on their grandchildren's saving is more variable (Webley and Nyhus 2011), though grandparents do have an indirect effect through their behavior as parents. Some grandparents, particularly maternal grandmothers and other grandparents who are involved and intimate with their grandchildren, are important agents of economic socialization, though it has to be admitted that their effect on their grandchildren's saving is limited. Overall, grandparents are not an important source of money for their grandchildren, though in some instances they do provide useful occasional income. Our findings are congruent with Hagestad's (2006) conclusion that much of the support of grandchildren by grandparents is indirect. In general, grandparents try not to step on the toes of parents, and providing regular pocket money would probably be seen as interfering too much. Whereas providing financial help indirectly (for example, by taking grandchildren on trips and helping grandchildren directly financially only when the need arises) would be seen as acceptable and would lead to the common irregular giving of money found in our study. Most grandparents are not involved in the economic socialization of their grandchildren; those who are involved tend to be conscientious and future-oriented individuals.

Grandparenting may not be particularly significant in children's saving, but parenting certainly is. The link between authoritative parenting and saving has been confirmed in two studies, one using American data (Elliot, Webley and Friedline 2011) and one using British data (Ashby, Schoon, and Webley 2011). The latter used information from the 1970 British cohort study, an ongoing inter-disciplinary longitudinal study that has been following all children born in a particular week in April 1970. These individuals have now been followed up six times. The particular analysis reported here used data collected at birth and at the ages of 16 and 34. The US study used data from the Panel Study of Income Dynamics, data on adolescents (aged 13–17) from the 2002 Child Development Supplement, and data on some individuals from the 2007 Transition into Adulthood supplement, when they were young adults (aged 18–22). These studies were not primarily concerned with adolescent economic behavior, so the savings measures used in both cases were very simple—for the US study, there were questions about the possession of a checking or savings account in their own name, and in the UK study there were straightforward direct questions (e.g., "Do you save money?" at age 16 and "Do you save on a regular basis or just from time to time when you can?" at age 34). In both the US and the UK saving was the norm: 78.5 percent of British adolescents said they saved, and 67 percent of American adolescents had savings. The economic socialization measures were also pretty simple, and captured whether adolescents received regular money from parents and whether they had to earn it.

These two studies yield two main findings. First, there is a clear link between parenting and saving in adolescence and adulthood. In the UK study, the respondents answered eleven questions on relationships with parents, parental interest, and involvement at age 16, and these were combined into a latent variable of authoritative parenting. In the US study there were measures of parental warmth available from the 1997 wave of the Child Development Supplement, when the children were aged 8–12. Ashby et al. found that those participants who in earlier years had rated their parents as more authoritative were more likely to save at age 16. There was no direct relationship between authoritative parenting and adult saving, but there was an indirect effect: authoritative parenting was linked to social status, which was itself linked to adult saving. Elliot et al. found that parental warmth is weakly associated with adolescent saving, but strongly linked to adolescents' future orientation, which is itself predictive of saving by young adults. Second, there are continuities in saving behavior. This might seem obvious, but it is important (if there was no continuity, studying the development of saving would be irrelevant to understanding adult saving and consumption) and it has not been demonstrated empirically before. In the British sample there is a small but significant association between saving in adolescence and saving in adulthood 18 years later. This relationship is stronger for those who live alone, which makes sense as individual characteristics will be more important in this context than in a household where two sets (or more) of personal characteristics matter. In the American sample there is a strong link between having savings in adolescence and having savings five years later in young adulthood. It may be that inertia plays a part in explaining the latter results, since once a savings account is opened it may well be maintained because of inertia. But since banks will close accounts if they have not been used for a while, and bank-account switching is quite common among the young, inertia can explain these findings only partially.

Conclusions

Saving is not just deferred consumption—not for children, adolescents or adults. There are now a large number of studies on motivations for saving, and these show that there are three general motivational orientations: self-gratification (essentially saving as deferred consumption), the need to avoid debt and achieve security (what economists usually label buffer stock saving, and what in colloquial terms is often called "saving for a rainy day"), and saving for old age (which might be thought as a mix of buffer saving and deferred consumption) (Canova, Rattazzi, and Webley 2005). But motives shift across the life span. (Also see the chapter by Webster et al.) Most obviously, children, as dependents, do not need money as a buffer against unforeseen contingencies, since that buffer is already provided by their parents. Saving to have money on hand when it is needed (the important motivation for older children's saving identified by both Furnham and Jundin) appears similar, but it is not quite the same, since this form of saving is not about dealing with emergencies but about being able to take advantage of opportunities. In terms of Keynes'

(1936) list of saving motives, it is psychologically more similar to the "independence" motive.

What starts as deferred consumption (saving as the classic way of solving the problem of adjusting the flow of income to the flow of expenditure) turns into something else: for some people, an end in itself (what Keynes memorably called the motive "to satisfy pure miserliness"), for others a general economic orientation (saving and being oriented to the future as a "way of life") or an individual disposition. And for others saving is never a palatable option, and probably always makes excessive demands on an individual's self-control. (A similar distinction between tightwads and spendthrifts is made in the chapter by Rick.)

From an individual perspective, the development of saving requires learning about what is valued, learning strategies, techniques, and habits for saving, and acquiring knowledge about one's one weaknesses so that one can plan appropriately for delayed gratification. It requires a modicum of mathematical ability, so one can calculate how long and how much saving is necessary in a particular instance. It also requires a belief in a stable economic and social world, and a sense of continuity over time: there would be no point in saving up for a computer game unless one believed that the computer game (and the store in which it was sold) would still exist when the necessary money had been accumulated.

Considering the context adds at least three features to this picture. First, there is the importance of current social structure. Institutional theory suggests that structural failures make it difficult for poorer families to provide their children and adolescents with the connections within and between financial institutions that they need to save and accumulate assets. From this viewpoint, the act of saving is not purely an individual matter; it also requires access to the capabilities that financial institutions provide. Sherraden (1991) puts it this way:

> Owning financial assets, for most people, is an educational process. People pay attention to the investment, manage it, make some successful decisions, make some mistakes, seek out information, and throughout this process, gain a greater financial knowledge and sophistication. With this experience, people are likely to display greater interest, greater effort, and greater success in additional financial endeavors. This added effort, on the average, leads to increased income and accumulation of assets.

Put simply, assets beget assets—and successful saving fosters more saving.

Second, we should note the importance of what we might call the technology of money (for humans, though, technology is also relevant in a biological context). Without an effective store of value, we cannot save effectively if what we are storing loses value—perhaps through inflation—or is susceptible to theft. Likewise, an animal cannot hoard effectively if too much of its hoard spoils or is lost. Technology and institutional arrangements have an effect that is probably taken for granted: for example, children below the age of 13 are not allowed to be employed in the United States or in Britain (with a few exceptions), and some banks don't allow children below a certain age to have access to their own accounts. These institutional arrangements condition both what is possible and behavior. Financial institutions try to provide technologies that are desirable—that have the right combination of liquidity, usability, and security. Changes in money technology can have unforeseen and unfortunate side effects: debit cards can reduce the pain of spending of which Rick writes in his chapter, and credit cards can permit individuals to take on unsustainable debt burdens. But such changes can also be positive—cards that can be charged up with money, for example, give people both control and convenience.

Third, parents (and other socializing agents) can try to inculcate saving as a "habit" and can foster the "pseudo-morality" of thrift. But we know from the studies of historians in Britain and the United States (Johnson 1985; Tucker 1991) that in the previous century there was a decades-long shift from a "thrift ethic" to a consumption ethic. (See also the chapter by Frank.) It is possible (though difficult, as such long-term cultural change is difficult to detect) that we are in the middle of another decades-long shift, from a consumption ethic to a "sustainable" ethic, which implies an approach to consumption where the very long term is the benchmark but also an approach where sensible borrowing can be good, as well as saving. Anderson and Nevitte (2006) have shown that there was a decline in the relative value placed on thrift in Canada over the period 1981–2000, and they see this as consistent with Inglehart's (1997) thesis that materialist values are gradually being replaced by post-materialist values, such as a need for belonging and self-esteem. (Also see the chapter by Griskevicius et al.) Parents' practices of economic socialization have changed significantly over the past 50 years (pocket money has become the norm, and children having to work for chores is much more common—see Webley, Nyhus, and Otto 2011), and can be expected to change as much in the next 50 years. And perhaps parents (and schools, and the media) are putting more stress on sustainability, with consequences we will see in the next few decades.

The studies discussed in this chapter focused on how children learn to save money and on the contextual variables that affect this learning. But learning to save money is just a specific example of more general issues that relate to consumption that is embedded in time, and the concepts outlined here are also relevant to learning how to regulate resources in the domains discussed in other chapters in this volume (e.g., for goods by Preston and Vickers, for human food by Todd and Minard, and for animal food by Lea and by Sherry). Understanding temptation and developing techniques for resisting it are highly relevant to regulating eating and drug taking, and lump-sum saving may also be relevant for spending to attract a mate (see the chapter by Griskevicius et al.). Understanding the evolutionary and biological context of saving is as important as understanding individual processes and the social context, which is why we need the interdisciplinary approach to consumption taken in this book.

Acknowledgments

My thanks to my collaborators, who are listed below in alphabetical order and who should take most of the credit for this research: Julie Ashby, Willie Elliott, Terri Friedline, Stephen Lea, Mark Levine, Alan Lewis, Michelle Mahdon, Ellen Nyhus, Annette Otto, Edmund Sonuga-Barke, Ingrid Schoon, Paul Schots, Joris Westerman.

References

Anderson, C. L., and Nevitte, N. 2006. Teach your children well: Values of thrift and saving. *Journal of Economic Psychology* 27: 247–261.

Ashby, J. S., Schoon, I., and Webley, P. 2011. Save now, save later? Linkages between saving behaviour in adolescence and adulthood. *European Psychologist* 16: 227–237.

Canova, L., Ratazzi, A. M. M., and Webley, P. 2005. The hierarchical structure of saving motives. *Journal of Economic Psychology* 26: 21–34.

Dickins, D., and Ferguson, V. 1957. Practices and Attitudes of Rural White Children Concerning Money. Technical report 43, Mississippi State College Agricultural Experimental Station.

Doss, V., Marlowe, J., and Godwin, D. 1995. Middle-school children's sources and uses of money. *Journal of Consumer Affairs* 29: 219–241.

Edwards, T. 1866. *The World's Laconics*. Dodd.

Elliot, W., Webley, P., and Friedline, T. 2011. Two Accounts for Why Adolescent Savings Is Predictive of Young Adult Savings: An Economic Socialization Perspective and an Institutional Perspective. Working Paper 11-34, Center for Social Development.

Furnham, A. F. 1999. The saving and spending habits of young people. *Journal of Economic Psychology* 20: 677–697.

Furnham, A. F., and Thomas, P. 1984. Pocket money: A study of economic education. *British Journal of Developmental Psychology* 2: 205–212.

Hagestad, G. O. 2006. Transfers between grandparents and grandchildren: The importance of taking a three-generation perspective. *Zeitschrift für Familienforschung* 18: 315–332.

Inglehart, R. 1997. *Modernization and Postmodernization: Cultural, Economic and Political Change in 43 Societies*. Princeton University Press.

Johnson, P. 1985. *Saving and Spending: The Working Class Economy in Britain 1870–1939*. Clarendon.

Jundin, S. 1985. *Adolescent Orientation towards Saving and Economic Planning*. Handelshögskolan EFI.

Katona, G. 1975. *Psychological Economics*. Elsevier.

Keynes, J. M. 1936. *The General Theory of Employment, Interest and Money*. Macmillan.

Leiser, D., and Ganin, M. 1996. Economic participation and economic socialization. In *Economic Socialization*, ed. P. Lunt and A. Furnham. Edward Elgar.

Lunt, P. K., and Livingstone, S. M. 1992. *Mass Consumption and Personal Identity*. Open University Press.

Mortimer, J. T., Dennehy, K., Lee, C., and Finch, M. D. 1994. Economic socialization in the American family: The prevalence, distribution and consequences of allowance arrangements. *Family Relations* 43: 23–29.

Nyhus, E., and Webley, P. 2013. The relationship between parenting and the economic orientation and behavior of Norwegian adolescents. *Journal of Genetic Psychology* 174: 620–641.

Otto, A. 2009. The Economic Psychology of Adolescent Saving. PhD thesis, University of Exeter.

Otto, A., Schots, P., Westerman, J., and Webley, P. 2006. Children's use of saving strategies: An experimental approach. *Journal of Economic Psychology* 27: 57–72.

Otto, A., and Webley, P. 2011. Saving, selling, earning, negotiating: How do adolescents acquire monetary lump sums? Unpublished manuscript, under review.

Sherraden, M. 1991. *Assets and the Poor: A New American Welfare Policy*. M. E. Sharpe.

Sonuga-Barke, E. J. S., and Paul Webley. 1993. *Children's Saving*. Erlbaum.

Steinberg, L., and Silk, J. S. 2002. Parenting adolescents. In *Handbook of Parenting*, volume 1: *Children and Parenting*, second edition, ed. M. Bornstein. Erlbaum.

Tucker, D. M. 1991. *The Decline of Thrift in America: Our Cultural Shift from Saving to Spending*. Praeger.

Ward, S., Wackmann, D. B., and Wartella, E. 1977. *How Children Learn to Buy*. Sage.

Webley, P. 2005. Children's understanding of economics. In *Children's Understanding of Society*, ed. M. Barrett and E. Buchanan-Barrow. Psychology Press.

Webley, P., Levine, R. M., and Lewis, A. 1991. A study in economic psychology: Children's saving in a play economy. *Human Relations* 44: 127–146.

Webley, P., and Nyhus, E. K. 2011. The grandparent role in economic socialization. Manuscript under review.

Webley, P., Nyhus, E. K., and Otto, A. 2011. The impact of economic socialization on adult saving and spending. Manuscript under review.

14 Consumer Behavior Across the Life Span: A Life History Theory Perspective

Chiraag Mittal, Vladas Griskevicius, and Bruce J. Ellis

The economist Harry Markowitz developed modern portfolio theory, which delineates how to optimally allocate investments to maximize financial gains. Yet Markowitz proved "incapable of applying" his theory to his own retirement fund, which he simply split 50/50 between stocks and bonds (Zweig 1998). "I should have computed the historical co-variances of the asset classes and drawn an efficient frontier," Markowitz recalled. "Instead, I visualized my grief if the stock market went way up and I wasn't in it—or if it went way down and I was completely in it." Optimally allocating resources is not an easy task, even for the man who wrote the book on it. Yet our human ancestors allocated resources for millennia, prioritizing some investments over others. Natural selection has endowed all modern humans to make decisions in ways that have consistently helped our genes survive and replicate. And we do this according to the rules of what can be described as evolutionary portfolio theory.

In this chapter, we examine how people allocate resources, as when consumers choose to spend money on one product rather than another. But we consider resource allocation from the perspective of evolutionary biology rather than from a traditional economic perspective. (For a similar perspective, see the chapter by Preston and Vickers and the chapter by Frank.) Evolutionary biologists also think in economic terms, in the sense that they ask how any animal allocates its scarce energetic resources. But evolutionary biologists consider how resource allocations maximize reproductive rather than economic success. One way biologists can study allocation decisions is by means of Life History Theory (LHT), a method that has important implications for consumer behavior and for economic decision making. Here we focus on the insights LHT provides into how consumer behavior changes across the life span, and on how individuals vary in their consumer preferences.

LHT and Core Tradeoffs

Life History Theory addresses how organisms allocate limited resources to maximize evolutionary fitness (Roff 2002; Stearns 1992). This framework has garnered considerable empirical support in the study of animal behavior (Ellis et al. 2009), and it has been central to empirical advances in human behavioral ecology and child development (Belsky, Steinberg, and Draper 1991; Del Giudice 2009; Hill and Kaplan 1999). LHT highlights that, although all organisms allocate resources to maximize fitness, the inherent scarcity of resources means that organisms cannot simultaneously maximize all critical life tasks, including survival, growth, and reproduction. All organisms must therefore make tradeoffs that prioritize the allocation of energy and resources to some life tasks and not to others.

LHT highlights that every organism must make tradeoffs between allocating resources to *somatic effort* and allocating them to *reproductive effort.* Somatic effort is the devotion of energy to growing and maintaining a healthy body (the "soma") so as to increase the likelihood of the survival of the individual. Somatic effort includes both maintenance (all the effort devoted to staying alive and maintaining basic functioning) and growth or development of "embodied capital" (all the energy allocated to processes and activities that increase physical size and socio-competitive competencies). Reproductive effort is the devotion of energy to producing and rearing offspring. Because energy spent on growing or repairing the body cannot be simultaneously spent on activities that facilitate reproduction, investing resources in somatic effort rather than reproductive effort represents a fundamental life-history tradeoff.

Reproductive effect can be further divided into another critical tradeoff: *mating effort* and *parental effort.* Mating effort is the energy expended on attracting mates and increasing the opportunities for reproduction. Because desirable mates are always a scarce resource, mating competition is inevitable, and thus dominance seeking, aggression, and risk taking are all functionally connected to mating effort (Trivers 1972). Parental effort is the energy spent on taking care of one's offspring and ensuring that they are able to survive and reproduce on their own. In the same way that it's difficult to be socializing at a bar and reading to your kids at home, mating effort and parental effort constitute another fundamental life-history tradeoff.

Life History Theory is relevant to consumer behavior and economic decisions because the aforementioned life-history tradeoffs have consequences for many behaviors that are not directly tied to reproduction or to parenting. LHT, therefore, provides a framework for understanding how, why, and when people make tradeoffs in consumer behavior, in economic decisions, in health, in diet, and in education. In the remainder of the chapter we discuss how LHT can inform the ways in which consumer behavior changes across the life span.

Developmental Life Stages

By looking through the lens of LHT, we can see that, like other animals, humans follow a specific developmental sequence across the life span. Our life histories can be divided into two primary stages: pre-reproductive and reproductive. The pre-reproductive stage is devoted to somatic effort; the reproductive stage includes major investments in mating and parenting, the allocations to parental effort increasing over time.

The pre-reproductive phase of the life span is dedicated to somatic effort, including heavy investment in developing physical, social, and cognitive competencies. Apart from developing physical capacities, such as building an efficient immune system, humans expend considerable resources on building a large brain, which is essential for navigating the social and ecological complexity of human life (Kaplan et al. 2000). The pre-reproductive stage generally lasts from conception until puberty, although somatic effort, such as DNA repair, continues throughout the life span, and most humans continue to invest significantly in building embodied capital even after puberty—for example, by continuing to build their competencies through further education.

Puberty marks the transition from the pre-reproductive to the reproductive phase of the human life span. Adolescence—the period between the onset of puberty and the onset of adulthood—is dominated by mating effort and growth. The developing individual reallocates energy and resources toward becoming reproductively competent (Ellis et al. 2012). From an evolutionary perspective, a major function of adolescence is to attain reproductive status—to develop the physical and social competencies needed to gain access to a new and highly contested biological resource: sex, and ultimately reproduction. Both sexual promiscuity and the intensity of sexual competition peak during adolescence and early adulthood (Weisfeld 1999; Weisfeld and Coleman 2005), when most people have not yet found a stable partner and the mating market is maximally open. A hallmark of adolescence is increased sociality: both males and females spend increasing amounts of time socializing with peers. This socialization serves two important evolutionary functions (Ellis et al. 2012; Weisfeld 1999). First, individuals in this stage need to determine where they stand in the social hierarchy, which is accomplished by constantly competing with and comparing themselves against other individuals of the same sex. Second, people in this stage also begin to evaluate their value on the mating market by exploring their mating opportunities and considering their own mate value.

The years beyond adolescence often involve major allocations to parental effort and are marked by "settling down," which generally occurs in early to mid adulthood. During "settling down," the focus shifts toward maintaining a long-term bond with a romantic partner and raising offspring. Whereas gonadal steroid hormones increase during adolescence, men's and women's testosterone levels decrease after marriage, and decrease even further after the birth of a child (Burnham et al. 2003; Gettler et al. 2011). As sex hormones decrease, so does mating effort. Parental effort lasts the rest of one's life, and grandparenting is an extension of parental effort.

Implications for consumer behavior

The bulk of research in consumer behavior and economic decision making has focused on young adults. Some studies of children (see, e.g., Bakir and Palan 2010; Chaplin and John 2005; Chaplin and Lowrey 2010) have sought to understand children's limited cognitive abilities and how communications media affect children's behavior. However, few if any studies have considered the systematic ways in which consumer behavior and economic decision making may change across the life span. This gap in our knowledge is especially important because decisions about money are being made by people of all ages. Life History Theory provides a powerful theoretical basis for understanding how, why, and when consumer behavior and economic decisions change across the life span. For instance, a life-history perspective suggests that people consciously or unconsciously use products in the service of achieving the evolutionary goals associated with each life stage. Furthermore, individuals in the different life stages may be differentially sensitive to particular types of environmental cues, advertisements, and persuasion strategies.

The different phases of the life span that are dominated by growth, mating effort, and parental effort are likely to be associated with the desire for and the purchasing of particular types of products and services. For example, children may be especially receptive to high-calorie diets of sugary and fatty foods that facilitate physical growth because building a bigger body and a larger brain are priorities in the pre-reproductive stage. A calorie-rich diet may also provide children with the energy they need to engage in vigorous play, which may help them to experience and sample their immediate environment so as to better prepare for later life stages. This kind of experiential play, which is facilitated by dolls and by action figures, is associated with superior social competence, a deferred benefit that persists throughout adulthood (Bjorklund and Brown 1998).

Whereas the evolutionary goals associated with the pre-reproductive stage are to grow and to learn new skills while remaining safe and healthy, the goals associated with the adolescent stage are to become a member of a group, to seek status within that group, and to impress potential mates. With an overriding emphasis on mating effort, these latter goals can often trump the need for safety and health. Teenagers and young adults are the demographic group highest in risk taking and sensation seeking; indeed, they often embrace danger. They are the people most likely to experiment with drugs and alcohol, to commit crimes, and to drive recklessly (Steinberg 2007). Teenagers achieve the evolutionary goals associated with the mating stage by increasing their interaction with peers—for example, by increasing their participation in group activities such as going to shopping malls and movie theaters. Wanting both to fit into a group and to stand out from the group, teenagers may also become much more concerned about brands, which can serve as displays of individual and group identity, preferences, and social means.

The third and final stage, in which resource allocations are dominated by parental effort, is associated with forming a long-term bond with another person (usually a marriage partner), which creates the foundation for producing and successfully raising offspring. These goals are facilitated by a decrease in aggression and competitiveness and accompanied by changes in consumer behavior. In this stage, resources are likely to be allocated to one's family. Besides spending on diapers and baby food, parents also begin investing in the long-term well-being of the child by setting up a college fund or vying for a spot at the best schools. With the sudden increase in long-term orientation, the impulsivity and the risky spending for short-term rewards that dominated in the mating stage may be reversed, and in the third stage people may become risk averse and forward looking.

In addition to providing many insights on how spending and economic decisions may change across the life span, Life History Theory suggests that individuals in different life stages may be differentially sensitive to specific types of social cues, advertisements, and persuasion strategies. For example, concerns about affiliation, status, and mate attraction should be most powerful at motivating behavior for individuals in the mating stage (teenagers and young adults). Accordingly, much research in social psychology finds that priming people with cues of attractive individuals of the opposite sex, status competition, or social exclusion has powerful effects on their psychology and their behavior. (See, e.g., Griskevicius, Tybur and Van den Bergh 2010; Sundie et al. 2011; Twenge et al. 2001; also see the chapter by Griskevicius et al. and the chapter by Saad.) The vast majority of this research has looked at college students in their late teens and early twenties, who are in the mating stage and are likely to be most responsive to such cues. However, we hypothesize that the same social cues regarding social exclusion, mate attraction, and status competition may have substantially smaller effects—or no effect at all—on older and younger individuals. Because Life History Theory predicts that people in the parenting stage and people in the pre-reproductive stage should be less concerned about affiliation, status, and mate attraction, these motives may be substantially less powerful at guiding the behavior in individuals who are not in the mating stage.

By contrast, certain types of environmental cues and messages may be particularly powerful at spurring the behavior of adults and children but not that of people in the mating stage. For instance, as we noted earlier, during adolescence the goals of affiliation, status, and mate attraction can often trump the desire for safety and health. This suggests that appeals to safety or health may be particularly ineffective for teenagers and young adults, who should be much more concerned about showing off by approaching dangerous situations. For example, most driver-education programs aimed at 16-year-olds implore them to drive safely by depicting gruesome injuries that can occur if one drives carelessly. (Some readers may recall watching the movie *Red Asphalt*.) However, because teenagers are more likely to seek out dangerous situations, such fear appeals may *increase* rather than decrease their desire to drive recklessly. By contrast, appeals to safety and health may be more powerful for older individuals, since people in the parenting stage should be more concerned about staying alive and healthy to raise their offspring. Overall, the question of whether people in different life stages may be differentially sensitive to particular environmental cues and persuasion appeals requires testing. Life History Theory provides a promising conceptual basis for specific novel predictions.

Fast and Slow Life-History Strategies

So far we have talked about how people's priorities change across the life span. When people are in the mating stage of young adulthood, for example, they tend to care more about the wants of today than about the needs and consequences of tomorrow. But Life History Theory also emphasizes that there are important differences between individuals. Although everyone goes through the mating stage, for example, some individuals make preparations for tomorrow but others seek to maximize the present.

As we mentioned at the outset of the chapter, Life History Theory highlights that all individuals must resolve several fundamental tradeoffs. These include whether to invest in somatic effort or in reproductive effort (sometimes referred to as current versus future reproduction), whether to invest in mating effort or in parental effort, and whether to invest in quality of offspring or in quantity of offspring. An important insight from Life History Theory is that individuals vary in how they resolve these tradeoffs, using different strategies to accomplish evolutionary goals. Thus *life-history strategies* are believed to vary on a slow-to-fast continuum, some individuals enacting a slower strategy and others enacting a faster one (Ellis et al. 2009; Figueredo et al. 2004; Nettle 2010; Promislow and Harvey 1990). For example, although the average age of first-time mothers in the United States is 25 years, more than 20 percent of first births occur to women under age 20, and 10 percent occur to women who are over the age of 35.

Slow and fast strategies are each associated with a distinct suite of cohering features. At the physiological level, slow and fast strategies are associated with earlier and later physiological development and sexual maturity. Slow strategists tend to have later onset of puberty and later sexual debut, and to prefer monogamous relationships, having fewer children and being married when they do so. In contrast, fast strategists experience puberty earlier, are sexually precocious, and have more sexual partners, having children at an earlier age and producing more children overall. Psychologically, the two strategies are associated with different psychologies and different orientations toward family, sex, and money (Belsky et al. 1991; Figueredo et al. 2004, 2006; Wolf et al. 2007). Whereas fast strategists are more likely to be short-term opportunists and to take immediate benefits with little regard for long-term consequences, slow strategists are more likely to be long-term planners who delay immediate gratification to increase future payoffs (Chisholm 1999; Daly and Wilson 2005).

A person's adult life-history strategy partially depends on his or her early-life experiences. Recent work emphasizes that adult life-history strategies relate to two critical aspects of people's childhood environment (Ellis et al. 2009). First, strategies speed up if people grow up in harsh environments—places that are poor and likely to be rife with violence or disease. In a study of 170 countries, local mortality levels (the likelihood of death) were strongly related to the age at which mothers had their first child, higher mortality being correlated with much earlier age at first birth (Low et al. 2008). Similarly, in a study of Chicago neighborhoods, the median age of women giving birth was 27.3 for the ten neighborhoods with the highest life expectancy but was only 22.6 for the ten neighborhoods with lowest life expectancy (Wilson and Daly 1997). The second factor that speeds up life-history strategies is *fluctuation* or unpredictability in the childhood environment, such as moving residences, having an unpredictable income, or having unstable bi-parental care (Ellis et al. 2009). For example, girls living in a household without a consistently present father figure start puberty significantly earlier than girls who have a steadily present father figure (Ellis 2004). Recent findings also show that experiencing fluctuating environments in the first five years of life was the strongest predictor of fast strategy behaviors in adolescence and at age 23, such as having more sexual partners, being more aggressive and delinquent, and having a criminal record as an adult (Belsky et al. 2012; Simpson et al. 2012).

It is important to note that Life History Theory does not consider either a fast strategy or a slow strategy to be inherently better. Instead, it emphasizes that a fast strategy and a slow strategy are evolutionarily adaptive in different environments. A fast strategy is adaptive in dangerous and fluctuating environments, where there is uncertainty about where people will get enough resources or whether they will survive for a long time. In such environments, a fast strategy characterized by desire for immediate rewards is adaptive because delayed payoffs may never be realized. By contrast, in environments that are less harsh and more predictable, an individual can expect to live longer and exert more control over the environment. In such environments, it can be adaptive to follow a slower strategy, forgoing immediate gains to improve long-term prospects.

Behaviorally and psychologically, the extent to which adults are following a faster or slower life-history strategy can be assessed using one of several validated instruments. The Mini-K (a short form of the 199-item Arizona Life History Battery; see Figueredo et al. 2006) contains 20 items assessing individual differences in life-history strategy, including differences in risk taking, in closeness to family, and in sexual promiscuity. For example, respondents are asked to agree or to disagree with the statements "I avoid taking risks" and "While growing up, I had a close and warm relationship with my biological father." One limitation of the Mini-K, however, is that it conflates potential determinants of life-history strategy (e.g., quality of early family relationships) with markers of life-history strategy (e.g., risk taking). Another instrument, the High-K Strategy Scale (Giosan 2006), is a 26-item measure that assesses a variety of indicators associated with slow life-history strategy; it includes items on health and attractiveness, economic prospects, and social support.

Because levels of environmental harshness and unpredictability are highly related to household income, socioeconomic status (SES) serves as an important predictor of life-history strategies (Belsky, Schlomer, and Ellis 2012; Miller et al. 2009; Simpson et al. 2012). However, as we will discuss in the next section, *childhood SES* is more predictive than current SES of whether adults have a faster or a slower life-history strategy. Age at sexual maturation (e.g., menarche) also serves as an indicator of life-history strategy, menarche at an earlier age being associated with a faster strategy.

Implications for consumer behavior

The bulk of research in consumer behavior and economic decision making has focused on identifying powerful main effects—factors that produce a change in the behavior of most individuals on average. Much less attention has been paid to individual differences between consumers. Although some studies have considered ways in which consumers differ (see, e.g., Becherer and Richard 1978; Moore and Lehmann 1980), these tend to be focused on individual differences with respect to specific motives, products, or domains. Life History Theory, however, suggests that all people differ on a fundamental biological dimension. The fact that some people follow a fast strategy and others follow a slow strategy has multiple important implications for consumer behavior and for economic decision making.

First, fast and slow strategists may have different consumption profiles. Because fast strategists are more focused on obtaining immediate rewards at the cost of long-term benefits, they may be more likely to purchase products and services that provide instant gratification and excitement, such as thrill rides, fast cars, and perhaps sweeter and fattier foods. They may also be more likely to be in financial debt and to take part in risky behaviors such gambling, playing the lottery, and excessive drinking and drug use. By contrast, slow strategists may be more likely to purchase products, such as books and education, that don't provide much immediate excitement or many thrills but provide more long-term benefits. Although these hypothesized differences have yet to be tested, fast and slow strategists may also be differentially attracted to what consumer researchers call "vices and virtues" (Read, Loewenstein, and Kalyanaraman 1999). Defined relative to one another, vices and virtue differ in the timing of their realized costs and benefits. Whereas vices provide more pleasure in the short run while inducing larger costs for later, virtues are seemingly costlier in the short run while being more beneficial in the long run. For example, binge eating, excessive drinking, and procrastinating are all vices relative to eating broccoli, exercising, and studying for an upcoming test. We hypothesize that whereas fast strategists may expend more resources on vices, slow strategists may spend more on virtues.

A second implication is that fast and slow strategists may differ in their desire to show off and draw attention to themselves by means of products. This is because a faster strategy is more strongly related to the motivation to display status and attract mates, which has been found to be associated with seeking conspicuous products (Griskevicius et al. 2007; Sundie et al. 2011). One possibility is that fast strategists may purchase more conspicuous luxury goods. But even within the luxury goods category, fast and slow strategists may seek different types of products. Because fast strategists should be more motivated to be noticed, they may seek products higher in name brand prominence and having bigger and more conspicuous logos. They may also prefer products that are more gaudy, more flamboyant, and louder. By contrast, slow strategists may prefer luxury goods that are quieter and less likely to draw attention. For example, whereas a fast strategist may purchase a bright red sports car, a slow strategist may purchase an equally expensive white luxury sedan. Future research is needed not only to ascertain whether fast and slow strategists differ in their luxury product preferences but also whether they may also be differentially susceptible to different types of advertising strategies and persuasion appeals.

Third, in the realm of economic decisions making, fast and slow strategists may differ in the extent to which they exhibit various decision biases. For example, they may differ in loss aversion—that is, tendency to weigh losses more strongly than gains (Tversky and Kahneman 1991). Because fast strategies are related to less sensitivity to risk (Griskevicius et al. 2011a), one possibility is that fast strategists may be less averse to loss than slow strategists. For instance, fast strategists may experience less negative affect as a result of losses than slow strategists. If so, this would suggest that fast and slow strategists may also differ in their experience of regret or anticipated regret, which has important implications for immoral behavior and cheating. More research is needed to test the many ways in which fast and slow strategists may differ in their consumption behaviors and in their economic decision making.

Expression of Life-History Strategies in the Face of Adversity

Thus far, we have discussed how early-life experiences can shunt individuals down faster or slower life-history trajectories, which can lead them to have different priorities, to make different purchases, and to make economic decisions differently in adulthood. Sometimes adults from varying childhood environments behave very similarly. Nevertheless, even when it may appear that different childhood environments do not lead to different adult behaviors, research is finding that behaviors associated with faster and slower strategies often emerge specifically in the face of adversity (Griskevicius et al. 2011a,b). This is because childhood experience can sensitize contingent expression of fast and slow life-history strategies. Sensitization models assert that early-life conditions can program individuals to respond in different ways to adversity encountered later in life. This means that adults who experienced different childhood environments may behave similarly in benign and non-threatening conditions, but the same individuals may behave very differently when facing adversity (such as resource scarcity or a sense of physical danger) in adulthood.

Griskevicius et al. (2011a,b) proposed that different life-history strategies may be sensitized by being reared in resource-scarce versus resource-abundant environments. Because socioeconomic status is a modern indicator of harsh and unpredictable environments, Griskevicius and colleagues hypothesized that low-SES environments sensitize faster life-history strategies, whereas high-SES early-life environments sensitize slower strategies. They tested the contingent expression of fast versus slow strategies by exposing people either to neutral conditions or to cues of mortality (e.g., news articles about increasing homicide rates) and then observing their risk preferences and delay of gratification. Under benign conditions lacking adversity, people had similar preferences, regardless of their childhood background. However, mortality cues led people to diverge in their behavior in ways that depended on their childhood SES (Griskevicius et al. 2011b). Whereas individuals raised in lower-SES environments became more likely to seek risk and more impulsive, seeking gambles and immediate rewards (consistent with a faster life-history strategy), those from higher-SES backgrounds became more averse to risk and more patient, avoiding gambles and seeking delayed but larger rewards (consistent with a slower life-history strategy). Importantly, people's responses did not differ as a function of their current levels of SES, but only differed as a function of their childhood SES.

The fact that stress and uncertainty can lead adults to behave very differently depending on their childhood SES has important implications for consumer behavior and for economic decision making. Adults often experience stress and uncertainty—for example, they see unpredictable acts of terror on the news, or they are affected by economic recessions, inflation, job insecurity, or divorce. The notion that life-history strategies are sensitized in childhood suggests that people's behavior in tough times may be less related to their current levels of wealth than to their childhood conditions. For example, Whether an economic recession prompts people to spend or to save depends on their childhood environment (Griskevicius et al. 2013). Individuals who grew up wealthier react to resource scarcity by saving money for the future (consistent with a slow strategy), whereas those who grew up poorer respond by spending money to improve their current quality of life (consistent with a fast strategy). For people who grow up feeling deprived of resources, resource scarcity appears to activate an impulsive "live fast and die young" orientation to life, motivating such people toward immediate consumption and potentially precipitating financial ruin. In contrast, for people who grow up in relative abundance, resource scarcity triggers a "weather the storm" orientation. Neither strategy is inherently superior from a life-history perspective. Although risk taking and a focus on short-term rewards can be associated with detrimental long-term outcomes, "living fast" is an adaptive evolutionary strategy in harsh and unpredictable environments.

Even when tendencies associated with fast and slow strategies may be dormant during good times, they emerge under duress. These kinds of childhood-SES-dependent patterns in response to stress are observable in people's desire to have children sooner versus later (Griskevicius et al. 2011a), in investing strategies with low versus high levels of diversification (White et al. 2013), and in the eating more versus fewer calories (Hill et al. 2012). Further research is required to uncover how responses to resource stressors affect a wider range of consumer attitudes and behaviors related to matters such as self-interest and pro-social behaviors. For example, it is possible that people's reactions to such behaviors are very different or even conflicting when they are under duress than when in a benign state. More research is also needed to investigate what environmental stressors have the most powerful effects on regulating life-history strategies. For instance, it may be that environmental unpredictability rather than harshness has a stronger effect on the expression of life-history strategies (Ellis et al. 2009). The research described in this section is finding than socioeconomic status during childhood is an important determinant of life-history strategies. However, SES is associated with many different things, and more research is needed to determine what specific aspects of childhood environment drive the sensitization of specific life-history strategies. Finally, it would be fruitful to ascertain whether there may be sensitive periods during which children's life-history strategies are most influenced by their environmental conditions. (See, e.g., Simpson et al. 2012.)

Conclusion

Consumer researchers readily acknowledge that people differ in their spending behaviors across their life spans, and that there are considerable individual differences between consumers. However, there has been little examination of the systematic ways in which consumer behavior changes throughout life, or of which universal individual differences may be most biologically critical. Life History Theory provides a powerful, interdisciplinary theoretical basis to inform both of these questions. By delineating that the human life span is separable into phases that differ in their underlying evolutionary goals, Life History Theory provides insight into how, why, and when consumer behavior and economic decisions change across the life span. It also suggests that all organisms, including humans, vary fundamentally in the speed of their life-history strategies. The fact that some people follow a faster life-history strategy and others follow a slower strategy has important implications for consumer behavior and economic decision making, most of which are yet to be tested. Overall, the framework of Life History Theory is poised to help answer such important questions as why individuals differ in their consumption patterns and what factors shape those differences.

References

Bakir, A., and Palan, K. M. 2010. How are children's attitudes toward ads and brands affected by gender-related content in advertising? *Journal of Advertising* 39 (1): 35–48.

Becherer, R. C., and Richard, L. M. 1978. Self-monitoring as a moderating variable in consumer behavior. *Journal of Consumer Research* 5 (3): 159–162.

Belsky, J., Schlomer, G. L., and Ellis, B. J. 2012. Beyond cumulative risk: Distinguishing harshness and unpredictability as determinants of parenting and early life history strategy. *Developmental Psychology* 48: 662–673.

Belsky, J., Steinberg, L., and Draper, P. 1991. Childhood experience, interpersonal development, and reproductive strategy: An evolutionary theory of socialization. *Child Development* 62: 647–670.

Bjorklund, D. F., and Brown, R. D. 1998. Physical play and cognitive development: Integrating activity, cognition, and education. *Child Development* 69 (3): 604–606.

Burnham, T. C., Chapman, J. F., Gray, P. B., McIntyre, M. H., Lipson, S. F., and Ellison, P. T. 2003. Men in committed, romantic relationships have lower testosterone. *Hormones and Behavior* 44 (2): 119–122.

Chaplin, L. N., and John, D. R. 2005. The development of self-brand connections in children and adolescents. *Journal of Consumer Research* 32 (1): 119–129.

Chaplin, L. N., and Lowrey, T. M. 2010. The development of consumer-based consumption constellations in children. *Journal of Consumer Research* 36 (5): 757–777.

Chisholm, J. S. 1999. Attachment and time preference: Relations between early stress and sexual behavior in a sample of American university women. *Human Nature* 10: 51–83.

Daly, M., and Wilson, M. 2005. Carpe diem: Adaptation and devaluing the future. *Quarterly Review of Biology* 80: 55–60.

Del Giudice, M. 2009. Sex, attachment, and the development of reproductive strategies. *Behavioral and Brain Sciences* 32: 1–21.

Ellis, B. J. 2004. Timing of pubertal maturation in girls: An integrated life history approach. *Psychological Bulletin* 130 (6): 920–958.

Ellis, B. J., Del Giudice, M., Dishion, T. J., Figueredo, A. J., Gray, P., Griskevicius, V., et al. 2012. The evolutionary basis of risky adolescent behavior: Implications for science, policy and practice. *Developmental Psychology* 48: 598–623.

Ellis, B. J., Figueredo, A. J., Brumbach, B. H., and Schlomer, G. L. 2009. Fundamental dimensions of environmental risk: The impact of harsh versus unpredictable environments on the evolution and development of life history strategies. *Human Nature* 20: 204–268.

Figueredo, A. J., Vásquez, G., Brumbach, B. H., and Schneider, S. M. R. 2004. The heritability of life history strategy: The K-factor, covitality, and personality. *Social Biology* 51: 121–143.

Figueredo, A. J., Vásquez, G., Brumbach, B. H., Schneider, S. M. R., Sefcek, J. A., Tal, I. R., et al. 2006. Consilience and life history theory: From genes to brain to reproductive strategy. *Developmental Review* 26: 243–275.

Gettler, L. T., McDade, T. W., Feranil, A. B., and Kuzawa, C. W. 2011. Longitudinal evidence that fatherhood decreases testosterone in human males. *Proceedings of the National Academy of Sciences* 108 (39): 16194–16199.

Giosan, C. 2006. High-k strategy scale: A measure of the high-k independent criterion of fitness. *Evolutionary Psychology* 4: 394–405.

Griskevicius, V., Ackerman, J. A., Cantu, S. M., Delton, A. W., Robertson, T. E., Simpson, J. A., et al. 2013. When the economy falters do people spend or save? Responses to resource scarcity depend on childhood environments. *Psychological Science* 24 (2): 197–205.

Griskevicius, V., Delton, A. W., Robertson, T. E., and Tybur, J. M. 2011a. The environmental contingency of life history strategies: Influences of mortality and socioeconomic status on reproductive timing. *Journal of Personality and Social Psychology* 100: 241–254.

Griskevicius, V., Tybur, J. M., Delton, A. W., and Robertson, T. E. 2011b. The influence of mortality and socioeconomic status on risk and delayed rewards: A life history theory approach. *Journal of Personality and Social Psychology* 100: 1015–1026.

Griskevicius, V., Tybur, J. M., Sundie, J. M., Cialdini, R. B., Miller, G. F., and Kenrick, D. T. 2007. Blatant benevolence and conspicuous consumption: When romantic motives elicit strategic costly signals. *Journal of Personality and Social Psychology* 93: 85–102.

Griskevicius, V., Tybur, J. M., and Van den Bergh, B. 2010. Going green to be seen: Status, reputation, and conspicuous consumption. *Journal of Personality and Social Psychology* 98: 392–404.

Hill, K., and Kaplan, H. 1999. Life history traits in humans: Theory and empirical studies. *Annual Review of Anthropology* 28: 397–430.

Hill, S. E., Rodeheffer, C. D., DelPriore, D., and Butterfield, M. 2012. A life history perspective on women's calorie regulation: Food, fat, and fertility suppression. Presented at annual meeting of Human Behavior and Evolution Society, Albuquerque.

Kaplan, H., Hill, K., Lancaster, J., and Hurtado, A. M. 2000. A theory of human life history evolution: Diet, intelligence, and longevity. Evolutionary Anthropology 9 (4): 156–185.

Low, B. S., Hazel, A., Parker, N., and Welch, K. B. 2008. Influences on women's reproductive lives: Unexpected ecological underpinnings. *Cross-Cultural Research* 42: 201–219.

Miller, G. E., Chen, E., Fok, A. K., Walker, H., Lim, A., Nicholls, E. F., et al. 2009. Low early-life social class leaves a biological residue manifested by decreased glucocorticoid and increased proinflammatory signaling. *Proceedings of the National Academy of Sciences* 106: 14716–14721.

Moore, W. L., and Lehmann, D. R. 1980. Individual differences in search behavior for a nondurable. *Journal of Consumer Research* 7 (3): 296–307.

Nettle, D. 2010. Dying young and living fast: Variation in life history across English neighborhoods. *Behavioral Ecology* 21: 387–395.

Promislow, D., and Harvey, P. 1990. Living fast and dying young: A comparative analysis of life-history variation among mammals. *Journal of the Zoological Society of London* 220: 417–437.

Read, D., Loewenstein, G., and Kalyanaraman, S. 1999. Mixing virtue with vice: Combining the immediacy effect and the diversification heuristic. *Journal of Behavioral Decision Making* 12: 257–273.

Roff, D. A. 2002. *Life History Evolution*. Sinauer.

Simpson, J. A., Griskevicius, V., Kuo, S. I.-C., Sung, S., and Collins, W. A. 2012. Evolution, stress, and sensitive periods: The influence of unpredictability in early versus late childhood on sex and risky behavior. *Developmental Psychology* 48: 674–686.

Stearns, S. 1992. *The Evolution of Life Histories*. Oxford University Press.

Steinberg, L. 2007. Risk taking in adolescence: New perspectives from brain and behavioral science. *Current Directions in Psychological Science* 16 (2): 55–59.

Sundie, J. M., Kenrick, D. T., Griskevicius, V., Tybur, J. M., Vohs, K. D., and Beal, D. J. 2011. Peacocks, Porsches, and Thorstein Veblen: Conspicuous consumption as a sexual signaling system. *Journal of Personality and Social Psychology* 100: 664–680.

Trivers, R. L. 1972. Parental investment and sexual selection. In *Sexual Selection and the Descent of Man 1871–1971*, ed. B. Campbell. Aldine.

Tversky, A., and Kahneman, D. 1991. Loss aversion in riskless choice: A reference-dependent model. *Quarterly Journal of Economics* 106: 1039–1061.

Twenge, J. M., Baumeister, R. F., Tice, D. M., and Stucke, T. S. 2001. If you can't join them, beat them: Effects of social exclusion on aggressive behavior. *Journal of Personality and Social Psychology* 81 (6): 1058–1069.

Weisfeld, G. E. 1999. *Evolutionary Principles of Human Adolescence*. Basic Books.

Weisfeld, G. E., and Coleman, D. K. 2005. Further observations on adolescence. In *Evolutionary Perspectives on Human Development*, second edition, ed. R. Burgess and K. MacDonald. Sage.

White, A. E., Li, Y. J., Griskevicius, V., Kenrick, D. T. and Neuberg, S. L. 2013. Putting all your eggs in one basket: Life history strategies, bet hedging, and diversification. *Psychological Science* 24: 715–722.

Wilson, M., and Daly, M. 1997. Life expectancy, economic inequality, homicide, and reproductive timing in Chicago neighborhoods. *British Medical Journal* 314: 1271–1274.

Wolf, M., van Doorn, G. S., Leimar, O., and Weissing, F. J. 2007. Life-history trade-offs favour the evolution of animal personalities. *Nature* 447: 581–585.

Zweig, J. 1998. America's top pension fund. *Money* 27 (1): 114.

15 Older Adults as Consumers: An Examination of Differences by Birth Cohort

Noah J. Webster, Toni C. Antonucci, Carolyn Yoon, Wayne R. McCullough, Debra N. Fin, and Debra L. Hartsell

It has been widely recognized that the United States, and indeed much of the developed world, is experiencing a demographic revolution (Kalache, Barreto, and Keller 2005). This demographic revolution is evidenced by a fundamental change in the age structure of the population. As recently as 100 years ago the population could be described as shaped like a pyramid, with a majority of people being children under the age of 16 and with very few older people. This has changed so drastically that the population structure is now most frequently described as a barrel-like shape, with the number of young and old people nearly equal. This change is a result of both reduced fertility and increased longevity. Reduced fertility has been attributed to the industrial and technological revolutions that have led to a decrease in the need for farm or factory workers, and also to educational and pharmaceutical advances that have rendered fertility largely a convenient matter of choice. Increased longevity, on the other hand, is attributed to advances in public health, such as improved sanitation and significant medical breakthroughs, both of which have reduced the spread of infectious diseases (Antonucci and Wong 2010).

Despite the successes cited in the preceding paragraph, the changes in the structure of the population pose a number of challenges for society. One challenge concerns the readiness of society to meet the needs of its aging population. In order to help industries and organizations prepare to meet the needs of the aging population in a responsive and competitive fashion, it would be particularly useful to understand the income and consumption patterns of older people and how they are changing with increased longevity. It is not clear whether the consumption patterns of older adults will largely remain the same as compared to previous cohorts of older adults, so that total consumption simply reflects an increase in the number of older consumers, or whether consumption patterns will change across cohorts of older people as a result of different gender ratios, racial compositions, or marital histories of the aging population across cohorts. In this chapter, we explore these issues by examining patterns of total consumption as well as specific consumption patterns among five cohorts of older adults in each of the following categories: food, transportation, trips and vacations, durable goods, health, and donations and gifts. We begin by considering changes in several socio-demographic factors that are likely to influence consumption patterns.

Changing Socio-Demographic Characteristics

An important component of the demographic revolution is the socio-demographic composition of the population. In this section we highlight three factors that may influence changes in consumption: gender, race, and marital status.

It has long been recognized that women now commonly outlive men. In 1950, women lived an average of 68 years and men only lived 66 years. By 2000, women lived an average of 78 years and men 75. It is projected that by 2050 women will live 83 years and men 81. Interestingly, life expectancy also differs for men and women once they reach the age of 65. In 1950 a woman who had reached the age of 65 could expect to live to the age of 80, a man to the age of 78. By 2000, a woman surviving to 65 had a life expectancy of 83 years, a man a life expectancy of 81 years. These figures are projected to have improved even further by 2050, when a woman surviving to 65 is projected to live to the age of 86 and a man in the same circumstance to live to the age of 84. It is not clear what these changing patterns of longevity by gender will mean for the future consumption patterns of older men and older women (U.S. Census Bureau 2008). The racial and ethnic composition of the society is also changing, with a decrease in the proportion of the population that is European-American and a concurrent increase in the numbers of racial and ethnic minorities, including African Americans, Hispanic Americans, and Asian Americans. The U.S. Census Bureau (ibid.) projects that the number of non-Hispanic whites will remain relatively stable from 2000 to 2050. They number approximately 200 million, which represented 65 percent of the population in 2000 and will represent approximately 46 percent of the population in 2050. On the other hand, the number of non-Hispanic Blacks will increase from approximately 31 million in 2000 to 52 million by 2050. Although their absolute number will increase, they will remain approximately 12 percent of the population. Hispanics have been identified as the fastest-growing population in the United States. In 2000 there were 38 million, about 14 percent of the population; by 2050 they are expected to number over 133 million and to constitute about 30 percent of the population. And the number of Asian Americans is expected to increase from approximately 15 million in 2000 to 33 million in 2050. This will represent an increase from approximately 4.5 percent of the population to 7.6 percent.

Changes in marital status often accompany old age. However, even the nature of that change varies by cohort. A common trend from 1950 to 2050 is that fewer older adults are married in more recent cohorts. Interestingly, the causes of non-marriage have changed with time. Whereas previously people most often became unmarried through widowhood, more people now become unmarried through divorce or separation, or were never married to begin with (Ryan, Smith, Antonucci, and Jackson 2012). Not only are the causes of being unmarried changing; the number of years people are living while unmarried also appears to be increasing.

Many questions about the effects of these socio-demographic changes on consumption over time have gone unanswered. In this chapter, we seek to begin addressing these questions by examining how changing socio-demographic characteristics (i.e., gender, race, and marital status) influence the consumption patterns of five cohorts of older people born during different periods in the twentieth century.

Models of Consumption and Aging

Several models have been suggested that predict how consumption patterns are likely to change with age. In this section we review the alternative predicted patterns.

As people age, their level of spending declines and their spending patterns related to consumption change. In general, they spend relatively more on health-care services, donations and gifts, and relatively less on trips and vacations, on automobiles, and on durable goods. The patterns of spending are of interest because they convey information about how people choose to allocate their resources as they age. These patterns also aid our ability to predict future demand for different types of goods and services, which is particularly important because this age group is increasing in raw numbers and in relative proportion to the entire population. This information will be especially useful for industries, because awareness of shifts in consumption will help them to time the introductions of new products to meet these shifts, thereby reducing the risks often associated with product adoption and market penetration.

One of the leading models for examining consumption by older adults is the life-cycle model of consumption (Gourinchas and Parker 2002). The life-cycle model captures the allocation of the consumption of one type of good or service at a time. Another approach accounts for the consumption of different types of goods (as a share of total spending) within a single time period, rather than across time periods (Deaton and Muellbauer 1980). By combining the approaches represented by the life-cycle model and the within-period choice model, it is possible not only to document the changes in total spending as the population ages, but also to document shifts in the demand for various goods that accompany aging and economic status as people approach retirement (Yoon, Cole, and Lee 2009).

In this chapter we utilize unique data (described in detail below) to examine age profiles of total consumption and its components for the U.S. population over the age of 50. According to the life-cycle model, the wealth of a person declines at advanced ages because spending becomes greater than income. As wealth declines, the fraction of total spending devoted to different categories of goods also changes. In addition, it is likely that the composition of spending will change because of a pure age effect. The utility of some types of goods is likely to change with age as a result of changes in physical and cognitive capacities and in needs. For instance, as people age, they may drive less because they have increased difficulty driving in bad weather or after dark. In some cases, older people may also have a reduced need to drive because friends and family members with whom they wish to maintain contact are likely to either live close to them or to visit, rather than the reverse. Thus, we expect that, with levels of total spending held equal, consumption of automobiles will decline with age, and that the rate of decline in such consumption will be greater than the rates for some other categories (e.g., food).

Below we describe the data used to examine the question of consumption among older people. Drawing on the age models of consumption mentioned above, we examine cohort differences in total consumption and in food, transportation, trips and vacations, durable goods, health, and donations and gifts.

A Study of Consumption Changes with Age and Cohort

Description of sample

The data analyzed for this chapter are drawn from Health and Retirement Study 2012, a nationally representative longitudinal panel study of more than 26,000 adults aged 50 and older in the United States who were interviewed every two years. The Consumption and Activities Mail Survey (CAMS) (Health and Retirement Study 2011) is a supplemental survey distributed to a subsample of the main HRS respondents every two years (in odd-numbered years), and specifically designed to assess household patterns of consumption. For the analyses reported in this chapter we included respondents who completed both the 2010 wave of HRS and the 2011 wave of CAMS (N = 2,363).

Measures

Demographics

The primary demographic characteristic examined in this chapter is age, indicated by birth year. The respondents were grouped into five unique birth cohorts. The cohorts are described in detail below. Other demographic variables examined for this chapter include gender (coded as 0 = male or 1 = female), race (coded as 0 = white or 1 = non-white), and marital status (measured in the 2011 CAMS and coded as 0 = not married or living with a partner—i.e., separated, divorced, widowed, or never married—or 1 = married or living with a partner). Household annual income was measured in the 2010 HRS using a single item assessing the primary respondent's and the spouse or partner's (if applicable) combined total income for the year.

Consumption

Household Annual Consumption was assessed in 2011 in units of dollars. Total Consumption was measured as the sum of six unique categories of household consumption. Most of the consumption items were measured as amount spent in the last 12 months. For some items, respondents could report money spent on specific items and activities on a per-week or per-month basis or in the last 12 months. We standardized all responses to indicate money spent in the last year by multiplying per week responses by 52 and per month responses by 12.

The six categories of consumption used to calculate total consumption were as follows:

Food, measured as a composite sum of two separate items including money spent on food and drinks (including alcoholic) bought in grocery or other stores and on dining and drinking in restaurants, cafés, and diners, including take-out food.

Transportation, measured as a sum composite of four items including vehicle insurance, vehicle maintenance (parts, repairs, and servicing), gasoline, and car payments (interest and principal).

Trips and vacations, measured with a single item assessing money spent on transportation, accommodations, and recreational expenses on trips.

Durable goods, measured as the amount of money spent in the past year on the purchase of a refrigerator, a washing machine and/or dryer, a dishwasher, a television, and a computer. If any of the items were not purchased, they received a value of zero for the item.

Health, measured as the sum of four items: health insurance (money spent out of pocket, including Medicare supplemental insurance), prescription and nonprescription medication costs not covered by insurance, and health-care services (out-of-pocket costs for hospital care, doctors' services, lab tests, eye care, dental care, and nursing-home care)

Donations and gifts, measured as the composite sum of two items, one including contributions to religious, educational, charitable, or political organizations and the other including cash and gifts to family members and friends outside of the household, including alimony and child support.

Cohorts

We examined the consumption patterns of five different birth cohorts, all within the age range 58–102. These included people born during different periods of history. Cohort 1 consisted of people born before 1924. This was a relatively small cohort, consisting of only 160 people, or 7 percent of our sample. We call them Parents of the Boomers. Cohort 2 included people born between 1924 and 1930. This was another small cohort, consisting of only 189 people, or 8 percent of our sample. Members of this cohort, most notable for having experienced the Great Depression during their formative years, are often called Children of the Depression. Members of cohort 3, which consisted of people born between 1931 and 1941 (during the Depression and before World War II), were labeled the Pre-War Babies. This relatively large portion of our sample—the focus of the original HRS consisted of 1,285 people, or 54 percent of our sample. Cohort 4 consisted of individuals born between 1942 and 1947, sometimes labeled War Babies because they were born during or shortly after World War II. They numbered 351, or 15 percent of the sample. Cohort 5 consisted of the early Baby Boomers—those born between 1948 and 1953. They numbered 378 people, or approximately 16 percent of the sample.

The total sample consisted of 2,363 people. As can be seen in table 15.1, there were more women than men. The 1,513 women constituted 64 percent of the sample. Approximately 16 percent of the sample (367 people) self-identified as non-white. Almost half of the subjects (1,119, or 47 percent) were married or living with a partner. Although we do not include age in the analyses, due to age being naturally confounded with cohort, it is useful to know that the mean age of the sample was 72 with a standard deviation of 8.6.

Results

Descriptive information about income and consumption

The sample's mean annual household income was \$51,067 (SD = \$54,814) and ranged from \$0 to \$400,200. Total household consumption averaged \$18,683 (SD = \$17,016) in the past year, ranging from \$0 to \$340,708. The sample spent an average of \$5,466 (SD = \$4,463) on food, \$4,450 (SD = \$4,780) on transportation, \$4,065 (SD = \$6,244) on health, \$3,241 (SD = \$9,155) on donations and gifts, \$1,492 (SD = \$3,071) on trips and vacations, and \$322 (SD = \$709) on durable goods.

Race, gender, and marital status

As expected, females, racial or ethnic minorities, and individuals not married or living with a partner reported significantly lower annual household income. (See table 15.2.) We found a similar pattern in total annual

Table 15.1
Descriptive statistics (N = 2,363).

	% (N)	Mean	(SD)	Range
Age		71.9	(8.6)	58–102
Birth cohort				
Parents of Boomers (1923 or earlier)	6.8 (160)			
Children of the Depression (1924–1930)	8.0 (189)			
Pre-War Babies (1931–1941)	54.4 (1285)			
War Babies (1942–1947)	14.9 (351)			
Baby Boomers (1948–1953)	16.0 (378)			
Gender (female)	64.0 (1513)			
Race (non-white)	15.5 (367)			
Marital status (married/living with partner)	47.4 (1119)			
Household annual income ($)		51,067	(54,814)	0–400,200
Household annual consumption ($)				
Total consumption[a]		18,683	(17,016)	0–340,708
Food		5,466	(4,463)	0–42,100
Transportation		4,450	(4,780)	0–73,500
Trips and vacations		1,492	(3,071)	0–49,000
Durable goods		322	(709)	0–14,000
Health		4,065	(6,244)	0–133,200
Donations and gifts		3,241	(9,155)	0–275,000

a. Total includes a sum of the six categories listed below.

consumption, with females, racial or ethnic minorities, and those who were not married reporting significantly less consumption in the past year. Females reported spending less on food, transportation, and donations/gifts. Race was significantly related to all six categories of consumption except transportation. In all cases racial or ethnic minorities reported spending less. Marital status was significantly related to every category of consumption we examined, with respondents who were married or living with a partner reporting greater consumption in all categories. This finding is not surprising, in view of the reality of spending for two people in a household compared to one. It is important to note that household income was not controlled for in these models, since age and declining levels of income are so intertwined. As a result, findings that link race, gender, and marital status to consumption may reflect income level differences between the groups.

Age and income

As expected, birth cohort was significantly related to income. Generally, we found that income levels in the older cohorts were less than in the younger cohorts. (See table 15.2 and figure 15.1.) However, this decrease, as demonstrated in the *post hoc* test results, was not perfectly linear. The youngest birth cohort, the Baby Boomers, the group most likely to still be employed, reported the highest annual income, which was significantly higher than the oldest three birth cohorts (Parents of Boomers, Children of the Depression, and Pre-War Babies). The second youngest birth cohort, the War Babies, reported significantly greater income when compared to the two oldest cohorts, but not the middle cohort (Pre-War Babies). This middle cohort, in addition to reporting income that was significantly smaller than the youngest cohort, reported income significantly greater than the oldest birth cohort. Lastly, the two oldest birth cohorts, Parents of Boomers and Children of the Depression, did not differ significantly from each other.

Age and consumption

We found that birth cohort was significantly related to total consumption and to all categories of consumption with the exception of health. (See table 15.2 and figure 15.1.) We observed that older cohorts generally consumed less, overall, than younger cohorts. However, as with income, the

Table 15.2

Model and parameter effects.[a]

	Household annual consumption of							
	Household annual income	Household annual total consumption	Food	Transportation	Trips and vacations	Durable goods	Health	Donations and gifts
	Tests of model effects (Wald χ^2)							
Birth cohort	48.63***	19.36**	27.19**	163.71***	248.85***	156.91***	8.64	70.22***
Female	10.67**	5.20*	4.91*	12.00**	2.51	3.46	0.21	3.87*
Non-white	39.95***	35.30***	26.18***	1.93	215.25***	59.23***	43.82***	121.64***
Married/living with partner	181.21***	153.87***	90.27***	133.84***	305.77***	187.66***	180.92***	259.57***
	Parameter estimates (b(SE))							
Female	–0.16 (.05)**	–0.10 (.04)*	–0.10 (.05)*	–0.16 (.04)**	–0.07 (.05)	0.09 (.05)	0.02 (.05)	–0.09 (.05)*
Non-white	–0.39 (.06)***	–0.35 (.06)***	–0.30 (.06)***	–0.08 (.06)	–0.87 (.06)***	–0.45 (.06)***	–0.39 (.06)***	–0.65 (.06)***
Married/living with partner	0.64 (.05)***	0.55 (.04)***	0.43 (.04)***	0.52 (.04)***	0.81 (.05)***	0.63 (.05)***	0.61 (.05)***	0.74 (.05)***

a. Data analysis: To examine how the five birth cohorts varied in annual household income, total consumption, and consumption by category we conducted eight generalized linear models. This technique allowed us to model the non-normal distributions (right skew) of the income and consumption variables as a negative binomial distribution with a log link function. These models included birth cohort as a five-category factor and gender, race and marital status as control variables. Bonferroni post hoc tests were conducted to examine if all pairwise combinations of birth cohorts significantly differed in terms of the estimated marginal means for income and consumption. Presented in the figures are the estimated marginal means in dollars for the eight outcome variables by birth cohort. Exact estimated marginal means are available from the authors upon request. *p < .05; **p < .01; ***p < .001.

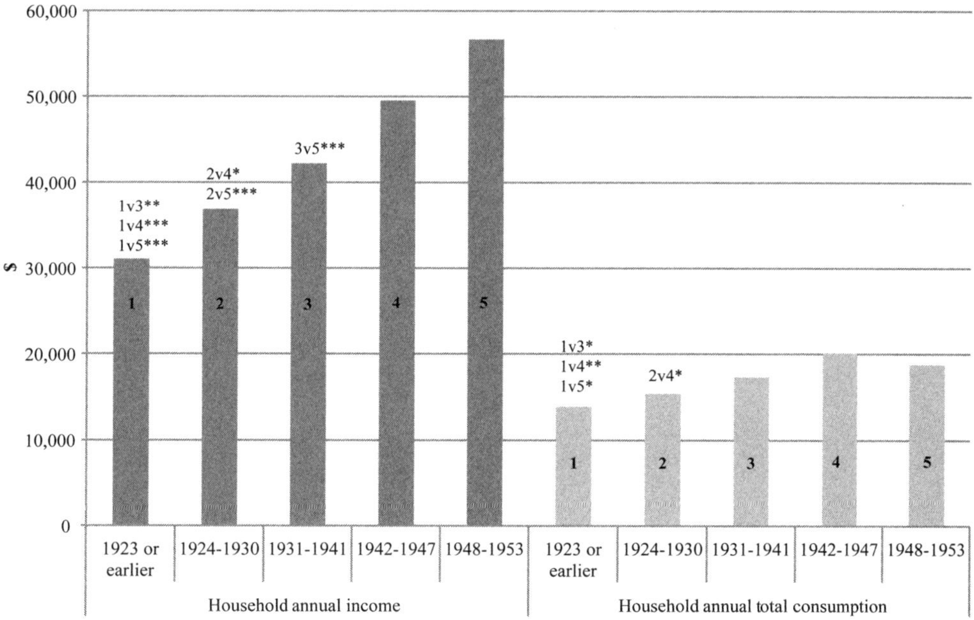

Figure 15.1
Household annual income and total consumption by birth cohort, with marginal means of income and consumption estimated. *Bonferroni pairwise *post hoc* test p value < .05; **p < .01; ***p < .001

negative relationship between birth cohort age and total consumption was not perfectly linear. The pairwise comparisons showed that the youngest three cohorts (Baby Boomers, War Babies, and Pre-War Babies) did not significantly differ in total consumption. The second youngest cohort, the War Babies, reported significantly greater consumption than the second oldest cohort, the Children of the Depression. Most of the observed differences were between the youngest three cohorts and the oldest one.

When we examined consumption within specific categories, we also found that the older cohorts generally spent less than the younger cohorts on food, transportation, trips and vacations, and durable goods. Pairwise comparisons of the birth cohorts on reported consumption of food expenses showed the exact same pattern as total consumption. (See figure 15.2.) This was not surprising, insofar as food represents the largest portion of total consumption. Although we expected food consumption to be lower among the older cohorts, we were surprised by the large significant difference

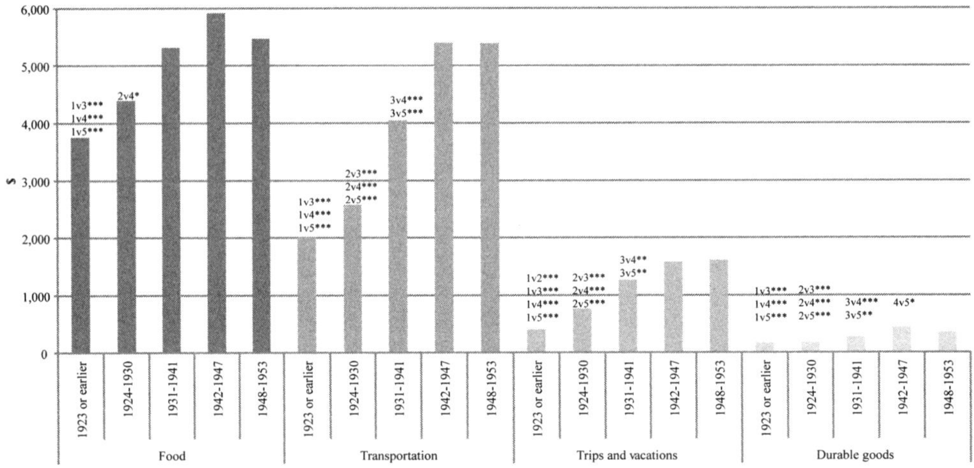

Figure 15.2
Household annual spending on food, transportation, trips and vacations, and durable goods by birth cohort, with marginal means of consumption estimated. *Bonferroni pairwise *post hoc* test p value < .05; ** $p < .01$; *** $p < .001$.

when the youngest three birth cohorts were compared against the oldest birth cohort. We believe this represents a true cohort difference in lifelong consumption. Older people are much more sensitive to food costs and are more likely to prepare foods at home if they are capable. Younger cohorts have been socialized to fast consumption out of the house, or at least to eating at home food that was prepared elsewhere and therefore was more expensive than home-prepared food. It is also the case that as people age their metabolism and activity levels slow down, which may reduce food consumption and the amount spent on food. Also, among the older cohorts, who are more likely to be on a fixed income, food may be viewed as a controllable expense that can be adjusted downward to ensure that resources will be available for other expenses that are less controllable (prescription drugs, utilities, and so on).

Next we consider transportation, the consumption category that represented the second-largest portion of total consumption. Older cohorts, as expected, generally spent less than younger cohorts. The two youngest birth cohorts did not differ from each other on money spent for transportation. However, both of these cohorts spent significantly more than all three older cohorts. The Pre-War Babies reported significantly greater consumption on transportation than the two oldest cohorts. The decline then leveled off as the two oldest cohorts, the Parents of the Boomers and Children of the Depression, reported no differences in transportation dollars spent.

Trips and vacations represented a smaller category of total consumption. This category of spending, as we expected, was highest among the younger cohorts and lowest among the older cohorts. We observed an almost perfect linear relationship between birth cohort and spending on trips and vacations. Every cohort spent significantly less on trips and vacations than the next younger cohort, with the exception that the two youngest cohorts reported similar levels of spending on this consumption category.

Consumption of durable goods was the smallest category of consumption. As expected, the oldest birth cohorts generally spent less on durable goods than the younger cohorts. However, there were some deviations from this general pattern, which were similar to the cohort patterns observed in food consumption. It is also important to note that the two oldest birth cohorts reported similar levels of consumption of durable goods. This was the same unexpected pattern observed for food and transportation consumption. Particularly surprising when examining this category of consumption was the finding that the youngest cohort, the Baby Boomers, spent significantly less on durable goods than the second youngest cohort, the War Babies.

Health was the only consumption category in which birth cohort had no effect. (See table 15.2.) As figure 15.3 shows, there were small descriptive differences between the five birth cohorts, but none were significant. The lack of a birth-cohort effect on health spending was unexpected. We hypothesized that respondents born in earlier cohorts would spend much more on health as their health declined. Inclusion of variables related to health, such as gender, race, and marital status, may explain why birth cohort had no independent effect on health consumption. In addition, the fact that approximately half of the War Babies and all of the Baby Boomers (i.e., those born after 1944) in the study sample were not yet eligible for Medicare at the time of the 2011 CAMS may have meant that these two cohorts incurred health costs that were covered by Medicare for the other cohorts. The surprising stability in health spending across the birth cohorts may actually indicate a cohort effect in this category of consumption. Since older adults utilized less in almost every consumption category examined, it is possible that the failure to show the typical decline in consumption

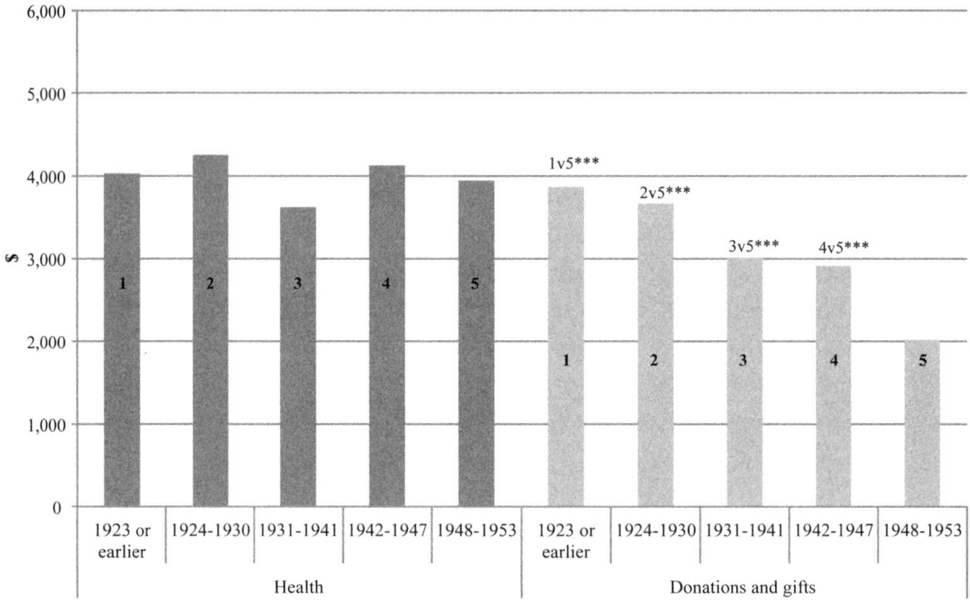

Figure 15.3
Household annual spending on health and donations/gifts by birth cohort, with marginal means of consumption estimated. ***Bonferroni pairwise *post hoc* test *p* value < .001.

in this domain actually represents a high level of utilization in older adults. Thus, while their spending decreases for almost all categories, it remains high for health services—arguably a less controllable expense that cannot be adjusted downward, even for those on a fixed income. In addition, surviving older adults may have been healthier and/or younger cohorts may have been sicker than we expected, and younger cohorts may have had more access to and use of over-the-counter health products (e.g., anti-aging products) and services (e.g., chiropractors) that typically are not covered by insurance.

The amount spent on donations and gifts was the only consumption category with significantly greater consumption among the older birth cohorts. Descriptively, the oldest birth cohort, Parents of the Boomers, reported spending the most in this category. However, as the *post hoc* test results indicate, only the Baby Boomers reported spending significantly less on donations and gifts than the four older cohorts.

The results provide an overview of how overall consumption patterns vary in later life. In general, our findings reinforce results from other studies that older adults report less income and consume less than younger adults (Gourinchas and Parker 2002). Our use of more detailed data on people's consumption of specific categories of goods and services allowed us to examine whether this trend differed across types of consumption. We found that adults in the older birth cohorts reported spending less on food, transportation, trips and vacations, and durable goods than those in the younger cohorts and more on donations and gifts. All cohorts reported similar levels of spending on health-related expenses. The examination of five birth cohorts within a sample of older adults also allowed us to observe patterns of consumption across birth cohorts. Specifically, we were able to examine at which stage in the life course spending on these specific categories begins to decline or to increase across age groups.

The results indicate a general decline in spending across most categories with age. Food, transportation, and durable goods show the greatest shift in the 70–80 age range and then remain the same at the lowest levels of spending among the two oldest birth cohorts. The only category of spending that showed a steady decline in spending across almost all the birth cohorts was trips and vacations. It is also important to note that the youngest two birth cohorts did not differ significantly from each other in their spending on food, transportation, and trips and vacations. This indicates little movement in these consumption categories in the earlier part of older adulthood. Results also suggest a plateau effect of age on consumption as the two oldest cohorts did not differ from each other in their spending on food, transportation, and durable goods.

Our data appear to have identified an age group—people between the ages of 70 and 80—in which the greatest changes in consumption patterns are evident. Industries and organizations would do well to recognize these changing patterns and to offer goods and products that meet their changing needs. However, it should be recognized that this middle group may in fact comprise two distinct groups: people who are healthy and still physically active and others who are declining in health and mobility. Though both of these groups would be consuming fewer durable goods (cars, washing machines, televisions), their needs and consumption patterns will obviously be quite different. People in the healthy group should continue to go out to eat, be physically active, and engage in vacationing and other leisure activities. In contrast, people in the less healthy group should be moving toward disability, with reduced mobility and reduced consumption across the same categories.

One might imagine intervention programs targeted at increasing the likelihood that pre-retirement individuals will be members of the former group rather than the latter (Antonucci et al. 2012). This would help the individuals to maintain both their health and their pre-retirement consumption patterns. On the other hand, people in the less healthy group becoming frail and disabled at younger ages will have negative effects on both their personal well-being and their consumption patterns, probably reducing all forms of consumption except for health-care costs.

The data suggest that these cohort differences may result from both life stage and life-experience phenomena. If we assume a rational consumption process on the part of aging consumers, we would expect more short-term focused decisions. For example, older consumers may be less likely to invest in a new furnace that might outlast them, and more likely to invest in less costly repair insurance. Changing patterns of transportation use indicate little decline in the two youngest cohorts, accelerated decline in the middle cohort, and a leveling off in the oldest cohorts. Perhaps this lack of a difference when comparing the two oldest birth cohorts reflects reduced or curtailed driving during this time period, which also reduces consumption in this category. Though the recently retired often spend time traveling, travel becomes less attractive with age (perhaps because of unwillingness or inability to spend money and time on it). For example, social networks decrease in size with age due to changing priorities and capabilities, including reduced interest in weak social ties, declining personal health, and loss of network members through death and disability. Transportation needs also change as family members and other close network members become more likely to visit elders and/or provide them with transportation. As the number of older people increases, these forms of transportation support may become less available. Offering alternative means of transportation might be especially beneficial to the middle and oldest cohorts.

The lack of demonstrated differences across birth cohorts in health consumption is not unimportant, since this is the third-largest consumption category. The fact that no differences are found could highlight the alarmingly increasing rate of relatively young older adults living with chronic conditions. In addition, these data could reflect a surprising degree to which younger birth cohorts spend more than expected on out-of-pocket health-care expenses while older cohorts continue spending in this category while reducing consumption in virtually every other domain (i.e., those that can be adjusted to make room for possible non-negotiable health-care expenses).

Although these findings are interesting and offer a preliminary glimpse into the consumption patterns of a number of older cohorts, several limitations to this study should be noted. We have provided a glimpse into the consumption patterns of only a limited number of categories. We were not able to capture all consumption categories, some of which are likely to provide a very different view of consumption across age cohorts. For example, the present chapter does not consider consumption patterns related to technology. As younger cohorts age, with increasing technological experience throughout their adult years, their consumption patterns in old age probably will look very different from those of earlier cohorts. Another notable limitation is the cross-sectionality of the data. Future studies should utilize longitudinal data to examine individual changes in consumption patterns over time.

Conclusion

Our findings suggest many differences in consumption patterns across age cohorts especially for food, transportation, trips and vacations, durable goods, and donations and gifts. Only health expenses did not differ across cohorts. Although we recognize, as we noted above, that there are limitations to the current data, the findings presented in this chapter suggest several areas in which industries and organizations might direct future product-development and marketing efforts.

Acknowledgments

This chapter resulted from meetings of the Consumption of Goods and Services workgroup of the University of Michigan's Society 2030 consortium, directed by T. C. Antonucci. Support was provided by the Institute for Social Research and the Office of the Vice President for Research at the University of Michigan.

References

Antonucci, T. C., Ashton-Miller, J. A., Brant, J., Falk, E. B., Halter, J. B., Hamdemir, L., et al. 2012. The right to move: A multidisciplinary lifespan conceptual framework. *Current Gerontology and Geriatrics Research* (http://www.hindawi.com).

Antonucci, T. C., and Wong, K. M. 2010. Public health and the aging family. *Public Health Reviews* 32 (2): 512–531.

Deaton, A., and Muellbauer, J. 1980. An almost ideal demand system. *American Economic Review* 70 (3): 312–326.

Gourinchas, P. O., and Parker, J. A. 2002. Consumption over the life cycle. *Econometrica* 70 (1): 47–89.

Health and Retirement Study. 2011. Data Description: 2011 Consumption and Activities Mail Survey (CAMS). Retrieved from http://hrsonline.isr.umich.edu.

Health and Retirement Study. 2012. About the Health and Retirement Study. Retrieved from http://hrsonline.isr.umich.edu.

Kalache, A., Barreto, S. M., and Keller, I. 2005. Global ageing: The demographic revolution in all cultures and societies. In *The Cambridge Handbook of Age and Ageing*, ed. L. Malcolm. Cambridge University Press.

Ryan, L. H., Smith, J., Antonucci, T. C., and Jackson, J. S. 2012. Cohort differences in the availability of informal caregivers: Are the Boomers at risk? *Gerontologist* 52 (2): 177–188.

U. S. Census Bureau. 2008. 2008 National Population Projections. Retrieved from http://www.census.gov.

Yoon, C., Cole, C. A., and Lee, M. P. 2009. Consumer decision making and aging: Current knowledge and future directions. *Journal of Consumer Psychology* 19 (1): 2–16.

16 Consumption as Pollution: Why Other People's Spending Matters

Robert H. Frank

In a 1978 book, the economist Thomas Schelling posed a question about hockey players, who when left to their own devices almost never wore helmets: Why, in secret votes, did they vote for a rule requiring helmets? If it is better to wear a helmet, Schelling wondered, why don't players just wear them? Why do they need rules?

Schelling's answer began with the standard assumption that most hockey players care about both their personal safety and winning their games. Because skating without a helmet lets a player see and hear a little better, and may help intimidate his opponents, it confers a competitive edge. Of course, it also increases the likelihood of serious injury. The standard rational-actor model assumes that the individual is in the best position to weigh tradeoffs of this sort. Whether or not that is true, hockey players have historically revealed by their choices that gaining an edge trumps concerns about injury.

The problem, Schelling noted, is that when all the players in a game follow this logic the inevitable outcome is that they all play without helmets. Even though all the players are exposed to greater risk, neither team gains the competitive edge it sought. Hence the attractiveness of the helmet rule.

Some object that, because the rule deprives individual players of the right to decide for themselves whether to wear helmets, it's an illegitimate restriction of their freedom. But that's an incoherent objection. The players themselves supported the rule because they understood that they would get a worse outcome without it. Of course the rule deprives individuals of the freedom to choose! That's the very reason they favor it!

Schelling's example illustrates Charles Darwin's fundamental insight that in competitive climates individual and collective interests are often sharply in conflict. (For a detailed exploration of this theme, see Frank 2011.) As two thought experiments will illustrate, this conflict is often present in ordinary consumption choices. In each of these thought experiments, your task is to choose between two otherwise identical worlds on the assumption that the lone difference between them will be permanent.

Experiment 1 Which of the following worlds would you choose? In World A, you and your family live in a neighborhood with 4,000-square-foot houses and others live in neighborhoods with 6,000-square-foot houses. In World B, you and your family live in a neighborhood with 3,000-square-foot houses and others live in neighborhoods with 2,500-square-foot houses.

Traditional economic models, which assume that utility depends on absolute consumption, imply that World A is the uniquely correct choice. Yet when people confront this question most choose World B, indicating a preference for a relatively large house over an absolutely larger one.

In most cases, that choice appears motivated less by a desire to feel superior to others than by an intuition that local context strongly shapes the standards that define adequacy. Decades ago, as a Peace Corps volunteer in rural Nepal, I lived in a two-room house that had no plumbing or electricity. I was never for a moment dissatisfied with that house. But if I had lived in a similar house in the United States I would have felt very differently, and my children wouldn't have wanted their friends to know where we lived.

Now consider the second thought experiment, which has exactly the same structure as the first:

Experiment 2 Which of the following worlds would you choose? In World A, you have two chances in 100,000 of dying on the job this year and others have one chance in 100,000. In World B, you have four chances in 100,000 of dying and others have six chances in 100,000.

Again you must choose between relative advantage and absolute advantage. This time, however, virtually everyone opts for absolute advantage by choosing World A.

Using terms coined by the economist Fred Hirsch (1976), I will use "positional good" to mean one whose value depends relatively strongly on how it compares with other similar goods in the same category. Similarly, I will use "nonpositional good" to mean one whose value depends much less heavily on context. In terms of the thought experiments just discussed, housing would be a positional good, safety a nonpositional good.

To call safety nonpositional is not to say that people don't care at all about relative safety. If you had two chances in 100,000 of dying and everyone else had one chance in 100,000, you would surely notice that difference, and it would probably be of some concern to you. But you wouldn't be willing to double your chance of dying to avoid the unfavorable comparison. Thus, "nonpositional" just means relatively less positional than other goods.

Adam Smith's celebrated theory of the invisible hand holds that individually rational consumption decisions generally steer scarce resources to their most highly valued uses. But if, as the modal responses in the two thought experiments seem to indicate, context shapes evaluation more heavily in some domains than in others, then all bets regarding the invisible hand are off. Instead, we expect to see expenditure "arms races" that focus on positional goods at the expense of nonpositional goods.

In terms of the examples in the thought experiments, someone may take a riskier job to earn the pay premium that would enable him to buy a larger house. But note the similarity to Schelling's helmet example: When all sacrifice safety to build bigger houses, they succeed only in raising the bar that defines adequate house size. And in return, they suffer a significant increase in risk of death. That's the kind of distortion in demand patterns I will focus on in this chapter.

It is clear that analogous distortions exist in many other domains. In a military arms race, for example, it is clear that equally matched antagonists are made worse off when each increases its stock of armaments. Since security depends on being relatively well armed, extra bombs for each leaves the balance of power unaffected. Enforceable arms-control agreements enable each society to improve the welfare of its citizens without having to sacrifice anything of real value.

Although military arms races are widely seen as problematic, few people complain that societies build too many schools and hospitals. Why this asymmetry? The simple reason is that context matters more for armaments than for schools and hospitals, since a nation with relatively few arms puts its political independence at risk. If context mattered more for schools and hospitals than for armaments, we would instead see escalating expenditures on schools and hospitals, paid for by reductions in expenditures on armaments. By analogy, if context shapes the evaluation of some consumption goods more than that of others, we will see a general tendency for "positional arms races"—mutual escalations in expenditures on positional goods.

It's a simple story, one that is difficult to challenge either in terms of first principles of logic or in terms of the foundational premise that context matters more for some goods than others. Yet it poses a profound challenge to the way economists have historically thought about the relationship between competition and social welfare.

The powerful effects of context on evaluation, long ignored by economists, are evident in virtually every domain. Making a fashion statement, for example, means to appear visibly different, at least in some minor way, from what people expect. A buzz of excitement occurred when women's hemlines first went above the knee in the 1960s, but people adapted quickly. For hemlines to continue to attract attention, they had to keep going up—and they did. And when it was no longer possible to make a fashion statement with still shorter hemlines, the mid-calf skirt burst onto the scene. Men's ties, similarly, got wider year by year, then suddenly got much narrower. Tailfins on cars got longer, then shorter. Such cycles are all about context and comparison.

When I was in high school, most Latinas wore pierced earrings, but almost no non-Latinas did. When the first non-Latina showed up with pierced earrings, there was a palpable ripple of excitement in the school. I first saw a woman with two earrings in the same lobe when I was in college. She was an instant fashion sensation. Today, of course, two earrings in one lobe no longer draw even a passing glance.

In recent years, being on fashion's cutting edge has required more and more varied piercings than was necessary the year before—not because the value of being on fashion's cutting edge is higher than before, but because the relevant context has shifted. Before long, the most effective way to make a fashion statement will be to have neither tattoos nor piercings, and at that point the cycle will begin anew.

In a 1980 paper (now quoted frequently), the economist Richard Layard wrote that "in a poor country, a man proves to his wife that he loves her by giving her a rose, but in a rich country he must give a dozen roses." But although virtually no one disputes the empirical reality on which that statement rests, traditional economic models continue to ignore the influence of context on demand.

Where do concerns about context and relative position come from? Are they hard-wired, or are we taught to develop them? Most parents not only don't attempt to encourage concerns about relative position; they invest considerable effort in discouraging them. "Pay attention to your own business, and don't worry about somebody having more or better than you," we say. That's good advice! People who are preoccupied with the fact that others have more tend to be miserable.

Long ago, I did an experiment that many people have told me would not be approved by a human-subjects committee today. It involved two of my sons, David and Jason. David was 7 years old at the time, and Jason was 5. It was a three-day experiment, and I kept careful notes. On day 1, I gave them each a glass of orange juice filled to the brim. Each drank his juice without comment. On day 2, I cut them back to half a glass each. Again, they drank without comment—no complaints about the portion reduction. On day 3, I gave David 7/8 of a glass, Jason just 3/4 of a glass. It was barely a noticeable difference. Jason's gaze darted back and forth between the two glasses as he assessed whether there was in fact a difference in levels. It quickly became clear to him that there was, and I could see him trying to restrain himself before exclaiming, at the top of his lungs, "That's not fair, he *always* gets more than me!" And that, of course, was my cue to explain patiently that there was plenty more orange juice, that it's better to pay attention to one's own business, and so on.

In similar situations, well-socialized adults don't voice similar complaints. At a dinner party, only a social moron would ask "How come he got a full pour of that Château Latour and I only got half as much?" But people notice such differences. And would you really want to wave a magic wand and strip your children of awareness of how they were doing in relative terms? What if your future son-in-law came home with a grade of D on his report card and said: "Well, I'm at a very selective school. A D there would be a B minus at the community college, so I'm pretty satisfied with that." You would be forgiven for wondering whether your daughter had chosen a suitable father for your grandchildren. Competition is an important dimension of life. You have to worry about where you are in the queue and pay some attention to that, but you don't want to be obsessive about it.

The Darwinian model is the only scientific framework we have for thinking about how human motivation came to assume its current form. In that framework, it is hard to construct a coherent narrative that wouldn't have relative position in a prominent place on the list of concerns. I will mention two obvious reasons. Famines were common as humans and other animals evolved. But there was always some food, even in the worst famines, and it was people of high rank who were most likely to get it. If caring about position made a person more likely to acquire and maintain high rank, people with that concern were going to be more likely to survive during famines.

Note also that most early human societies were polygynous. But if some men took more than one mate, others were inevitably left with none. Typically, it was the high-ranking males who took more than one wife.

Darwin's central insight was that life is graded on the curve. It's not how big, fast, or strong you are; it's how you compare along those dimensions with those with whom you compete most directly. (For more on the importance of social signaling on consumption, see the chapter by Saad and the chapter by Griskevicius et al.) Our deeply embedded concerns about relative position are rooted in that simple fact.

Those concerns focus more heavily on some domains than on others. And because the competition for spots in a rank ordering is zero-sum, competition for high-ranking spots in a hierarchy often results in substantial waste, as the following series of examples will illustrate.

I once participated in an interdisciplinary seminar that brought social scientists and humanists together with the stated aim of developing a common language for discussing issues related to ethics. Participants would take turns leading the discussion, and each leader would suggest readings for that week's session. It quickly became evident that the non-humanists in the group had great difficulty understanding the articles assigned by the humanists. Yet the authors of those articles, like nearly all academic humanists, almost certainly had scored high on the verbal portion of the Scholastic Aptitude Test. Why, then, weren't they writing in terms the rest of us could understand? Consider this passage from Maria Lugones's 2003 article "Tactical strategies of the streetwalker":

> I propose to embrace tactical strategies in moving in disruption of the dichotomy, as crucial to an epistemology of resistance/liberation. To do so is to give update to the disaggregation of collectivity concomitant with social fragmentation and to theorize the navigation of its perils without giving uptake to its logic. . . .

Why would a humanist write in such a way? My conjecture is that at one point, not long ago, most humanists wrote in clear English. Then someone discovered that, by throwing in an erudite phrase, he or she could startle the others into thinking "Wow, he must be smart. He knows what that means and I don't." And then others began to emulate that strategy, which resulted in a steady accretion of similar locutions. But although this pattern may be explainable in terms of rational pursuit of individual interest, there is no reason to presume that it is socially optimal.

Similar dynamic forces shape many spending patterns that matter for people's well-being. For example, the fact that virtually all income gains in the last 30 years have been at the top of the income ladder has given rise to a process of expenditure cascades that have made it more costly for middle-income families to achieve basic goals. The people at the top spend more money simply because they have more money. That's what people of all income levels do when they get more money. People in the middle don't get angry about the higher spending of the wealthy. On the contrary, they often seem eager to see pictures of their mansions and yachts. But the people just below the top are influenced by the new houses that the people at the top build. Maybe they need to have their daughter's wedding reception at home now too. So they build bigger. And then the group that they rub elbows with one level down, they build bigger too. That continues in a cascade all the way down the ladder, and now it is much more expensive than it used to be for middle-income families to meet the standards set by the spending of their peers.

Consider, for example, a family's aspiration to send its children to a good school. Now, a good school is an inherently relative concept. A good school is one that's better than other schools in the area. And in virtually every jurisdiction, the relatively good schools are located in the more expensive neighborhoods. So in order for the median earners to send their children to a school of even average quality, they must spend at least the median price for housing in their area. That is problematic because the median house has gotten much more expensive. In 1980, median earners could send their children to a school of average quality by purchasing a 1,600-square-foot house. But by 2007, the size of the median newly built single-family home had increased to more than 2,300 square feet.

Some criticize parents when they spend more on housing than they could afford. But if other middle-income families were spending more, any family that didn't follow suit would have to send its children to schools whose students scored poorly in reading and math, and that had metal detectors at their entrance doors.

The expenditure cascade spawned by higher spending at the top leaves middle-income families with no attractive options. No matter how intensely families bid for houses in the better school districts, half of all students must attend bottom-half schools. This brings to mind the familiar stadium metaphor: everyone stands up to get a better view, yet no one sees better than if they all had remained seated.

Since the real median hourly wage rate has risen little for women during the past three decades, and has fallen slightly for men, how have median earners managed to keep up? They have had to cut corners at every margin. Savings rates declined steadily over the past several decades, and even became negative at the peak of the housing boom. Using U.S. Census data for the largest counties, Adam Seth Levine, Oege Dijk, and I found that the counties in which inequality had increased the most also recorded the biggest increases in direct and indirect measures of financial distress (Frank et al. 2013). Those counties, for example, registered the largest increases in bankruptcy rates.

Another adjustment commonly made by families in financial distress is to move farther from the center of town, to a place where land is cheaper. We found that the counties in which inequality increased the most were also those that recorded the longest increases in long commute times (more than an hour).

Marriage counselors report that financial problems figure prominently among the concerns of couples who come to see them. We found that the counties in which inequality had increased the most were also those that registered the biggest increases in divorce rates.

Other investigators have found additional links between inequality and indications of financial distress. For example, Bowles and Park (2005), using both cross-country time-series data and cross-section data within countries, found that people tend to work longer hours when income inequality increases.

Of course, the mere fact that competition for position can be wasteful doesn't imply that regulation will necessarily make things better. Regulation can also be inefficient. In the end, we must look to evidence as to whether regulation is likely to help in each specific instance. That's essentially a pragmatic cost-benefit question. Yet proposals to regulate are, unfortunately, all too often evaluated in ideological terms. Some presume that all government intervention makes matters worse, while others insist that unregulated markets always lead to bad outcomes.

If positional competition often leads to waste, we also should expect to see private attempts to regulate individual behavior. Schelling's hockey-helmet example is one. Other examples include the engine-displacement limits adopted by auto-racing associations and the equipment standards enforced by many sailboat-racing groups.

Consider also the regulation of duels in centuries past. Honor codes in many countries held that if one was insulted, one was required to challenge the offending party to a duel. But when duelists met, their seconds were empowered to enforce strict rules. A pistol could be used to fire only a single shot, for example, and its barrel could not have spiral grooves (whose purpose is to make the weapon more accurate). Duelists were also required to stand back to back and then march a certain number of paces before they could turn and fire. The clear purpose of each of these restrictions was to reduce the likelihood of duelists' being killed. In one sample from England, only one duelist in six was struck by a bullet, and only one in 14 died (Wilkinson 1979). The norms of dueling were intended to promote civil discourse by making it more costly to be rude to others. To be effective, duels had to be costly. But it was the clear purpose of the rules to reduce the odds of duelists' being killed. Most societies now outlaw dueling altogether, and that seems better still.

One last example of this sort is provided by mandatory start dates for kindergarten. Without them, a parent could say "If I hold my 6-year-old back a year, he'll be bigger, stronger, and more socially skilled than others in his class. And since school performance is graded on the curve, he'll get better grades, be more likely to succeed athletically, and more likely to win admission to a good university when the time comes." But if all parents were to follow the same logic, the result would be kindergartens full of 7-year-olds instead of 6-year-olds. Individually, it may be rational for parents to "red shirt" their kindergarten-age children, but collectively the practice makes no sense at all. And that's why most jurisdictions have laws saying that a child who reaches the age of 6 by a certain date must start kindergarten that year.

Again, there can be no general presumption that, because regulations improve matters in some instances, they must therefore be desirable in all cases. The mere fact that much of today's consumption is wasteful from a collective vantage point does not mean that it would be better to empower a bureaucratic commission to make detailed consumption decisions for individuals.

Yet there are simple steps that would almost surely lead to more desirable outcomes. One would be to abandon the federal income tax altogether and adopt in its place a much more steeply progressive consumption tax.

Roughly speaking, a family's income flows into consumption and into savings. Under a progressive consumption tax, each family would report its income to the IRS, and also its annual savings, as many families now do with 401(k) accounts and other tax-exempt retirement accounts. The difference between those two numbers—income minus savings—is how much the family consumed this year. That amount minus a large standard deduction—say, $30,000 for a family of four—would be the family's taxable consumption. If, for example, the Jones family earned $50,000 and saved $5,000, its taxable consumption would be $50,000 – $30,000 – $5,000 = $15,000. Rates would start low, so that families with low levels of taxable consumption would pay less, or no more, than under the current system.

But marginal tax rates would rise as taxable consumption rose, and there would be no fear that high marginal rates would choke off savings and investment (a worry under the current income tax), because a higher tax rate on consumption actually encourages additional savings and investment.

Think about how this simple change in the tax structure would affect a rich family that is currently spending $4 million a year on consumption and is considering a $2 million addition to its mansion. Under the existing tax scheme, the family has to come up with $2 million to pay the contractor. Under the progressive consumption tax, let's assume a marginal rate of 100 percent on all consumption beyond $4 million annually, which means that to do the project as originally planned the family would have to come up with $2 million for the contractor and another $2 million for the IRS. The addition would thus cost them $4 million. Confronted with that big an increase in price, even the rich are likely to respond by scaling back their plans. (Those who doubt that the rich respond in this way to higher prices should consider the fact that the rich in Manhattan's expensive real-estate market choose to live in much smaller spaces than the rich in most other cities.) Other families would respond in a similar way. Because of the power of social contagion, the norms that define how big a mansion the rich feel they need would change quickly.

Note the element of fiscal alchemy inherent in the progressive consumption tax: if each rich family were to build a smaller mansion, the smaller mansions would serve just as well—indeed, probably better—than the larger ones would have. And that, in turn, would slow the expenditure cascade that has been putting pressure on middle-income families.

Yet no one would suffer. If all CEOs had mansions that were 20 percent smaller, they would still be able to entertain in the style expected of them. But they would have to recruit and train fewer domestic employees, and there would be fewer tell-all memoirs to worry about.

Phased in gradually after the economy was back at full employment, a progressive consumption tax would gradually shift resources from consumption to investment. As a result, productivity and incomes would increase more rapidly. These changes would not cause any rise in unemployment, because investment creates employment the same way that consumption does. In the process, we could gradually make the transition back to being a save-and-invest economy rather than a borrow-and-spend economy.

Cutting taxes on high-income families so they could build bigger mansions and trying to balance the budget deficit by cutting "wasteful government spending" was a bad idea. Everyone favors cutting wasteful spending in the abstract; however, most government programs have constituents who want them, and that makes them inherently hard to cut. When we do cut, it's often the programs with the least vocal constituents, not the most wasteful ones, that get the axe. For example, budget deficits led George W. Bush to cut the budget for the Energy Department's program to lock down poorly guarded nuclear materials in the former Soviet Union. A century from now, puzzled historians will look back in wonder. Those materials were being guarded by soldiers who drank too much and didn't get paid regularly. Their facilities were poorly fortified. Terrorists desperately wanted those materials, and they could easily smuggle them out if they got them. On any reasonable cost-benefit analysis, we should have been spending more on programs like that, not less. Yet because most voters don't know that such programs even exist, it is precisely those programs that are most likely to be cut.

Consumption does not occur in a social vacuum. The spending of others in the community establishes frames of reference that strongly shape the spending patterns of each individual. (See also the chapter by Saad and the chapter by Griskevicius et al.) This is a normal and inescapable fact of the human condition.

In recent decades, virtually all significant income gains have accrued to those who already had the highest incomes. This group has responded the same way all others have responded to income growth: by spending more. Higher spending at the top has shifted the frames of reference that shape judgments by those just below, causing *them* to spend more—and so on, all the way down the income ladder. In many cases, the resulting expenditure cascades have made it more costly for middle-income families to achieve basic goals.

Negative externalities from consumption are thus much like negative externalities stemming from noise, smoke, and other forms of pollution. To ignore that simple fact when designing of our laws and institutions is to pass up clear opportunities for everyone to lead a more fulfilling life.

References

Bowles, S., and Y. Park. 2005. Emulation, inequality, and work hours: Was Thorsten Veblen right? *Economic Journal* 115 (November): F397–F412.

Frank, R. H. 2011. *The Darwin Economy*. Princeton University Press.

Frank, R. H., A. S. Levine, and O. Dijk. 2013. Expenditure cascades. *Review of Behavioral Economics*, forthcoming.

Hirsch, F. 1976. *Social Limits to Growth*. Harvard University Press.

Layard, R. 1980. Human satisfactions and public policy. *Economic Journal* 90: 737–750.

Lugones, M. 2003. *Pilgrimages*. Rowman and Littlefield.

Schelling, T. 1978. *Micromotives and Macrobehavior*. Norton.

Wilkinson, F. 1979. *The Illustrated Book of Pistols*. Hamlyn.

Contributors

Joshua M. Ackerman Sloan School of Management, Massachusetts Institute of Technology

Toni C. Antonucci Institute for Social Research and Department of Psychology, University of Michigan

Kent C. Berridge Department of Psychology, University of Michigan

Sarah F. Brosnan Departments of Psychology and Philosophy, Language Research Center, and Neuroscience Institute, Georgia State University

Frans B. M. de Waal Yerkes National Primate Research Center, Emory University

Bruce J. Ellis John and Doris Norton School of Family and Consumer Sciences, University of Arizona

Debra N. Fin Healthcare Industries, Dow Corning Corporation

Robert H. Frank Johnson Graduate School of Management and Department of Economics, Cornell University

Vladas Griskevicius Carlson School of Management, University of Minnesota

Debra L. Hartsell New Business Creation, Procter & Gamble Company

Uma Karmarkar Harvard Business School

Brian Knutson Department of Psychology, Stanford University

Morten L. Kringelbach Department of Psychiatry, University of Oxford

Stephen E. G. Lea Department of Psychology, University of Exeter

Wayne R. McCullough Institute for Social Research, University of Michigan

Sara L. Minard School of International and Public Affairs, Columbia University

Chiraag Mittal Carlson School of Management, University of Minnesota

Hilke Plassmann INSEAD and Ecole Normale Supérieure

Stephanie D. Preston Department of Psychology, University of Michigan

Darby Proctor Yerkes National Primate Research Center, Emory University

Joseph P. Redden Carlson School of Management, University of Minnesota

Scott I. Rick Stephen M. Ross School of Business, University of Michigan

Michael J. F. Robinson Department of Psychology, University of Michigan

Terry E. Robinson Department of Psychology, University of Michigan

Gad Saad Department of Marketing, Concordia University

David F. Sherry Department of Psychology, University of Western Ontario

Peter M. Todd Department of Psychological and Brain Sciences, Indiana University

Brian D. Vickers Department of Psychology, University Of Michigan

Tor D. Wager Department of Psychology and Neuroscience, University of Colorado, Boulder

Paul Webley School of Oriental and African Studies

Noah J. Webster Institute for Social Research, University of Michigan

Peter C. Whybrow Semel Institute for Neuroscience and Human Behavior, University of California, Los Angeles

Carolyn Yoon Institute for Social Research and Stephen M. Ross School of Business, University of Michigan

Index